Multiple Choice on English Synonyms and Antonyms

The Synonyms and Antonyms form an integral part of the English Language. Acquaintance with the vocabulary of the English language is a necessity for effective expression either in the written or in the oral form.

Synonym is nothing but the similar meaning of a particular word or its semantic relation. So, it is a word or a phrase that means the same as another word or a phrase in the same language.

Antonyms are the negative connotation of a particular word. An Antonym is a word or phrase that is opposite in meaning to a particular word or a phrase in the same language.

So enjoy this list and then get around for preparing your own list of Synonyms and Antonyms. There is no better way of boosting your word power.

List of Words with Antonyms and Synonyms

Abandon (Transitive verb)

Since the political situation changed drastically, the company abandoned the project.

Synonyms:

Relinquish	Resign	Forgo
Discontinue	Waive	Abdicate
Leave	Quit	Evacuate
Discard	Desert	

Examples:

He relinquished all hope that she was alive.

Alan may forgo some of his rights, but he need not give up the right of doing something.

The conditions of the agreements can be waived if both the parties agreed to.

The party decided to abdicate from its role in the coalition Government.

The seaman evacuated the ship as soon as they discovered it was drowning.

Selfish people desert their friends in difficult times.

Paul was discarded by his brothers because he wanted to become a doctor and his brothers wanted him to take to family business.

Antonyms:

| Pursue | Hunt | Follow |
| Chase | Prosecute | Undertake |

Examples:

I wish I could pursue my studies further.

The Police chased the criminal for some distance but gave up there after.

In ancient times, the human had to hunt for food in the forest.

The Government has prosecuted quite a number of officers for betraying against the country.

Abash (Transitive verb)

His uncivilized behaviour in the company function abashed his parents and his relatives.

Synonyms:

Humiliate	Humble	Debase
Degrade	Reduce	Depress
Mortify	Denigrate	Embarrass
Disconcert	Astound	Confound

Examples:

Napoleon was humiliated in the Battle of Waterloo by the humble British fleet under Lord Nelson.

You debase yourself by telling such lies. Giving up smoking reduces the risk of heart of disease.

She suffered the mortification of seeing her assistant promoted above her.

The rise in oil prices will depress the car market.

Antonyms:

Immodesty	Self-esteem	Self-love
Self-praise	Complacency	Smugness
Dignified	Upgrade	Exalt

Examples:

The ceremony was dignified by the presence of ambassador.

He was exalted as the pillar of the community.

She was upgraded to the post of senior designer.

In certain modern societies of west, immodesty has become a part of civilization.

To judge your standing in the society, you must develop self-esteem.

Self-love and self-praise are the new traits used in modern advertisements.

Abate (Intransitive Verb)

After the heavy rains for the last one week, the flood has abated to the safe level.

Synonyms

Decrease	Lessen	Moderate
Diminish	Subside	Ally
Slacken	Subdue	Alleviate
Dwindle	Ease	Grow less
Reduce		

Examples

Interest in the sports is steadily decreasing.
Antiseptics lessen the chance of infection.
We must moderate our temper.
The unequivocal image diminishes gradually.
The tension generally subsides but intransigence always expands.
The Doctor gave him an injection to alleviate the pain.
Their savings have dwindled to almost nothing.
The situation is beginning to ease.
The unabated rains subdued the sprits of the farmers.
He had slackened in his duties, was therefore punished.
The police tactfully allayed the commotion of the picketers.

Antonyms

Increase	Augment	Extreme
Enlarge	Extend	Dilate
Sprout	Expand	Swell
Grow	Advance	Develop
Rise	Ascend	Enhance
Deepen	Heighten	Intensify
Magnify	Aggravate	Spread
Disperse	A exaggerate	

Examples:

The volume of the gas increases as we decrease the pressure on it.
Dirty food augments the chances of infection.
Too extreme our temper is to be invariably destructive.
It is the amplifier in a radio that magnifies the sound.

Abbreviate (Transitive Verb)

WHO is the abbreviated form of World Health Organization?

Synonyms

Abridge	Condense	Contract
Shorten	Curtail	Truncate
Trim		

Examples:

The abridged edition of the book greatly curtailed the cost.
The condensed ideas have not only reduced the size of the book, but also presented it in a better form.
Shorten the length of the précis to its requirement.

They published my article in a truncated form.

I trimmed the boundary wall of my garden to give it a refined look.

We must try to curtail our spending.

Anonyms

Lengthen	Extend	Elongate
Stretch	Prolong	Protract
Draw out		

Examples:

Daily exercise lengthens one's life.

The Government extended his service by three years due to good health.

This looking glass gives an elongated view to one's face.

They prolonged their visit by a few more days.

The cardigan stretched when I washed it and it's far too big for me.

Abundant (Adjective)

Definition plentiful, large in number

Synonyms

Abounding,	Ample,	Bounteous,
Bountiful,	Copious,	Crawling with,
Cup runs over with,	Eco-rich,	Exuberant,
Filled,	Full,	Generous,
Heavy,	Lavish,	Liberal,
Lousy with,	Luxuriant,	Mucho,
No end of,	Overflowing,	Plate is full of,
Plenteous,	Plenty,	Profuse,
Rich,	Rolling in,	Stinking with,
Sufficient,	Teeming.	

Antonyms

Lacking,	Rare,	Scarce,
and sparse.		

Abduct (Transitive Verb)

The gang which abducted a boy from the school demands ransom to release the boy.

Synonyms

Kidnap	Carry off
Steal	Spirit away

Examples

The kidnapped child was restored to its exasperated parents.

He was carried off by the ostentatious overture of his officer.

The stolen goods are still untraceable.

Constant failures spirited away his over-confidence.

Antonyms

| deliver | Give away | Surrender |

Examples

He delivered a beautiful speech in the meeting.

The rich man gave away his property to the local orphanage.

The thief surrendered to the police when his conscience pricked.

Aberration (Abstract Noun)

An aberration in our behaviour is unavoidable for many of us.

Synonyms

| deviation | Variation | Distortion |
| Disorientation | Error | |

Examples

We should not deviate from the path of morality.

There was a conspicuous variation between the two figures.

The culprit narrated a distorted version of the episode.

The 19th century masses could not assimilate the disorientation of Galileo.

Just one error cost him his job.

Antonyms

| Truth | Sanity |

Examples:

Mahatma Gandhi propagated the spiritual values of truth.

If sanity dawns on humanity, there will be no wars in the world.

Abet (Transitive verb)

Those who abetted the culprit in the conspiracy were arrested by the police two days ago.

Synonyms:

| Aid | Assist | Support |
| Encourage | Incite | Instigate |

Examples:

The generous aid by the society has assisted him to support his family through thick and thin.

The glare of monetary encouragement culminates in inciting lethargy and instigating the people to resort to evil doings.

Antonyms

Hinder	Prevent	Obstruct
Interrupt	Intercept	Restrict
Restraint	Inhibit	Block
Close	Affect	Prohibit

Examples

Hot weather greatly caused hindrance top his farming work.
Prevention is always better than cure.
The lack of capital causes obstruction in the growth of my business.
The birth of a son to her was the interruption to her career.
She has no inhibitions about making her opinions known.
He voted in favour of the prohibition of smoking in public area.
The threat of closure affected the workers' morale.

Abhor (Transitive verb)

The foreigners who come to this country as tourists abhor the beggars who roam around the cities.

Synonyms

Hate	Dislike	Detest
Loathe	Despise	Abominate

Examples:

We should hate sin, not the sinner.
His dislike for the type of work resulted in his very slow rise in position.
The noble person loathes crime.
The rich should not despise the poor.
The conqueror should not abominate the defeated enemy.

Antonyms

Love	Fondness	Liking
Inclination	Desire	Admiration
Affection	Attachment	Yearning
Passion	Devotion	Infatuation
Advocating	idolatry	

Examples:

Love of humanity is the first condition of prayer to GOD.
The father developed more fondness for his second daughter due to her great care for him.
Deepak has a great attachment with his cousin, but you cannot call it love.

Abiding (Adjective)

The abiding principles of this school should not be violated at any moment in our approach.

Synonyms:

Everlasting	Constant	Continuing
Durable	Enduring	Eternal
Immortal	Permanent	Persistent
Steadfast	Unending	

Examples:

I am tired of her everlasting complaints.
This entrance is in constant use. Do not block it.
The fabric has a special baking for extra durability.
I am tired of your eternal arguments.
China is a permanent member of UN Security Council.
She eventually married the most persistent of her admirers.

Anonyms:

Brief	Fleeting	Momentary
Short-lived	Temporary	Transitory
Ephemeral		

Examples:

For a fleeting moment, I thought the car was going to crash.
This arrangement is only temporary.
Their sweets were only transitory.
Her interest in tennis was very short-lived.
Journalism is important but ephemeral.

Ability (Noun)

Mr. Kuala alone has the required ability to get things done in the government.

Synonyms:

Power	Skill	Competence
Competency	Capacity	Efficiency
Capability	Aptitude	Faculty
Talent		

Examples:

An artisan earns fame for his skill in the craft.
According to the latest instructions, he has the power to sign the agreement and we can doubt his competence in this regard.
Efficiency of a worker can increase if he is given the required facilities.
The capability of an individual can be gauged by his background.

He has a good aptitude towards arts but his father compels him to study science. In India, even many talented people may remain unemployed.

Anonyms:

| Unskillfulness | Impotence | Incompetence |
| Weakness | Incapability | |

Examples:

Unskillfulness is still a common phenomenon in the country, although facilities for general education are being increased.

Consuming more alcoholic drinks will result in impotence among men.

The incompetence of the workers resulted in heavy lose to the company.

Abject (Adjective)

The abject condition in which the poor people live caught the attention of the world body which decided to do something.

Synonyms

Degraded	Contemptible	Miserable
Wretched	Base	Mean
Worthless	Grovelling	Repulsive

Examples:

By indulging in such an immoral act simply to earn the money, he has very much degraded himself.

His contemptible rudeness to the guests cannot be forgiven.

Poverty is the biggest bane. It makes the life of man quite miserable.

He is a wretched fellow. He does not pay attention to others' feelings.

Greed, anger and lust are few of the base qualities of man.

Anonyms

Insolence	Arrogance	Haughtiness
Presumption	Pomposity	Snobbery
Domineering	Defiance	

Examples:

The subordinate's insolence made him lose his job.

Arrogance is the enemy of good education.

Haughtiness and pride always lead to failure in any walk of life.

Abjure (Transitive verb)

The King abjured his right over the neighbouring country in order to provide peace to the people.

Synonyms

| Forswear | Renounce | Relinquish |

| Abandon | Recant | Repudiate |

Renunciation

Examples:

The astronomer Galileo was forced to forswear his theory of the rotation of the earth.

He has recanted the sinful ways after his release from jail.

It is not necessary to renounce the world for worshipping God.

John relinquished his right to property of his father voluntarily to help his sister.

If we can abandon our vices of anger, hatred and physical attachments, we are on the right path of progress.

It is very difficult to the level of renunciation world attachments.

Anonyms:

| Desire | Like | Worship |
| Long for | Wish | Earn |

Examples:

I desired to go to USA for my higher studies, but the fate was in another way.

All those who wish to succeed in the politics will not do so.

Mt father is still longing for the old classical music.

Earn while you are young. Otherwise it will be difficult for all of you.

Able (adjective)

Only those students who are able to score very high marks in GMAT will apply to this business school.

Synonyms:

Capable	Accomplished	Adept
Adequate	Adroit	Clever
Competent	Efficient	Expert
Fit	Masterful	Proficient

Examples:

I am sure he is capable of running a mile in four minutes.

He is very adept in mending computers.

Fuel resources are barely adequate for our needs.

She is competent to look after young children.

He revealed himself to be surprisingly practical and efficient.

She has become reasonably proficient at her job.

Antonyms:

Incapable	Inadequate	Incompetent
Inefficient	Inept	Weak
Mediocre	Unskilful	Unfit

Examples:

The children seem to be totally incapable of working quietly by themselves.
The safety precautions are totally inadequate.
I suppose my application has been lost by an incompetent clerk.
I have heard anyone so inept at making speeches.
His books are obviously mediocre.

Abnormal (Adjective)

The abnormal growth in the economy of India was possible because of the drastic changes in the economic policies of that country in 1990s.

Synonyms

| Aberrant | Eccentric | Irregular |
| Anomalous | Insane | Monstrous |

Examples:

He is too aberrant taking the medicine and exercise; hence we cannot guarantee any great improvement in his health.
He is not a fool, he is an eccentric and no one can predict his behaviour.
His contradictory statements at different times have put him in an anomalous situation.
The mental torture and agony have made him insane.
Greed and lust take a monstrous form in due course.

Antonyms:

Sanity	Conformity	Soundness
Reason	Rationality	Normality
Sobriety	Lucidity	

Examples:

Only sanity at the highest political levels in super power countries can save the world from destruction.

Conformity to the ideals of peace and development is needed to make the youth of our country use its power in the right direction.

Abolish (Transitive verb)

The social system of untouchability was abolished a long time back in India.

Synonyms:

| Annul | Cancel | Nullify |
| Abrogate | Exterminate | |

Examples:

When two equal forces act on a point in opposite direction, they annul each other.
His orders for transfer to New York have been cancelled.
It is generally believed that homeopathic medicines nullify the effect of the allopathic medicines.

Hitler wanted to exterminate the Jews from the world. That is why he killed them so ruthlessly.

Antonyms:

Approve	Retain	Continue
Fabricate	Build	Erect
Establish	Achieve	Complete

Examples:

The non-aligned nations have unanimously approved the resolution on keeping arms-free the Indian Ocean Zone.

The principal decided to retain the old teacher for three more years.

The established companies have more responsibilities than the new ones in safe guarding the environment.

Abominate (Transitive verb)

The students abominated the uncivilized attitude of the teachers towards the girls.

Synonyms:

Hate	Abhor	Detest
Dislike	Loathe	Recoil from
shudder at		

Examples:

I hate people to take advantage of me.
He detests having to get up early.
I loathe having to go to these conferences.
He recoiled from the idea of killing another man.

Anonyms:

Admire	Adore	Cherish
Dot on	Esteem	Love
Revere	Idolize	Worship

Examples:

I admire him for his success in business.
He adores his wife and children.
Children feel the need to be cherished.
Every mother loves her children.
A good teacher is revered by generations of students.

Above (Preposition & Adjective)

One should deal with the politicians above the board.

Synonyms:

Over	Atop	Upon
Exceeding	Beyond	Higher than

On top of	Superior to	

Examples:
The wind must have blown it over.
The road continues beyond the village up into the hills.
You should not exceed the speed limit.
She is certainly superior to other candidates.

Antonyms:
Below	Beneath	Under
Underneath	Inferior	Lesser

Examples:
The temperature remained below freezing point all day.
He threw himself under the bus.
They found the body buried beneath a pile of leaves.
She found a lot of dust underneath the sofa.

Above board (Adjective)

We should deal with the politicians above board in order to remain safe.

Synonyms:
Honest	Candid	Fair and square
Frank	Legitimate	Covert
Trustworthy		

Examples:
He was honest enough to admit that he knew nothing about the subject.
Let me be absolutely candid with you. Your work is not good enough.
To be frank with you, CI think your son has little chance of passing the exam.
Politicians are legitimate targets for satire.

Antonyms:
Clandestine	DeceitfulCrooked	Deceptive
Devious	Dishonest	Fraudulent
Furtive		

Examples:
All the officials are crooked.
Her simple style is deceptive. What she has to say is very profound.
He became rich by devious means.
It would be dishonest of me to pretend that I enjoyed the evening.

Abrupt (Adjective)

The abrupt manner in which he concluded the Board meeting indicated that he was not in normal condition.

Synonyms:

Sudden	Hasty	Headlong
Hurried	Precipitate	Quick
Surprising	Swift	Unanticipated
Unforeseen		

Examples:
Their departure was very sudden.
I do not want to make a hasty decision.
To go ahead without further consultation would precipitate even foolhardy.

Antonyms:

Leisurely	Slow	Thoughtful
Unhurried	Gradual	

Examples:
The rest of the day may be sent at leisure.
She was not slow to realize what was happening.
Improvements will be gradual at first.

Abridgment (Noun)

The act of abridgment of the holy books is not liked by the respective religious scholars.

Synonyms:

Abbreviation	Epitome	Summary
Abstract	Compendium	Outline
Synopsis	Analysis	Digest

Examples:
In Chemistry, the use of abbreviations helps solve the chemical equations.
We may have an epitome of religion but not its abridgement.
An investigator can analyse the data and reach a conclusion where others get confused.
An abstract or digest is an independent statement of what the book contains.
A summary is the most condensed statement of results or conclusions.
This is an abridged form of The Webster's Dictionary.
My uncle is very fond of English Literature. He keeps a compendium of English Literature always with him.
In an essay one should first give the synopsis and then the description.

Antonyms:

Elaborate	Expand	Dissect
Elongate		

Examples:
This book beautifully elaborates the theory of business cycle.
This is an expanded version of Ramayana.

Unless we dissect the basic constituents of this statement, we cannot get at an accurate conclusion.

Abscond (Intransitive verb)

Since he has been looked upon by his friends themselves as one of the culprits involved in murder case, he absconded a few days ago.

Synonyms:

Hide	Slip away	Conceal oneself
Leave	Steal away	Decamp
Retire	Depart	Retreat
Take oneself off	Disappear	Run away
Withdraw	Flee	Run off

Examples:

The traveller decamped in fear of lurking robbers.
A frightened horse runs as a bolt is from a bow or a gun.
He leaves his home for office in time but does not get a bus and is generally late.
The traveller had some fears in mind when he departed on his journey.
A bonded labour may run away from his master but the master generally succeeds in catching him again.
A public man may try to hide himself from the reporters but the reporters somehow will find him out.
One may slip away from a company, which he does not wish, to break up.
Army retreats from an untenable position.
The hunted thief disappeared in the crowd and the police failed to catch him.
The Jews had to flee from Germany when Hitler ordered their General massacre.

Antonyms:

Hold one's ground	Reappear	Arrive
Remain	Be present	Present one self.
Come into view	Put in appearance	Stay
Emerge		

Examples:

The Army held its ground against heavy firing from the enemy posts.
The great leader reappeared after oblivion.
The witness presented himself in the court after great prompting.
It is difficult for the Indo-US warm friendship to put in reappearance under the present circumstances.
The recession is over and brighter prospects for the industry have now emerged.

Absent (Adjective)

When I spoke to him, he looked at me in an absent way, but he did not answer.

Synonyms:

Missing	Away	Gone
Lacking	Non-existent	Not present
Not attachment	Elsewhere	

Examples:
Christmas is only a week away.
The hammer is missing from my tool box.
The book was interesting but lacking in originality.
Our favourite restaurant was full, we had to go elsewhere.

Antonyms:

Attendant	Present	Alert
Attentive	Aware	
Conscious		

Examples:
Were you present when the news was announced?
Although he is eighty, his mind is still remarkably alert.
A good hostess is always attentive to the needs of her guests.
She became aware that something was burning.

Absolve (Transitive Verb)

The Investigation Committee absolved his from all the charges levelled against him by his company.

Synonyms:

Forgive	Acquit	Clear
Deliver	Discharge	Exempt
Pardon	Release	Remit.
Shrive	Vindicate	Set
free		

Examples:
I forgave her a long time ago.
The Jury acquitted him of the charge of murder.
A courier delivered the parcels to our office.
The accused man was not found guilty and discharged.
I consider that I have been completely vindicated.

Antonyms:

Blame	Censure	Charge
Convict	Denounce	Excoriate
Reprehend	Sentence	Upbraid

Examples:
A bad workman blames his tools.
Two MPs were censured by the speaker.

There was not enough evidence to convict him.
She has completed his sentence and will now be released.

Absolute (Adjective)

When giving evidence in the court of law, we must tell the absolute truth.

Synonyms:

Arbitrary	Compulsory	Haughty
Positive	Arrogant	Controlling
Imperative	Supreme	Authoritative
Despotic	Dictatorial	Irresponsible
Unconditional	Commanding	Domineering
Overbearing	Unequivocal	Compulsive
Exacting	Peremptory	Unlimited
Imperious	yrannical	autocratic

Examples:

Shah of Iran was an absolute monarch but the rule of Khomeini and other religious leaders is arbitrary, tyrannical, autocratic, dictatorial and over-bearing.

In India, The President is the supreme commander of all the three wings of defence- Army, Navy and Air Force.

A person of an independent spirit in inclined to resent the imperious manner in any one whose authority is not clearly felt and acknowledged.

Knowledge of an Indian language is compulsory for the Indian Civil Service officers.

Although he is an educated person, no one takes him seriously because of his haughty nature.

The politicians generally become arrogant after assuming power.

There is an imperative need to control the politicians from assuming unlimited powers to them. They should be made to share it with other people at large.

Antonyms:

Accountable	Contingent	Lenient
Mild	Docile	Limited
Responsible	Complaint	Lowly
Submission	Conditional	Gentle
Neck	Yielding	Constitutional
humble		

Examples:

The Prime Minister is accountable to the Parliament for the actions of his cabinet.

A contingent of twenty teams visited Bangkok to participate in the last Asian Games.

It is good to be lenient in principles but bad to be docile in practice.

Absorb (Transitive Verb)

Paper that absorbs ink is called blotting-paper.

Synonyms:

Spend	Waste	Squander
Destroy	Exhaust	Devour
Assimilate		

Examples:

A wise man spends the money and a fool wastes it.
The wounds of a stove-burn destroy certain parts of the skin and hence take long to be healed up.
The untimely cyclone squandered the crop away.
Overwork will exhaust him shortly.
In a clash between the police and the porters, the latter destroyed many vehicles of the police.
The hordes of Attila, the Hun burned and wasted what they could not carry away.

Antonyms:

Save	Hoard	Reserve
Pressure	husband	

Examples:

Wise men always save something for the rainy day.
The government has built storage facilities to hoard food grains for any emergency.
We should reserve 25% of our income for the emergency period.

Abstain (Intransitive Verb)

After his college days, he abstained from both alcoholic drinks and non-vegetarian foods.

Synonyms:

Forbear	Refrain	Desist
Withhold	resist	

Examples:

We should refrain from reading cheap and sensational literature.
Although already jailed once, he cannot resist from gambling.
Government has the right to withhold his pension as a measure of penalty.

Antonyms:

Pursue	Adopt	Persist
Offer		

Examples:

Dr. Jones is pursuing his profession nicely.
Rajneesh had adopted a definite progressive policy for his firm.
It we persist on the path of success; we shall certainly achieve it in due course.

Abstract (Adjective)

A flower is beautiful, but beauty itself is abstract.

Synonyms:

Abstruse	Arcane	Complex
Conceptual	Deep	Hypothetical
Indefinite	Occult	Subtle
Unpractical	Unrealistic	

Examples:
The situation was more complex that we realized.
Losing passport will land you in deep water.
She shall be away for an indefinite period.
All his claims are extremely hypothetical.
I thought the film was rather unrealistic.

Antonyms:

Concrete	Definite	Factual
Real	Specific	

Examples:
Physics deals with the forces acting on the concrete objects.
It is definite now that she is going to be promoted.
Real life is sometimes stranger than fiction.
The money is to be used for one specific purpose: building of the theatre.

Absurd (Adjective)

It was absurd of you to suggest such a thing.

Synonyms:

Foolish	Stupid	Ridiculous
Irrational	Senseless	Silly

Examples:
It is foolish to think of selfish interests in modern society.
He looked stupid in the narrow jeans.
It is ridiculous to think of business without capital.

Antonyms:

Logical	Sound	Rational
Sensible	Consistent	Reasonable

Examples:
Congress victory in recent elections makes us reach a logical conclusion that people want a socialist system.
This proposition is quite sound if worked out properly.
Unless the modern youth develops a rational attitude, he cannot make due contribution to the country's progress.

Abundance (Noun)

The wealthy people live a life of "food and drinks in abundance."

Synonyms:

Plenty	Affluence	Ampleness
Bounty	Copiousness	Plentitude
Profusion	Exuberance	

Examples:
They always gave us plenty to eat.
Royal bounty supplied the central parks of London.
We can excuse his behaviour as youthful exuberance.
Roses grew in profusion against the old wall.

Antonyms:

Dearth	Deficiency	Lock
Need	Paucity	Scarcity
Sparseness		

Examples:
There seems to be a dearth of good players at the moment.
Vitamin deficiency can lead to illness.
Her voice lacked conviction.
The scarcity of food forced prices up.

Abusive (Adjective)

Using abusive language is considered uncivilized tendency.

Synonyms:

Insulting	Calumniating	Castigating
Contumelious	Disparaging	Libellous
Maligning	Offensive	Scolding
Reviling	Slanderous	

Examples:
The government has been widely castigated in the press for its handling of the economy.
He was most insulting to my wife.
In meeting she always takes the offensive before she can be criticized.
The government is regularly reviled for running down the welfare state.
He scolded me before I left the window shop.
He was charged with slandering a government minister.

Antonyms:

Approving	Complimentary	Eulogistic
Laudatory	Praising	Panegyric

Examples:
She received many approving glances.
She was highly complimentary about my paintings.
He received high praising for his scientific research.

Accept (Verb)

No one would accept the ideas that he presented in the seminar on Population Control.

Synonyms:

Believe	Take	Assent
Agree	Honour	Admit
Confirm		

Examples:
Most of the religions believe in the presence of some supernatural Power.
Smith was joking but his friends took it otherwise. Hence there was misunderstanding between the two.
He was requested to give his consent in writing to be posted outstation or face dismissal for his misadventure.
I will agree to his proposal if it does not harm anybody.
He should not feel guilty while admitting his fault.
He is a man of principle. He always honours his words.
His crime was confirmed by a number of eye witnesses.

Antonyms:

Disbelieve	Refuse	Reject
Disagree	Non-consent	

Examples:
There is no reason to disbelieve his personal observations in this matter.
I already had such fears and had rejected the original statement.
He refused to avail of my services.
I have many reasons to disagree with your proposal.

Accidental (Adjective)

The company set aside some amount for accidental expenses.

Synonyms:

Unintentional	Adventitious	Casual
Chance	Contingent	Fortuitous
Haphazard	Incidental	Random
Uncertain		

Examples:
This may not be obvious to the casual observer.

Is there any chance of getting tickets for tonight's performance?
The resemblance between the two books is certainly fortuitous.
The approach of the government towards the problem is haphazard.
The terrorists fired into the crowd at random.
The outcome is still uncertain.

Antonyms:

Intended	Intentional	Planned
Prepared	Foreseen	Expected

Examples:
I am sorry I left you off the list. It was not intentional.
I'd intended visiting you this week. But I was not able to make it.
I'd planned on having a quiet evening at home. But it happened to be otherwise.
A hotel room is being prepared for their arrival.
Train fares are expected to rise sharply.

Accompany (Verb)

Her father accompanies her where ever she goes in this town.

Synonyms:

Escort	Join	Attend
Chaperon	Conduct	Convoy
Consort		

Examples:
The security guard escorted the political leader throughout the journey.
I will join hands with you in this mission.
Let us attend to this task with devotion.

Antonyms:

Discard	Leave	Abandon

Examples:
It is high time you discard bad company if you wish to achieve something in life.
It is good to leave bad habits in order to achieve something worthwhile in your life.
Let us abandon old traditions which stand in the way of our progress.

Accomplish (Verb)

He accomplished many achievements at the very young age.

Synonyms:

Achieve	Attain	Complete
Conclude	Effectuate	Finish
Perform	Fulfil	

Examples:
They could not achieve their target of less than 30% inflation.

When will you complete the construction of this building?
We must conclude from these remarks that all hope of a settlement is dead.
Wait, I have not finished yet.
The play was first performed in 1991.
You must first fulfil the terms of your contract.

Antonyms:

Fail	Fall	Short
Forsake	Give up	

Examples:
The letter failed to arrive in time.
He forsook the glamour of the city life for the small and simple cottage in the country.
She does not give up easily.

Accumulate (Verb)

They accumulated a lot of wealth for his son. But he expired very young.

Synonyms:

Assemble	Gather	Congregate
Rally	Hoard	Store
Convene		

Examples:
The members of the Managing Committee assemble every month to review the progress of the work and take necessary measures to step up construction of the houses.
The thief was gathering the articles when the police came there.
The strikers congregated at the gates of the factory and took out a rally in the city.
Now it has been made illegal to hoard the essential commodities in large quantities.
The medicines should be stored in a cool place.

Antonyms:

Disperse	Scatter	Broadcast
Spread	Dissipate	Distribute

Examples:
The police used tear gas to disperse the crowds.
The people scattered in the nearby streets to save themselves from the crowds.
The leaders broadcast the futility of the determinations taken out by the labourers.

Accurate (Adjective)

The accurate number of students who discontinued their studies is not known.

Synonyms:

Correct	Precise	Exact
Nice	Right	True

Examples:
The correct answers can be found at the end of the question paper for the reference of the students.
The Prime Minister tried to be as precise as possible in his statement on public policy.
We should try to be exact in our calculations.

Antonyms:

Incorrect	Inaccurate	Inexact
Wrong	False	Erroneous

Examples:
This attitude on your part seems to be incorrect. You may easily annoy the public.
The statistical statement seems to be inaccurate and erroneous. It needs to be done afresh for exact conclusion.

Accuse (Verb)

The people accused the politician of having swindled the money allotted for constructing a bridge across the river.

Synonyms:

Allege	Arraign	Attribute
Blame	Censure	Cite
Denounce	Impute	Indict

Examples:
The prisoner alleges that he was at home on the night of the crime.
A bad workman blames his tools.
Union officials have denounced the action as a breach of the agreement.
He was indicted for the charge of corruption.

Antonyms:

Absolve	Defend	Exonerate
Vindicate		

Examples:
The inquiry absolved the driver of all the responsibilities for the accident.
A commission of enquiry exonerated him from all charges of corruption.
I consider that I have been completely vindicated.

Accustomed (Adjective)

We are accustomed to go a long walk in the morning before sunrise.

Synonyms:

Usual	Common	Conventional
Customary	Expected	Habitual
Normal		

Ordinary	Regular	Routine
Adopted	Familiar	

Examples:
She arrived later than usual time.
Robbery is not common in this area.
She is very conventional in her views.
He gave the customary speech of thanks to the chairman.
Start work at the normal time.
We were dressed up for the party but she was still in her ordinary clothes.
She writes a regular column for the national newspaper.

Antonyms:
Abnormal	Infrequent	Occasional
Odd	Peculiar	Rare
Strange	Unusual	

Examples:
Such cases are relatively infrequent.
There will be occasional shows during the day.
The odds are that she will win.
It is unusual for him to be so rude.
I had a peculiar feeling that I had been the before.

Achieve (Verb)

He achieved a score of 100 per cent in Mathematics in the National Competition.

Synonyms:
Attain	Accomplish	Do
Win	Effect	Fulfil
Gain	Perform	Finish
Execute	Acquire	

Examples:
A Yogi's only desire is to attain Moksha.
Rakish Sharma, India's first cosmonaut was able to accomplish the job successfully.
In spite of his best efforts, he could not effect any change in the system because it was corrupt to the grass-root.
The gymnasts performed such fests that we could not help praising them.
His loan was cancelled because he did not execute the requisite agreement in time.

Antonyms:
Fail	Miss	Miscarry
Loss	Give in	

Examples:
The school Doctor failed to save the lives of the injured students.

Rajesh missed first class by few marks.
Abita took such risks that her baby in the womb could not help miscarriage.

Acknowledge (Verb)

We have to acknowledge the little achievements of our children so as to give them emotional support.

Synonyms:

Admit	Own	Profess
Avow		

Examples:

I admit my statement is not up to the mark but it does show the accurate position of the case.
I can own all the blame for making a mess of this issue.
I profess a religious attitude on material affairs of society to inspire social confidence.

Antonyms:

Contradict	Foreswear	Deny
Disown	Disclaim	

Examples:

I cannot but contradict your stiff stance on this issue.
I can foreswear the doom of this country, unless its citizens raise their national character in some ways.
I disown responsibility for this severe action you propose on this small issue.

Acme (Noun)

The acme of the growth of this company will be reached not in the near future.

Synonyms:

High point	Apex	Climax
Crest	Crown	Culmination
Optimum	Peak	Pinnacle
Top	Vertex	Zenith

Examples:

At the age of 40 had reached the apex of his career.
The climax of the celebration was the firework display.
Her appointment was the culmination in his career.
The optimum temperature of plants is not very low.
At the very young age, he reached the pinnacle of his career.
At its zenith, the Mughal Empire covered almost from Kabul to Bangladesh.

Antonyms:

Bottom	Depths	Low point
Minimum	Nadir	Zero

Examples:
The book that I want is right at the bottom of the pile.
Water was found at the depth of fifty feet underground.
In this area, temperature will fall to a minimum level by the end of December.

Acquire (Verb)

My parents acquired wealth by their hard and diligent works.

Synonyms:

Achieve	Amass	Attain
Buy	Collect	Earn
Gain	Gather	Get
Obtain	Procure	Realize
Receive	Score	

Examples:
I have achieved only half of what I did hope to do.
They amassed enough evidence to convict him.
We gained from our investment.
This room gets very little Sunshine.
I managed to obtain the book I wanted.
The party failed to procure sufficient votes.
We received a warm welcome from our hosts.

Antonyms:

Be deprived of	Forfeit	Forgo
Give up	Lose	Relinquish
Renounce	Surrender	Waive

Examples:
It's wrong to suddenly deprive your body of certain foods.
Passengers who cancel their reservations will forfeit their deposits.
The workers agreed to forgo a pay increase for the sake of greater job security.
She relinquished possession of the house to her sister.

Acquit (Verb)

He was acquitted of the murder charges by the Supreme Court.

Synonyms:

Absolve	Deliver	Discharge
Exonerate	Free	Fulfil
Release	Relieve	Vindicate

Examples;
The inquiry absolves her of all responsibility for charges.
Did you deliver my message to my mother?

The accused man was not found guilty and was discharged.
My pant caught in barbed wire and it took me some time to free it.
The bullet is released from the gun at a very high speed.
The bypass relieves traffic jams in the city centre.

Antonyms:

Blame	Charge	Condemn
Convict	Sentence	Dam

Examples:
If you fail the exam you will only have yourself to blame.
I resent the charges of incompetence made against me.
She is often condemned as uncaring.
She has been twice convicted of fraud.
Damn this computer. What is the matter with it?

Acrimonious (Adjective)

In this acrimonious political situation, we could not remain peace and calm.

Synonyms:

Acerbic	Astringent	Biting
Caustic	Censorious	Churlish
Cutting	Irascible	Mordacious
Peevish	Petulant	Pungent
Rancorous	Sarcastic	Severe
Sharp	Spiteful	Tart
Trenchant	Vitriolic	

Examples:
She was uncharacteristically acerbic in her response.
It seems churlish to refuse such a generous offer.
He tore up the letter in a fit of petulance.
People who did not like him said he was very sarcastic.
He is just being spiteful.
The stewed apple needs a bit more sugar. It is still a bit tart.

Antonyms:

Affable	Benign	Forgiving
Good-tempered	Kind	

Examples:
He found her parents very affable.
She is benign by nature.
Mt parents are very kind and forgiving.

Active (Adjective)

All the active students will be given a chance to join military services.

Synonyms:

Busy	Bustling	Engaged
Hard-working	Alert	Animated
Diligent	Industrious	Nimble
Vibrant	Vigorous	Vital

Examples:
We have been terribly busy at work recently.
The city centre was bustling with life.
She was engaged as an interpreter.
The alert listener would have noticed the error.
The letter was found after a diligent research among the files.
She is sewing the clothes with nimble fingers.

Antonyms:

Dormant	Dull	Idle
Inactive	Inoperative	Lazy
Slow	Sedentary	Sluggish
Torpid	Unimaginative	

Examples:
The virus can lie dormant for years.
The conference was deadly dull.
We spent very idle hours just sitting under the Sun.
We spent a lazy day on the beach.
The tortoise lies around in a torpid state.

Acute (Adjective)

The acute observation of the young children is admirable.

Synonyms:

Serious	Critical	Crucial
Grave	Decisive	Important
Severe	Urgent	Vital

Examples:
We are at critical time in our country's history.
Winning this contract is crucial to the future of this company.
He is in a grave condition and needs immediate medical treatment.
The bomb-threats caused a severe disruption to flights from New York.

Antonyms:

Dense	Dim	Dim-witted

Dull	Obtuse	Slow
Stupid	Unintelligent	

Examples:
How can you be so dense?
His eyesight is getting dim.
The conference was deadly dull.
She cannot possibly be so obtuse.
Political evolution is a long slow process.
I do not want to hear your stupid secret.

Adamant (Adjective)

Being adamant on every issue will make you unpopular among your relatives.

Synonyms:

Firm	Fixed	Immovable
Inexorable	Inflexible	Insistent
Intransigent	Obdurate	Relentless
Resolute	Rigid	Stiff
Stubborn	Unbending	Uncompromising
Unshakable	Obstinate	

Examples:
"I do not want to be unkind", he said in a firm voice.
Has the date of the next meeting fixed?
Lock your bike to something immovable like a railing or a pillar.
She is obstinate and inflexible.
He remained obdurate. He would press ahead regardless.
She sat at her chair, rigid and staring.

Antonyms:

Compliant	Compromising	Easy-going
Flexible	Lax	Pliant
Receptive	Responsive	Susceptible

Examples:
The government, compliant as ever, gave in to their demands.
The photographs showed the couple in a highly compromising circumstance.
You need to be more flexible and imaginative in your approach.
The law is rather lax on this point.
Her easy-going tendency made her popular among her in-laws.

Actual (Adjective)

We were not aware of the actual conditions prevailed in that Country when we took that decision.

Synonyms:

| Authentic | Real | Certain |

Demonstrable

Examples:

The statistics of the position about food grains in this country are collected from authentic sources.

The real cause of discontentment among the people in the country is all around poverty.

I am certain that poverty can be eradicated in the country only by changing the basic socio-economic system.

Antonyms:

| Fabulous | Virtual | Unreal |

Examples:

Do make fabulous stories. I know the real facts.

The virtual situation in this country smacks of acute localism.

Adapt (Verb)

People have the natural ability to adapt to the situation in which they are destined to live.

Synonyms:

| Fit | Regulate | Conform |

Suit

Examples:

He is a fit for services but he is a misfit for business.

Trade union leaders want adequate legislative measures being passed to regulate the working and service conditions of different classes of workers.

A private company will accept the supply only if they strictly conform to the specifications laid down by them in their order.

The terms and conditions of this agreement do not suit me.

Antonyms:

| Misfit | Irregularities | Differ |

Disagree

Examples:

He is misfit for the work assigned to him.

He indulges in irregularities which cause the failure of the projects. And then he dares to differ with his colleagues over the minor issues of business.

He will not differ from us in this matter.

Adjust (Verb)

Please, adjust the knob at the top to make this remote-control work.

Synonyms:

Set in order	Arrange	Set right
Regulate	Accommodate	Settle
Set	Compose	

Examples:
One needs a lot of courage and skills to set the system in order in a corrupt department.
It took him two hours to arrange the articles and set them right.
A person has to accommodate himself to many unpleasant things in life.
We need not resort to war to settle our territorial disputes with the neighbouring countries if we keep ourselves in a good military strength.

Antonyms:

Displace	Disarrange	Dislocate
Disconnect	Derange	Disjoint

Examples:
When he entered the room, he found everything in a shattered and displaced.
Our lives, in war ridden Gulf countries, are dislocated and disjointed.
The failure to affect a happy marriage left him gravely deranged.

Admire (Verb)

The whole nation admired The President for the New Economic Policies introduced by him.

Synonyms:

Applaud	Extol	Approve
Praise		

Examples:
The public applauded the sentimental speech made by the orator.
The politician extolled the people to reform their character by giving up selfishness.
The government has approved the proposal for the expansion of Small Scale Industries.
Let us praise those who deserve it.

Antonyms:

Despise	Blame	Condemn
Disapprove		

Examples:
You are following the wrong path hence you despise my best advices.
It is no use blaming others for the social ills. First we have to look within.
Such attitude on the part of the administration needs to be condemned.

Admit (Verb)

They admitted that it was only they who mixed water with milk.

Synonyms:

| Own | Avow | Grant |
| Concede | Give | Yield |

Examples:

We could locate no one to own the box found on the railway platform.
He avowed to be not guilty in very strong terms but the Judge remained unconvinced and sentenced him to imprisonment for five long years.
He has conceded to me a big loan for starting the construction of my house.
You ought to give the porter a nice trip.
Her parents yielded at last to let her marry with the boy of a low cast.

Antonyms:

| Disown | Disavow | Deny |
| Dispute | Disclaim | |

Examples:

We disowned any control over the property after the dispute was settled by the court.
He did not deny his involvement in the crime.
Your sole proprietorship over this house is disputed by your sons.
They have disclaimed that they are not responsible for the absence, if any, of accuracy in the information given by the newspaper.

Adopt (Verb)

The Clinton Foundation adopted more than thousand children from India and Sri Lanka affected by Tsunami

Synonyms:

Accept	Appropriate	Approve
Assume	Embrace	Endorse
Espouse	Follow	Maintain
Ratify	Sleet	Support

Examples:

He proposed marriage and she accepted.
Some of the opposition policies have been appropriated by the government.
I approve of your trying to earn some money but do not neglect your studies.
I think we can safely assume that the present situation is going to continue.
She was quick to embrace the opportunity.

Antonyms:

Abandon	Abnegate	Cast aside
cast off	Disclaim	Disown
Give up	Reject	Renounce

| Repudiate | Spurn |

Examples:
They abandoned their properties and lands to the invading forces.
She has cast her old friends aside.
I never give up my ambitions just to save few bucks.
The players who were previously rejected have been brought back into the team.
They have renounced their old criminal ways of life.

Adore (verb)

He adored his fiancée for her beauty and sharp intelligence.

Synonyms:

Admire	Bow to	Cherish
Dote on	Esteem	Exalt
Glorify	honour	Idolize
Revere	Venerate	Worship

Examples:
I admire him for his success in his business.
We are tired of having to bow to authority.
Children feel the need to be cherished.
By restructuring the ministry, the Prime Minister has esteemed the sentiments of public.
He was exalted as pillars of this community.

Antonyms:

Abhor	Abominate	Despise
Detest	Execrate	Hate
Loather		

Examples:
Strike-breakers are often despised by their fellow workers.
He detests having to get up early in the morning.
He hates to be kept waiting.
I loathe having to go to this conference.

Adversity (Noun)

Our Company is prepared to face an adversity of any kind.

Synonyms:

| Affliction | Misery | Poverty |
| Misfortune | | |

Examples:
Although aware of the affliction of his son, the father did not lend him any help.
Gambling was the root cause of the misery that befell this family.

In Pakistan poverty is wide spread than it is in Sri Lanka.
It was his misfortune that despite all his training he could not be selected to become an space-flight.

Antonyms:

| Prosperity | Lick | Fortune |
| Happiness | Progress | |

Examples:
India cannot gain prosperity until the village folk attain a better standard of living.
I wish you good luck on your journey on your trip abroad.
It is my good fortune to be your friend.
It gives me great happiness to release this book.

Advise (Verb)

If you advise your son on this matter, he will not like it.

Synonyms:

| Warn | Admonish | Recommend |
| Counsel | Suggest | |

Prompt **Examples:**
India has warned Pakistan that any accumulation of warms will go against its own interest.
His officer admonished him for carelessness in handling the official work.
The measures now recommended by the Planning Commission to improve the Pakistan economy are very practical.
One has to repent if one goes against the council of elders.
He could not suggest even a single practicable solution for resolving the problem.
He was prompted by his father to embark upon such an ambitious plan.

Antonyms:

| Deter | Dissuade | Restrain |
| Hinder | Discourage | Criticize |

Examples:
This warning need not deter the brave but rather prepare them to face the even more bravely.
Mohan continues dissuading his son from going to USA.
I had to restrain my outbursts on the arrival of the unwanted guest.

Affable (Adjective)

Her affable nature gained her more friends in this alien environment.

Synonyms:

Amiable	Amicable	Benevolent
Benign	Congenial	Cordially
Courteous	Genial	Gracious

Mild	Pleasant	Sociable

Examples:
Her parents seemed very amiable.
An amicable settlement was reached between him and his brother over the properties of their father.
I find this aspect of my job particularly congenial.
He was courteous but did not encourage conversation.
He was most courteous to everyone, smiling and thanking them all.
She gave a mild answer in spite of his annoyance.

Antonyms:
Brusque	Cold	Discourteous
Distant	Haughty	Ride
Surly	Unfriendly	Ungracious
Unpleasant		

Examples:
His reply was typically brusque.
Here expression was one of haughty contempt.
It is rude to interrupt when somebody is speaking.
He was distinctly unfriendly towards me.
It was ungracious of me not to acknowledge your help.

Affecting (Adjective)

What is affecting him the most is the indifferent attitude of his father?

Synonyms:
Touching	Melting	Moving
Pathetic	Eloquent	Impressive
Changing		

Examples:
His performance was so touching that the audience could not help weeping.
Wax solidifies again after melting and drying.
Siddhartha's heart was moved on seeing the pathetic condition of the old lady.
Swami Vivekananda's speech was so eloquent that Americans became his fans within no time.
The data furnished by him was so impressive that none of the members of the Society could oppose any of his suggestions.

Antonyms:
Amusing	Droll	Ridiculous
Absurd	Funny	Comic
Laughable	Farcical	

Examples:
It is amusing to find him going up to a tree.
Your proposal to break this partnership is ridiculous.
Do not act funny. Do as I say.

Afraid (Adjective)

Now a day, the children are not afraid of their parents.

Synonyms:

Frightened	Scared	Fearful
Panicky	Fainthearted	Anxious

Examples:
The child was frightened to see a snake.
Though he is very rich he is always scared of the adversities of life.
When it was announced that the ship was in danger everybody aboard became panicky.
He could not do well in his examination. But he is anxious to know the result now.
When communalism erupts, even the neighbours are fearful of each other.
He is posing as a brave man. But I know it certain that he is fainthearted when it becomes a matter of emergencies.

Antonyms:

Brave	Bold	Courageous
Unafraid	Daring	Upright

Examples:
Atul is a brave boy. He is bold and courageous when he faces emergencies.
He can take a daring decision on the spun of the moment.
He is also upright on principles.

Alarming (Adjective)

The alarming rises in the prices of essential items caused intolerable problems to the ordinary people.

Synonyms:

Frightful	Terrible	Ominous

Examples:
The scene of the rail accident was frightful.
War clouds always bring terrible circumstances.
The present day atmosphere round the world is changed with ominous fear of destruction.

Antonyms:

Hopeful	Bright	Auspicious

Examples:
The new peaceful atmosphere in the country is hopeful of a brighter future.
US-USSR decision on disarmament gives a bright picture of the future world.
The growth rate of 5 % per annum for the Seventh Five Year Plan is considered auspicious.

ALLAY (Verb)

Your presence did allay my fear when I was caught in the traffic jam.

Synonyms:
Ease	Lighten	Abate
Relieve	Palliate	Soothe
Get rid of	Assuage	

Examples:
A person can ease himself by admitting his fault.
You can lighten your heart by telling your difficulties to your friends.
We should sincerely fight and abate the communal forces.
This medicine has a soothing effect and is likely to relieve the patients of their pain immediately.
His words sounded eloquent but could not palliate the sorrow of his friend.
Ambitious young people try to get rid of the traditions.
A stone-hearted person may repress his own feelings but cannot assuage the feelings of others.

Antonyms:
Aggravate	Enhance	Worsen
Heighten		

Examples:
Timidity always aggravates a bad situation.
It does not enhance resistance to dangers.
It tends to worsen the overall circumstances.
His lack of co-operation heightens the fear-complex and dislocates high spirits and courageous action.

Allegiance (Noun)

Members of Parliament took the oath of allegiance to the Queen.

Synonyms:
Adherence	Constance	Devotion
Duty	Faithfulness	Fealty
Fidelity	Homage	Obedience
Obligation	Consistency	

Examples:
The Gold leaf will adhere to any clean metal surface. We prefer Gold only for its adherence.
She has played with great consistency all season.
Her devotion to the job left her with little free time.
Marital fidelity is not valued as highly as it once was.
He describes his book as homage to his father.
They attended the party more out of a sense of obligation than anything else.

Antonyms:

Disloyalty	Faithfulness	Falseness
Inconstancy	Infidelity	Perfidy
Treachery	Treason	

Examples:
He has been accused of disloyalty to the party.
She tolerated her husband's frequent infidelities.
In the second part of the drama he learns of Giovanni's perfidy swears revenge.
In this country treachery and treason are considered criminal offences

Alliance (Noun)

Democratic Party formed an alliance with Labour Party with the sole intention of defeating Republic Party.

Synonyms:

Affiliation	Affinity	Agreement
Association	Coalition	Combination
Compact	Concordant	Confederacy
Connection	Federation	League
Pact	Partnership	Treaty

Examples:
This College has sought affiliation to Columbia University.
She has strong affinity for music and classical dance.
Do you belong to any professional association?
It is the combination of wit and analysis that makes his article so readable.
The two states have made a compact to co-operate in fighting terrorism.
They made a pact not to tell anyone.
She worked in partnership with her sister.

Antonyms:

Alienation	Breach	Break
Disaffection	Dissociation	Disunion
Disunity	Division	Rapture
Separation	Severance	Split

Examples:
His criminal activities lead to complete alienation from his family.
There are signs of growing disaffection among his followers.
I wish to dissociate myself from the views expressed by my colleagues.
Separation from his friends made him sad.
The children split up into small groups.

Altruistic (Adjective)

The altruistic services rendered by Mother Teresa got her the Nobel Peace Prize.

Synonyms:
Benevolent	Charitable	Considerate
Generous	Humanitarian	Philanthropic
Self-sacrificing	Unselfish	

Examples:
You should try to be more charitable to your neighbours.
It was generous of you to share your food with your friends.
Since he is old and sick, doctors say he should be released from prison on humanitarian grounds.
Her work with refugees involved considerable self-sacrificing.

Antonyms:
Egoistical	Egotistical	Greedy
Mean	Self-centred	Self-interested
Selfish	Self-seeking	

Examples:
I had always thought him to be egotistical and attention-seeking.
The starving child looked at the cake with greedy eyes.
When you have children, you have to become less selfish.

Always (Adverb)

He is always ready to extend his helping hands for the up lift of the poor people.

Synonyms:
Aye	Consistently	Constantly
Eternally	Ever	Everlasting
Evermore	Forever	Invariably
Perpetually		

Examples:
We drove through constantly changing scenery.
For the invaluable help that you rendered to me, I will be eternally grateful to you.
Paul ever the optimist, agreed to give it one last try.
The land will remain our national heritage evermore.
She invariably arrives late.

Antonyms:

Hardly ever	Infrequently	Once in a blue moon
Once in a while	Only now and then	Rarely
Scarcely	Ever seldom	

Examples:
He hardly ever goes to bed before midnight.
Such cases are relatively frequent.
I only see her once in a blue moon.
Once in a while we go to restaurant, but usually we eat at home.
She is rarely seen in public nowadays.

Allure (Verb)

Money allures all.

Synonyms:

Charm	Invite	Entice
Draw	Fascinate	Endear

Examples:
Her exuberant beauty can charm even the stoics.
There are occasions when the government invites opposition parties to discuss important issues.
Unscrupulous and snit-social elements always entice criminals to commit more crimes.
The thief was so much fascinated by the speech of the priest that he gave up thieving and became his disciple.
The more we endear a child, the more it will become to obey us.

Antonyms:

Repulse	Rebuff	Reject
Repel	Deter	Check

Examples:
The very presence of the villain repulsed the good atmosphere of the scene.
Rajesh rebuffed the satirical remark of the competitor about his product.
Ram rejected the reconciliation offer of his supplier.
Similar poles of magnets repel each other.
The noisy atmosphere did not deter him from his studies.
The opposition forces tried to check his advance but he was too determined to be held back.

Ally (Noun)

The Political ally of Republic Party for the forthcoming election is Labour Party.
Synonyms:

Friend	Accessory	Abettor
Spy	Companion	Co-operator
Colleague	Partner	Accomplice

Examples:
A friend in deed is a friend indeed.
An abettor is usually involved, either actively or passively whenever there is a crime.
Two Pakistanis spies were caught by the police in Ferozepur.
Members of congress from the same state are colleagues, though they may be political opponents.
Their business flourished very much when they were partners but now both of them have become paupers.
One of the pick-pockets was caught by the police, but his accomplice managed to flee.

Antonyms:
Enemy	Opponent	Rival
Competitor	Oppose	Foe
Antagonist		

Examples:
The rulers of Pakistan have always considered India an enemy country mainly for the sake of maintaining themselves in power or to check internal antagonists, opposes or rivals.

Almighty (Noun)

The Almighty blesses all.

Synonyms:
Absolute	All-powerful	Invincible
Omnipotent	Omnipresent	Omniscient
Supreme	Unlimited	

Examples:
She has an invincible belief in God.
A theist believes that God is omnipresent.
After a year without defeat, the team now reigns Supreme as the finest team in the country.
Our car hire rate includes unlimited mileage.

Antonyms:
Helpless	Impotent	Powerless
Weak	Feeble	Insignificant
Paltry	Poor	

Examples:
Without weapons we are helpless.
Without a chairman's support, the committee is impotent.
I feel powerless in your absence.
The level of dangerous chemicals present in the river is now so low as to be insignificant.
She is still weak after her illness.

Alone (Adjective)

I am alone. But, I do not feel lonely.

Synonyms:

Abandoned	Apart	By itself
Deserted	Desolate	Forlorn
Lonely	Single	Lone
Isolated		

Examples:
She keeps herself apart from other people.
The machine will start by itself in few minutes.
The road was completely deserted.
We all felt absolutely desolate when she left us.
Empty house quickly takes on a forlorn look.
Several villages have been isolated by heavy snowfalls.
I live alone but I never felt lonely.

Antonyms:

Accompanied	Aided	Among others
Assisted	Escorted	Helped
Joint	Together	

Examples:
He was accompanied on the expedition by his wife.
His absence aided the rebels to gain control of the city.
Check that the joints of the pipes are properly sealed.
Get all the ingredients together before you start cooking.

Amazing (Adjective)

The amazing performance of The Hero in this movie will create a record of its genre.

Synonyms:

Extraordinary	Surprising	Miraculous
Marvellous	Wondrous	Stupendous
Wonderful	Astounding	

Examples:
One can attain extraordinary powers through Yoga.
The comet seemed to approach the earth at a surprising speed.
The vehicle was totally smashed but the drivers had a miraculous escape in the accident.
Taj Mahal is a marvellous piece of architecture.
The super powers spend stupendous amounts on nuclear weapons.
When a villager comes to city, everything looks wonderful to him.
The recent earth quake had filled the local citizens with astounding grief.

Antonyms:

Ordinary	Normal	Common
Everyday	Commonplace	Average
Habitual	Usual	

Examples:
Ordinary citizens in India can spend a life of normal comfort.
The common man in the country does not enjoy everyday needs like food, cloth and shelter.
Radio and television have become commonplace items.
An average individual has a reasonable scope for a minimum earning.

Ambition (Noun)

His only ambition in his life is to become a doctor that is why he has taken up the study of Biology.

Synonyms:

Purpose	Desire	Wish
Hope	Intention	Goal
End	Destination	End post
Aim		

Examples:
Selfish people develop friendship for one or the other purpose.
I wish if I were a king.
Hope is the zest of life.
His action belied his intention.
His only ambition in his life is to become a doctor that is why he has taken up the study of Biology.
Hinduism lays more emphasis on the goal of life.
Revolutionaries and extremists hold the view that quality of means does not matter so long as the end is achieved.

Antonyms:

Indifference	Purposelessness	Aimlessness
Hopelessness		

Examples:
He is indifferent to the means. What matters to him is the objective.
He keeps busy without a mission. His life is marked by purposelessness.
Aimlessness causes wastage of time, money and effort.

Amorous (Adjective)

It can't be expected that she should discuss her amorous matter with all of us.

Synonyms:

Affectionate	Amatory	Ardent
Attached	Doting	Enamoured
Erotic	Fond	Impassioned
In love	Lovesick	Lustful
Passionate	Tender	Loving

Examples:
He is very affectionate towards his children.
She is enamoured with the boy next door.
The photographs are profoundly erotic.
The children performed a short play watched by their fond parents.
She needs a lot of tender loving care.

Antonyms:

Aloof	Cold	Distant
Frigid	Frosty	Indifferent
Passionless	Stand-offish	Undemonstrative
Unfeeling	Unloving	

Examples:
She kept herself aloof from her fellow students.
He seems distant until you get know him.
She appeared indifferent to their sufferings.
She often appears cold and unfeeling.

Ample (Adjective)
You have ample time to develop your personality and skills.

Synonyms:

Full	Broad	Unrestricted
Unlimited	Sufficient	Large
Spacious	Abundant	Extensive

Examples:
For a man who has a smile, broad and liberal outlook, life is full of joy and happiness.
If a man were given unrestricted liberties, he will tend to become a slave to greed and crime.

It was a large house. There was sufficient room in it to accommodate the marriage party.
Our college has a spacious building.
In our library we have collected abundant materials for the study of public utility services.
The politicians out of necessity undertake extensive tours to their constituencies at the time of election.

Antonyms:

Scarce	Short	Restricted
Limited	Insufficient	Small
Skimpy	Narrow	

Examples:
When a product becomes scarce in its supply, its price tends to go up.
Kerosene is in short supply these days.
We in India restricted yet abundant rights.
In an incorporated company, the financial responsibility of the shareholders is limited to the value of the shares held.
The space at our disposal is insufficient; therefore, we cannot undertake additional activities.

Amuse (Verb)

The performance of the animals in the circus amused the children.

Synonyms:

Please	Enliven	Entertain
Gladden	Charm	Cheer

Examples:
No one can please every body.
A shrewd speaker enlivens the audience by quoting various jokes from daily life.
The artists were very glad to meet the soldiers and entertain them.
The audience was charmed by the personality of Mrs. Gandhi and cheered her with great applauses when she proceeded to the dais to deliver her speech.

Antonyms:

Bore	Annoy	Tire
Fatigue	Wax	

Examples:
The politician proved a poor speaker by boring the audience with his insipid speech... He was therefore hooted down by the audience.
The subordinate happened to annoy his boss by his irresponsible behaviour.
Rajesh got tired of the routine and employed a clerk to relieve him of routine duties.
It is natural for the old man to feel fatigued after a whole day's hard work.
His health was giving ways, but he waxed his way by tact.

Animated (Adjective)

All his life, this great man was animated by a passion for truth and justice.

Synonyms:

Active	Airy	Alive and kicking
Ardent	Brisk	Buoyant
Dynamic	Ebullient	Elated
Energetic	Enthusiastic	Excited
Fervent	Gay	Passionate
Quick	Sparky	Vivacious
Vivid	Zealous	Zestful

Examples:

She takes an active part in local politics.
You will be glad to hear that The Will is alive and kicking.
Despite all the setbacks, she remained buoyant.
She was elated to hear the news that Indian cricket team beat Pakistan Cricket team.
You must take few energetic exercises.
We hoped that his fervent approach will make him succeed.
I feel quite sparkly this morning.

Antonyms:

Apathetic	Boring	Dejected
Depressed	Dull	Inactive
Lethargic	Lifeless	Listless
Monotonous	Passive	

Examples:

He is totally apathetic about world affairs.
Repeated failure had left him feeling very dejected.
He felt deeply depressed even suicidal at times.
The hot weather made him listless and lethargic.

Animosity (Noun)

The animosity between India and Pakistan will come to an end sooner by the efforts of well-wishers of both countries.

Synonyms:

Acrimony	Animus	Antagonism
Antipathy	Bad blood	Bitterness
Enmity	Hatred	Ill will
Malevolence	Malice	Rancour
Virulence	Resentment	

Examples:
The dispute was settled without acrimony.
The antagonism he felt towards his old enemy was still very strong.
She made no attempt to hide her feelings of antipathy.
The pay cut caused bitterness and resentment among the staff.
I do not understand his enmity towards his parents.
She certainly bears you no malice.

Antonyms:

Amity	Benevolence	Congeniality
Friendliness	Friendship	Goodwill
Harmony	Kindness	Love
Rapport	Sympathy	

Examples:
The aim of the conference is to promote international friendship.
He did it entirely out of kindness, not for money.
He shows little love towards her.
He has developed very good rapport with his pupils.
Given goodwill on both sides I am sure we can reach agreement.
She showed no sympathy when I told her I am in trouble.

Anger (Verb)

Def: - make someone mad, become mad.

Synonyms:

Acerbate,	Affront,	Aggravate,
Agitate,	Annoy,	Antagonize,
Arouse,	Bait,	Blow up,
Boil over,	Boil, bristle,	Burn,
Burn up,	Chafe,	Craze,
Cross,	Displease,	Egg on,
Embitter,	Enrage,	Exacerbate,
Exasperate,	Excite,	Fret,
Gall,	Get mad,	Get on one's nerves,
Goad,	Incense,	Inflame,
Infuriate,	Irritate,	Lose one's temper,
Madden,	Make sore,	Miff,
Nettle,	Offend,	Outrage,
Pique,	Provoke,	Raise hell,
Rankle,	Rant,	Rave,
Rile,	Ruffle,	Seethe,

| Steam up, | Stew, | Stir up, |
| Tempt, | Umbrage, | Vex. |

Antonyms:

| Calm. | Forbear, | Make happy, |
| Quiet, | Soothe on. | |

Annexation (Noun)

Annexation of part of India by China in 1962 was condemned by United Nations.

Synonyms:

Increase	Expansion	Supplement
Augmentation	Accession	Extension
Appendix		

Examples:

The expenses of man increase with income.

There is much more expansion in gases than in liquids or in solids.

The scientists are now engaged in supplementing the efforts of agriculturists for augmentation of produce.

India has occasionally protested the accession of its territories by China in its 1962 attack.

In the view of the unabated local disturbance extension of curfew another 24 hours was announced.

The note should be brief and precise. The details may be added as an appendix if necessary.

Antonyms:

Decrease	Contraction	Curtailment
Subtraction	Diminution	Reduction
Fall		

Examples:

India's annual death rate had greatly decreased since Independence owing to better medical and health facilities made available to the common people.

A gap is left between rails to provide for expansion and contraction of steel.

There is curtailment of demand for goods even with increase in prices.

Annihilate (Verb)

The invaded forces were annihilated by Our Army.

Synonyms:

Destroy	Cancel	Annul
Suppress	Extinguish	Supersede
Repeal		

Examples:
The enemies kept bombing the city until all the buildings were destroyed.
The Minister cancelled his tour of North Eastern States to preside over the non-aligned meet in New Delhi.
The policies adopted by the new Mayor annulled the good results of the schemes initiated by his predecessor.
The fireman struggled the whole night to extinguish the fire.
Two of his junior officers superseded him because of a vigilance case pending against him.
An Act passed by the parliament cannot be repealed by any State Legislature.

Antonyms:

Establish	Confirm	Support
Encourage	Promote	Forward
Produce	Testify	

Examples:
The non-aligned meet in New Delhi agreed to establish an independent news agency for covering reports on the activities of the movement around the world.
The Geneva Conference of the Super-Powers on disarmament confirmed the need to have a nuclear free outer space.
India and other non-aligned countries have supported the move to have a nuclear-free outer space.

Annoy (Verb)

He was annoyed with his wife because the dinner was badly cooked.

Synonyms:

Worry	Torment	Trouble
Vex	Irritate	Disturb
Bother	Harass	Tease

Examples:
A man who believes in luck does not worry about his future.
The opposition parties always try to trouble and vex the government by politicizing the national issues.
A sportsman should not feel irritated if he is defeated by his opponent.
His habit of flouting his subordinates disturbs the whole business.
This drastic and unfair law gives ample opportunities to officers to harass the public.
In colleges the students are nowadays prone to tease the teachers.

Antonyms:

Please	Charm	Oblige
Gratify	Gladden	Delight

Examples:
She has a pleasing personality.
Her charm leaves the onlookers spellbound.
You can oblige me by helping in solving my little financial problem.
It will delight me if you pay an early visit.

Annoy

Def: - irritate, upset.

Synonyms:

Abrade,	Agitate,	Ask for it,
Badger,	Be at,	Be on the back of,
Bedevil,	Beleaguer,	Bore,
Bother,	Break,	Bug,
Burn up,	Chafe,	Displease,
Distress,	Disturb,	Egg on,
Exasperate,	Fire up,	Get,
Gnaw,	Harass,	Harry,
Heat up,	Henpeck,	Hit where one lives,
Irk,	Madden,	Make waves,
Miff,	Nag,	Needle,
Nettle,	Nudge,	Peeve,
Perturb,	Pester,	Plague,
Provoke,	Push,	Button,
Ride,	Rile,	Ruffle,
Tease,	Tick off,	Trouble,
Turn off,	Vex,	Work on,
Worry.		

Antonyms:

Aid,	Gratify,	Make happy,
Please,	Soothe	

Examples:

His own crabbed sentences go far to exasperate even a reader who must needs respect his scholarship.

Limited growing regions where the climate is acceptable for apricot, further exasperate the situation.

Additionally, it would also only exasperate the problem of meeting the local demand for firewood.

Answer (Verb)

He answered that he knew nothing about that.

Synonyms:

Reply	Retort	Repartee
Rejoinder	Response	Solution

Examples:

It is advisable to reply the business letters the same day.
I retorted to his charges in a rejoinder.
George Bernard Shaw always carried a sense of repartee to match every situation.

Antonyms:

Query	Interrogation	Defiance
Question		

Examples:

Nowadays business queries have to be answered the same day.
In day-today affairs of business there are many interrogations to be tackled and answered.
Over-expectation usually brings defiance.

Antiquated (Adjective)

No antiquated idea is welcome in this meeting.

Synonyms:

Antediluvian	Antique	Archaic
Date	Old-fashioned	Outmoded
Out-of-date	Obsolete	Outworn
Passé	Old	Superannuated

Examples:

His ideas are positively antediluvian.
Thou art' is an archaic form of you is.
Kids which are now becoming obsolete will not be taught in this institution.
Five years-old should be able to read.

Antonyms:

Current	Fashionable	Fresh
Modern	Modish	New
Stylish	Up-to-date	Young

Examples:

It is becoming fashionable to have long hair again.
Terrorism is one of the major problems of the modern world.
She wears clothes that are right up to date.
Though he is sixty, he is young in his outlook.

Anxiety (Noun)

We waited with anxiety for the news of her safe arrival.

Synonyms:

Restlessness	Apprehension	Disquiet
Dread	Worry	Misgiving
Foreboding	Uneasiness	Concern

Examples:

I do not know why he is feeling the intense form of restlessness.
It is only an apprehension that he may not come today as he promised.
The news about the death of his father gave him disquiet.
The moment the news that he was not selected for the army reached him, a sense of uneasiness crept in him.
The misgivings about the wellbeing of the Minister are still alive.

Antonyms:

Assurance	Calmness	Composure
Confidence	Ace	Security
Quietude	Equanimity	

Examples:

There is no assurance that he will marry your daughter.
The calmness prevailed among the students was disturbed by the news that the Principal of the college dismissed a student.
There is security for the postmen who travel a long distance to deliver letters.
The quietude that prevails in a forest can be seen anywhere else.

Aplomb (Noun)

In the interview, he answered all the questions with a perfect aplomb

Synonyms:

Self-possession	Balance	Calmness
Composure	Confidence	Coolness
Equanimity	Poise	Self-assurance
Stability.	Self-confidence	

Examples:

He showed a remarkable composure in a difficult situation.
There is a lack of confidence in the current government.
I admire his coolness under pressure.
She is facing the prospect of her operation with cheerful equanimity.

Antonyms:

Awkwardness	Chagrin	Confusion
Discomfiture	Discomposure	Embarrassment
Self	Consciousness	

Examples:
Much to his chagrin, he came last in the race.
There is some confusion about what the right procedure should be.
He persisted with his question despite his obvious discomfiture.
She was overcome with embarrassment at the idea.

Apocryphal (Adjective)

His books on England are treated with an apocryphal look by the scholars.

Synonyms:

Doubtful	Dubious	Equivocal
Fictitious	Legendry	Mythical
Spurious	Unauthenticated	Uneconomical

Examples:
She looked rather doubtful.
I remain dubious about his motive.
He gave an equivocal reply, typical of politicians.
All the characters and places in my novel are fictitious.

Antonyms:

Attested	Authentic	Authorized
Canonical	Credible	Factual
Substantiated	True	Undisputed
Verified		

Examples:
I have authorized him to act in my place when I am away.
Is there is credible alternative to the nuclear deterrent?
Can you substantiate your accusation against him?
Unfortunately, what you say about the company is all too true.

Appearance (Noun)
We must not judge people by their appearance.

Synonyms:

Sight	View	Show
Outlook	Scene	Tableau
Scenery	Setting	Picture
Landscape		

Examples:
Rhinoceros is deadly to sight.
What a beautiful view of the sea from this window!
Your outlook on life seems quite constructive.
The scenery of Kashmir attracts our poetic admiration.
The landscape of Switzerland is comparable to that of London.

Antonyms:

Formless   Distorted   Skeleton
Insulting

Examples:
The area surrounding this coal mine is the least interesting. It is almost formless.
The scene in Baghdad today gives a grim distorted picture of the war-torn great city.

Appreciation (Noun)

She showed little appreciation of good music.

Synonyms:

Love   Regard   Respect
Praise

Examples:
Love for humanity is the greatest service to God.
The rich should pay due regard to the poor.
Respect for religion and community makes a complete man.
A just praise is gift and unjust one is nothing but a flattery.

Antonyms:

Hate   Disrespect   Disregard
Condemn   Disapprove

Examples:
The worst disrespect one shows to God is to hate a human being.
All relations unanimously disapprove the use of violence in human relations.
Strong condemnation of violence is what we need at this hour of crisis in personal lives.
Never disregard your parents. Nor your relatives

APPROPRIATE (Verb)

$ 20,000.00 has been appropriated for the new school building.

Synonyms: Confiscate

Take   Allot   Seize
Correct

Examples:
This Act will empower the Government to confiscate the properties of the smugglers.
Anita took my advices on all important issues.
Deepak was allotted a piece of land in the heart of this city.
The documents seized by the police proved that he was guilty.
The action taken by the government is correct for the solution of the problem.

Antonyms:

Release   Relinquish   Open

Loosen   Incorrect

Examples:
The principal released the plot of land which had been inappropriately occupied by the college.
The government has lost its hold on the private sector by announcing its new industrial policy.
The new policies have opened the scope for new ventures in industry and trade.

Approve (Verb)

Her father will never approve of her marriage with you.

Synonyms:

Acclaim	Admire	Applaud
Appreciate	Commend	Esteem
Like	Regard highly	Respect
Accept	Advocate	Allow
Confirm	Bless	Give the green signal
Mandate		

Examples:
It was acclaimed as a great discovery.
I admire him for his success in business.
The crowd applauded him for five minutes.
The school appreciated her for her shining results in the final board examinations.
The Journalist was commended for his reporting of the case.
The changes provide an opportunity for The President to recapture the public esteem.

Antonyms:

Blame	Censure	Condemn
Deplore	Deprecate	Disapprove
Dislike	Frown upon	Object to
Disallow	Discountenance	Veto

Examples:
The bad work man always blames his tools.
Two students were censured by their class teacher for their low performance in the examination.
The newspapers were quick to condemn him for his mistakes.
The President said that he deplored the killings of the innocent people by the extremists.
The article deprecates the negative attitude of the politicians.

Apt (Adjective)

He is very apt at picking up a new subject.

Synonyms:

Suitable	Fitting	Liable
Likely	Prone	Ready
Apposite	Befitting	Correct
Germane	Meet	Pertinent
Proper	Relevant	Quick-witted

Examples:

You will be liable for any damage caused.
The most suitable dress for this occasion is pant and shirt.
Your response is not the most fitting reply to his remarks.
This U-turn is the most accident prone area in this highway.
What he said is not pertinent to the question on the table.
She is the most quick-witted girl in the whole school.
Whatever you say, that should be relevant to the issue.
The correct answer for this question can be found in the page number 45 of the book.

Antonyms:

Ill-fitted	Improper	Inapplicable
Inapposite Infelicitous	Irrelevant	Awkward
Clumsy	Dull	Gauche
Incompetent	Maladroit	Slow
Stupid		

Examples:

It is thought improper for the old ladies to wear bright clothes.
The rules seem inapplicable to this situation.
The handle of this tea pot has an awkward shape.
The conference was deadly dull.
The boy is not as stupid as you think.

Arbitrary (Adjective)

Taking an arbitrary decision will not boost your image.

Synonyms:

Capricious	Chance	Discretionary
Erratic	Fanciful	Inconsistent
Optional	Personal	Subjective
Unreasonable	Whimsical	Illogical
Irrational		

Examples:
The scheme is not as fanciful as it sounds.
Such behaviour is inconsistent with her high-minded principles.
The CD-Player is an optional element in this car.
We will join you later. We have something personal to discuss first.
Our perception of things is often influenced by subjective factors such as tiredness.
Much of his works have a whimsical sense of humour.

Antonyms:

Consistent	Judicious	Logical
Objective	Rational	Reasonable
Sensible	Sound	

Examples:
You are not very consistent. First you condemn me then you praise me.
It is the only logical thing to do.
He finds to remain objective when it becomes a matter of his son.
No rational person would behave like this.
She is perfectly reasonable in her demand.

Archaic (Adjective)

Thou art' is the archaic forms of you are.

Synonyms:

Ancient	Antique	Bygone
Olden	Primitive	Obsolete
Out of date	Passé	Superannuated

Examples:
I feel pretty ancient when I see how the younger generation behaves.
The cave provided a primitive shelter from the storm.
Skills which are becoming obsolete now will not be taught in this institution.
He was a fine actor, but he is a bit passé.

Antonyms:

Contemporary	Current	Modern
New	Present	Recent Fresh
Latest	Novel	

Examples:
Palikir Bazaar is one of the modern shopping complexes in this country.
Everything in this department still seems very new to her.
There were 500 people present in the meeting.
She was keen to forget her recent failures.

Ascent (Verb)

We watched the mists ascending from the valley.

Synonyms:

Further	Go forward	Progress
Proceed		

Examples:

Gandhi sacrificed his life to further the cause of the humanity.
He went forward with his technique of non-violence in spite of severe criticism from many quarters.
Hard work and firm determination are the two planks to progress.
He is a clever man. He takes necessary precautions before proceeding further.

Antonyms:

Bend	Go backward	Regress
Recede	Descend	

Examples:

Gandhi made British Government bend at last.
Some people are criticizing the Chinese Government for its going backward from its socialistic attitude.
The stiff attitude of The President Reagan of the United States on the issue of nuclear disarmament means a regress in international relations.

Assist (Verb)

Def: - help.

Synonyms:

Abet,	Aid,	Back,
Bail out,	Benefit,	Boost,
Collaborate,	Cooperate,	Do for,
Expedite,	Facilitate,	Further,
Give a boost,	Give a leg up,	Give a lift,
Go down the line for,	Fo for, go to bat for,	Go with,
Grease the wheels,	Hype, lend a hand,	Make a pitch for,
Open doors, plug,	Puff, push,	Put on the map,
Reinforce,	Relieve,	Ride,
Shotgun,	Root for,	Run interference for,
Serve, stand up for,	Stump,	Support,
Sustain,	Take care of,	Thump,
Work for,	Work with.	

Antonyms:

Hinder,	Hurt,	Stop,
Thwart.		

Associate (Verb)

We associate Egypt with the Nile.

Synonyms:

Connect	Ally	Band
Fraternize	Join	Combine
Unite	Relate	Link

Examples:

This road connects New York with many important cities.
Germany betrayed its many allies during the Second World War.
It is necessary to keep admiring the band of martyrs for the sake of keeping the patriotic spirit among the youth.
The combination of these ideas may resolve the problem.
In India the opposition parties get united during the elections only.

Antonyms:

Disconnect	Separate	Defy
Break apart	Dissociate	Desert

Examples:

The electrician disconnected the electrical supply at the mains to test the safety of wires.
We cannot reach the right conclusion without separating the discussion of the two issues involved.
The opposition political parties broke apart as they could not fit their irrespective ideologies in one frame.

Assure (Verb)

The sum assured by him is more than what he could pay premium for.

Synonyms:

Ensure	Guarantee	Certify
Uphold	Encourage	Promise
Inform		

Examples:

We have to ensure necessary circumstances before taking up the proposed measures.
It is very difficult to guarantee the right to work to everybody in a newly independent country.
The Constitution of India upholds the six Fundamental Rights to the citizens in the country.

Antonyms:

Imperil	Unsettle	Discourage
Mislead	Warn	Jeopardize

Examples:
It is very difficult to undertake this project without imperilling the economy of this firm.
The personal misuse of the company's funds by directors tended to unsettle its very continuance.
Lack of law and order discourages the propensity to save.

Assume (Verb)

But we assumed other way that he married your sister.
Synonyms:

Pretend	Affect	Feign
Shame	Suppose	Imply
Presume	Presuppose	Simulate

Examples:
She pretended that she was not at home when we rang the bell.
What makes you suppose I am against it?
His silence seemed to imply agreement.
I presume that you still want to come.

Antonyms:

Abandon	Cast-off	Discard
Reprove	Substantiate	Confirm
Establish	Verify	

Examples:
They abandoned their land and property to the invading force.
As a boy I often wore my elder brother's cast-off.
The grass was littered with discarded cans and cardboard boxes.
The priest reproved people for not attending church more often.
Could you substantiate your accusation against him?

Astonish (Verb)

His escape from the fire accident astonished all of us.
Synonyms:

Surprise	Amaze	Astound
Startle	Confound	

Examples:
The final reversal in election fortunes surprised the masses.
People stood amazed at the feat of the jugglers.
Victory of the Indian team over the Pakistan team in the World Cup Cricket astounded the whole world.
The deviations in the Pyramids of Egypt startled the intellectuals.

Antonyms:

Forewarn	Caution	Warn
Threaten		

Examples:
The Doctor forewarned the parents of the sick child against optimism about quick recovery.
The Government cautioned the Police against complacence.
Let me warn you about your health, so that you may take care to improve your diet.

Attach (Verb)

He wants to purchase a house with a garage attached.

Synonyms:

Unite	Link	Join
Conjoin	Couple	Combine

Examples:
The two political parties have united to form a coalition.
Television stations around the world are linked by satellite.
Hydrogen combines with Oxygen to form water.
The bad light coupled with the wet ground made the play very difficult.
The island is joined to the main land by the bridge.

Antonyms:

Disunite	Separate	Cut
Sever	Divide	Part
Detach	Dissever	

Examples:
She keeps herself parted away from other people.
Opposing views on health care are threatening to disunite the party.
The children were divided in small groups.
He jumped as a dark shape detached itself from the wall.
The children sleep in a separate bed.
In the accident, his hand was severed form his arm.

Attract (Verb)

Bright colours attract babies.

Synonyms:

Allure	Bewitch	Captivate
Charm	Decoy	Draw
Enchant	Endear	Engage
Entice	Fascinate	Incline
Induce	Interest	Invite
Lure	Tempt	

Examples:
Deepak was bewitched by her beauty.
She is a woman of great charm.
He managed to endear himself to everybody.
Advertisements are designed to entice people into spending money.
She was fascinated to discover that once she lived in China.
Handsome salary is used as a lure to attract skilled staff.
They tried to tempt her with offers of promotion.

Antonyms:

Disgust	Give one the creeps	Put one off
Repel	Repulse	Revolt
Reject	Deter	Check
Rebuff	Detest	

Examples:
The idea of smoking fills me with disgust.
He detests having to get up early.
Her kindness to him was met with cruel rebuff.
Same magnetic poles repel each other.

Augment (Verb)

He augmented his income by writing short stories.

Synonyms:

Add to	Amplify	Boost
Build up	Dilate	Enhance
Enlarge	Expand	Extend
Grow	Intensify	Magnify
Multiply		

Examples:
Many new words have been added to this edition of the Dictionary.
He asked you to amplify your earlier statement.
The unexpected win helped to boost the team's morale.
The pupils of your eyes get dilated when you enter a dark room.
The photograph is considerably enlarged.
The terrorists have intensified their bombing campaigns.

Antonyms:

Contract	Curtail	Cut down
Decrease	Diminish	Lessen
Lower	Reduce	Shrink

Examples:
Metals contract as they get cooler.

We must try to curtail our expenditure.
The Doctor told him to cut down his drinking.
Interest in this sport is steadily decreasing.
His strength has diminished over the years.

Attention (Noun)

A teacher must know how to secure the attention of his pupils.

Synonyms:

Care	Study	Heed
Regard	Notice	

Examples:
God will take care of us if we take care of humanity.
The proper study of all the aspects of a problem will help us to find a solution for the problem.
Heeding others before taking the final solution is must to keep the organization united.
Let us pay due regard to the views of others before passing any judgment.
Take notice of what is around you before you move further.

Antonyms: Absence

Distraction	Remission

Examples:
Your absence was greatly felt in the party.
The presence of ladies in the party caused unwanted distraction.
The poor student applied to The Principal for remission of tuition fees.

Auspicious (Adjective)

He is waiting for the auspicious time to launch his project.

Synonyms:

Successful	Hopeful	Happy
Fortunate	Lucky	Reasonable

Examples:
India has been successful in sending its own satellite to space.
Pankaj has fared well in the examinations. He is hopeful of getting first division.
She is fortunate that she could avoid the accident by turning her car suddenly.
A man who is indifferent towards sorrow and joy is always happy.
None of the demands made by the agitators was reasonable.

Antonyms:

Despairing	Hopeless	Unhappy
Unfortunate	Unlucky	Luckless
Ill-fated		

Examples:
With the possibilities of Star Wars occurring in the outer space, the world is going through a despairing period.

The situation seems quite hopeless unless negotiations between the super powers at Geneva take a more concrete and constructive turn.

The people of the world are so unhappy over the dim prospects.

Authority (Noun)

We should not question the authority of our Boss.

Synonyms:
Power	Right	Title
Jurisdiction	Influence	Prestige
Control	Command	Rule
Sway		

Examples:
Power corrupts a man and absolute power corrupts absolutely.

Freedom is my birth right and I shall have it.

He cannot sell the house to you because the title to the property vests with the President.

The jurisdiction of each state is clearly stated in the constitution.

He was under the influence of liquor when he met an accident.

She is an orthodox and so makes even a small thing involving her issue of prestige.

In modern times, the government does have control not only over the political preferences of the masses but also over the economic conditions of them.

Only a Field Marshal can take command of all the three forces upon the advice of the President.

At the lost moment, his speech swayed the voters and he won the election.

Antonyms:
Submission	Obedience	Subjection
Thralldom	Slavery	

Examples:
The papers are at present under submission to the President for orders.

The state is authorized to exact obedience of the citizens.

The bonded labour is put to subjection by the village landlords in some places even in this last quarter of the 20th century.

Avoidance (Noun)

Avoidance of bad companions is what will save him from disaster.

Synonyms:
Elusion	Retract	Abstinence
Evasion	Truant	The brush-off
The go-by	Escape	Regression

Examples:

He was under an illusion that I had complained against him to the boss.
Retract is the only option that The Pakistan army had then after it was heavily shelled.
His abstinence from the meetings has helped the Secretary to take arbitrary decision.
The statement made by him was utilized by the authorities to substantiate the charges of evasion levelled against him.
The game is experience by itself to enjoy playing truant during school times.
She longed to escape form her mother's domination.
Deepak's regression from public life resulted in his total defeat in the election.

Antonyms:

Continuation	Firmness	Status-quo
Pursuit	Discipline	

Examples:

This process involves continuation of the old techniques.
Only firmness on the facts of officers can restore honesty in the administration.

Awkward (Adjective)

The handle of this teapot has an awkward shape.

Synonyms:

Unskilled	Uncouth	Rough
Ponderous	Heavy handed	Maladroit
Bungling		

Examples:

His unskilful handling of the situation led to violence by the mob.
His friend was drafted in uncouth language, so his friend did not care to reply him.
I have a rough idea of the location of his house but I do not know the exact address.
The drama presented by the society was maladroit and boring.
He was sentenced to one-year rigorous imprisonment for bungling in the election.

Antonyms:

Skilful	Dexterous	Clever
Adept		

Examples:

Suresh brought success to the project by his skilful handling.
The new manager introduced dexterous techniques in the administration of the company to pull it out of morass.
Sarah is adept at mending clocks.

Backward (Adjective)

This part of the country is still backward in economic advancement.

Synonyms:

Unwilling	Behind	Dull
Sluggish	Late	Tardy
Reluctant		

Examples:
An introvert is unwilling to work in the company of other people.
Bangladesh is much behind USA so far as technological advancement is concerned.
When India was not free, Indians were considered dull and sluggish by the Developed Countries.
Some people are habitual late comers to office. They present a very tardy picture of government offices.
First of all, he was reluctant to accept the help offered by me, later on he accepted it.

Antonyms;

Willing	Ahead	Anterior
Quick	Alert	Early
Advancing	Forward	Prompt
Eager		

Examples:
A smart person is generally more willing to cooperate with people.
Rajesh is far ahead of Suresh in Science.
The student gave a prompt reply to the question asked by the teacher.

Baffle (Verb)

His strange behaviour baffled all of us.

Synonyms:

Amaze	Astound	Bewilder
Confound	Confuse	Daze
Disconcert	Elude	Flummox
Mystify	Nonplus	Perplex
Stump	Stun	Balk
Defeat	Hinder	Thwart
Upset	Foil	

Examples:
We were amazed by the change in his appearance.
They were astounded that anyone could survive such a crush.
I am totally bewildered by the crossword clues.
The sudden rise in the edible items has confounded the city.
He was dazed for a moment by the blow to his head.
I was disconcerted to find the other guests formally dressed.

Antonyms:

| Clarify | Elucidate | Explain |
| Explicate | Interpret | Spell out |

Examples:
I hope that what I say will clarify the situation.
The notes help to elucidate the difficult parts of the texts.
Please, explain why you are late.
She interpreted your silence as acceptance.
Could you spell that word out for me again?

Balance (Verb)

How long can you balance yourself on your foot?

Synonyms:

| Equalize | Adjust | Poise |
| Weight | Pit | |

Examples:
The new Finance Act provides the opportunities to equalize wages between man and woman in the public sector.
Let us adjust out differences, because they become public.
The hawk poised in the mid-air ready to swoop.

Antonyms:

| Overbalance | Tilt | Upset |

Examples:
With no strong opposition political party in India, The Congress overbalances political power.
Because of a democratic constitution, the power is tilted in favour of the masses.
Gas tragedy in Bhopal, India upset the life of the city.

Banal (Adjective)

His talk was full of banal remarks.

Synonyms:

Clichéd	Commonplace	Everyday
Hackneyed	Humdrum	Mundane
Ordinary	Pedestrian	State
Stereotyped	Tired	Trite
Vapid	Uninteresting	

Examples:
In the words of the old cliché, I am over the moon.
Western clothes are now commonplace in Beijing.
I lead a pretty mundane life – nothing interesting ever happens to me.

We were dressed up for the party but she was still in her ordinary dress.

Antonyms;

Challenging	Distinctive	Fresh
Imaginative	Interesting	New
Novel	Original	Stimulating
Unique	Unusual	

Examples:

He was dressed in the highly distinctive black and white coat.
Most of the original inhabitants have left for the main land.
This success stimulated him to ever greater efforts.
It is unusual for him to be so rude.
The Synonyms and Antonyms form an integral part of the English Language.

Bankrupt (Adjective)

The newspapers accused the government of being bankrupt in ideas.

Synonyms:

| Insolvent | Penniless | Ruined |
| Indigent | Destitute | |

Examples:

Deepak became penniless in a single transaction because his speculation proved entirely wrong in the share market

His company was declared insolvent and his properties were auctioned.
His greed for money ruined him completely.
In spite of his indigent circumstances, he always ready to help others.
The hermit believes that man is a destitute soul destined to die one day.

Antonyms:

| Solvent | Credit-worthy | Well-off |
| Prosperous | Rich | |

Examples:

This firm is strong and solvent. We may buy its shares with benefit.
This firm has enough credit-worthiness. People are prepared to supply it raw-materials on credit.
Its Directors are well-off people, prosperous and rich.

Bargain (Noun)

The Foreign Secretary was in a good bargaining position in his dealings with his opposite number in France.

Synonyms:

| Deal | Inexpensive | Transaction |
| Agreement | Contract | |

Examples:
Dishonest officers sometimes try to make a deal with the income-tax assesses.
Because of its comparative inexpensiveness, the new designs of the furniture became popular.
A shrewd businessman believes in cash transaction only.
In legal terminology, marriage is regarded as a contract.

Antonyms:

Account	Closed	Expensiveness
Quittance	Payment	

Examples:
The use of local parts in this machine accounts for its economical price.
China, which was closed country until now, has been reopened to the visitors from other countries under ordinary international law regulations.
The balancing of sales and purchases of a firm means that the firm is sound for making all payments on liabilities in time.

Barren (Adjective)

He made an attempt that was barren of results.

Synonyms:

Arid	Boring	Desert
Desolate	Dry	Empty
Unfruitful	Waste	Fruitless
Unsuccessful	Useless Boring	Childless
In fecund	Sterile	Vapid
Unproductive		

Examples:
Many deserts are covered by sand. Sahara desert is one of them.
We all felt absolutely desolate when she left.
It is good to drink alcohol on an empty stomach.
Our efforts to persuade her proved fruitless.
Medical tests proved that she was sterile.
A car is useless without petrol.

Antonyms:

Fecund	Fertile	Fruitless
Lush	Productive	Profitable
Rich	Useless	Interesting

Examples:
The inner cities of this state are fertile ground for military purpose.
I spend a productive hour in the library.
Air America is one of the most productive air lines in the world.

Videos are useful things to have in the class room.

Base (Adjective)

He was acting in base motives.

Synonyms:

Corrupt	Shameful	Mean
Sordid	Low	Dishonourable
Vile		

Examples:
Corrupt practices among the government officials are being investigated by a special commission appointed for the purpose.
It is shameful that even few decades after Independence, the poverty has not been eradicated in South Africa.
How mean the landlords in India behaved to exploit the poor people as the bonded labours!

Antonyms:

Above-board	Pure	Honoured
Esteemed	Noble	Exalted
Lofty		

Examples:
Most of the officers today are above-board but a few corrupt ones spoil the purity of the administration.
Honoured are those who render selfless services to their countrymen.
Hindustan Times is one of the esteemed dailies in India.

Bashful (Adjective)

After we heard the news about the failure, we were bashful.

Synonyms:

Abashed	Blushing	Confused
Coy	Diffident	Easily
Embarrassed	Overmodest	Reserved
Reticent	Sheepish	Shrinking
Timid	Timorous	

Examples:
His boss's criticism left him feeling rather abashed.
She blushed crimson with embarrassment when I kissed her.
Do not be so coy about your achievement.
I was embarrassed by his comments about my clothes.
He seemed strangely reticent about his past.
She came into the room looking rather sheepish.

Antonyms:

Aggressive	Arrogant	Bold
Brash	Conceited	Confident
Egoistic	Fearless	Forward
Immodest	Impudent	

Examples:
A good sales man should be aggressive if he wants to succeed.
He has reputation for rudeness and intellectual arrogance.
I do not feel bold enough to ask for a pay increase.
Her brash and abrasive style made her unpopular.
I have always thought him to be egoistical and attention-seeking.

Bear (Verb)

The only way for him to overcome the pain is to bear away the palm.

Synonyms:

Cherish	Entertain	Exhibit
Harbour	Have	Hold
Maintain	Possess	Shoulder
Sustain	Uphold	Bring
Beget	Breed forth	Develop
Engender	Generate	Abide
Admit	Brook	Endure

Examples:
Children feel the need to be cherished.
They entertain a stream of visitors throughout the summer.
He has exhibited his skills and his works in several galleries.
Several boats lay at anchor in the harbour.
The winning captain held the trophy in air.
The improvement in his health is being maintained.
He decided to give away everything he possessed and to become a monk.

Antonyms:

Abandon	Cease	Desert
Discontinue	Drop	Give up
Leave	Quit	Relinquish
Put down		
Shed		

Examples:
They abandoned their land and property to invaders.
Hostilities between the two sides ceased at midnight.

We do not sell those any more. They are discontinued line.
I give up. Tell me what the answer is.
If I do not get a pay rise, I will quit.

Bend (Verb)

It is not easy to bend a bar of Iron.

Synonyms:

Bow	Submit	Stoop
Yield	Condescend	Lean
Tend	Incline	

Examples:
Mohan bowed before his grandfather.
The Company submitted its accounts to the Income-Tax officer.
The corrupt officer stooped to accept the bribe.
The bride's father condescended at last to raise a loan for the dowry of his daughter.

Antonyms:

| Break | Stiffen | Stand |
| Advance | Rise | Straighten |

Examples:
Atoll has broken new ground in the field of Hindi Poetry.
The demand for dowry in such an open way stiffened the bride's father.
Ram's father took a brave stand on the issue of dowry.
Let us straighten this issue in the general meeting of the company.

Before (Preposition, Conjunction & Adverb)

Do not hesitate to speak before every one.

Synonyms:

Preceding	Ahead	Prior to
In front of	Previous to	Formerly
Above	Already	

Examples:
In an essay each paragraph should be connected by sequence with the preceding one.
Will you go ahead with this project?
The picture must be painted prior to its fitting in the frame.
They have built a factory in front of my house. It will always be a source of noise and nuisance.
He had already visited France prior to his present tour to Moscow.
Formerly he was an ambassador. Now he has been appointed as Governor.
The hare was surprised to see that the tortoise had already reached the destination.
The passage quoted above has been taken from Hamlet- the famous play of Shakespeare.

Antonyms:

Succeeding	After	Behind
Alter	Following	Subsequently
Afterward		

Examples:
We have added a few notes on the subject in the succeeding chapter.
The minister also addressed the meeting after the Secretary had finished his introductory address.
Afterwards the local leaders spoke one by one.

Brave (Adjective)

We are not brave enough to meet the headmistress in her Room.

Synonyms:

Bold	Courageous	Dauntless
Gallant	Heroic	Intrepid
Plucky	Undaunted	Valiant
Valorous		

Examples:
Rave is bold and courageous person.
Subhash Chandra Bose was a dauntless and gallant freedom fighter.
Heroic adventures of the characters in Jonathan's stories have always inspired the children round the world.

Antonyms:

Afraid	Cowardly	Daunted
Timid	Intimidated	Unheroic

Examples:
Mahatma Gandhi was never afraid of the consequences of his non-violent Satyagraha.
The cowardly attitude of the police caused failure in their mission.
The cat is a timid animal as it runs to safety on the slightest noise of any other animal.

Break (Noun)

A break in the water mains is the cause of the water problem that we face.

Synonyms

Interlude	Intermission	Interval
Let-up	Full	Pause
Recess	Respite	Spell

Examples:
Most of the feature films have interludes of jokes to break the seriousness of the story.
Feature films also have an intermission around the middle part of their duration.
Five-minute respite in the heavy rain gave us the chance to slip away to our destination.

Antonyms
Continuation	Connection	Attach
Fasten	Join	Unite

Examples:
This serial is a continuation of the earlier series.
There is a great connection between the budgetary policy and the industrial development of a country.
Please fasten the rope tightly otherwise it will break again.
The house has a balcony attached to every room.
Come and join us in the party.
Let us unite together to fight against racial discrimination.

Breed (Verb)
Birds bread in the spring.

Synonyms:
Produce	Raise	Beget
Conceive	Train	Hatch
Incubate		

Examples:
Our gardener produces many nice vegetables in our new farm.
The farmer sells his produce at the marker.
Nowadays the army is raising a special fund for the assistance of the ex-soldiers.
Love begets love and even a spoiled child can be reformed through love.
Only a genius like him can conceive of such a utopian situation.
My cousin is being trained as a hospital nurse. Her training is near completion.
The batches have to be fastened down firmly when a storm expected.
The old hen has hatched eight chicks.
Animals incubate twice in a year during the period of their heat.

Antonyms
Destroy	Slay	Murder
Annihilate	Kill	

Examples:
The grasshoppers badly destroyed his crop.
The villain had slayed the very hoodlum who had helped him to hide the stolen treasure.

The wicked man has after all been arrested for a rape by the police.
Atomic warfare can annihilate the whole of mankind in no time.
We went to the Coffee House to kill time.

Breeze (Noun)

There is no much of breeze in the summer.

Synonyms:

Storm	Gust	Hurricane
Wind	Typhoon	Blast
Gale		

Examples:
The weather office has predicted a storm in the coastal areas within next 48 hours.
It was only the courage and ability of the Captain that the ship has survived the hurricanes of the Bay of Bengal.
Due to a stormy wind the leaves were blown off the trees.
The blast of the explosion shook the building.
Don't go out into the gale.

Antonyms:

Calm	Lull	Placidity
Doldrums		

Examples:
After five days of storm, we have a calm, weather today.
There is often a lull before the storm.
His placidity has won him the little "man of peace".
The failure of his son in the examination has put him in doldrums.

Brevity (Noun)

The beauty of her communication is its brevity.

Synonyms:

Short	Concise	Succinct
Brief		

Examples:
The short size of the committee has made its President, run the local affairs, in an arbitrary manner.
In précis writing, the matter remaining concise is of the utmost importance.
The period of the training was so short that all the participants felt sorry for its being brief.
He is famous for the brevity of his speeches.
His statements were detailed yet succinct.

Antonyms

| Confused | Loquacious | Addle headed |

Examples:
His ideas are good but his style is so loquacious, his writings get confused.
His habit of non-stop speech during his walking hours has made him addle headed.

Beget

Part of speech: - verb.
Def: create bears.

Synonyms:

Afford,	Breed,	Bring
About,	Cause,	Effect,
Engender,	Father,	Generate,
Get,	Give	Rise to,
Multiple,	Occasion,	Procreate,
Produce,	Regenerate,	Reproduce,
Result in,	Sire,	

Belief (Noun)

I have not much belief in his honesty.

Synonyms:

| Trust | Credit | Faith |
| Opinion | Idea | View |

Examples:
We should not trust those politicians who make big promises only at the time of elections.
Some traders sell their goods on credit but then they charge higher rate of interests.
People had great faith in the leadership of Abraham Lincoln.
Students generally hesitate to express their opinion frankly when it concerns their teacher.
They have been selected with a view to reflect both the thought and action of the writer's life.
Daps will not mind spending more money provided he is sure that this venture will fetch him huge profit.
Belief gives you more energy.

Antonyms:

Distrust	Whim	Discredit
Suspicion	Doubt	Disbelief
Misgiving		

Examples:
Distrust between the husband and wife was the main reason their divorce.
The officers who are whimsical cannot be depended upon to perform their duty effectively.
Ram has of late developed some misgivings about Sham.

Beneath (Preposition)

His accusations are beneath contempt.

Synonyms:

Below	Underneath	Under
Down	Not worth	

Examples:
The footnote given below from the text of the speech must be read to know the mind of the speaker correctly.
The archaeologist excavated the earth underneath to trace the structure's origin.
Everyone wanted to dig the treasure hidden under the tree.
A man walked down the aisle selling popcorn and balloons.

Antonyms:

Up	Overhead	Above
High		

Examples:
Up and up goes the balloon.
An airplane flew overhead us.
The above sentence is critically related to the main text.
Our pilots can fly very high.

Benefit (Noun)

Did you get much benefit from your holiday?

Synonyms:

Profit	Gain	Favour
Advantage	Avail	Service
Boon		

Examples:
The whole district will profit form this industrial opening.
Each day that fortune give to us be what it may is set down for gain.
The government selected electronics as an industry for special favour in the seventh plan.

Antonyms:

Harm	Loss	Disadvantage
Damage	Injury	Calamity

Examples:
Laziness does more harm to studies that gossiping.
This factory is now running under a loss of $20,000,000.00 per month.
The new budget is rather damaging to this industry.

Benevolence (Noun)

His benevolence made it possible for many poor boys to attend college.

Synonyms:

God's Grace	Selflessness	Kindness
Kindliness	Charity	Humanity
Fellow Feelings	Good Nature	Brotherly Love
Mercy	Pity	Bounty
Good Offices	Public Service	

Examples:
With god's grace, he could survive the accident.
Swami Ramakrishna was a living example of selflessness and kindness.
He believes in the maxim "Charity begins at home".
Doris has a benign personality. She has good nature and she does feel pity for others.
UNESCO has done tremendous work for the betterment humanity.
Mechanical life makes a man lose fellow feeling and brotherly love for others.
Officers of Industrial Relations machinery are supposed to use their good offices to bring harmony between the employers and the employees.

Antonyms:

Ill Nature	Spite	Cruelty
Inhumanity	Evil eye	Evil intent
Enmity	Hate	Hatred
Malice	Venom	Churlishness
Outrage		

Examples:
His ill-nature is the cause of his unpopularity.
He has earned spite of many friends due to his churlishness.
He does work with cruelty against his enmities.

Bewilder (Verb)

The old woman from the country was bewildered by the big crowds and traffic in the big city.

Synonyms:

Problem	Poser	Mystery
Enigma		

Examples:
All problems have a solution but one needs determination to solve them.
Existence of god was a great poser for the priest to prove.
Even the scientists have failed to unveil the mystery of cosmos completely.
His behaviour has become an enigma for the psychiatrist which the latter are trying to analyse for the last two months.

Antonyms:

Enlighten	Teach	Illuminate
Inform	Edify	Instruct

Examples:
I do not know to edit a book. Would you enlighten me?
Will you teach me English?
The banquet hall is illuminated by bright lights.
My friends informed me about Raja's evil intentions.
Ram was appointed to instruct some ten boys on first-aid.
The charity show was not an edifying spectacle.

Bitter (Adjective)

His failure to pass the examination was a bitter disappointment.

Synonyms:

Acrid	Intense	Sad
Harsh	Sour	Severe

Examples:
As our bus passed by the drain, we felt a severe acrid smell.
With the passage of April, heat is becoming more intense.
The news of failure in the Examination made him very sad.

Antonyms

Mild	Sweet	Pleasant
Genial	Light	

Examples:
I prefer mild drinks.
Spending a few minutes with the poetess was a sweet experience.
Her company was very pleasant and genial.

Blame (Verb)

He blamed his failure on his teacher.

Synonyms

Criticism	Reproach	Censure
Guilt	Rebuke	

Examples:
Politicians may do their best but they cannot avoid criticism by their opponents.
He has done the job so honestly that he cannot be reproached.
The teacher censured the boy trying to cheat his class fellows.
He was rebuked by his father for scoring such a low percentage of marks.
Some reformers forget their own guilt and try to teach others.
What a farce!

Antonyms:

Praise	Appreciation	Approval
Exhort	Applaud	Extol

Examples:
We should praise our military personnel for the great amount of risk and sacrifice they take during an emergency.
They deserve our appreciation if they succeed in defending the country.
We should applaud their valour.

Blessing (Noun)

What a blessing it is, you did not get in the storm yesterday!

Synonyms:

Good wishes	Prayer	Thanks
Praise	Consecration	

Examples:
Dr. Abdul Kalam, the President of India, receives good wishes from people all over the world on his birthday every year.
He arrived as if in answer to her prayers.
Deepak received high praise for his scientific research.
Many thanks for all your hospitality.
Consecration of the male child is a very important religious ceremony of the Muslims.

Antonyms

Bad wishes	Curse	Evil thought

Examples:
He is so popular, even his enemies cannot dare to have bad wishes for him.
There is hardly a soul that curses him.
There is no place for evil thought in his mind for any human being.

Bountiful

Part of speech: - adjective
Definition: - abundant
Synonyms:

ample,	aplenty,	bounteous,
copious,	crawling with,	dime a dozen,
Exuberant, free,	galore,	generous,
handsome,	lavish,	liberal,
luxuriant,	magnanimous,	munificent,
no end of,	plenteous,	plentiful,
plenty,	prolific,	stink with,
Unsparing.		

Antonyms:

insufficient,	lacking,	meagre,
sparse,	Wanting.	

Example:

The accelerated state tends to be exuberant in invention and fancy.
Scientists studying complexity are particularly exuberant these days.
She is also a student of life, exuberant nerd, and musician.

Bliss (Noun)

The fact that I passed this examination gave me the greatest bliss that I have experienced so far.

Synonyms:

Joy	Pleasure	Happiness
Rapture		

Examples:

A thing of beauty is joy forever.
Children get pleasure out of playing truants.
Happiness lies in selfless service of others.
A yogi believes that he could live in a state of rapture after attaining Moksha.

Antonyms

Sorrow	Sadness	Pain
Dejection		

Examples:

Every life has its share of sorrows.
Sadness and happiness are two sides of the life of every individual.
Pain and pleasure flow side by side in human life.
It if dejection that shatters our personality sometimes.

Blithe (Adjective)

Our excursion to the hill station was blithe days for all of us.

Synonyms

Careless	Casual	Indifferent
Nonchalant	Thoughtless	Untroubled
Animated	Buoyant	Carefree
Cheerful	Cheery	Debonair

Examples:
This may note obvious to the casual observer.
She appeared indifferent to their sufferings.
I had rarely seen him so animated.
The raft would be more buoyant if it was less heavy.
Deepak strolled about, looking very debonair in his elegant new suit.

Antonyms:

Concerned	Preoccupied	Thoughtful
Dejected	Depressed	Gloomy
Melancholy	Morose	Sad
Unhappy		

Examples:
He didn't seem in the least concerned for his safety.
She seemed preoccupied all the time I was talking to her.
Repeated failure had left them feeling very dejected.
He felt deeply depressed even suicidal at times.
What are you so gloomy about? Cheer up.

Blunt (Adjective)

The blunt fact is that our soccer team was defeated in the match.

Synonyms

Direct	Insensitive	Dull
Undiplomatic		

Examples:
The Politicians, being practical and realistic men, avoid direct confrontation with their opponents.
This salesman is insensitive to the complaints of the customers.
The difficulty Deepak faced was the result of his undiplomatic handling of the affairs in the beginning.
The debate in the council over the budget was rather dull and boring.

Antonyms

Diplomatic	Sensitive	Sharp
Sophisticated		

Examples:
If we handle our affairs diplomatically there is no need for annoyance later.

He is too sensitive to remain in composure during controversies.
His reaction is too sharp to allow for healthy discussion on any disputed subject.
Pankaj's sophisticated manners win him acclamation everywhere.

Boost (Noun)

His work got a welcome boost.

Synonyms

Encouragement	Aid	Help
Recommendation	Hoist	Lift

Examples:

At the time of frustration and disappointment, my father is a great source of encouragement.
They were getting a lot of aid from CIA and other foreign agencies.
We should always be ready to help our relatives.
It was on the recommendation of an Architect that we opted for his design of the furniture of our new house.
The Principal hoisted the flag at the school ground on the Independence Day.
Dara Singh was called modern Bheema as he can lift as much weight as four persons together

Antonyms:

Rebuke	Discouragement	Hindrance
Obstacle	Rebuff	

Examples:

Only incitement can better reform a modern young man than the rebuke.
Inequality is the biggest hindrance in the way of social and economic development.
Lack of close connection between the public and private sectors is the biggest obstacle to the speedy expansion of small scale industries.

BORDER (Noun)

We camped on the border of the lake.

Synonyms

Edge	Brink	Limit
Margin	Boundary	Brim
Rim		

Examples:

Don't put that glass so near the edge of the table.
Pankaj is a very short tempered man. He ignores the limits of decency while talking to others.
The typist was instructed by his boss to leave wide margin on the left while typing a draft.
Manoj has erected a wall along the boundary of his plot so as to stop its trespassing.

The sorcerer filled the glass with water up to its brim and tilted it but the water did not fall out.

Raja loaded the truck beyond the prescribed limit. The result was the breakdown of the rim of its rear wheel.

Antonyms:

| Centre | Midst | Point |
| Middle | Axis | |

Examples:
Draw a circle in the centre of this line.
The culprit was spotted in the midst of the crowd.
A circle has a point in its centre.
The tailor cut the cloth at its middle.
The earth revolves round the sun at an axis of 66 ½.

Bore (Noun)

We could not bear with a person who is a bore.

Synonyms:

| Troublesome | Talker | Nuisance |
| Talkative | Pest | |

Examples:
Surely they will not put up with such a troublesome member in their society.
Pallavi is a sheer talker and cannot inspire confidence in her friends.
Their ruined child has become a great nuisance in the family.
Women are supposed to be talkative by nature, but it is not always true.

Antonyms:

| Thinker | Genial | Listener |
| Entertainer | Amusing | |

Examples:
Marx and Angels were great thinkers and philosophers of their time.
Saurabh has a genial temperament. He has therefore made a circle of good friends.
P.C. Sarkar was not only a great magician but also a great entertainer.
His manners are so amusing that many of his obvious lies go unnoticed.

Borrow (Verb)

Do not borrow books from. Do them from the library?

Synonyms

Receive	Appropriate	Take
Adapt	Adopt	Steal
Imitate	Pilfer	Pirate
Copy		

Examples:

You can determine your net loss on investment for the year only if you know the exact amount you received and spent during the year.

Haryana administration has appropriated all the vacant land in Haryana.

We shall have to take the children away from their parents during such a function.

You will have to adapt your food habits to items that increase his sales.

The Poor child was so hungry that he could not help stealing some bread from the shop.

Decide what you want to do; don't imitate others.

Salman has copied the style of his writing from the essays of Rabindra Nath Tagore.

In the Army also there may be back-stabber who would pilfer away the secret information to the enemy.

Captain Kidd was a notorious pirate.

Antonyms

Lend	Advance	Give
Invents	Improve	Make
Credit		

Examples:

Could you lend me US$ 5000 for a month?

The publishers gave the author an advance of US$15000.

I have given a word of honour to my friend to keep the information confidential.

Brace (Verb)

He braced himself to meet the blow.

Synonyms

| Strengthen | Invigorate | Prop |
| Support | Refresh | |

Examples:

Balance diet strengthens our body and mind.

The kind rich man supported many poor students.

Sleep refreshes us when we feel tired.

I feel invigorated by all this fresh air.

As the only son he should prop up his old parents.

Antonyms

| Weaken | Degenerate | Raze |
| Knock | Enfeeble | |

Examples:

The fall in productivity has weakened the economy.

Too much materialism has degenerated our youth.

The Earthquake razed many buildings to ground.

Deepak knocked at every door during his financial crisis to save his firm from collapse.

Breed

Part of speech: - verb.

Def: - generate, bring into being.

Synonyms:

Bear,	Beget,	Bring
About,	Bring forth,	Cause,
Create,	Deliver,	Engender,
Give birth to,	Give rise to,	Impregnate,
Induce,	Make,	Multiply,
Originate,	Procreate,	Produce,
Regenerate,	Propagate,	Reproduce.

Antonyms:

Not produce.

Example

Attacks on the namesake engender strong visceral reactions and calls to defend it at all costs.

The unions and the left were repressed, but not so severely as to engender a guerrilla movement.

Either course-curtailing support for personnel or curtailing personnel-is likely to engender resentment in the military.

Bring

Part of speech: - verb.

Def: - Cause, influence.

Synonyms:

Bring,	Compel,	Contribute to,
Convert,	Convince,	Create,
Dispose,	Effect,	Engender,
Force,	Induce,	Inflict,
Make,	Lead,	Move,
Occasion,	Persuade,	Prevail on,
Prevail	Upon,	Produce,
Prompt,	Result in,	Sway,
Reek.		

Antonyms:

Avoid,	Back out,	Desist,
Give up,	Hold back,	Pass up

Bring about

Part of speech: - verb.
Def: - cause success.
Synonyms:

Accomplish,	Achieve,	Beget,
Bring to pass,	Compass,	Create,
Do,	Draw on,	Effect,
Effectuate,	Engender,	Generate,
Give rise to,	Make happen,	Manage,
Occasion,	Produce,	Realize,
Secure,	Succeed.	

Antonyms: - halt, kill, stop.

Bring on

Part of speech: - verb.
Def: - provoke.
Synonyms: -

Accelerate,	Advance,	Cause,
Expedite,	Generate,	Give rise to,
Induce,	Inspire,	Lead to,
Iccasion,	Precipitate,	Prompt,

Example

Be willing to help expedite the work of the committee.

Some people need an over-the-counter lubricant to expedite insertion of the catheter.

When you get one reviewer, it may mean the editor had to cut some corners to expedite the process.

Bright (Adjective)

The leaves on the trees are bright green in the spring.
Synonyms

Shining	Quick-witted	Intelligent
Luminous	Resplendent	Sparkling

Examples:
A streetlight was shining through the window.

Deepak is an intelligent boy; he scores very good marks in board exam.
The champion was in sparkling form.
A glittering career has been predicted for her.

Antonyms

Dull	Dim	Foolish
Dark	Ignorant	Faint

Examples:
Political evolution is a long slow process.
The stage lights were dimmed as the curtain rose.
There's never a dull moment when John is around.
It's rather dark in here can we have the lights on.

Barrier

Part of speech: - Noun.
Def: - obstruction to goal

Synonyms:

Bar	Check	Difficulty.
Drawback	Encumbrance	Handicap
Hindrance	Hurdle	Impediment
Limitation	Obstacle	Pale,
Preventive	Restraint	Restriction
Stumbling block		

Antonyms:
Opening.

Burden

Part of speech: - Noun.
Def: - Mental weight, stress.

Synonyms:

Herculean task,	Accountability,	Affliction,
Albatross,	Anxiety,	Ball and chain,
Blame care,	Charge,	Clog,
Concern,	Deadweight,	Difficulty,
Duty,	Encumbrance,	Excess
Baggage,	Grievance,	Hardship,
Hindrance,	Load,	Millstone,
Misfortune,	Mishap,	Obstruction,
Onus,	Punishment,	Responsibility,
Sorrow,	Strain,	Task,

Tax,	Thorn in one's side,	Trial,
Trouble,	Weary,	Work,
Worry.		

Antonyms: - aid, help, relief

Brusque (Adjective)

The brusque manner in which she delivered her speech in the opening ceremony spoiled the joviality of the atmosphere.

Synonyms

1. Discourteous　　　　2. Gruff　　　　3. Cut
4. Abrupt

Examples:

Although he is an educated person, he is often discourteous to his elders.

The Sergeant always gave a gruff answer to the soldier's questions.

The program came to an abrupt end when the lights went off.

I was surprised at his curt reply.

Antonyms

1. Courteous　　　　2. Smooth　　　　3. Polite
4. Polished

Examples:

Remy was highly courteous to us when we visited him.

He was smooth and soft whenever we went to seek his favour for a party not so well known
to him.

His polite behaviour in fact greatly surprised us.

His behaviour proved that he is a man of polished manners.

Brutal (Adjective)

Her approach was so brutal that we all maintained a distance from her.

Synonyms

| Inhuman | Merciless | Cruel |
| Savage | Pitiless | Barbarous |

Examples:

Deepak treated his servant in an inhuman way.

The prince of England was merciless to his attendants.

Deepak behaves like a savage when he is angry.

He is so pitiless that nobody likes to talk to him and share feelings with him.

In ancient times there were many barbarous kings, who killed people for the sake of keeping an atmosphere of terror.

Antonyms

| Humane | Merciful | Kind |
| Sympathetic | Compassionate | Tender |

Examples:
Mahatma Gandhi measured the Quality of life by the element of humanity ingrained in it.
God is merciful to those who are merciful to humans.
Lal Bahadur Shastri was sympathetic to the interest of the poor.
Mrs. Indira Gandhi was highly compassionate to the bonded labour and got passed adequate legislation to free them from the clutches of the Zamindars.
Atul is kind to the animals.

Busy (Adjective)

He was busy getting ready for his journey.

Synonyms

| Active | Occupied | Diligent |
| Industrious | Engaged | Engrossed |

Examples:
Although he is quite old he is still very active.
Studies keep the youth occupied during the examination
Atul is a diligent student taking serious interest in all subjects.

Antonyms

Indolent	Idle	Inactive
Lazy	Unoccupied	Inert
Passive	Relaxed	

Examples:
Since his visit to the hill station, he has become rather indolent and idle in temperament.
This child is inert and passive but can be toned up with the help of better diet.
The news of favourable result has given me great relief. I now feel well relaxed.

Cajole (Verb)

We had to cajole him out of going to USA for higher studies.

Synonyms:

| Inveigle | Beguile | Coax |
| Flatter | Blandish | Wheedle |

Examples:
The smugglers managed to inveigle their colleague from the clutches of the police somehow.

The innocent girl was beguiled into thinking she could become a famous actress.
Smith coaxed his father to let him use his new car.
The servant flattered his master telling him he was a good writer.
Even her blandishments could not win him over.
Mother tried to wheedle father into going to the party.

Antonyms

Cool	Dampen	Flaunt
Dam	Dissuade	

Examples:
Jane was in a high temper. It took me some time to cool him down.
I was in very high spirits. Maria has dampened these by asking for a loan.
The subordinate flouted the order of the manager.
The water of the river has been well dammed by this barrage project.
You should dissuade him from undertaking this risky project.

Calamity (Noun)

AT last, we had to face the calamity.

Synonyms

Distress	Misfortune	Trouble
Misery	Catastrophe	Affliction
Disaster		

Examples:
The minister was move to see the misery of the distressed child labour employed in the weaving industry.
The loss of her job was a big misfortune.
Sometimes the members of opposition party create lot of trouble in the Parliament and obstruct the proceedings of the House.
The land reforms may have benefited the poor but not proved to be a catastrophe for the rich land-owners.
Our country is afflicted with twin disaster of food shortages and an exploding population.

Antonyms

Prosperity	Fortune	Peace
Joy	Tranquillity	Happiness

Examples:
Recent agricultural research has made the farmers quite prosperous.
Land reforms have also brought fortune for the small farmer.
Peace is essential for the economic development of Punjab.
It gives me immense joy to inaugurate this library of the village.

Calculate (Verb)

Please, calculate once again. I think you are wrong.

Synonyms

Reckon	Count	Assess
Estimate	Number	Computer

Examples:

Corruption is a problem the government must reckon with more seriously.
Some children are intelligent and learn to count very fast.
The achievements of scientific research cannot be assessed in monetary terms.
The engraver could not estimate the cost of enlarging the emblem without first calculating the price of the metal to be used.
The number of vehicles passing through the Jan path crossing is not less than 5000 a day.
Although the rules have been amended, his pension has been computed at old rates.

Antonyms

Imagine	Conjecture	Surmise
Suppose		

Examples:

Imagine the beauty of nature in this season on a hill station.
Do not conjecture the price of this present. It is invaluable.
My calculation of the cost of this project is based on mere surmise.
It is no use supposing negative things without rhyme or reason.

Call (Verb)

I called to see Mr. Green.

Synonyms

Bid	Recall	Invite
Summon	Muster	Convent
Invoke		

Examples:

Tears rolled down his cheeks when he bade farewell to his mother.
The Ambassador of India to Pakistan has been recalled by the government for the time being.
I have been invited to participate in local committee meetings.
He was summoned court for giving evidence in case.
A meeting of the General Body was convened by the Secretary of the Society to discuss some urgent matters.
He could barely muster the strength to raise his head from the pillow.
Once it was believed that witches could invoke the evil powers and harm anybody.

Antonyms

Remove	Dismiss	Discharge
Exile	Banish	

Examples:
The general body of the company in a meeting removed Mr. Mukesh Jain from chairmanship.
The Officer dismissed the corrupt subordinate.
The railway employee who had caused an accident through negligence was discharged from service.
The extremist leader who was responsible for creating disturbances in the capital was exiled from the country.

Calm (Adjective)

We had to keep calm to hear what she said.

Synonyms

Pacify	Hush	Compose
Quiet	Solace	Palliate
Mitigate	Lull	

Examples:
The Government hushed the affair up to avoid a public outcry.
Ram is a quiet little man who does his work inconspicuously but well.
The assurances given by him could give no solace to the mourners.
The new medicine is designed to mitigate the after-effects of sun strokes.
This drug has a palliative effect but cannot cure the disease.
Before every storm there is a lull for some time.

Antonyms

Agitate	Excite	Perturb
Crisis	Disturb	Fluster

Examples:
The workers are agitating for higher wages.
Modern civilization excites our nerve at every step.
The clouds of war are presently perturbing the whole mankind.
Deepak does not seem to have a solution for this crisis.
It is a disturbing sign.

Cancel (Verb)

Because of heavy rain, the musical program stands cancelled.

Synonyms

Destroy	Abolish	Obliterate
Blot out	Efface	Nullify
Invalidate	Erase	Bit

Examples:
An atom bomb can destroy the whole city within a few minutes.
The post of junior investigator has been abolished in our office.
The murderer tried to obliterate all the evidences against him but the handkerchief found in his pocket become the needed evidence.
This act of yours will nullify all the good you have done to him.
His nomination for election was invalidated because he is not a citizen of India.
If you erase the last paragraph of the story, it will lose all its literary charm.

Antonyms

Establish	Ratify	Corroborate
Substantiate	Endorse	Confirm

Examples:
Let us establish new rules and regulations for our society.
Any amendment passed by the U.S. congress has to be ratified by at least 2/3rd number of states to go on the statute.
This fact is so well-known it needs no corroboration.
There is no evidence to substantiate your theory.
I endorse your views on the present political situation in the country.

Capacity (Noun)

This book is within the capacity of young readers.

Synonyms

Capability	Ability	Competence
Aptitude	Faculty	Skill
Wit	Talent	Power

Examples:
It is beyond his capability to tackle such a complex problem.
We cannot challenge his ability to handle this newly developed machine.
His termination orders were set aside by the court because these were not within the competence of the director who issued them.
Prankish has an aptitude for science but his parents are compelling him to study commerce.
His faculties are not sharp enough to understand the complexities of the new technique.
A shrewd salesman possesses wit, humour and skill to convince the customer to buy his articles.
Knowledge is power.

Antonyms

Incapability	Inability	Incompetence

Examples:
Don't exhibit your incapability to handle this computerized machine.

Pankaj has expressed his inability to help us in this project not because he is incompetent but because he is going abroad.

None amongst us has the relevant in aptitude for this kind of work.

Capture (Verb)

This advertisement will capture the attention of the readers everywhere.

Synonyms

Arrest	Seize	Snatch
Catch	Apprehend	

Examples:
At last the police was able to arrest the culprit.
The army has seized three check posts of the enemy.
The incidents of robbery are on the increase in the capital these days.
Although Deepak ran fast, he could not catch the bus,
The Police have apprehended a number of criminals during the last two days.

Antonyms

Liberate	Release	Acquit
Free	Disengage	

Examples:
The United Nations is now seriously trying to liberate East Timor from Indonesia.
The Government has released a number of political prisoners recently.
The judge has acquitted one of the accused in the bank robbery case.
My examinations are over. I am a free bird now.
Unless you disengage yourself from drinking we cannot offer you this whole-time job.

Care (Noun)

Care should be taken to see that no theft takes place on Sundays in this shop.

Synonyms

Prudence	Thrift	Wariness
Custody		

Examples:
Your good prudence alone can save your family from break-up.
Only thrift and hard work can pull this factory through the present crisis.
The present circumstances need some wariness in financial dealings.

Antonyms

Remissness	Temerity	Neglect

Examples:
Any remissness on your part can land you in trouble.
He ran the company like a dictator and no one had the temerity to question his judgment.

A little neglect today causes great loss tomorrow.

Careful (Adjective)

Be careful not to break the eggs.

Synonyms:

Meticulous	Conscientious	Scrupulous
Punctilious		

Examples:
Anil's meticulous manners won him the high job at a young age.
Gandhi was too conscientious and scrupulous to compromise with other leaders on basic principle of non – violence as a technique of fighting against the British rule.
He proposes to celebrate his marriage punctiliously.

Antonyms:

Negligent	Heedless	Sloppy
Slipshod		

Examples:
If you become negligent of your duty, you will not rise much in life.
He became heedless in the civil case and in the end lost it.
His writing is sloppy and slipshod.

Carry (Verb)

Can you carry all these figures in your head?

Synonyms:

Bear	Bring	Haul
Convey	Take	Transport

Examples:
Pankaj bears all the features of his father.
Bring the entire luggage here and store it on the top floor.
The police hauled all the smuggled goods.

Antonyms:

Leave	Abandon	Drop

Examples:
I left the luggage at the railway station.
I abandoned the idea of going abroad.
I have dropped the proposal of marriage with a rich girl.

Casualty (Noun)

Casualty list was published after the train accident.
Synonyms:

Mishap	Incident	Chance

Calamity   Misadventure

Examples:
Further inquiries show that he had visited the place of incident a few days earlier.
The police gave pick pocket another chance to mend himself.
His family was shocked to know of the calamity that befell him.
Sarah's attempt to scale the Himalayas without proper equipment proved a misadventure.

Antonyms:

Design	Purpose	Intent
Meaning	Adventure	

Examples
The architectural design of this building was prepared with great care.
The purpose of my visit is to apprise you of the present circumstances.
Deepak is intent on buying a car very soon.
There is a definite meaning to his frequent visits.
I am out for adventure in the hilly terrain this summer.

Catching (Adjective)

The eye-catching colour of the dress he wore got the attention of all the people present in the function.

Synonyms:

Charming	Attractive	Appealing
Enchanting	Captivating	Winning
Fascinating		

Examples:
Riana's charming face, shinning like moon, left speechless everybody present on the occasion.
The priest was preaching sermons in an attractive and appealing manner. The people listened to him in pin drop silence.
The enchanting personality of the class teacher made the student attentive in the classroom.
His resistance entirely gave way to her captivating figure and moonlit eyes.
Madhuri's strong appeal for help won Deepak's heart. He sacrificed himself to save her.
Ravi found himself caught up by the fascinating and sensuous movements of her body.

Antonyms:

Unpleasant	Ugly	Unattractive
Revolting	Loathsome	Repellent
Odious	Disagreeable	

Examples:
The weather has become unpleasant with the onset of high temperature.
The pig is an ugly creature to look at.
Magma is very intelligent but her outward facile is rather unattractive.
Everybody condemned him for the odious crime he committed.
The situation was loathsome, so he felt irritated.

Cause (Verb)

This has caused us much anxiety.
Synonyms:

Produce	Bring about	Originate
Evoke	Create	Effect

Examples:
The region has produced over half the country's wheat crop.
In spite of his best efforts he could not bring about any tangible change in her attitude.
The new syllabus will evoke a radical change in the standard of teaching.
The style of architecture originated with the ancient Greeks.
The pilot effected a take-off despite the bomb packed runway.
Praveen is a great novelist. He can create a unique view of life by using latter aspects which showed little attractiveness.

Antonyms:

Destroy	Demolish	Kill
Devastate	Ruin	Desolate

Examples:
An atomic bomb can destroy the whole universe in no time.
This building is now too old. It should be demolished and built a new.
This insecticide is enough to kill all the little germs in the house.
His new thinking has devasted the logic of all old theories of management.
Let's not ruin the present happy atmosphere by talking of unpleasant history.

Cease (Verb)

The Old German Empire ceased to exist in 1918.
Synonyms:

End	Discontinue	Stop
Halt	Pause	

Examples:
They decided to end their relation.
After the death of his father he had to discontinue his studies.
As the bus stopped far from its stand, the passengers had to run fast to catch it.
Some miscreants pulled the chain and the train came to a halt suddenly.

As the duke paused on his way downstairs, he was at ease and looked like an eagle standing at the edge of a cliff.

Antonyms:

Start	Continue	Begin
Carry on	Pursue	

Examples:

Now don't start crying over the split milk.
Let us continue our best efforts to achieve the goal leaving the result to God.
Marry began her studies with renewed vigour after her initial failure in the examination.
Let's carry on the work, come what may.
Veranda Singh has pursued the new profession with greater zeal.

Celebrated (Adjective)

He is a celebrated painter.

Synonyms:

Notable	Distinguished	Eminent
Noted	Illustrious	

Examples:

The town is notable for its ancient harbour.
I think grey hair makes you look very distinguished.
Bertrand Russell is an eminent prose writer of the modern times.
Rattan has been awarded Ashok Chakra for his illustrious services.
Deepak was hopeful of winning the case because it was pleaded by a noted lawyer.

Antonyms:

Unnoticed	Undistinguished	Unknown
Unnoted	Nameless	

Examples:

His brilliant performance at the meeting went unnoticed because the press people had a prejudiced view of him.
He has many literary works to his credit, yet he remains in the category of undistinguished writers.
Most of his literary pieces are still rather unknown. The press still regards him an unnoted literary critic.

Celibacy (Noun)

He maintains his state of celibacy in order to become a Priest.

Synonyms:

Single	Singleness	Bachelorhood
Virginity	Blessed	Maidenhood
Chastity		

Examples:
There was no single evidence which could prove that he was guilty.
He had decided to get married because now he feels that his singleness is too boring.
Hinduism lays great emphasis on bachelorhood of man and virginity of woman.
A Yogi believes that he will live in a perpetual state of blessedness after his communion with God.
India has lodged a strong protest against the chastity tests of Indian women carried out by the British Government at Heathrow Airport before allowing them entry into Britain.

Antonyms:

| Engagement | Wedlock | Married state |
| Matrimony | Union | Nuptial tic |

Examples:
Their engagement was announced in the local church.
In due course the two will enter into wedlock.
They will be called as being in a married state.
Their matrimony is attributed to a chance meeting in a tea party at a common relation's place.
Their union is likely to be very happy as their temperaments match very well.

Censorship (Noun)

All the feature films in India should undergo censorship before their release.

Synonyms:

| Criticism | Blame | Disapproval |

Examples:
Government's disapproval of his request for import of machinery has caused him great loss.
In a democratic state, criticism of the Government by opposition parties is allowed to check its arbitrary functioning.
He has put all the blame for his failure on his predecessors.

Antonyms:

| Approval | Commendation | Appreciation |
| Approbation | | |

Examples:
She knew that the industrial policy of the government will lead to the approval of her application for import of the desired machinery.
The management has issued a commendation note praising the services rendered by the retiring executive.
In this way the retiring executive has won the appreciation of the management.

Central (Adjective)

The central theme of this book is that democracy is not good for all countries.

Synonyms:

Inner	Interior	Mean
Median	Mid	Chief
Essential	Focal	Fundamental
Key	Principal	Primary

Examples:

I have never been the inner side of the monument.
Pasha is in her mid-thirties.
Smoking is one of the chief causes of lungs cancer.
The government is proposing a ban on strikes in essential services.
There are fundamental differences between these two government departments.
We need to establish the primary cause of the problem.

Antonyms:

Exterior	Outer	Outermost
Minor	Secondary	Subordinate
Remote		

Examples:

The outermost layer of the earth is crust.
Such considerations are secondary to our main aim of improving efficiency.
All other issues are subordinate to this one.
I did not have even a remote idea that the exhibition of our produces will bring such response.

Certain (Adjective)

Synonyms:

Positive	Definite	Indisputable
Sure	Actual	Unequivocal
Incontestable		

Examples:

We have to no positive evidence of her involvement.
Although he has undergone several check-up, the doctors have not yet reached a definite conclusion about his disease.
This piece of land is a part of his indisputable property.
The minister was sure that the proposed legislation will stop the exploitation of the emigrants completely.
Deployment of missiles in Europe by America was criticized by India in unequivocal terms.
Hindu law gives an incontestable right to the daughters over the property of their parents.

Antonyms:

Doubtful	Indefinite	Disputable
Uncertain	Ambiguous	Equivocal
Contestable		

Examples:
I am doubtful about the prospects of any early settlement of dispute between Iran and Iraq.
Mahatma Gandhi went on an indefinite fast to persuade the people of India to maintain communal harmony.
The wisdom of your complacent attitude on this issue is disputable.
It is no use undertaking new business projects in the present uncertain circumstances.
His speech was quite effective but some of his assessments were rather ambiguous.

CHANGE (Verb)

I must change these trousers. They have got oil on them.

Synonyms:

Alter	Veer	Shift
Diversity	Modify	Convert
Transform	Transmute	Transfigure

Examples:
I gave my old coat the tailors to alter its inner lining.
The boss veered round to my point of view when I gave him complete facts of the case.
We will have to shift our stand on policy matters if we want to augment the state resources.

Antonyms: Hold fast

Stand	Clinch	Fix
Maintain	Sustain	Stabilize
Give way		

Examples:
I still hold fast to my old belief that only non-violent methods can solve our national problems.
The old boss gave way to his position at last to make room for a younger manager.
The two leaders decide to clinch the issue by yielding on disputed points.

Chaos (Adjective)

Synonyms:

Disorder	Confusion	Jumble
Abysmal	Void	

Examples:
Everyone began shouting at once and the meeting broke up in disorder.
When you are in a hurry, you make confusion worse confounded.
Shankar is very quick in making words from the jumbled letters.
He tried to conceal his abysmal ignorance of the subject by side tracking the issue.
Negotiations made void the disputed clause in the contract, thereby invalidating its provisions.

Antonyms:

| Organization | Government | Orderliness |

Examples:
Our Prime Minister has the capability to create orderliness out of chaos.
What we need is an efficient organization to look after our economic interest.
Democracy is defined as a government of people, by the people and for the people.

Charity (Noun)

Charity begins at home.

Synonyms:

Kindness	Benignity	Generosity
Philanthropy	Benevolence	Beneficence
Alms	Giving	Liberty

Examples:
The kindness and generosity of the hermit kindled new light in the heart of the culprit.
The institutions engaged in philanthropic activities have been exempted from the new taxes.
Religious – minded people consider alms – giving a sacred act.
Indian constitution gives the citizen liberty to pray in any manner one likes.
You can observe his benevolence when a poor man approaches him for help.
St. John's attitude as a good teacher is one of beneficence to the students.
Malignancy and benignity can be tested through response of a person in marginal cases of abnormal growth.

Antonyms:

| Meanness | Liberality | Greediness |
| Selfishness | | |

Examples:
To criticize the activities of a dead person is nothing but meanness.
The lukewarm response of the U.S. President to Soviet gestures on disarmament is characteristic of his liberality.
Most of the calamity in the world is caused by inherent greediness of the selfish people.

Chase (Verb)

Synonyms:

| Follow | Hunt | Pursue |
| Track | Run after | Course |

Examples:
All religions teach us to follow the principles of non-violence and morality.
The hunter was warned not to hunt in the reserved forests or face consequence.
In spite of his domestic problems, he has decided to pursue his studies.
The murderer ran into the forest but the police were able to track him.

Antonyms:

| Forgo | Renounce | Withdraw |
| Leave | Forsake | Abandon |

Examples:
Nita was advised to return to India or forgo the property rights for ever.
The U.N. advised the warring nations to renounce violence and sit round the negotiating table for settlement of their disputes.
Sarah withdrew his resignation upon satisfactory settlement of the pending dues.
Leave the fish in the mixture for at last an hour.

Cheap (Adjective)

We had to travel by the cheap route to reach our home town.

Synonyms:

| Worthless | Inferior | Mean |
| Inexpensive | Common | Paltry |

Examples:
Sanjay's parents considered salesmanship as a worthless career.
The job of a sweeper is by no means inferior to that of a priest.
Deepak was poor but not mean. He had no complexes.
He always wears inexpensive yet sober dresses.
She captures in her writings the turbulence of the common man.
He will never agree to work for such a paltry sum.

Antonyms:

Worthy	Superior	Noble
Lofty	Honourable	Eminent
Expensive	Dear	Costly

Examples:
This work is not worthy of your qualifications. You have a more superior talent than the one demanded for this job.
Vijendra is a noble soul, always serene and inspired. He has lofty ideals in life.
We have to address the members of the jury with the prefix Honourable.
Subhas Chandra Bose was an eminent freedom fighter and politician.

Cheat (Verb)

You cannot cheat money out of him.

Synonyms:

Deceive	Swindle	Dupe
Hoodwink	Defraud	Fleece
Gull	Hoax	Bilk
Delude		

Examples:

Sushi's heart was filled with rancour when he found that this dearest friend had deceived him.

Investors were swindled out of millions of funds by stock broker.

Beware of the door-to-door salesmen who defraud the housewives by taking advances for the articles which they never deliver.

An art collector was fleeced of a million rupees by a cheat who sold him counterfeit paintings.

The lawyer tried to hoodwink the judge by confusing the main issue.

The fire brigade answered the emergency call but there was no fire – It was all a hoax.

The innocent villagers are often duped by swindler when they come to the cities.

You are deluding yourself if you think things will get better

Antonyms:

| Fair | True | Above-board |
| Just | | |

Examples:

This in a nutshell is a fair assessment of the present situation.

I shall be grateful if you give us a true picture of the problems.

In that case I will offer you my above-board opinion.

The government tries to be just while setting industry labour disputes.

Check (Verb)

We had checked the enemy's advance.

Synonyms:

Stop	Impede	Hinder
Control	Curb	Subdue
Repress		

Examples:

They put up all the resistance but could not stop the enemy forces from advancing.

The crowd at the scene of accident impeded the arrival of the police.

Bad weather hindered the military operation.

He was able to control normal impulse to tell his boss what the thought of him.

The movement became so overwhelming and unwieldy that the police force could not curb it.

It has become difficult for him to subdue his spoiled child.
The situation has exploded. The Government cannot repress the rebellion.

Antonyms:

Speed	Hurry	Expedite
Accelerate	Quicken	Hasten
Precipitate		

Examples:
In large cities the government fixes a maximum limit on the speed of vehicles.
You should expedite the completion of this book.
In his hurry he forgot his passport.
The driver accelerated the speed of the car to catch up with the on-going traffic.

Cheer (Verb)

Your visits have cheered up the sick man.

Synonyms:

Comfort	Solace	Gladden
Enliven	Exhilarate	Applaud
Clap	Praise	

Examples:
Some politicians are more worried about their own comfort than about the welfare of the public.
The Caption did his best to solace the wounded and dying soldiers during the battle.
He was gladdened by the news of his success in the examination.
He felt gladdened until the sea breeze exhilarated him and steadied his nerves.
The outspoken couple can always be counted on to enliven a dull party.
The audience clapped forgive minutes when the film stars appeared on the stage.

Antonyms:

Deject	Depress	Dishearten
Sadden	Discourage	Damp
Decry	Deprecate	Disparage
Vilify	Condemn	Condole

Examples:
I felt dejected on hearing the news of my brother's failure in the examination.
The rise in oil prices will depress the car market.

Cheerful (Adjective)

His cheerful conversation with his friends gave him more energy and confidence to face the challenges.

Synonyms:

Joyous	Blithe	Sunny

Happy	Bright	Gay
Lively		

Examples:
Vicky felt joyous on his success in the examination.
The blithe colours of the painting made the viewers so happy.
It is always advisable to look at the sunny side of life in this era of clouded intentions of jealous nations.
I won't be happy until I know she's safe.
I am not very bright early in the morning.
I am afraid I don't feel very lively today.

Antonyms:
Sullen	Gloomy	Downcast
Miserable	Sad	Woebegone

Examples:
The father became sullen on going through the shaded progress report of his only son.
He said to his son: "Instead of looking gloomy, get ready to work harder next year".
The mother felt miserable on her child's indifferent attitude to studies.

Chief (Adjective)

The chief composition of this album is all about love and friendship

Synonyms:
Premier	Main	Leading
Supreme	Cardinal	Principal

Examples:
The premier's conduct was exemplary in the handling of a very difficult situation.
Delhi Public School is a leading educational institution in Delhi.
One of our main atomic scientists was killed in an air crash.
U.S. A. and U.S.S.R are two supreme powers in the world today.
A minister can appoint anybody as his principal secretary.
Carelessness is a cardinal cause of highway accidents.

Antonyms:
Petty	Lesser	Minor
Inconsiderable	Inferior	Subordinate
Junior	Subsidiary	

Examples:
He is a petty officer in a public sector firm.
He has lesser influence than his brother who is a boss in the same company.
Madhu is still a minor. She cannot open an independent account in the bank.
The number of scenes exhibiting him as a dance was considerable.
He holds an inferior position in the school than a junior teacher.
Tooth brush is a subsidiary product of the Palmolive ltd.

Chief (Noun)

The Chief Minister of this state is very young man.
Synonyms:

| Leader | Head | Captain |
| Chieftain | Ruler | Commander |

Examples:
The opposition parties have failed to elect a common leader.
The Indian delegation to Gulf countries was headed by the Foreign Secretary.
The captain of our hockey team was injured during the last Olympics.
For the tribal, the word of their Chieftain is as good as law.
After the French revolution, most of the European rulers had to honour the wishes of the masses.
The commander loved to narrate the story of his adventurous life to the soldiers.

Antonyms:

| Follower | Servant | Dependent |
| Parasite | Minion | |

Examples:
My grandfather was a staunch follower of Mahatma Gandhi.
Our boss has started treating some of us as his domestic servants.
He thinks we are dependent on him for our two times meals.
Jack behaves as if he were a parasite of the boss.

Chill (Adjective)

There is a quite chill in the air in the morning.
Synonyms:

| Coldness | Chilliness | Shivering |
| Bite | Frost | |

Examples:
Mountain climbers should make due preparations to stand the coldness of the peaks they wish to scale.
Chilliness is the first symptom of Malaria.
The poor boy was wearing only a shirt in the shivering cold and chilly winds.
It is amusing to see the windows turning frosty at Hill stations.

Antonyms:

| Warmth | Fire | Gleam |
| Glow | Bonfire | Fervour |

Examples:
The warmth of his welcome pleased me.
Set out some fire in the centre to the room to make its cold tolerable.
The new gas stove has a strong blue flame.

Her colour glows red in the morning sunshine.
We made a bonfire of the waste material.
Rajeev Gandhi displayed a strong patriotic fervour like Jawaharlal Nehru.

Choice (Noun)

Be careful in your choice of your spouse.

Synonyms:

Selection	Option	Alternative
Adoption	Preference	

Examples:
His selection of the art pieces is marvellous
He has given his option for his pension being calculated under new rules.
He had no alternative to accepting the invitation
He had become so materialistic that he gives preference to money than to his friends.
Adoption of an orphan child by him was greatly resented by his relatives.

Antonyms:

Refusal	Denial	Rejection
Cancellation		

Examples:
His refusal to accept knighthood from the British government made his word famous.
Culprits' denial of the crime in the court greatly upset the public prosecutor.
Rejection by the party high command of his candidature for membership of the Parliament made him defect to the other party.
The cancellation of his tour programme abroad depressed him.

Choke (Verb)

Her voice was choked with sobs.

Synonyms:

Strangle	Suffocate	Smother
Stifle	Throttle	

Examples:
The government's monetary policy is slowly strangling the economy.
The room was so suffocating that I could not stay there for even a minute.
The Caravan was smothered in dust while passing through Rajasthan.
We were stifling in that hot room with all the windows closed.
The guards throttle the burglar with his bare hands.

Antonyms:

Oxygenate	Freshen	Ventilate
Air		

Examples:
The patient was first oxygenated and then put on glucose.
A good clean will really freshen up the house.
This house is O.K. except for its ventilation.
We need fresh air to keep healthy.

Choose (Verb)

The greedy boy had to choose the largest apple in the dish.
Synonyms:

Select	Prefer	Pick
Elect	Cull	

Examples:
She was so confused to see the large variety of saris that she could not select one for her.
Baja Singh preferred death to yielding to the British.
The beginning of the trial had to be delayed owing to difficulty in picking the right kind of jurors.
The high school cricket team elected John as the Captain.
A sheep breeder culls the weak animals from his flock.
A housewife in a supermarket confronted by several tins of tomato of identical size and quality, often picks the one nearest to her.

Antonyms:

Reject	Discard	Renounce
Spurn	Disapprove	

Examples:
I rejected the over-ripe apples but bought the rest.
I have discarded the old furniture, so I need new one.
The old bachelor has renounced this world and gone to the Himalayas for meditation.
I am a democrat but spurn the overcrowded and underfed poor.
He has disapproved the purchase of this building.

Circulate (Verb)

Blood circulates through our body.
Synonyms:

Propagate	Spread	Advertise
Publish	Diffuse	Disseminate

Examples:
Some politicians even today propagate the concept of racial superiority for their dubious ends.
Ideas spread more rapidly in the present age of instant communications.

Only big companies can afford to advertise their products through the television.
The editors have formed a guild to publish a new magazine.
The diffused light of the candles on every table lent a pleasant intimate air to the restaurant.
In recent times, it was Gandhi who disseminated the gospel of truth and non-violence.

Antonyms:

Quieting	Silence	Hush
Repress		

Examples:
Calm posed tables will be quieting the patient and let him sleep.
There was complete silence in the room after Satish left the meeting abruptly.
The police have hushed the murder case to avoid damage to their reputation.
Any controls on news media will only repress the anti-government circles.

Claim (Verb)

Every citizen in the democratic country may claim the protection of law.

Synonyms:

Maintain	Require	Assume
Challenge	Demand	

Examples:
The improvement in his health is being maintained.
Law requires him to pay heavier taxes.
Bureaucrats have, of late, assumed greater importance in the governance of the country.
For its smooth functioning, the society demands your sincere compliance of all norms.

Antonyms:

Waive	Drop	Forgo
Yield	Renounce	

Examples:
We have decided to waive the tuition fees in your case.
The crane drops the cargo on the truck after picking it up from the seaplane.
We can forgo many small privileges in order to enjoy the main ones.
At last, the American forces yielded to Vietnamese pressure and withdrew.

Class (Verb)

Is it advisable to class the people according to their financial background?

Synonyms:

Arrange	Group	Rank
Distribute	Dispose	Classify

Examples:
Deepak was busy arranging his vast library subject wise and author wise.
The soldiers were grouped according to their rank and ordered to march.
Pankaj ranked first in the school board Examination.
The teacher distributed the answer sheet among the students.
He is the sole owner of his property and can dispose it off in any manner he likes.
He sorted out the books and classified them as per the international systems.

Antonyms:

Disarrange	Display	Upset
Disorder	Confuse	Derange

Examples:
The children disarranged his books in heaps when he was away.
We found the books displayed haphazardly at the counter.
We had to upset our drawing room to accommodate more guests.
Everything in the room was lying in disorder.
Let us confuse the main issue by side-tracking the discussions on minor issues.
The divorce has led to derangement of his mental make – up.

Clean (Verb)

Wash your hands and clean your nails.

Synonyms:

Purify	Clarify	Cleanse
Faultless	Immaculate	Spotless
Unblemished		

Examples:
Most of the religions believe that fasting purifies the heart.
The lawyer tried to clarify the issue further but the judge refused to listen to him anymore.
The doctor cleansed the wound of the injured patient and dressed it.

Antonyms:

Corrupt	Infect	Defile
Soil	Pollute	Taint

Examples:
Marx felt that religion always corrupted society by its fundamental belief in fate and God.
The dogs bite has infected the body of the boy. Hence he should be immediately vaccinated.
The western movies of crime, horror, sex and violence defile the character of the youth.

Clear (Adjective)

The clear water of the mountain lake is the major attraction for the tourists to visit the mountains in the summer.

Synonyms:

Definite	District	Unmistakable
Explicit		

Examples:

Your stay in the hostel seems to have brought a definite change for the better.
There is a district improvement in your personality and all round demeanour.
There is an unmistakable boost in your personality.
Will your make this explanation of your theory more explicit?

Antonyms:

Blurred	Confused	Doubtful
Foggy	Vague	

Examples:

The politician could give only blurred impressions of his visit to Algeria.
We should not make a final decision on this important subject in the present confused situation in the trade.
You are yourself doubtful whether to make or to avoid this driving the scooter.
The weather is quite foggy today. we should avoid driving the

Clever (Adjective)

He is cleaver at arithmetic.

Synonyms:

Talented	Gifted	Capable
Sharp	Dexterous	Smart
Natural		

Examples:

He is a very talented actor he can even stage and direct plays.
God had gifted him with a sharp sense, poet's sensibility and verbal acumen.
The company pays him so well because he is capable of doing many odd jobs.
Sportsmen are always active and smart.
A surgeon should be manually dexterous.
I cannot help praising his natural awareness of International politics.

Antonyms:

Foolish	Dull	Doltish
Incapable	Stupid	

Examples:

His foolish activities have spoiled his reputation in society.
He is a dull student and takes long times to grasp a simple point.

He is too doltish to grasp wit and humour.
He is incapable of performing intricate jobs.
The boy is not as stupid as you think.

Cling (Verb)

They had to cling together when the time came for part.

Synonyms:

Attach	Adhere	Stick
Cleave	Together	Hold
Embrace	Hug	

Examples:
A door is attached to the doorpost by hinges.
Deepak always adheres to his principles.
Pankaj sticks doggedly at his physics homework until midnight.
A Hindu considers it his duty to cleave to his marriage partner through thick and thin.
Religion has a force which can hold the masses together for long.
They turned to hug each other as soon as they were in a secluded corner for the park.
This thesis embraces the major ideas you suggested.

Antonyms:

Surrender	Give up	Forgo
Relinquish	Resign	Cede

Examples:
After long discussion I surrendered to his way of thinking.
I gave up the hope of her passing in Board Exam.
I cannot forgo my respect for matrimony.
I relinquished the charge of my old post the other day.
I resigned from the old post last month.

Cloudy (Adjective)

The cloudy sky is the indicator of rainy season.

Synonyms:

Dark	Dim	Gloomy
Murky	Foggy	Overcast

Examples:
His gloomy comments on the trouble they would face in customs clearance upset me very much.
Dark shades loomed out of the steam and acrid fumes.
The room was veiled with dim light of the candles.
The light was too murky to continue playing.

My idea on the subject is a little foggy.
Antonyms:

Sunny	Undimmed	Unclouded
Clear	Bright	

Examples:
Sunny weather is welcome after so many days of dark clouds.
The undimmed rays of the sun fall on the eastern wing of our house every morning.
The discussion between us has unclouded the controversial points.
We have already cleared the problematic issues.

Clutch (Verb)

A drowning man will clutch at a straw.
Synonyms:

Grip	Seize	Catch
Grab	Grasp	

Examples:
A good administration is one that can have a grip of the circumstances and tackle each problem on merit.
The shrewd seize the opportunity of accomplishment at the right moment.
I threw a ball to her and she caught it.
Antonyms:

Release	Liberate	Emancipate

Examples:
The government released all the aged prisoners on the Independence Day.
The government has ordered all agricultural landlords to liberate the bonded labour from compulsory work.
This has led to the emancipation of the bonded labour that now has their wider opportunities of work of their choice.

Course (Adjective)

A dress made of coarse is the fashion-dress today.
Synonyms:

Unpolished	Harsh	Indelicate
Unrefined	Rude	Gross

Examples:
The unpolished surfaces do not reflect light.
He is very harsh in dealing with his subordinates.
His popularity among his friends has reduced because of his unrefined manners.
The teacher has condoned the student for his rude behaviour.
We were shocked at his gross ignorance of the subject under discussion.

Antonyms:

| Polished | Polite | Elegant |
| Refined | Civilized | Genteel |

Examples:
His polished manners win him new friends.
His polite behaviour is responsible for his success with subordinates.
He looks elegant in his new suit.

Cold (Adjective)

This is a hotel with hot and cold water in every room.

Synonyms:

Chilled	Chilly	Cool
Frigid	Frosty	Gelid
Icy		

Examples:
Chilled Coco Cola gives great refreshment in the summer.
With the onset of winter the weather has become somewhat chilly.
Let us discuss this subject in a cool atmosphere.

Antonyms:

| Hot | Passionate | Warm |
| Balmy | | |

Examples:
It is very hot today: The day's temperature has touched 40-degree C.
The boss has taken a passionate attitude towards the young girl.
Jim offer of writing off old debt against Jack has proved very balmy.

Combat(Noun)

A combat with the wind and waves is inevitable for a sailor.

Synonyms:

| War | Battle | Action |
| Contest | Conflict | Broil |

Examples:
The border incident led to war between the two countries.
Their whole life was a constant battle against poverty.
The army action in Bangladesh was praised by all.
It is little use contesting the election as an independent candidate.
The policies they are following will surely bring them in conflict with each other.
The travellers were broiling in the sun as they crossed the desert.

Antonyms:

| Harmony | Peace | Concord |

| Amity | Agreement | Quite |

Examples:
Communal harmony is the first condition to keep India strong and united.
After years of fighting, the people of India and Pakistan longed for peace.
India and Pakistan must reach a concord to avoid disturbances in the Indian subcontinent.
They should develop amity among the people of the two countries.
They have to work out agreement on disputes of various types.

Comfort (Noun)

Become fond of comfort as we grow old.

Synonyms:

| Ease | Rest | Leisure |
| Relaxation | Repose | Relief |

Examples:
The electrification of the village gave great ease to the villagers.
The old patient needs complete rest.
Modern life leaves little scope for leisure.
The president doesn't have much time for relaxation.

Antonyms:

| Unrest | Discomfort | Restlessness |
| Agitation | Nervousness | |

Examples:
There is unrest in most of the underdeveloped countries.
He still suffers considerable discomfort from his injury.
Restlessness is a regular feature of the modern youth in all big cities.
National Trade Union has ordered an agitation in all coal mines until settlement of new wage rates in the UK.
Nervousness is a common disease among the unemployed youth.

Comfortable (Adjective)

Please, make yourself comfortable.

Synonyms:

Pleasant	Agreeable	Pleasing
Delightful	Homely	Relaxing
Restful	Convenient	Cozy

Examples:
The diffused light of the candles lent a pleasant aura to the rooms.
If you are agreeable to our proposal, we'll go ahead.
The salesman had a pleasing personality which could convince the customers easily.
Kindly make it convenient to attend the meeting.

This restaurant has a very cosy atmosphere because of its soft furniture, mild air-conditioning, delicious and food and non-violent music.

Antonyms:

Irritating	Disagreeable	Displeasing
Aggravating	Distressed	Disturbed

Examples:
The atmosphere in this locality is rather irritating because of foul smell, smoke, noise and dirt.
All this gives disagreeable nauseas to my senses.
The speech of the general manager about the conditions of the factory workers was displeasing to the managing committee.
Presently aggravating tension on nuclear disarmament can be checked only by an understanding among the super powers.

Command (Noun)

General Shah is in the command of the Army.

Synonyms:

Commandment	Order	Directive
Mandate	Rule	Behest
Decree	Direct	

Examples:
Every Muslim considers it his sacred duty to follow the commandments of the Holy Quoran.
The boss orders and the subordinate obey.
In view of the new directive issued by the government, our co-operative society will have to amend its bye – laws.
The mandate given by the masses through vote is the main characteristic of democracy.
He did not present himself before the court. Therefore, the court has passed ex-parte decree against him.
The Supreme Court is empowered to direct the High Court on any substantive matter of law.

Antonyms:

Comply	Submit	Obey
Beg	Beseech	Plead

Examples:
The teacher asked the students to comply with the regulations pertaining to the examination.
I have submitted my income – tax returns for the current year.
As sportsmen we should strictly obey the laws of the game.

Commemorate (Verb)

Christmas commemorates the birth of Christ.

Synonyms:

Celebrate	Honour	Immortalize
Keep	Memorialize	Pay tribute to
Recognize	Remember	Salute
Solemnize		

Examples:

Large crowds turned out to honour the winning team.
If your hands are cold, keep them in your pocket.
Her colleagues paid tribute to her outstanding loyalty and commitment to the firm.
I recognized him from the photograph you showed me.
Have you met my brother? Not as far as I remember.

Antonyms:

Disregard	Forget	Ignore
Omit	Overlook	Pass over
Take no notice of		

Examples:

His argument completely disregards the facts.
I will never forget seeing my daughter sing in public for the first time.
I said hello to her, but she ignored me completely.
Despite her qualifications she has been repeatedly overlooked for the job.
They close to pass over her rude remarks.

Common (Adjective)

They have English as a common language.

Synonyms:

Usual	Frequent	Ordinary
Familiar	Vulgar	Mean
Hackneyed	Trite	Low

Examples:

Father has gone out for his usual evening walk.
His visits became less frequent as time passed.
We travelled in an ordinary compartment.
It is nice to be back in the old familiar room.
His vulgar table manners shocked all the guests.
He is so mean that he looks down upon the poor.
This is a story written beautifully but concerned with the trite theme of adolescent loneliness.
I don't like hackneyed jargon of movie – romance magazines.

His low position in the society was exploited by his neighbour.
Antonyms:

Unusual	Frequent	Extraordinary
Exceptional	Unfamiliar	Choice
Refined	Cultured	Polished
Gentle		

Examples:
It is unusual of the Director to visit the factory without prior notice.
The Director's visits to our establishment are infrequent.
The extraordinary meeting of the Non-aligned members was held in New York to press for an early freedom of Namibia.
There are many topics in our syllabus which need exceptional treatment.
These premises are unfamiliar to our pet dog.
Zimbabwe was the unanimous choice of the Non-aligned Countries to have their meetings this year.
Nescafe is one of the refined brands of Indian coffee.

Compact (Adjective)

Compact Disc is the mostly used to transmit data in Computers.
Synonyms:

Compressed	Condensed	Dense
Firm	Impenetrable	Impermeable
Pressed	together	Thick
Compendious	Concise	Epigrammatic
Laconic	Solid	

Examples:
Still dense forests are found in Africa.
She is now the firm favourite to win the championship.
It was so cold that the village pond had frozen solid.
The ice on the lake is over six inches thick.
His observations were concise and to the point.
Antonyms:

Dispersed	Large	Loose
Roomy	Scattered	Spacious
Sprawling	Garrulous	Lengthy
Prolix	Rambling	Verbose
Wordy		

Examples:
Security forces tried to disperse the crowd with teargas.
A large family needs a large house.

Be careful with that sauce pan – the handle is loose.
In Arunachal Pradesh thinly scattered populations live.
He was sprawling in an arm chair in front of the T.V.

Companion (Noun)

He is an excellent companion.

Synonyms:

Friend	Colleague	Pen-pal
Comrade	Shadow	Accomplice
Associate		

Examples:
Jonathan, a close, friend of mine, stands by me in thick and thin.
One of my colleagues is very kind – hearted and helps every one.
I have made many pen-pals through the science master monthly.
In Hindu religion wife is considered to be a shadow of her accomplice.
These two men are business associates.

Antonyms:

Enemy	Rival	Pieties'
Unsportsmanlike		

Examples:
Jill and Sam are staunch enemies of each other.
They are rivals in studies and sports.
They always carry pietism attitude against each other.
They are considered unsportsmanlike by the students and teachers.

Company (Noun)

He stayed at home to keep his wife company.

Synonyms:

Collection	Crowd	Troupe
Assemblage	Group	Gathering
Firm	Assembly	House
Gang	Conclave	

Examples:
Rotary Club is a collection of educated and kind hearted persons who occasionally organize charitable programmes for the poor.
The angry crowd raised slogans against the leader because he did not keep his word of honor on an important issue.
There was an assemblage of workers at Boat Club who were on strike.
The group of leaders elected by the students has given a presentation to the Vice Chancellor.

There was a large gathering of villagers at the cattle show.
A large number of stores were purchased by a new firm.
The school assembly begins at 9 am morning.
A gang of robbers looted the whole village.
The conclave of opposition leaders will meet at Bangalore next month.
This dance troupe is setting out on a world tour very shortly.

Antonyms:

| Individual | Isolated | Alone |

Single

Examples:
The Indian constitution provides numerous freedoms to the individual.
These freedoms are part of the Fundamental Rights but not isolated from the Directive Principles.
The freedoms are not alone. They are accompanied by Fundamental Duties of citizens.
My uncle is single i.e. he is not married.

Comparison (Noun)

The tallest buildings in London are small in comparison with those in New York.

Synonyms:

| Similitude | Illustration | Simile |
| Collation | Juxtaposition | Correlation |

Resemblance

Examples:
His poetry is full of similitude and makes a very interesting reading.
He threw in two humorous anecdotes as illustrations of his main point.
He was so brave that in his biography, writers refer to lion as a simile to describe his bravery.

Antonyms:

| Difference | Contrariety | Contrast |

Contrary

Examples:
There is a world of difference between this printing machine and the one fitted at Okhla.
The two machines are opposite in their costs and functioning and are characterized by contrariety in many ways.
One is letter press. It prints composed matter. The other is an offset press. It prints off prints of sheets already made-up. They are thus contrasted to each other.

Compassion (Noun)

He was filled with compassion for the refugees.

Synonyms:

Kindness	Charity	Clemency
Sorrow	Tenderness	Mercy
Sympathy	Condolence	

Examples:
Impressed by the kindness of the priest, the thief became his follower.
The new medicine will maintain the tenderness of your skin.
He shows no mercy towards his horse and flays it with baton continually.
The boss expressed his sorrow but pointed out his inability to attend the condolence gathering.

Antonyms:

Cruelty	Malignity	Barbarity
Savagery		

Examples:
Highly prosperous himself, his attitude to the poor shows his basic selfishness and cruelty.
The boss shows malignity towards those subordinates who come late to office.
Although known for his civilized manners in his high circle, he often shows acute barbarity to his low-paid workers.
The beginning of the industrial revolution in England showed an attitude of savagery of the barons to the working classes.

Compel (Verb)

His conscience compelled him to confess.

Synonyms:

Bind	Coerce	Drive
Oblige	Constrain	Force
Necessitate		

Examples:
Our government has done well to amend the constitution to bind citizens to Fundamental duties while they enjoy Fundamental Rights.
There is found an element of coercion in establishing state authority in every country.
With some embarrassment she felt constrained to point out his mistake.
You are not obliged to answer these questions, but it would help us if you do.

Antonyms:

1. Acquit   2. Induce   3. Allure

Examples:
The court acquitted the accused of all charges after examining the evidence.
Instead of compelling the people to family planning it is desirable to induce them to

it through proper media like the radio and T.V.
Family planning can be presented in such a way that the couples at large are allured to it in their own interests.

Competent (Adjective)

Is Miss Matura competent in her work as a teacher?

Synonyms:

Able	Adapted	Adequate
Appropriate	Capable	Clever
Endowed	Equal	Fit
Pertinent	Proficient	Qualified
Sufficient	Suitable	

Examples:
I have never been able to understand such complicated things.
Your work is adequate but I'm sure you could do better.
His formal style of speaking was appropriate to the occasion.
I'm sure he is capable of running a mile in four minutes.
He keeps himself fit by running several miles away every day.
She has become reasonably proficient in her work.

Antonyms:

Inadequate	Incapable	Incompetent
Inexperienced	Inexpert	Unqualified
Unskilled		

Examples:
I felt completely inadequate to cope with this job.
The children seem to be totally incapable of working quietly by themselves.
I suppose my application has been lost by an incompetent clerk.
To bob's inexpert eye it looked like a camera.

Complacent (Adjective)

With a complacent smile, he sent us off to our native place.

Synonyms:

Content	Gratified	Pleased
Pleased	With oneself	Resting on one's
laurels	Satisfied self	Assured
Self-contented	Self-satisfied	Serene
Smug	Unconcerned	

Examples:
He is content to stay in his present job for the time being.
It is extremely gratified to see one's effort rewards.

Your mother will be pleased with you for your brilliant result.
I felt quite satisfied with my day's work.
Throughout the crisis she remains serene and in control.

Antonyms:

Discontent	Dissatisfied	Insecure
Troubled	Uneasy	Unsatisfied

Examples:
The strikes are a sign for growing discontent.
Many women feel dissatisfied with their appearance.
She feels very insecure about her marriage.
I had an uneasy suspicion that all was not well.

Compose (Verb)

She composed herself to answer the letter from her father.

Synonyms:

Write	Pacify	Form
Calm	Allay	

Examples:
The poet wrote most of his poems sitting in a garden.
His poetry was meant to pacify the aggrieved lovers.
He formed images of love and romance better amidst the natural surroundings than in the air-conditioned room of his villa.
The news about the new economic policy calmed fears in the business community.

Antonyms:

Excite	Irritate	Criticize
Dissect		

Examples:
Marx's writings greatly excited the workers to revolt against the capitalists.
Don't irritate me by repeating you're here to say something.
Let us criticize the government in a constructive way i.e. by making suggestions.

Compress (Verb)

After he compressed cotton into bales, he set out to bank.

Synonyms:

Abridge	Contract	Crowd
Compact	Condense	

Examples:
Better compress your ideas in a page or two and leave them with me for consideration.
Metals contract when they are cooled.
Crowded cities are a menace to nature.

Antonyms:

Diffuse	Dilate	Expand
Extend		

Examples:
We can diffuse the negative aspects of elections by educating the voters with more constructive campaigning.
I dilated upon the scheme to provide due guidance to my subordinates.
Let us expand this paragraph into an essay.
There are plans to extend the no smoking area.

Compromise (Noun)

The strike was not ended until they resorted to compromise.

Synonyms:

Accommodation	Accord	Adjustment
Agreement	Concession	Half measures
Settlement		

Examples:
The two sides failed to agree on every point but came to an accommodation.
Such an act would not be in accord with our policy.
I have made a minor adjustment to seating plan.
An agreement with the employers was finally worked out.
The company was finally forced to make important concessions to the workers.
The strikers have reached a settlement with the employers.

Antonyms:

Contention	Controversy	Difference
Disagreement	Dispute	Quarrel

Examples:
It is my contention that you are wrong, and I shall try to prove it.
The appointment of the new director aroused a lot of controversy.
Why don't you settle your differences and be friends again?
The union is in dispute with management about overtime rates.

Compulsory (Adjective)

Is military service compulsory in your country?

Synonyms:

Binding	Forced Imperative	
Mandatory	Obligatory	Required
Requisite		

Examples:
The agreement is binding on both parties.
I found his reasoning rather forced.

It is absolutely imperative that we make a quick decision.
Tuition is mandatory for all students in France.
It is obligatory to remove your shoes before entering the mosque.
The firm employs the requisite number of women.

Antonyms:

Discretionary	Elective	Optional
Unimperative	Unnecessary	Voluntary
Non-requisite		

Examples:
Sanskrit is an optional subject in Indian school.
My presence at the meeting was unnecessary.
The firms want on voluntary liquidation.
Military board has discretionary power in the matter of defence purchases.

Conceal (Verb)

He tried to conceal the fact that his son scored very low marks in the public exam.

Synonyms:

Suppress	Screen	Disguise
Hide	Bury	Camouflage
Cover	Obscure	Secret

Examples:
Every individual has good and bad points. The one who can suppress the bad points and bring out the good ones becomes great.
Feature films screened this year at the film festival were all superb.
The actor has to disguise himself to give a real picture of the character he plays.

Antonyms:

Expose	Confess	Avow
Manifest	Disclose	Divulge
Expose Reveal		

Examples:
It is always better to avoid exposing one's bad thoughts in public.
Let us confess faults before God.
He avowed his responsibility for the failure of the project.

Concede (Verb)

He conceded ten points to his opponents.

Synonyms:

Admit	Accept	Acknowledge
Allow	Confess	Grant
Cede	Hand over	Relinquish
Surrender	Yield	

Examples:
I wrestled with the problem for weeks but finally had to admit defeat.
You must accept the consequences of your action.
She acknowledged that the equipment had been incorrectly installed.
He allowed that I had the right to appeal.
She finally confessed to having stolen money.
I grant you that she's clever woman, but I wouldn't want to work for her.

Antonyms:

Contest	Deny	Disclaim
Dispute	Protest	Refute
Reject	Boat	Conquer
Defeat		

Examples:
He denied that he had been involved in this scam.
They disclaimed all the responsibility of the explosion.
They disputed at great length what they should do.
General public protested strongly at the cut of public spending.
He refuted all his suggestions that he was planning to resign.

Conceited (Adjective)

His self-conceited tendency cost him success in the recently concluded election.

Synonyms:

Arrogant	Egotistical	Immodest
Narcissistic	Overweening	Too big for one's boot
Vain		

Examples:
He has a reputation for rudeness and intellectual arrogance.
I had always thought him to be egotistical and attention-seeking.
If I may be immodest for a moment, I'd like to quote from something I have just written.
Women are said to have narcissistic tendencies.
Radhika is too big for her boot, she always boosting his intelligent ship.

Antonyms:

Humble	Modest	Self-effecting
Unassuming		

Examples:
Be bumble enough to learn from your mistakes.
It's not good to boasting with everybody, be modest about your achievements.
She is charming and pretty but self-effecting.
Deepak is a gentle and unassuming person.

Concentration (Noun)

This book requires a high power of concentration to complete.

Synonyms:

Absorption	Application	Heed
Bringing	To bear Centralization	Consolidation
Convergence	Accumulation	Aggregation
Collection	Horde	

Examples:
His work suffered because of his total absorption in sport.
Success as a writer demands great application.
I've warned him of the risk but he pays little heed to what I say.
We must bring all our energies to bear upon the task.
The two companies consolidated for greater efficiency.
Accumulation of toxic chemical in river causes fatal-diseases to aquatic life.

Antonyms:

Absentmindedness	Disregard	Distraction
Inattention	Diffusion	Disperse
Scattering	Spreading–out	

Examples:
Deepak failed in board exam due to absent mindedness.
His argument completely disregards the facts.
I find it hard to work to home because there are too many distractions.
Deepa is inattentive to her studies.

Concerted (Adjective)

The concerted action taken by them produced the wanted results.

Synonyms:

Collaborative	Agreed upon	Combined
Coordinated	Joint	Planned
Prearranged	United	

Examples:
Circumstances have combined to run our plans for holiday in a successful manner.
The plan was not very will coordinated.
We should apply joint effort for upliftment of our nation.
United we stand. Divided we fall.

Antonyms:

Disunited	Separate	Uncontrived
Uncooperative	Unplanned	
Divided		

Examples:
Opposing principles on passing the 30% reservation bill are threatening to disunite the party.
Separate sitting arrangements were made in the theatre for the VIP's and common people.
There was a lot of commotion in the hall as the function uncontrived.
The city is unplanned, so the drains overflowed and made the streets dirty.
The general people were very uncooperative which created difficulties to the police to find out the culprit.
United we stand. Divided we fall.

Concord (Noun)
Live in concord with nature.
Synonyms:
Unity	Peace	Amity
Accord		

Examples:
People showed an immense sense of unity at the meeting.
There was an implied atmosphere of peace at the inter-religious conference held in Allahabad-India
Indo-USSR amity has become a well-known fact.

Antonyms:
Animosity	Variance	Discord
Disagreement		

Examples:
It is asking unduly long to end Indo–Pak animosity.
There was variance of views on some issues at the India-Lanka meet in New Delhi.
US-USSR discord on disarmament proposals can lead to serious consequences for the whole world.

Concrete (Adjective)
A lamp is concrete but its brightness is abstract.
Synonyms:
Consolidated	Compact	Firm

Examples:
There is immense need for consolidating all races into one human race irrespective of colour, creed or religious affiliation.
Indian national is a compact of numerous races, religions, regions and tribes.
Ashoka had firm ideas on the goodness of soul and non-violence in human affairs.

Antonyms:

Loose   Shifting   Bogy
Sloppy

Examples:
The Janata Party is a loose combination of politicians with divergent views.
Lok Sabha has passed the Anti–defection Law to stop shifting loyalties of politicians.
The heavy rains left the roads with sloppy around.

Confess (Verb)

He confessed that he had stolen the money.
Synonyms:

Acknowledge   Reveal   Own
Aver

Examples:
It is good to acknowledge one's weaknesses before indulging in self-praise.
The working of the economy has revealed many weaknesses in the basic economic policies of the country.
There is nothing wrong in owning one's faults. Self – analysis is good for self – development.

Antonyms:

Deny   Suppress   Disavow
Cover   Hide

Examples:
One who denies his imperfections is telling a lie. Suppress your ego, if you want to develop good–self.
Nobody can disavow responsibility for the consequences of bad actions.
His words had hidden meaning.

Confine (Verb)

Please, confine your remarks to the subject we are discussing.
Synonyms:

Bind   Narrow   Bound
Limit   Immune   Impute

Examples:
I am bound by the limits of my little knowledge.
Narrow thinking never makes a great man.
Let us not impute bad intentions to others and good ones to self.
We mortals cannot be immune to disease and death.

Antonyms:

Extend   Expand   Loosen
Widen   Dilate

Examples:
It is wise to extend the frontiers of knowledge as far as possible.
Metals expand on heating.
This knot needs to be loosened with knife.
Widen the mind's horizon if you want to be poet.

CONFIRM (Verb)

Please, confirm your telephone message by a letter.

Synonyms:

Fix	Prove	Strengthen
Settle		

Examples:
The firm has yet to calculate its cost to fix the price of this product.
Proper evidence is called for to prove the authenticity of this statement.
This latest development has only strengthened by determination to leave.
One can settle the accuracy of this remark without any fuss.

Antonyms:

Cancel	Upset	Refute
Repeal	Shake	

Examples:
Our arguments certainly cancel the logic propounded in this historical theory.
The law relating to the puny purses was repealed long back.
The disturbances in some states in India have shaken my faith in the concept of the open state.

Conquest (Noun)

The Roman conquests in Africa are now part of history.

Synonyms:

Overthrow	Victory	Triumph

Examples:
In recent decades' monarchies have been over thrown in many countries.
Socialist democracies have won victories in many states.
Democracy has triumphed over political dictatorship in most countries although military dictatorships persist in some states.

Antonyms:

Forfeiture	Surrender	Retreat
Defeat		

Examples:
In communist countries they have followed the forfeiture of private properties by the state.

English Synonyms and Antonyms 'C' 133

Many imperialist regimes have surrendered to the popular movements of independent countries.
Military occupation of foreign powers has been compelled to retreat.

Conscientious (Adjective)

What we lack now days is conscientious worker.

Synonyms:

| Careful | Diligent | Faithful |
| Uncorrupted | Meticulous | Responsible |

Examples:
We should the very careful while handling glass utensils as they are easily breakable.
It is difficult to find an uncorrupted politician in our country.
The student must be faithful to their teachers.
She has done a meticulous and painstaking research on Golden Lagoons.
The company is proud of its diligent workers.

Antonyms:

Careless	Corrupt	Negligent
Slack	Profligate	Wicked
Vile		

Examples:
Corruption is evident in every field of politics.
A number of corrupt officials have been dismissed from our Minister recently.
They were charged of profligate activities connected with selling confidential information to foreigners.
The wicked persons could not conceal their evil designs for long.
Their vile habits gave way to the security of their service.
She is very careless about her dresses.

Considerable (Adjective)

He gets considerable income from his website. That is not adequate to meet all his expenses.

Synonyms:

| Thoughtful | Attentive | Heedful |
| Circumspect | Kind | |

Examples:
She is thoughtful of her friends.
The teacher asked him to be attentive in the class.
The driver was heedful but the brakes of his vehicle failed and he met with an accident.
The circumspect investor put his money in blue-chip stocks.

The rich should be kind to the poor.

Antonyms:

| Thoughtless | Inattentive | Heedless |
| Negligent | Unconcerned | |

Examples:
For a moment he became thoughtless of the consequences.
Vicky is inattentive in his class. No wonder he secures low marks in his examination.
Deepak is heedless of lessons taught and is rather low in results.
Ahmed is equally negligent of his studies and hence he keeps failing in the exam.
Their teacher is unconcerned with the individual progress of his students. He cares only for those who work hard.

Considerate (Adjective)

It was considerate of you not to play the piano while I was having a sleep.

Synonyms:

Attentive	Careful	Reflective
Unselfish	Factful	Helpful
Thoughtful		

Examples:
The students listened to the speech of the Principal attentively.
The Principal advised the students to be careful against mixing of politics with education.
She refused their invitation firmly but tactfully.

Antonyms:

| Rude | Heedless | Negligent |

Examples:
The manner of his conversation with the boss was rather rude.
Rude behaviour led to the rejection of his demand for promotion.
When an institution is heedless to the genuine demands of its staff, its standard of teaching is bound to dwindle.
The teachers became negligent of their duties and concentrated on the agitation for better salaries.

Constant (Adjective)

He has been constant in his devotion to his scientific studies.

Synonyms:

Steady	Firm	Unswerving
Ceaseless	Everlasting	Incessant
Steadfast		

Examples:
Slow and steady wins the race is a well-known maxim.
India takes a firm stand on international issues.
The crew had an unswerving faith in the caption.
The steadfast attitude of Muslims has made the Muslim Law static.

Antonyms:

Unsteady	Flexible	Variable
Inconsonant	Unreliable	Unstable
Fickle		

Examples:
He is so unsteady in his career. He keeps changing jobs every six months.
He is flexible. He draws deep every influence that comes his way.
His is of variable temperament. He therefore keeps shifting his attitude with the environment.
He is so inconstant in his objectives that he has to change his policy frequently.

Contemptible (Adjective)

The manner in which he treated all of us was highly contemptible.

Synonyms:

Despicable	Paltry	Pitiful
Vile	Detestable	Execrable

Examples:
The attitude of some high caste members towards the scheduled castes is still despicable and should be condemned by all sane people.
Vile attitude of some rich is still responsible for class divisions in society.
The snobs in society look down at the poor with pitiful attitude.

Antonyms:

Respectable	Admirable	Excellent
Weighty	Grave	Important

Examples:
India has earned a respectable position among suppressed nations after independence by her support to freedom movements in Asia and Africa.
The role played by Jawaharlal Nehru and his daughter, Mrs. Indira Gandhi in this country is admirable.
The Indian team played excellent cricket in the last international match.

Consumption (Noun)

The consumption of beer did not go down when the price was raised.

Synonyms:

Extinction	Decline	Waste
Expenditure	Dissipation	Destruction

Examples:

Government has taken several steps to protect he species of animals facing extinction.
The number of lions in India is on the decline these years.
The enemy laid waste in a number of villages before retreated.
The typhoon caused great destruction in Manila last year.
Although his income has increased considerably, his expenditure still exceeds his income.
He dissipates his energies in productive works. That is why he remains short of funds.

Antonyms:

Preservation	Increase	Gain
Income	Accumulation	Addition

Examples:

Preservation is the first law of a healthy life.
There has been a tremendous increase in food grains production during the last decade.
There is a phenomenal gain in the national product this year.
My income has increased more than my expenditure in recent years. Hence I have accumulated some savings.

Contented (Adjective)

With a contented smile, he sent us off to our native place.

Synonyms:

Satisfied	Gratified	Pleased
Cheerful	Comfortable	Serene
Happy		

Examples:

John is satisfied with the progress of his son.
Mr. Samson was gratified to know that his son had secured a top position in the higher secondary examination.
I was pleased with the sincere attitude of my employee and gave him an increment.

Antonyms:

Discontent	Frustrated	Malcontent
Miserable		

Examples:

There is general discontent among salaried classes owing to galloping inflation in the economy.
Deepak felt frustrated with his routine work and resigned to take up a more creative job.

I feel miserable when I look at the way slum–dwellers live.

Contract (Noun)

There are so many works to be done as per the contract.

Synonyms:

Agreement	Arrangement	Bargain
Bond	Commitment	Compact
Convention	Covenant	Engagement
Settlement	treaty	

Examples:
An agreement with the employers was finally worked out.
I have an arrangement with the bank to cash cheques here.
The bargain they reached with their employers was to reduce their wage claim in return for a shorter working week.
I will honour my existing commitment but I am reluctant to take on any more work at present.
The two states have made a compact to co-operate in fighting terrorism.
Their engagement was announced in the local paper.

Antonyms:

Decline	Disagree	Refuse
Enlarge	Expend	Grow
Increase	Multiply	Spread
Stretch	Swell	

Examples:
Manufacturing output is in decline.
The reports from Rome disagree with those from Milan.
The building has been considerably enlarged.
He had already expended large sum in pursing his claim through the court.

Controversy (Noun)

That is the question that has given rise to much controversy.

Synonyms:

Dispute	Argument	Contention
Bickering	Debate	

Examples:
The judge advised the parties to settle their dispute mutually.
He tried to win the case by furnishing ingenious arguments.
The lawyer failed to produce any witness to prove his contention.
He is miser and starts bickering if he has to spend even a meagre amount on an avoidable item.

He was awarded the first prize in the college debate competition.
Antonyms:

| Agreement | Compromise | Accord |

Unanimity

Examples:
India and Yugoslavia have signed a new bilateral agreement to expand their trade.
The disputing parties came to a compromise owing to the mediation of a well-wisher.
Opposition parties have reached an accord on the nomination of candidates for Membership of the Legislative Assembly.
There was unanimity of opinion on the basic issue among the participants.

Convenient (Adjective)

Will it be convenient for you to start work tomorrow?
Synonyms:

| Suitable | Comfortable | Adapted |
| Handy | Advantageous | |

Examples:
He was not considered suitable for the job of an engineer.
The journey by air is fast as well as comfortable.
He has adapted himself to the environment of his new job.
The students must always keep a dictionary handy with them.
Being on the hill top, our soldiers were in advantageous position as compared to the enemy.

Antonyms:

| Untoward | Inconvenient | Cumbersome |

Heavy

Examples:
We all behaved as if nothing untoward had happen.
This house is too inconvenient for my living.
The procedure adopted by the Committee for distribution of essential commodities is still cumbersome.
We come back from the site of accident with heavy hearts.

Conventional (Adjective)

This is a conventional design for a carpet.
Synonyms:

Accepted	Formal	Habitual
Normal	Correct	Common
Orthodox	Prevailing	Prevalent
Traditional	Usual	Stereotyped
Hackneyed		

Examples:
He accepted the proposal whole heartedly.
Reema belong to an orthodox Hindu family.
She looks more beautiful in traditional attire.
The prevailing caste system in India is a grave problem and threat to the unity of the country.
My old mobile handset in hackneyed.

Antonyms:

Uncommon	Off-the-wall	Left–field
Unconventional	Unorthodox Unusual	

Examples:
The girl is gifted with uncommon qualities.
The boy behaved in a very unusual way.
The person is rather unorthodox.
His views regarding polygamy are unconventional.

Convict (Verb)

To convict him of his errors is what we have to do at once.

Synonyms:

Condemn	Sentence	Imprison
Culprit		

Examples:
The spy was condemned to long imprisonment by the court.
The thief was sentenced to one year's rigorous imprisonment.

Antonyms:

Discharge	Acquit	Innocent

Examples:
The corrupt official was discharged from service.
The accused was acquitted by the judge as the prosecution failed to produce adequate evidence against him.
The law should take every measure so that the innocent people are not punished.

Cooperate (Verb)

Please, cooperate with your friends in starting a social club.

Synonyms:

Work together	Abet	Concur
Aid	Assist	Contribute

Examples:
Mohan and Johan work together, both in studies and sports.
They abet each other to perform better in both class tests and sports events.
Their methods of work are identical and they concur on most of the ideas and proposals of work.

Antonyms:

Conflict	Opposed	Rival
Thwarting	Fight	Hamper
Hinder	Obstruct	Prevent

Examples:
Rachel and Atilt are classmates in the college but they are opposed to each other on most of the important issues.
They behave as rivals in and outside the class.
They are always bent upon thwarting each other's progress.

Cordial (Adjective)

Your cordial smile put us at ease.

Synonyms:

| Hearty | Sincere | Warm |
| Earnest | | |

Examples:
Ravi and Mukul are classmates and close friends. They are both hearty and sincere to each other.
Their friendship is quite warm. They help each other in and outside the class.
They are earnest in their endeavour to perform better and better.

Antonyms:

| Formal | Distant | Ceremonious |
| Cold | | |

Examples:
Ajay and Deepak are also classmates. But they are formal in their attitude to each other.
Their friendship is rather cold and distant.
Their personal relationships are ceremonious.

Correspond (Verb)

This house exactly corresponds with my needs.

Synonyms:

Accord	Agree	Coincide
Complement	Conform	Correlate
Dovetail	Fit	Harmonize
Match	Square	

Examples:
This information does not accord with the evidence of earlier evidence.
Your account of the affair does not agree with his.
Her arrival coincides with our departure.

His business skill complements his flair for design.
His idea does not conform to mine.

Antonyms:

Be at variance	Be dissimilar	Be inconsistent
Belie	Unlike	Differ
Disagree	Diverge	

Examples:
The two of them are at variance with each other over certain key policy issues.
His cheerful manner belied a deep feeling of sadness
Her mood varied from optimism to extreme depression
We differ over many things.
I disagree with the idea of spending more money on the project.

Corrupt (Verb)

In this town, there are many young people whose morals have been corrupted.

Synonyms:

Pollute	Impair	Spoil
Putrefy	Defile	Infected
Decayed	Violated	Defiled

Examples:
Insincere friends pollute the word friendship.
Their relationship is impaired and spoiled at one stage or the other.
They tell lies to each other and thus putrefy their minds.
It may defile their character.

Antonyms:

Cleanse	Purify	Repair
Mend	Pure	Undefiled
Uncorrupted	Uninfected	

Examples:
It is high time the Prime Minister should cleanse the administration of corruption of all type.
Factors polluting the atmosphere should be mended to purify day-to-day life of the people.
I left the car in the garage to get it repaired.

Cover (Verb)

Put your skirt down and cover your knees.

Synonyms:

Hide	Screen	Shield
Veil	Project	Mask

Examples:

The ravines of Chambal areas provide a very good hide to dacoits.
The police screened the whole village but could not trace the thief.
People would vanish under a veil of secrecy if they excited the vengeance of the old tyrant.
The mother shielded the son when the father was beaming him.
It is the responsibility of the police to protect the life and property of the people.
The doctors had covered their faces with masks when they operated on the patients.

Antonyms:

Expose	Unveil	Uncover
Exhibit		

Examples:

The interview of Pakistan's President with a foreign correspondent has exposed his hypocrisy on the Atomic bomb issue.
The President unveiled the portrait of Mahatma Gandhi to celebrate his 100th birth anniversary.
The newspapers have uncovered the mystery of a bride's recent death in London.

Courage (Noun)

Courage and wisdom are two important traits that we should have to succeed.

Synonyms:

Bravery	Boldness	Heroism
Intrepidity	Valour	Mettle

Examples:

The child was awarded medal for his bravery from the principal.
The Principal taught their students boldness and bravery.
Heroism of Bhagat Singh has no parallel in history of India.
He was praised for his intrepidity in climbing a peak that no one else had dared to climb.
The fireman exhibited his valour when he saved several persons trapped in a burning building.
If you want him to do his best, put somebody on his mettle.

Antonyms:

Cowardice	Timidity	Diffidence
Pusillanimity		

Examples:

To throw down arms at this stage will be show our cowardice.
The labour leader advised the workers to shed off timidity in their bargaining with the management.
The speech delivered by the Chairman of the Company showed his diffidence on the issue of labour welfare.

Creed (Noun)

With more creeds, Hinduism is a network of more castes.

Synonyms:

Belief	Faith	Confession
Catechism	Dogma	Doctrine
Tenet		

Examples:

It is our belief in the principle of human dignity which makes us work for the welfare of the poor.
She started to question the dogmas of the church.
I thank you for the faith you have placed in men by re-electing me as the Chairman of the Company.
The robber made a confession of his guilt when handled by the police.

Antonyms:

Disbelief	Recantation	Protest
Abjuration		

Examples:

Disbelief in God recants when they find human power never superseding natural power or destiny.
The workers held a protest demonstration against the management's stiff attitude on wages.

Crime (Noun)

It is the business of the Police to prevent and detect crime.

Synonyms:

Sin	Evil	Wrong-doing
Offence	Outrage	Guilt
Felony		

Examples:

Untouchability is a sin against humanity.
The evil habits have estranged him from his kith and kin.
The Hindus believe that everyone is punished by God for his wrong-doing to others.
The motorist was fined for the offence of illegal parking.
He was punished for the felony of raping a girl.
Six persons were killed in the outrage committed by the mob.
He confessed his guilt before the priest and prayed for his guidance.

Antonyms:

Modesty	Incorruption	Guiltlessness
Blamelessness	Artlessness	

Examples:

Modesty is the first virtue of a successful individual.

Incorruption is the first virtue of a successful socialist democracy.

Very seldom can one enjoy the bliss of guiltlessness as humans may commit one guilt or the other consciously or unconsciously.

Cripple (Verb)

That is the ship that was crippled in a storm in 1987.

Synonyms:

Disable	Curtail	Cramp
Impair Weaken		

Examples:

The accident disabled him from attending the meetings of the Board.

It also curtailed his other day-to-day activities of business.

The new law has cramped the powers of the government to curb individual liberties.

Antonyms:

Free	Ease	Renovate
Augment		

Examples:

You are now free to go anywhere you like.

I eased myself before undertaking the bus journey.

Let us renovate the shop before the next Deepavali.

Cruel (Adjective)

It was a cruel of him to make the donkey carry such a heavy load.

Synonyms:

Inhuman	Merciless	Inexorable
Callous	Pitiless	

Examples:

Orphans are brought up in inhuman conditions in this so called orphanage.

The dacoits were merciless upon the villagers and killed a few of them to terrorize the others.

His inexorable propaganda against his opponents brought him temporary victory but ultimate defeat.

Don't be callous to the suffering of others.

His work is generally compared with the pitiless efficiency of machine.

Antonyms:

Human	Merciful	Sympathetic
Tender	Kind	Compassionate

Examples:

O God! Take mercy on the humans. Save them from mutual warfare and destruction.

Although a rich man, Rajesh has always exhibited sympathy and kindness to the poor.

The Principal remitted the tuition fee of the poor child on compassionate grounds.

Cunning (Adjective)

His cunning smile revealed his malicious intention.

Synonyms:

Crafty	Artful	Astute
Devious	Guileful	Machiavellian
Skilful	Adroit	Shrewd
Sly	Subtle	

Examples:

School children had a crafty smoke in the corridor.

Deepak is an artful Devil.

It was an astute move to sell the shares just then.

The main road was blocked so we came by a ratter devious route.

She succeeded by a combination of adroit diplomacy and sheer good luck.

Antonyms:

Artless	Dull	Ethical
Frank	Honest	Ingenious
Maladroit		

Examples:

There is never a dull moment when John Lever is around.

His behaviour has not been strictly ethical.

To be perfectly frank with you, I think your son has little chance of passing the exam.

He was honest enough to admit that he knew nothing about the subject.

Curious (Adjective)

I am curious to know what he said about me.

Synonyms:

Inquiring	Inquisitive	Interested
Puzzled	Searching	Inquisitive
Meddling	Peeping	Pressing
Unusual	Extraordinary	Mysterious
Peculiar		

Examples:
What is that you are reading? Don't be so inquisitive.
I tried to tell him about it but he just wasn't interested.
She listened with a puzzled expression on her face.
It seems quite extraordinary that the Prime Minister can claim these figures as a triumph.
He resigned in mysterious circumstances.

Antonyms:

Incurious	Indifferent	Uninterested
Common	Everyday	Familiar
Ordinary		

Examples:
She appeared indifferent to their sufferings.
Car thefts are becoming increasingly common.
There was something vaguely familiar about him.
We were dressed up for the party but she was still in his ordinary clothes.

Customary (Adjective)

There is a customary vote of thanks to the Chairman.

Synonyms:

Usual	Accepted	Accustomed
Common	Confirmed	Conventional
Established	Everyday	Familiar
Fashionable	General	Habitual
Normal	Ordinary	Popular
Regular	Routine	Traditional
Wanted		

Examples:
When the accident happened, the usual crowd gathered.
My eyes slowly grew accustomed to the darkness.
Doctors are still trying to find a cure for the common cold.
She is very conventional in her views.
Hinduism is the established religion in India.
Such accounts of environmental pollution are now depressingly familiar.

Antonyms:

Exceptional	Infrequent	Irregular
Occasional	Rare	Uncommon
Unusual		

Examples:
I could only condone violence, in exceptional circumstances.

Such cases are relatively infrequent.
I don't drink much alcohol, just the occasional glass of wine.
The Jains are a rare community in this locality.
Instances of the disease are uncommon in this country.

Cynical (Adjective)

His cynical smile revealed his malicious intention.

Synonyms:

Sceptical	Contemptuous	Derisive
Distrustful	Ironic	Misanthropic
Mocking	Mordacious	Pessimistic
Sarcastic	Sardonic	Scoffing
Scornful	Sneering	Unbelieving

Examples:
I'm rather sceptical about his chances of winning despite what the paper say.
She has always shown herself to be contemptuous of public opinion.
It is ironic that she became a teacher, because she used to hate school when she was a girl.
I think the original sales figures were too pessimistic.
People who don't like him said he was very sarcastic.

Antonyms:

Credulous	Green	Gullible
Hopeful	Optimistic	Trustful
Trusting	Unskeptical	
Unsuspecting		

Examples:
He must have been pretty gullible to fall for that old trick.
I feel hopeful that we'll find a suitable house very soon.
She is not optimistic about the outcome.
He had crept upon his unsuspecting victim from behind.

Current (Adjective)

The current issue of the magazine carries an article on the controversial subject.

Synonyms:

Popular	Present	Ordinary
Prevalent		

Examples:
Loren has become the most popular student in the college by his sweet manners and innate intelligence.
The present position of the company is rather bad. The value of its shares has fallen by 25%

He is rich wealth but ordinary in intellect.
Antonyms:

Rejected	Private	Confined
Secret		

Examples:
Sarah passed the examination but was rejected in the final interview.
John D'Souza has been admitted in the private medical college hospital.
The thief was confined to custody until the decision in his case.

Dainty (Adjective)

A dainty child got the attention of all the people present in the function.
Synonyms:

Delicate	Charming	Elegant
Exquisite	Fine	Graceful
Neat	Petite	Pretty
Choice	Delicious	Palatable
Savoury	Choosy	Fastidious
Finial fancy	Sweetmeat	Tidbit

Examples:
Only a very delicate thermometer can measure such changes in temperature.
She writes with great elegance and economy.
This is arguably the finest collection of paintings in Europe.
We managed to get the garden looking neat and tidy.
This dish is absolutely delicious with sour cream.
She is very choosy about whom she goes out with.

Antonyms:

Awkward	Clumsy	Coarse
Gauche	Inelegant	Maladroit
Uncouth	Ungainly	

Examples:
The handle of this teapot has an awkward shape.
Your clumsy oaf – that's the second glass you've broken today.
A coarse, red-faced man yelled something across the road.
I find him terribly gauche.

Dally (Verb)

Don't dally with the idea of marrying this girl.
Synonyms:

Dawdle	Delay	Drag one's feet or

heel	Linger	Loiter
Procrastinate	Tarry	Caress
Fondle	Tamper	Tease
Toy	Trifle	

Examples:
She doesn't get his work done because she's always dawdling.
The train has been delayed due to snow on line.
I want to sell the home but my husband is dragging his feet.
She was still lingering around the theatre long after the other fans had gone home.
He procrastinated until it was too late to do anything at all.

Antonyms:
Hasten	Hurry	up Make haste
Push	Forward or on	Run
Step on it		

Examples:
He repeatedly pushed forward his own claim.
He cannot run because he is patient of high blood pressure.

Danger (Noun)

Is there any danger of fire?

Synonyms:
| Risk | Peril | Hazard |
| Menace | Threat | Jeopardy |

Examples:
The element of risk justifies some margin of profit in all business.
All great achievements like conquest of Mount Everest can be made with great peril to life.
The journey to Shilling proved to be rather hazardous.

Antonyms:
| Protection | Safeguard | Defence |
| Safety | Security | |

Examples:
Modern aircraft provide complete protection to the passengers.
The aero planes are equipped with numerous mechanical safeguards.
India is well-equipped militarily for defence against any foreign attack.

Dark (Adjective)

It is getting too dark to take photographs.

Synonyms:
| Cloudy | Dim | Dingy |

Murky	Overcast	Pitchy
Shadowy	Dusky	Sable
Bleak	Dismal	Morbid
Morose	Sad	Sombre
Abstruse	Arcane	

Examples:
The water looked cloudy and not fit to drink.
The light was too murky to continue playing
It is bit overcast. It might rain.
The news was as dismal as ever.
It was a sad day for us all when the village school closed down.

Antonyms:

Blond	Blonde	Fair
Fair-haired	Flaxen-Haired	Light
Bright	Cheerful	Clear
Genial	Glad	Hopeful
Pleasant		

Examples:
We have to be fair to both players.
He had lost a lot of weight. He is three kilos lighter than he used to be.
The sitting is brighter in the afternoon.
The news isn't very cheerful I'm afraid.
I'm glad about your passing the test.

Dazzling (Adjective)

The dazzling sunshine brought the poet out of me.

Synonyms:

Brilliant	Divine	Glittering
Glorious	Radiant	Scintillating
Shining	Sparkling	Stunning
Sublime	Superb	Virtuoso

Examples:
A glittering career has been predicted for her due to seriousness of her study.
Mahatma Gandhi, the father of nation has died a glorious death.
She was radiant with joy, hearing the news of passing her exam.
That was a very scintillating conversation.
He shows a sublime indifference to sufferings of others.

Antonyms:

| Dull | Ordinary | Tedious |

| Unexceptional | Unexciting | Uninspiring |
| Uninteresting | Unmemorable | Unremarkable |

Examples:

The day began grey and dull in host summer seasons.

We had to sit through several tedious speeches.

The book is fascinating, despite its uninspiring title.

He is completely uninterested in anything to do with politics.

Damn (Verb)

The book was damned by the critics.

Synonyms:

Blast	Castigate	Censure
Condemn	Denounce	Denunciate
Excoriate	Inveigh	Abuse
Blaspheme	Execrate	Imprecate
Revile	Sentence	

Examples:

The film was blasted by the cities.

The government has been widely castigated in the press for its handling of the economy.

Two MPs were censured by the speaker.

The papers were quick to condemn him for his mistake.

Union officials have denounced the action as a breach of the agreement.

Antonyms:

Acclaim	Admire	Applaud
Approve	Cheer	Compliment
Congratulate	Extol	honour
Laud	Praise	Adore
Bless	Exalt	Glorify
Pay homage to		

Examples:

It was acclaimed as a great discovery.

I admire him for his success in business.

The crowd applauded the performance for five minutes.

I approve of your trying to earn some money but please don't neglect your studies.

He was extolled as a hero.

Deepak was exalted a pillar of the community.

Damp (Adjective)

Don't sleep between damp sheets.

Synonyms:

Clammy	Dark	Dewy
Dripping	Drizzly	Humid
Misty	Muggy	Sodden
Sopping	Vaporous	Wet
Allay	Check	Chill
Cool	Dash	Deaden
Dull	Reduce	

Examples:
He is far too dewy–eyed to succeed in business.
Her clothes were still dripping wet.
There was a hot and humid atmosphere in Kolkata.
My shoes are sodden from walking in the rain.
Your clothes are sopping.

Antonyms:

Arid	Dry	Watertight
Encouraging	Gee	Up
Hearten	Inspire	

Examples:
Nothing grows in these arid conditions.
Don't use this door until the paint is dry.
This basement is totally watertight.
This year's sales figures are very encouraging.

Deadly (Adjective)

Fog is a deadly enemy for a sailor.

Synonyms:

Fatal	Baleful	Mortal
Noxious	Pernicious	Poisonous
Venomous		

Examples:
Alfred met with a fatal accident. He was run over by a fast moving truck.
His activities against the stage are rather baleful. He was caught red-handed passing on strategic confidential information to the foreign powers.
Each man is mortal but mankind as a species is immortal.

Antonyms:

Vital	Healthful	Life-giving
Nutritious		

Examples:

This is one of the vital medicines for human beings. Hence its production and supply is controlled by the state.

Carrot and peas are healthful vegetables.

Modern biotic is trying to invent life-giving enzymes. \

Decay (Noun)

Old civilizations may fall into decay.

Synonyms:

| Deterioration | Sinking | Decline |
| Wearing | Degeneracy | |

Examples:

Some deterioration in the quality of workmanship of this jewellery had set in from this year.

The boatman reached in time and saved the sinking man.

Cheap and sensational literature sets a decline in the moral standard of the children.

The water flowing underneath is wearing out the stone gradually.

Drug addiction is the main cause of degeneracy among teenagers.

Antonyms:

| Improvement | Progress | Expansion |
| Development | Growth | |

Examples:

There is great scope for improvement in the quality of workmanship in this piece of jewellery.

India has greatly progressed since independence.

There is growth in the enrolment of school-going children in this state.

Development programme of the company includes computerization of machines.

Deceive (Verb)

You can't pass the examination without hard work. So, do not deceive yourself.

Synonyms:

| Betray | Dupe | Entrap |
| Cheat | Trick | |

Examples:

Smugglers of foreign goods try to make big money by betraying national interest.

They dupe the customers and the officials in one way or the other. Sometimes the officials are able to entrap them but often are cheated badly.

The smugglers have many tricks up their sleeves.

Antonyms:

| Enlighten | Guide | Deliver |
| Advise | | |

Examples:
Unless the masses are enlightened about their individual, social and national interests, they cannot be expected to enjoy their right of vote wisely.
It is for the educational and mass communication system to guide the people.
The transport company delivered the goods at the destination in time.

Deception (Noun)

Politicians are used to practice deception on the public.

Synonyms:

Fraud	Deceit	Trickery
Chicanery	Equivocation	

Examples:
The supplier has played a fraud upon me by delivering sub–standard products.
It is an open case of deceit against which I can move the court.
Buying votes is the worst kind of trickery against democracy.

Antonyms:

Sincerity	Veracity	Honesty
Candour	Frankness	

Examples:
It requires all the sincerity at your command to prove a successful administration.
Mrs. Indira Gandhi inherited the desired veracity from her father.
It is only through honesty to your principles that you can become a great man.

Decide (Verb)

It is difficult to decide between the two singers.

Synonyms:

Settle	Fixed	Determine
Choose	Conclude	Decree
Elect	Resolve	

Examples:
The super–powers should settle their differences over the disarmament issue amicably.
The Seventh Five-year plan of India has fixed high targets of production in every field.
An evaluation process needs to be formulated before we can determine the viability of a project.

Antonyms:

Hesitate	Doubt	Fluctuation
Vacillate	Be indecisive	

Examples:
Do not hesitate if you consider this action as righteous.
If you have any doubt in your mind, I will be happy to clear it.
The rising prices have caused unexpected fluctuation in our estimates of cost of production.

Declare (Verb)

Australia declared when their score reached 500.

Synonyms:

Announce	Broadcast	Publish
Proclaim	Advertise	Enunciate

Examples:
The Government has announced its export policy for the next three years.
The new policy was broadcast on the radio last evening in full detail.
She enunciated each word slowly for her student.
It proclaims some incentives for the manufacturer exporters.
This book was published by Oxford University Press.

Antonyms:

Conceal	Censor	Withhold
Deny		

Examples:
She concealed her excitement on his arrival and hugged him.
The government has the power to censor all news during an emergency like a war.
The Judge withheld his judgment on the case till the next date.

Decline (Verb)

He declined to discuss his plans with press people.

Synonyms:

Reject	Refuse	Discard
Renounce	Sink	Degenerate
Decrease	Lessen	Fall
Drop		

Examples:
The court rejected his appeal for bail.
The doctor refused to go and see the patient at midnight.
All the traditions cannot be discarded out rightly.
He has renounced the world and become a Sanyasi.
When the patient's pulse started sinking, the nurse rushed to call the doctor.
The decline of this degenerate empire is imminent.
The number of students opting for science has decreased over the year.
The drug lessened his pain and he slept well.

Because of the slump in the market the prices will fall further.
He dropped his voice to a whisper.

Antonyms:

Accept	Accede to	Agree to
Admit	Grow	Aggravate
Enhance	Increase	

Examples:
I accepted his offer of a long–term loan.
The judge acceded to my request for fixing a new date for evidence in the case.
India has agreed to Pakistan's request for postponing the meeting of the Indo – Pakistan Joint Commission.
The principal has admitted my son into his college.

Decrease (Verb)

The population of this village has decreased by 150 to 500.

Synonyms:

Reduce	Decline	Subside
Diminish	Lessen	

Examples:
The doctor has advised her to reduce her weight.
The crime rate in Delhi has been on the decline for last four months.
This medicine will subside the disease but cannot cure it.
Lack of rainfall diminished the water supply.
The drug lessened his pain and he slept well.

Antonyms:

Increase	Enlarge	Enhance
Extend	Argument	Advance
Intensify		

Examples:
The recent increase in prices has upset many a family budget.
The teacher asked the students to enlarge the paragraph into a full essay.
India's role in Non-Align movement has greatly enhanced India's prestige in the committee of nations.
Each of the super–powers is interested in extending its sphere of influence.
The Public Sector in India can greatly augment the resources of the state.

Deed (Noun)

Deeds are better than words when people are in need of helps.

Synonyms:

Action	Feat	Exploit

Work	Achievement	

Examples:
To every action, there is an equal and opposite reaction.
Playing several chess games simultaneously is a rare feat.
Are you aware of the exploits of Daniel Boone?
Some of his works are well known all over the world.
He was awarded for distinguished and scholastic achievements.

Antonyms:

Inertness	Restful	Unemployment
Passivity	Dullness	Fatigue
Dawdling	Dormancy	Delay

Examples:
He used to be very active in his young days. Old age has set in a sort of inertness and brought a decline in the quality of his poetry.
He is spending restful days since his retirement.
The rate of unemployment has fallen in India with liberalization of the economy.
The new incentives have wakened up the private sector from its passivity.

Defeat (Verb)

They were defeated in their attempt to reach the top of the mountain.

Synonyms:

Overcome	Rout	Outwit
Frustration	Fail	

Examples:
The brave overcome all difficulties to achieve their aim.
They have started a new organization to rout out the social evils.
The thief outwitted the policeman and escaped.
The course commercialism of some of the publishers has frustrated the talented playwrights.
This year the crop has failed because of the usually hot summer.

Antonyms:

Prevail	Triumph	Win
Overthrow	Vanquish	

Examples:
An atmosphere of fear and distrust prevails in the international sphere today.
The crook triumph easily in modern complex societies.
Our college team won against the Siddhartha College.
The Military general overthrew the civilian ruler and became a dictator.

Definite (Adjective)

I want a definite answer: Either Yes or NO.

Synonyms:

Exact	Certain	Specific
Fixed	Definite	Explicit
Express	Unconditional	Unqualified
Categorical	Unequivocal	

Examples:
The exact time at this moment is 1.05 pm.
I am quite certain about the availability of this new apparatus from a specific firm.
Students leave for school at a fixed time every evening.

Antonyms:

Indefinite	Unspecified	Unspecific
Vague	Obscure	Tentative
Ambiguous	Implicit	Uncertain
Conditional		

Examples:
My question brought forth only an indefinite answer from the official.
The time for holding next meeting of the Board of Directors of the company has been left unspecified.
The Chairman seemed unspecific about the value of the next meeting.

Delay (Verb)

I was delayed by traffic.

Synonyms:

Hold	Keep	Detain
Retard		

Examples:
The congress held its annual session recently.
The police are keeping strict vigilance on the activities of the extremists.
The alleged was detained in police custody until the rise of the court.
The population growth is responsible for retarding economic growth.

Antonyms:

Quicken	Speed	Send
Accelerate	Advance	Expedite
Rush	Hasten	Hurry
Further		

Examples:
He accelerated away from the traffic light.
The climbs have advanced two miles from the base camp.
I have some news for you – good news, I hasten to add.
He picked up his bag and hurried along the platform.

She made a rush for the door.
Deepak sped downstairs and flung open the door.

Delicacy (Noun)

Everyone admired the delicacy of her features.

Synonyms:

Smoothness	Softness	Nicety
Elegance	Refinement	Slenderness
Lightness		

Examples:
Reflection of light depends upon the smoothness of the surface.
Some of the metals have extraordinary softness.
The picture frame and modern furniture have added to the elegance of the room.
The parents were very happy to see trends of refinement in the behaviour of their spoiled son.
He was aware of the slenderness of chances of success, yet his lightness.

Antonyms:

Roughness	Hardness	Robustness
Crudeness	Heaviness	

Examples:
The roughness of this cloth is in contrast to the softness of the nylon fabric.
The hardness of the Indian farmer is now bringing good results, thanks to the improved provision of irrigation facilities.
Dara Singh has become world Champion in wrestling, thanks to his robustness.

Deliver (Verb)

A Post-Man is a man who is employed to delivered letters at the door.

Synonyms:

Free	Discharge	Liberate
Surrender	Release	Rescue
Save	Yield	Relinquish
Handover		

Examples:
My coat caught in some barbed wire and it took me some time to free it.
The accused man was not found guilty and discharged.
In many countries women are still struggling to be fully emancipated.
Large areas of the country had already been liberated.
He had relinquished all hopes that she was alive.

Antonyms:

Arrest	Imprison	Capture
Apprehend	Catch	Seize

Adopt   Withhold   Keep
Appropriate

Examples:
Five people were arrested for drug–related offence.
The thief was apprehended in the act of stealing a car.
The terrorist was imprisoned and tortured.
I threw a ball to her and she caught it.
He seized my bag and ran off with it.

Denigrate (Verb)

If you denigrate a girl in this campus, it will be treated as a cognizable offence.

Synonyms:

Asperse	Belittle	Besmirch
Blacken	Calumniate	Decry
Defame	Disparage	Impugn
Malign	Revile	Slander
Vilify		

Examples:
She felt belittled by her husband's arrogant behaviour
He decried her efforts as a waste of time.
The article is an attempt to defame an honest man.
The government is regularly reviled for running down the welfare state.
She was vilified by the press for his unfashionable views.

Antonyms:

Acclaim	Admire	Approve
Cheer	Compliment	Eulogize
Extol	Honour	Laud
Praise	Take one's hat off to	

Examples:
It was acclaimed as a great invention.
Aren't you going to admire my new hat?
The crowd cheered loudly as the Pope appeared.
She is always eulogizing her children's achievements.
I must say I take my hat off to him. I never thought he would get into the first team.

Deny (Verb)

I deny that this statement is true.

Synonyms:

Contradict	Disagree with	Disprove

Oppose	Rebuff	Rebut
Refute	Refuse	Begrudge
Decline	Disallow	Forbid
Reject	Veto	Abjure

Examples:
The speaker had got confused and started contradicting himself.
The reports from Rome disagree with those from Milan.
She wants to be an actress, but her parents disprove.
He refuted all suggestions that he was planning to resign.
The car absolutely refused to start.

Antonyms:
Accept	Acknowledge	Admit
Affirm	Agree	Allow
Concede	Confirm	Recognize
Grant	Let	Permit
Receive		

Examples:
She offered me a lift so I accepted.
She refused to acknowledge what had happened.
George would never admit to being wrong.
She continued to affirm her innocence.
I agree with his analysis of the situation.

Dependence (Noun)

Why don't you find a job and end this dependence?

Synonyms:
| Slavery | Helplessness | Thralldom |
| Reliance | | |

Examples:
America was the first country in the world to abolish slavery.
Pakistan showed its helplessness in dealing with the hijackers of Indian Airlines plane.
In villages the Zamindars keep some people in their thraldom.
His too much reliance on his secretary was criticized by management.

Antonyms:
Delivery	Permission	License
Independence	Discharge	Play
Latitude	Release	Free
Trade	Swing	Foolscap

Examples:
The delivery of post in the village has been delayed owing to postman's sickness.
The principal has granted permission to deserving students to take the scholarship test.
In India, one does not need a licence to start the small scale industry.
Ever since independence, the government has discharged its responsibility in the field of economic development with proficiency.

Depraved (Adjective)

The depraved persons will come forward to raise this issue against the Company.

Synonyms:

Abandoned	Corrupt	Debased
Debauched	Degenerate	Degraded
Dissolute	Evil	Immoral
Lascivious	Lewd	Licentious
Perverted	Profligate	Shameless
Sinful	Vicious	Vile
Wicked		

Examples:
He debauched many innocent girls.
Pornography degrades human dignity.
You cannot pretend there's no evil in the world.
Some people still think it is immoral to have sex before marriage.
Bribery is vile practice.
That was wicked thing to do.

Antonyms:

Chaste	Decent	Ethical
Good	Honourable	Innocent
Moral	Proper	Pure
Upright	Virtuous	Wholesome

Examples:
The hospital has no decent equipment.
His behaviour has not been strictly ethical.
Is the height good enough to take photograph?
His intentions are entirely honourable.
They have imprisoned an innocent man.
Students do a year's foundation course before they start this degree course proper.

Depreciate (Verb)

Shares of this company have depreciated last week.

Synonyms:

Decrease	Deflate	Devaluate
Lessen	Lower	Reduce
Disparage	Denigrate	Deride
Detract	Ridicule	Scorn
Traduce	Underestimate	

Examples:
The government has decreased the size of grants.
His influence was already lessening.
She lowered herself slowly into a chair.
Giving up smoking reduces the risk of heart disease.
The poor service detracted from my enjoyment of the evening.
The opposition ridiculed the government's attempt to explain the mistakes.
She did nothing to conceal his scorn for the others.
We underestimated the time it would take to get there.

Antonyms:

Add to	Appreciate	Augment
Enhance	Enlarge	Expand
Grow	Increase	Use
Admire	Cherish	Esteem
Like	Prize	Regard
Respect	Value	

Examples:
Many words have been added to this edition of the Dictionary of Antonyms and Synonyms.
You can't appreciate foreign literature in translation.
Those clothes do nothing to enhance her appearance.
A tire expands when you pump air into it.
You must invest if you want your business to grow.
Children feel the need to be cherished.

Describe (Verb)

Words cannot describe the beauty of the scene.

Synonyms:

Explain	Relate	Illustrate
Tell	Draw	Define
Narrate	Recount	

Examples:
The science teacher explained the phenomenon with the help of illustrations.
The politicians try to relate unconnected incidents to blame their opponents.

He illustrated his point with a number of examples to convince the audience.
The father drew blank when his son asked him to tell about his love affair with another lady.
One cannot define God as it is not possible to define what is supernatural.
The hunter rejoiced in narrating his adventures.
His heart is filled with sorrow to recount his unlucky childhood.

Antonyms:

Falsify	Mystify	Misrepresent
Suppress	Obscure	Misinterpret

Examples:
His failure in the final examinations falsified all his past record of brilliance.
The phenomenal growth of the young man mystified the expectations of the old leader.
The salesman booked the order by misrepresenting the virtues of the product.

Despair (Noun)

Your stupidity will drive me to despair.

Synonyms:

Despondency	Dejection	Desperation
Hopelessness	Discouragement	

Examples:
The news of Mrs. Indira Gandhi's assassination sent a wave of despondency and rage in the whole of India.
His dismissal from the high position has caused acute dejection in his family.
"Pluck courage, my dear" said the father. "This look of desperation will take you nowhere".

Antonyms:

Confidence	Encouragement	Elation
Hopefulness	Expectation	Hope
Optimism		

Examples:
The leader spoke with confidence. No wonder he got elected with thumping majority.
I must thank you for the encouragement your ideas have given me.
I felt elated for having taken to topping the list of successful candidates.

Despise (Verb)

A dish of strawberries and cream of chocolates is not to be despised.

Synonyms:

Hate	Abhor	Scorn
Loathe	Disdain	

Examples:
To hate a human is inhumane.
His negative thinking abhors me.
We had a scorn for all weaklings.
I loathe the company of bores.
He disdains to sit with people like us.

Antonyms:

Admire	Adore	Like
Love	Respect	Appreciate

Examples:
I admire your courage and sagacity.
I cannot help adoring your spirit of selflessness.
I like the very look of our Prime Minister.
I love to see a movie every Sunday.

Destroy (Verb)

The forest was destroyed in fire.

Synonyms:

Ruin	Raze	Uproot
Wreck	Waste	Demolish
Annihilate	Eradicate	Exterminate
Extinguish		

Examples:
He ruined his career by showing impertinence to his new boss.
The earthquake razed hundreds of houses to ground.
The cyclone uprooted many old thick trees. It also wrecked numerous ships anchoring on the sea coast.

Antonyms:

Make	Repair	Restore
Reinstate	Build	Create
Devise	Establish	

Examples:
It is easy to destroy but difficult to make.
My car needs repairs.
This medicine restores my energy.
The court passed orders reinstating the suspended employee.

Destruction (Noun)

The destruction of a town in earthquake in Iraq bitterly goes into our memory lane.

Synonyms:

Devastation	Demolition	Desolation
Annihilation	Subversion	

Examples:
The storm has caused unprecedented devastation of the city.
Demolition of unauthorized houses was withheld at the instance of the Mayor of the city.
Desolation of towns on the borders is a common sign of the coming war.
Annihilation of Hiroshima and Nagasaki has put a great check on warlike tendencies in man.
He was acquitted by the Court because the charge of subversion and sabotage levelled against him could not be proved.

Antonyms:

Creation	Production	Making
Construction		

Examples:
All the beauty of nature, including mankind, is the creation of God.
The production of food grains has picked up since independence.
Education through doing helps making the character of the young.
The local government has undertaken the construction of a new industrial estate.

Detrimental (Adjective)

He works long hours every day to the detrimental of his health.

Synonyms:

Adverse	Baleful	Damaging
Deleterious	Destructive	Disadvantages
Harmful	Inimical	Injurious
Mischievous	Pernicious	Prejudicial
Unfavourable		

Examples:
The cuts will have an adverse effect on our research programme.
How damaging does you think this will be to the Congress Party?
Publication of the report might be harmful to the interest of the company.
The polices are inimical to national unity and harmony.
Present conditions are unfavourable for sailing.

Antonyms:

Advantageous	Beneficial	Efficacious
Favourable	Good	Helpful
Salutary		

Examples:
The slump in the housing market is advantageous to home buyers.
Fresh air is beneficial to everybody.
She decided it would be more efficacious to remain silent.
The public reaction to the new text was generally favourable.
He is always very helpful to his mother.
The accident is a salutary reminder of the dangers of climbing.

Develop (Verb)

A chicken develops in the egg.

Synonyms:

Expand	Clear	Unfold
Disclose	Lay	Open

Examples:
The facilities for technical education are expanding year by year.
There is no clear official policy yet on environment in India.
Recent political events in Pakistan have unfolded fresh dictatorial tendencies.

Antonyms:

Obscure	Conceal	Wrap
Envelop		

Examples:
The outcome of super- power talks in Geneva is still very obscure.
The thief concealed the stolen goods in an underground pit of his house compound.
Better wrap the bread in the plastic bag to save it from moisture.

Deviate (Verb)

Don't deviate from the path of truth.

Synonyms:

Diverge	Swerve	Stray
Ramble	Wander	Err
Vary	Differ	

Examples:
The bus drivers diverged from their usual route because of a traffic jam.
The truck swerved to avoid knocking the boy down.
The driver lost his way and strayed the passengers into a jungle track.
The couple liked to ramble about the countryside in search of a secluded picnic spot.
His speech wandered badly from one example to another without every coming to the core point.
To err is human, to forgive is divine.
The results of his new experiment very much vary from his earlier experiments.
They differ in their approach but their aim is the same.

Antonyms:

Coverage	Stay	Perpetuate
Continue	Pervade	Abide

Examples:
The coverage of this book is exhaustive yet to the point.
The theme of the book stays within the prescribed syllabus.
The socio-economic system in the country perpetuates the general poverty of the masses.
The features of inequality continue to pervade the social fabric.

Devoted (Adjective)

She is devoted to her children.
Synonyms:

Affectionate	Assiduous	Dedicated
Fond	Ardent	

Examples:
The parents were ready to sacrifice anything for the happiness of their affectionate son.
He got his Ph.D. Degree after an assiduous research for seven years.
He has dedicated his new book to his late mother.
The young wife is fond of her husband. Her open gestures in public are, however, despised.
An ardent patriot will not allow the separatist tendencies to grow.

Antonyms:

Unfaithful	Faithless	Indifferent
Cool	Disloyal	

Examples:
His employee proved to be unfaithful in the emergent circumstances and deserted him.
His faithless wife has applied for divorce in order to pick up a new husband.
The husband was indifferent to the divorce sought by the faithless wife.
The husband and the wife were rather cool to each other right from the day of their marriage.

Diligent (Adjective)

Diligent work is what will take you to higher places in your profession.
Synonyms:

Careful	Laborious	Attentive
Busy	Painstaking	

Examples:

The Prime Minister has asked the people to be careful of the divisive forces.
The engineer was praised for the laborious job of cleaning up the river after the floods.
The teacher flayed him for being not so attentive in the class.
Now-a-days he is busy in social work.
It was the result of the painstaking efforts of the Chairman that the society was saved from closure.

Antonyms:

Slack	Lazy	Indolent
Idle	Slothful	

Examples:
My business is rather slack these days.
He is a lazy fellow and does not get up before 9 a.m.
He is a man of indolent habits. You cannot expect him to succeed in business.
Don't idle away your time if you want to succeed in business.

Dim (Adjective)

Your face is not visible in this dim light of the candle.

Synonyms:

Cloudy	Dark	Darkish
Dusky	Overcast	Tenebrous
Bleary	Blurred	Faint
Obscured	Dense	Dull
Obtuse	Unclear	Stupid

Examples:
The weather is cloudy. It may rain any time.
It is too dark to play outside.
The origin of the disease is still rather obscure.
She cannot possibly be so obtuse.
The boundaries between east and west have become blurred.
The road is unclear due to dense fog.

Antonyms:

Bright	Clear	Cloudless
Fair	Pleasant	Sunny
Brilliant	Limpid	Acute
Astute	Clever	Intelligent
Keen	Sharp	Smart

Examples:
In summer, days are bright and clear.
Cloudless sky is usually seen in winter.

Deepak is a brilliant boy; he always stood first in his class.
The water of this bottle is quite limpid and fit for drinking.
She is keen that we should go with her to Australia.

Diplomatic (Adjective)

He is refined person in diplomatic approach.

Synonyms:

Discreet	Prudent	Shrewd
Sagacious	Judicious	Sharp
Astute		

Examples:
How can one be discreet if one does not know about the past career of one's opponent?
It was not prudent to undertake climbing of the steep slope. It has put her life in constant danger.
He was shrewd enough to understand how far he could go in criticizing the existing regime.
I like his sharp awareness of social niceties.
The secretary made an astute assessment of the strengths and weakness of the plans for reorganizing the department.
His judicious judgment has saved the family form its breakup.
In this matter you should ask a sagacious man for advice.

Antonyms:

Indiscreet	Imprudent	Tackles
Injudicious	Silly	Bungling

Examples:
His indiscretion has made him to lose the contract.
He was so imprudent in dealing with his boss that he could retain his job for just one month.
His tactless behaviour lost him his best friend.

Dirty (Adjective)

I am glad that I have not to go out in such a dirty night.

Synonyms:

Foul	Filthy	Squalid
Soiled	Unclean	Sordid
Impure		

Examples:
Sher Singh played a foul game and hence lost.
The villain used filthy language against the hero but the hero remained unsullied.

The shopping-mall near the Chowpaty had a squalid atmosphere owing to dirt and din of the poor.

Antonyms:

Clean	Pure	Unsoiled
Unsullied	Virginal	

Examples:
I can play a clean game of chess.
Buddha preached for pure habits, pure thoughts, pure action and pure dealing.
Anita is a mother of two children. But she still has virginal looks.

Disappoint (Verb)

I am sorry to disappoint your expectations.

Synonyms:

Defeat	Vex	Baffle
Foil	Deceive	Betray

Examples:
Ashoka defeated the Kalinga forces but the loss of life changed his heart. It left him vexed and betrayed.
The military coup in Thailand was foiled in time.

Antonyms:

Satisfy	Gratify	Fulfil
Justify		

Examples:
Service to humanity in various ways satisfied his conscience.
It gratified his ego and fulfilled the purpose of his existence as a human being.
It also justified his faith in God.

Disclose (Verb)

She refused to disclose her name and address to me.

Synonyms:

1. Reveal	2. Uncover	3. Confess
4. Expose	5. Unveil	6. Betray
7. Unfold		

Examples:
His business secrets were revealed to the income tax department by his secretary.
When he unveiled the status, he was amazed at its beauty and artistic excellence.
A true Christian confesses his guilt in the Church.
The caption was blamed to have exposed the soldiers to the enemy's fire to save his own kin.
When the police uncovered the box they found a dead body in it.
The king was defeated because his own general had betrayed him.

The grandmother unfolded a new story to the children every night.
Antonyms:

Conceal	Cover	Suppress
Hide	Veil	Dissemble
Cloak		

Examples:
His expressionless face concealed the shock of the tragedy.
He covered the face of the dead person.
He could not finally suppress his shock and burst into tears.

Disgrace (Noun)

A man who commits suicide brings disgrace on himself and on his family.
Synonyms:

Dishonour	Shame	Degrade
Discredit	Disparage	Humiliate
Desert		

Examples:
The accusations were intended to degrade him and destroy his reputation.
She felt thoroughly humiliated at her own lack of insight.
They shamed him for his timid behaviour in the emergency.
No one liked their caustically disparaging each new production just to prove the play Wright's worthlessness.
He attempted to discredit his opponent by disparaging references from his personal life.
The soldier was convicted of wilful desertion causing dishonour to the army.

Antonyms:

Honour	Reverence	Respect
Exalt	Dignify	Elevate
Venerate		

Examples:
Mrs. Indira Gandhi was honoured with the award Lenin Peace Prize in Moscow.
It was also the Soviet people's respect to the world's greatest woman of the century.
The house is in an elevated position far away from the city.
Nation heritage of a country is a thing of veneration.

Displace (Verb)

The volunteers were displaced by the professional army.
Synonyms:

| Dislocate | Remove | Oust |
| Supplant | Supersede | |

Examples:
The boss ordered the peon to remove the files from his table.
The accident not only broke his leg but also dislocated his joints.
The Chief Minister was ousted from party leadership by a non-confidence vote.
He was superseded by his junior. He has therefore decided to resign from service.
Electric light has superseded gaslight in many towns.
Trains are being supplanted by buses in this great city.

Antonyms:

Establish	Settle	Set
Secure	Root	Plant

Examples:
My College was established in 1970.
Let us settle our differences and live like friends.
The factory is now well set to bring profits.
We can now feel quite secure. Thanks to the restoration of law and order in city.

Dissolve (Verb)

Water dissolves salt.

Synonyms:

Divide	Disunite	Separate
Break up	Disperse	Part
Disconnect		

Examples:
British followed the policy of divide and rule to continue their occupation of the country.
It seems quite certain that Remy will separate from his father after his marriage.
In modern society joint families have a tendency to break up into smaller units.
The thunder–storm dispersed the picnickers.
If he joins the new office, he will have to disconnect relations with his present friends.
When the strings of the rope parted, the load fell to the ground.

Antonyms:

Unite	Combine	Concert
Join	Conjoin	Amalgamate
Connect		

Examples:
The party is united behind its leader.
Let us combine our resources; if you want the firm to proper.
Unless we take concerted action, we cannot make our scheme a success.
I have joined the office as a chief editor.

Distant (Adjective)

The school is three miles distant from the station.

Synonyms:

Far–away   Inaccessible   Remote
Asunder

Examples:

Our objective of making the firm pay for its past losses seems far-away dream.
The new Governor has become inaccessible even to his close associates of the past.
There is now a remote possibility of resurrecting the old relationship.

Antonyms:

Accessible   Close Proximate   Contiguous
Adjacent

Examples:

Our principal is easily accessible for discussing reasonable demands of the students.
Our college is quite close to my residence.
The status of a bank manager approximates to that of a joint secretary in a government department.

Diversity (Noun)

Unity in diversity is the strength of this nation.

Synonyms:

Variegate   Modify   Alter
Vary

Examples:

Nehru had a variegated personality. He was a humanist, scientist economist, politician all rolled into one.
The government has modified its stand on economic issues. It is moving towards liberalization of the private sector.
I have asked the tailor to alter my pant so as to adapt it to new fashion.

Antonyms:

Solidify   Unity   Fix
Conserve

Examples:

Modern educationists want to solidify all subjects at the primary level into one integrated whole.
Economic institutions in modern societies help to unify all religions, races and sects.
Political parties tend to develop fixed ideas on national and international issues.

Dogged (Adjective)

Her dogged tendency is the main reason for her success in this international examination.

Synonyms:

Determined	Firm	Immovable
Indefatigable	Obstinate	Persevering
Persistent	Pertinacious	Resolute
Steadfast	Stubborn	

Examples:

I am determined to go to U.S.A for higher studies but at the mean time I had to postpone due to severe accident of my mother.
He is a firm believer of socialism.
Lock your bike to something immovable like a railing or lamp post.
Deepak is very obstinate in his views.
Despite persistent denials, the rumour continued to spread.
A few preserving climbers finally reached the top.

Antonyms:

Doubtful	Half-hearted	Hesitant
Irresolute	Undetermined	Unsteady

Examples:

It is extremely doubtful that anyone survived the explosion.
Being an introvert Ahmed made a half-hearted attempt at conversation.
She is still unsteady on her feet after the illness.

Doubt (Noun)

I have no doubt that you will succeed.

Synonyms:

Suspicion	Scepticism	Uncertainty
Dubiety		

Examples:

I have no suspicion about your noble intentions but I expect early action in the matter.
The present international atmosphere is surcharged with scepticism on the issue of nuclear disarmament.
Uncertainty in law and order situation in Punjab has upset many a business house in the country.

Antonyms:

Certainty	Confidence	Conviction
Assurance		

Examples:

Only conditions of continued certainty and security can restore relations between different communities.

The Prime Minister displayed positive confidence in his polices at his press conferences in Moscow and Washington.

All his statements showed his deep conviction in international peace and cooperation among states.

Doubtful (Adjective)

The future looks doubtful.

Synonyms:

Uncertain	Dubious	Questionable
Problematic	Equivocal	Ambiguous

Examples:

Mohit is uncertain about his appointment in the air force.

John is dubious about the intentions of his boss in the matter of his promotion.

The speaker considered the behaviour of the opposition leader in the Parliament questionable.

Antonyms:

Clear	Confident	Definite
Decided	Sure	Certain

Examples:

The new government has enunciated its politics in a clear manner.

The government is confident of its ability to tackle the problem of law and order in the country.

The new law is quite definite on the responsibility of political parties in maintaining law and order.

Dreadful (Adjective)

What a dreadful story!

Synonyms:

Frightful	Dire	Afraid
Alarming	Horrible	Awful
Terrific		

Examples:

Frightful howls pierced the air in the graveyard when the relations of the deceased arrived there.

The union leader threatened that refusal to meet his demands will result in dire consequences.

We were afraid she might harm herself.

A terrific earthquake woke the whole town.

The situation had become so alarming that the officer had to order firing on the violent mob.

He was found guilty of the awful crime of raping the minor girl.
It was horrible to see the railway accident.

Antonyms:

Pleasing	Pleasurable	Propitious
Reassuring	Auspicious	

Examples:
The sound of the soft music was very pleasing to the ear.
Your dream is pleasurable but it is also practicable.
The meeting between the disputed parties took place under propitious circumstances of international boom.

Dry (Adjective)

Is this wood dry enough to burn?

Synonyms:

Parched	Arid	Barren
Tedious	Dehydrated	Crisp
Desiccated		

Examples:
The acute drought left the soil very much parched making it unfit for cultivation.
The Institute of Agriculture Research has invented a new technique of framing for aridtracts of land.
A good part of land on the high hills has to be left barren due to inaccessibility.

Antonyms:

Damp	Wet	Moistened
Fresh	Lively	Moist
Soggy		

Examples:
Mumbai's climate is damp throughout the year owing to the sea.
This towel is wet it may not soak the water of my body.
Let me moisten my hands. They are too dry to be activated for operating this machine.

Dull (Adjective)

His last book is dull one.

Synonyms:

Monotonous	Uninteresting	Irksome
Boring	Dreary	

Examples:
The view from the train window grew monotonous after an hour or two and I found myself dozing off.

The film was so boring that I left the theatre hall an hour before the end.
It was a tiresome day filled with a number of exhausting house-hold tasks.
For him even the job of a first class magistrate is uninteresting.
She rented a dreary little room on the top floor of a building.

Antonyms:

Interesting   Spirited   Enthralling
Lively

Examples:
This novel is too interesting to be left unread in one sitting.
The happy news of passing her exam enthralled her completely.
Today's picnic was pretty lively. I enjoyed it to the full.

Eager (Adjective)

His eager for success is the source of motivation for him to score more marks in this exam.

Synonyms:

Desirous   Anxious   Fervent
Impatient   Zealous   Enthusiastic
Keen

Examples:
My friend is desirous of her hand in marriage.
Children watched the clown with keen delight.
He is very enthusiastic about the plans he has made for his higher studies.
Deepak is very anxious to join the military service.
The lawyer made a fervent plea for clemency.
The class was impatient for the vacations to begin.
Saurabh is the most zealous worker in the whole office.

Antonyms:

Unconcerned   Indifferently   Apathetic
Loath   Disinterested

Examples:
Mahatma Gandhi was a cool and calculated politician. He always found the non-violent way to his objective.
The government cannot remain unconcerned about the atmosphere of violence let loose by the extremists.
Of late Raja has become indifferent to studies.

Earn (Verb)

His achievements earned him respect and admiration.

Synonyms:

Gain	Win	Achieve
Acquire	Merit	

Examples:
The students gained in knowledge from the lecturers of the visiting professor from Boston University.
Dara Singh has again won the wrestling championship.
Our college has achieved very good results in recent years.
Deepak acquired handsome amount in his internet business.

Antonyms:
Lose	Waste	Spend
Forgo	Forfeit	

Examples:
The doctor has advised the patient to lose weight by stages in order to normalize his blood pressure.
Let's not waste time, but start the studies right now.
The government must spend more money on the schemes meant for the upliftment of the poor.
Work harder in life even if it means forgoing some leisure if you want better results.

Easy (Adjective)

To lead an easy life in your last days, you should work hard in your prime period.

Synonyms:

A bed of roses	Child's play	Clear
Effortless	Facile	Light
Simple	Carefree	Calm
Comfortable	Contented	Peaceful
Serene	Tranquil	Tolerant
Lenient	Mild	Affable
Easy–going		

Examples:
Working here isn't exactly a bed of roses.
It's not a difficult to climb. It should be child's play for an experienced mountaineer.
She plays with seemingly effortless skill.
It is important to stay calm in an emergency.
She made herself comfortable in a big chair.
Throughout the crisis he remained serene and in control.
He was very tolerant of his daughter's passion for loud music.
My mother doesn't mind, who comes to stay with us, your presence. She's very easy-going.

Antonyms:

Arduous	Complex	Difficult
Formidable	Onerous	Stressful
Hard	Harsh	Rigid
Stern	Anxious	Formal
Unnatural	Impossible	

Examples:
The work is very arduous.
The situation was more complex than we realized.
This mathematical problem is quite difficult to solve.
The situation was formidable to cope with.
It is quite impossible to stay here without proper supply of drinking water.
She sat in her chair, rigid and staring.

Ebb (Verb)

After the accident in which he lost his left-arm, his fortunes began to ebb.

Synonyms:

Wane	Decline	Decay
Sink	Recede	Retire

Examples:
High morals of the olden days are on the wane due to greater emphasis on material aspects in modern life.
There is a decline in the real balanced values among the youth.
The patient has been decaying fast since he developed symptoms of cancer.

Antonyms:

Flow	Increase	Abound
Swell		

Examples:
There is an increased flow of water in this canal owing to recent rains.
He increased his speed to overtake the bus.
A number of criminal rackets abound in all metropolitan cities.

Elegant (Adjective)

When he was in his college, he was an elegant young man.

Synonyms:

Elaborate	Luxurious	Grandiose
Sumptuous		Deluxe

Examples:
The organizers have made elaborate arrangements for the successful holding of the seminar.

Modern aircraft have good luxurious seating arrangements.
The new airport has a set of grandiose paintings collected from the best artists of the country.

Antonyms:

Inexpensive	Plain	Mediocre
Unadorned	Simple and vulgar	

Examples:
The Satabdi Express launched by the Railway ministry has inexperience yet comfortable fittings.
I intend to have a simple plain talk with my girlfriend before deciding upon matrimony.
Our new manager is a mediocre in talent but has strong will-power to make up for this deficiency.
Amitabh is top in every field – studies, sports and debates. He is like an unadorned prince of the college.

Emit (Verb)

A volcano emits smoke and ashes.

Synonyms:

Breathe forth	Cast out	Diffuse
Discharge	Eject	Emanate
Exhale	Exude	Give out
Give	Vent to	Issue
Radiate	Send forth	Send out
Throw out	Transmit	

Examples:
Social planning has led to greater equality and a more diffused prosperity.
The accused man was found not guilty and hence discharged.
Police ejected a number of violent protesters from the Rallis ground.
Delicious smells are emanated from the kitchen.
We inhale oxygen and exhale carbon dioxide.
After a month, their food supplies gave out.
The police have issued an appeal for witnesses to the accident.

Antonyms:

Absorb	Assimilate	Consume
Devour	Digest	Drink in
Incorporate	Ingest	Receive
Soak up	Such up	Take in

Examples:
Aspirin is quickly absorbed by the body.
Children need to be given time to assimilate what they have been taught.
The fire quickly consumed the wooden hall.
In no time at all they had devoured the entire loaf.
He stood drinking in the beauty of the landscape.

Emotion (Noun)

He thought of his dead child with deep emotions.
Synonyms:

Agitation	Tremor	Passion
Feeling	Sentiment	Desire

Examples:
The employees of the factory propose to launch an agitation for higher wages.
The earthquake gave a strong tremor to the buildings in the city.
Her passion for tennis took her to glorious heights.

Antonyms:

Stoicism	Insensibility	Rationality
Reason	Indifferences	

Examples:
Modern socialists are characterized by a strange sense of stoicism in their attitude.
Modern management is marked by insensibility to galloping inflation so far as the question of increasing the wages of their workers is concerned.
Worker's participation in management of factories is justified on the principles of rationality in human behaviour.
There is every reason for managements to accede to worker's participation.

Enchanted (Adjective)

She was enchanted with the flowers you sent her.
Synonyms:

Fascinated	Bewitched	Captivated
Enraptured	Enamoured	Entranced
Spell-bound	Charmed	

Examples:
The scenic view glimpsed through the window of the train charmed me.
I was fascinated by beauty of the girl from India.
Meena Kumari bewitched a generation of movie goers.
The actor's performance and good looks captivated the audience.
Her beautiful voice enraptured audiences everywhere.
Most visitors are enamoured by the marble beauty of the Taj Mahal.
A hypnotist looks for subjects which can be easily entranced.
Everyone was spellbound by the mimicry of young boy at the concert.

Antonyms:

Disgusted	Repulsed	Replied
Nauseated		

Examples:
The teacher was disgusted by the continued indifference of the student in studies.
He was advised by the Principal to attract the interest of students in studies by reforming his mode of speech which perhaps repulsed his students.
I have not yet replied to my mother's last letter.

Encourage (Verb)

I feel encouraged by the progress that I have made in my works.

Synonyms:

Back up	Animate	Urge
Reassure	Incite	Cheer
Embolden	Foster	Hearten
Support	Promote	

Examples:
Every project needs to be backed up with finance before implementation.
Cartoon films involve animation technique of still pictures.
The director has urged the employers to withdraw their strike in order to enable him to recommend higher salaries.

Antonyms:

Dissuade	Discourage	Abash
Dishearten	Thwart	Hinder

Examples:
The Principal has dissuaded the lecturers from going on a strike.
Nothing can discourage me from my resolve to proceed on a mountaineering mission.
I hope the weather will, not thwart my mission.

Encroach (Verb)

The sea is encroaching upon the land.

Synonyms:

Infringe	Violate	Invade
Intrude	Trespass	

Examples:
I cannot tolerate anybody infringing my right to worship God the way they like.
Violation of law is punishable in every state.
The state does not intrude into the personal life of individuals in a democracy.

Antonyms:

Desist	Observe	Respect
Withdraw		

Examples:

I desisted from slapping him on this face, although he did his worst to annoy me.
We can travel safely if we observe the rules of traffic seriously.
With due respect to your sentiments, I beg to withdraw my comments.

Endanger (Verb)

Brushing the wrong side of one's boss will endanger one's success.

Synonyms:

Hazard	Jeopardize	Risk
Imperil		

Examples:

Don't hazard your reputation by supporting that crook.
He has insured his business against the risk of failure.
It is not advisable to jeopardize your health for this petty gain of money.
He imperilled his life to save a burning child from the fourth floor of the building.

Antonyms:

Protect	Safeguard	Shield
Defend	Screen	

Examples:

I can protect my rights, but do I protect the rights of others or of the society at large?
Traditional weapons cannot safeguard a country against the evil designs of an atomic power.
USA is providing shield to those countries in Asia who can take a stand against the USSR.

Endless (Adjective)

A mother should be a woman of endless patience.

Synonyms:

Unceasing	Boundless	Eternal
Infinite		

Examples:

Mahatma Gandhi had unceasing patience to withstand opposition.
Shiva had boundless courage in war and peace.
Nobody can break our eternal friendship.

Antonyms:

Temporary	Brief	Fugitive
Limited		

Examples:

UN aid can give only a temporary relief; what we need is hard work to become self-sufficient in food grains.

What I need is a brief loan from the bank to tide over the present crisis.
Great men do not behave like fugitives. They face the problems and solve them with courage.

Endorse (Verb)

His driving license has been endorsed by the authorities.

Synonyms:

Approve	Accredit	Ratify
Confirm	Sanction	

Examples:
I whole – heartedly approve your stand on this issue.
Samuel is an accredited representative of the newspaper.
India has ratified the Indo-Indonesian Trade Agreement of 1984.

Antonyms:

Discredit	Censure	Disapprove
Reject	Reprehend	

Examples:
Communal disturbances in India bring discredit to the image of unity and integrity of the country.
The communal elements anywhere need to be condemned in strong words.
All politics parties that stand for unity of the country should censure the divisive elements.

Enduring (Adjective)

She can't endure to see animals cruelly treated.

Synonyms:

Abiding	Continuing	Durable
Firm	Immortal	Immovable
Imperishable	Fasting	Living
Perennial	Permanent	Persistent
Prevailing	Remaining	Surviving

Examples:
These kitchen wares are made of durable material.
To his eternal credit, he did not mention it to anyone.
She is now the firm favourite to win the championship.
The company is now taking on workers on a permanent basis.
Despite persistent denials, the rumour continued to spread.

Antonyms:

Brief	Ephemeral	Fleeting
Momentary	Passing	Short

Short-lived   Temporary   Transient
Transitory

Examples:
Journalism is important but ephemeral.
In summer, days are short but nights are long.
Her interest in tennis was very short-lived.
This decoration is only temporary.
Every living being is transitory by nature.

Enlarge (Verb)

I need not enlarge upon this matters. You know all this very well.

Synonyms:
Augment	Expand	Amplify
Magnify	Increase	

Examples:
A modern welfare state has to augment its financial resources to launch more welfare schemes for the common people.
It needs to expand state activities on larger scale.
State policies are amplified for public discussion, so that in due course maximum cooperation in implementation of new schemes can be ensured.

Antonyms:
Contract	Condense	Narrow
Shorten	Reduce	Decrease

Examples:
In terms of their defence agreement, India and China have signed a few contracts in the industrial field.
This long paragraph can be condensed in two lines without losing its significant points.
Recent meeting of the leaders of the super powers at Geneva has narrowed their difference over space disarmament.

Enmity (Noun)

Don't be at enmity with your neighbours.

Synonyms:
Hostility	Hate	Discord
Animus	Rancour	Animosity
Antagonism		

Examples:
Recent extremist activities in Jammu and Kashmir are designed to create an atmosphere of hostility between India & Pakistan.
Some innocent persons have fallen victim to hostility with seeds of hate and

discordbred in their mind.
Certain forces outside India are jealous of India's economic progress and have fanned the spirit of antagonism by secret interference.

Antonyms:

Amity	Love	Harmony
Fellowship	Sympathy	

Examples:
Recent cricket match has helped to increase the amity between India & Pakistan to play cricket.
I love all my hobbies.
There is perfect harmony among the different communities of this state.

Enormous (Adjective)

I notice enormous changes in this town since my last visit two years back.

Synonyms:

Astronomic	Colossal	Elephantine
Excessive	Gargantuan	Gigantic
Gross	Immense	Mammoth
Massive	Monstrous	Mountainous
Prodigious	Titanic	Tremendous
Vast		

Examples:
He's been offered an astronomic salary.
Their daughter is quite plump but their son is positively elephantine.
He is not just fat; he is positively gross.
Yesterday I drank a massive amount of alcohol in the party.
The waves are rising like mountainous in the ocean during storm.
The government sank prodigious amount of public money into the scheme.

Antonyms:

Diminutive	Dwarf	Infinitesimal
Insignificant	Lilliputian	Little
Meagre	Microscopic	Minute
Petite	Small	Tiny
Trivial	Wee	

Examples:
She was a diminutive figure before her husband.
The level of dangerous chemical present in the river is now so low as to be insignificant.
Even America's largest banks look Lilliputian in comparison with those of Japan.
There's a little shop on the corner that sell bread.
We lived in the country when I was small.

Enough (Adjective)

There is enough food for everybody.

Synonyms:

Sufficient	Adequate	Plenty
Abundant	Ample	

Examples:

Our hotel room was not luxurious, but it had adequate space for comfortable sleep.
Despite the forecasting of draught, there wasn't abundant rain this year.
I had ample time today.
We wish you peace and plenty in the New Year.
I do not have sufficient book to study.

Antonyms:

Insufficient	Inadequate	Scarcity
Deficient		

Examples:

This much evidence is insufficient for proving the case.
The supply of electricity in this city is inadequate for industrial progress.
Scarcity of power is responsible for the slow progress of industries in this district.
He is quite healthy in physique but is deficient in brains.

Enrage (Verb)

He was enraged by Raja's stupidity.

Synonyms:

Anger	Madden	Incense
Infuriate		

Examples:

Anger is the enemy of success.
His rough behaviour maddened me and I felt compelled to leave his premises.
His illogical remarks infuriated me.

Antonyms:

Pacify	Mollify	Soothe
Tranquilize	Placate	

Examples:

He was furious at first, but I managed to pacify him.
The new medicine soothed my nerves.
Compose is a kind of tablet that acts as a tranquillizer.

Entire (Adjective)

The entire village is destroyed by the storm.

Synonyms:

Whole	Full	Complete
Intact	Total	

Examples:

The whole world is at my disposal through the T.V. & Radio.
The cupboard was full of old newspapers.
They came as a complete surprise to me.

Antonyms:

Broken	Partial	Divided
Damaged	Destroyed	Empty
Imperfect	Incomplete	Limited

Examples:

Quick fix joins everything except broken heart.
This noon is going to be a partial eclipse of the sun.
United we stand. Divided we fall.

Erase (Verb)

Please erase all these pencil marks in these documents before you submit them to the College.

Synonyms:

Efface	Eradicate	Obliterate
Cancel	Delete	

Examples:

Time and weather had long since effaced the inscription on the monument.
Poverty cannot be eradicated unless the working conditions of the farmers and workers are improved by legislation.
The basic weakness in the economic structure is obliterating the concept of economic equality in our country.

Antonyms:

Impress	Imprint	Insert
Confirm	Establish	Reinstate

Examples:

The system of education prevalent in this country impresses the foreign tourists as the most undemocratic in the world.
There is an imprint of acute inequality among students of government schools and the so-called public schools.
I have inserted an advertisement in the local newspaper for the sale of my old car.

Eternal (Adjective)

Does the Christian religion promise eternal life?

Synonyms:

Perpetual Ceaseless Deathless
Unending

Examples:

Poverty is a perpetual problem of India.
The administration in the country is working ceaselessly to eradicate the root cause of poverty.
The poor people are always engaged in a deathless struggle to subsist.

Antonyms:

Temporal Fleeting Swift
Passing

Examples:

The Pope emphasized on the temporal nature of mankind and counselled his audience to avoid all kind of conflicts.
He said that life was fleeting and that each of us should make the best contribution to the good of society.
Machine has made human life swift and colourful.

Evasion (Noun)

His answers to my questions were all evasion.

Synonyms:

Quibble Subterfuge Prevarication
Excuse Pretext

Examples:

I only have a few minor quibbles about your essay. Basically it's very good.
Why didn't they tell us immediately instead of resorting to this subterfuge?
The robber used the ringing of the doorbell as a pretext to the holdup robbery.
Ignorance of the law is no excuse.

Antonyms:

Refutation Reply Rejoinder
Response Defence Answer

Examples:

The minister's prompt refutation of the allegations made by a Member of Parliament saved the situation.
I am awaiting a reply to my letter from the authorities.
The opposition leader sent a rejoinder to the party in power on the issue of opposition involvement in the spy episode.

Evident (Adjective)

He looked at his children with evident pride.

Synonyms:

Clear	Visible	Obvious
Evident	Patent	Manifest
Distinct		

Examples:

He tried to give many examples but could not make his point clear.
The airship was not visible because of the fog.
It is an obvious gimmick to compensate for the playwrights arranging innovation.
From the quick success of the business, it was evident that he had invested his money wisely.
Every law has a patent as well as latent meaning.
The referee's manifest towards the home-side was criticized by the audience.
He failed to realize the distinct note of annoyance in her voice.

Antonyms:

| Hidden | Obscure | Secret |
| Covert | Latent | Masked |

Examples:

Her charming face was hidden behind the veil but the impact of her beauty could not be contained.
The autobiographies of great men are rather obscure for a common man to comprehend.
The defence ministry has kept the message received from the RAW as top secret.

Exact (Adjective)

What is the exact size of this room?

Synonyms:

| Truthful | Correct | Careful |
| Precise | Strict | |

Examples:

The witness gave a truthful account of the accident.
She was wearing the correct dress for a formal dinner.
The parts of a computer must be precise, or else it does not work.
The laws on speeding have been made stricter for observance.
Children should be taught to be very careful while crossing the road.

Antonyms:

| Inexact | Erring | Incorrect |
| Careless | Negligent | Untruthful |

Examples:
The statistics used for this conclusion seem to be inexact; therefore, they need rechecking.
The erring figure spoilt the final result of the computer programmer.
It is incorrect to say that I deliberately evaded discussion on the controversial issue in the last meeting.
A bus driver should not be careless.

Excellent (Adjective)

His excellent performance in the show got him more accolades.

Synonyms:

| Select | First–class | Prime |
| First–rate | Choice | |

Examples:
Look at his dress, manners, movements he seems to belong to the select class.
The entertainment provides was first class.
She is in the prime of her youth.

Antonyms:

| Mediocre | Faulty | Imperfect |
| Poor | Second–class | |

Examples:
Aril Mishra is a mediocre student. He secured only 40% marks in the board examination.
This motor - bike is imperfect in many ways.
The lighting system of this studio is rather faulty.

Excite (Verb)

Everybody was excited by the news of the victory of our team.

Synonyms:

Stimulate	Provoke	Arise
Awake	Inflame	Animate
Kindle	Irritate	

Examples:
His remarks have stimulated my curiosity.
The arbitrary police action provoked public outcry for an investigation.
Arise, awake and stop not until you reach your goal.
Poor performance of the actors in the theatre aroused a sense of disgust among the spectators.
A smouldering cigarette can kindle a devastating bonfire.
The crowd was inflamed by the brutality of the police.

A smile animated her face, when she met her boyfriend after a long time.
He is very short-tempered and gets irritated on trivial matters.

Antonyms:

Compose	Soothe	Allay
Hush	Mollify	Quell
Appease	Quietness	Pacify
Lull		

Examples:
His mind was in such a whirl that he could hardly compose his thought.
The new promises made by the leader soothed many a poor man.
The major allayed the fears of the frustrated folk of the industrial estate.

Exertion (Noun)

Exertion of authority is not always wise. Persuasion is better.

Synonyms:

Energy	Strain	Effort
Stretch	Pull	Tug
Spurt	Struggle	Pain
Trouble	Endeavour	

Examples:
Einstein has proved that matter and energy are convertible into each other.
I can realize your strain of working while suffering from a painful back ailment.
In spite of his best efforts he could not win any prize.
He worked for six hours at a stretch.
The pull of current carried as downstream.
She gave her sister's hair a sharp tug.
The Red Cross endeavoured to alleviate the suffering of mankind.
Fruits of one's struggle are most enjoyable.
The President of the society has taken pains to save it from being wound up.
We are having trouble with our new car.

Antonyms:

Rest	Repose	Peace
Tranquillity	Idleness	Laziness
Lethargy		

Examples:
I switched off the machine and it came to rest.
Her face is mirror of her sweet repose.
I have made peace with my boss by clarifying all the misunderstandings.
Laziness and lethargy makes man dull.

Extend (Verb)

Can you extend your visit for a few more days?

Synonyms:

Lengthen	Protract	Wide
Stretch	Elongate	Prolong

Examples:

Protracted negotiations are being held between US and USSR in Geneva on the disarmament issue.
India and France have decided to widen the area of economic cooperation.

Antonyms:

Contract	Shorten	Narrow
Shrink	Terminate	Truncate

Examples:

In winter the metallic articles contract.
Shorten this essay into a paragraph.
The path leading to his house is too narrow to let this car pass.

Extravagant (Adjective)

His extravagant tastes and habits explain why he is always in debt.

Synonyms:

Unreasonable	Excessive	Immoderate
Inordinate	Spendthrift	Lavish
Profuse	Wasteful	Prodigal

Examples:

He is a spoiled son of a rich father, unreasonable in demands and not amendable to argument.
Government is trying its best to economize on wasteful expenditure in day-to-day administration.
His excessive love for money was brought him all these difficulties.
The old man consumed an immoderate amount of wine and fell asleep, never to rise.
Inordinate delay in finalization of minor details can cause failure of the project.
He consumed his inherited wealth with too lavish a hand.
The prodigal number of eggs laid by the fish ensures the survival of the species.
They gave profuse thanks to the industrialist for his contribution to the orphanage.
He is bit worried about his spendthrift brother who squanders a fortune on each dress.

Antonyms:

Reasonable	Judicious	Moderate
Temperate	Economical	Provident
Thrifty	Sparing	

Examples:
The price of these shoes seems reasonable.
We must make judicious use of our voting right.
The climate of Bombay is moderate throughout the year.
The girl is very thrifty, so many of her friends dislike her.
An economic use of water and electricity is required to get rid of water and power crisis in the cities.

Fabulous (Adjective)

Fabulous heroes could be found only in fictions.
Synonyms:

Brilliant	Fantastic	Marvellous
Spectacular	Superb	Amazing
Breath-taking	Fictitious	Immense
Incredible	Wonderful	Astounding

Examples:
She has a brilliant mind. She always stood first in her class.
Bachendri Pal was a fantastic mountaineer.
It's marvellous that we can at last own our house.
The weather was absolutely superb.
I find it amazing that you can't swim.
It was an absolutely astounding performance.
The ACCOUNT he gives of his childhood is quite fictitious.
It's wonderful that they managed to escape from the danger.

Antonyms:

Actual	Common	Commonplace
Credible	Genuine	Natural
Ordinary	Real	

Examples:
The actual cost is much higher than we had expected.
Car thefts are becoming increasingly common.
Is there a credible alternative to the nuclear deterrent?
She seems genuine, but I can't trust her.
Earthquake is a natural calamity.

Fame (Noun)

His fame as a poet did not come until his death.
Synonyms:

Reputation	Honour	Glory
Renown	Esteem	Celebrity
Credit	Repute	Reputation

Examples:
Justice Bhagwati is a jurist of high reputation.
Children must be taught to show honour to their elders.
The old soldier had won glory on the battle field.
Shankar Jai Krishna is musician of great renown.
The photographer was given due credit for his participation in the programme.
He is a writer of world repute.

Antonyms:
Disrepute	Dishonour	Notoriety
Oblivion		

Examples:
The involvement of the high official in the spy scandal brought him disrepute.
Dishonouring the national flag is a serious crime punishable with imprisonment and fine.
Dacoit Veerappan of Tamil Nadu had notoriety for his ruthlessness and cruelty towards innocent citizens.

Famous (Adjective)
This town is famous for its hot springs.

Synonyms:
Noted	Celebrated	Renowned
Well-Known		

Examples:
Ashok Kumar is not only a great actor but also a noted poet and writer.
Ravi Shankar is a celebrated Sitarist of India.
He is renowned for creating sweet melodies on sitar.

Antonyms:
Obscure	Fugitive	Inglorious
Unknown		

Examples:
His writings are uninteresting and obscure.
Some of the offenders who caused riots have recently become fugitive.
He is obviously feeling sorry for his inglorious behaviour.

Fanciful (Adjective)

His fanciful paintings are more popular in USA than in England.

Synonyms: Imaginary
Unreal	Imaginative	Fantastic
Capricious	Whimsical	

Examples:
He is always haunted by his imaginary fear of failure in business.

The actions of diplomats must never be capricious.
She lives in an unreal world of make-believe.
His essay on the car and feeding of husbands is pleasantly whimsical.
The artist's imaginative use of colour delighted the critics.
The director received fantastic praise from the audience for his new play.

Antonyms:

Positive	Realistic	Existent
Substantial	Factual	Veritable

Examples:
His positive role in organizing the meeting so successfully was greatly appreciated.
His role in this film is highly realistic. It seemed he actually lived the character he played.
A substantial amount of oil has been dug and drilled in this terrain.

Fasten (Verb)

Have you fastened all the doors and windows?

Synonyms:

Join	Bind	Fix
Anchor	Bolt	Grip
Connect		

Examples:
Many people joined the movement for economic freedom of the bonded labor, after distributing a good part of his own land to his old workers.
India has refused to bind itself to any of the power blocs in the world. It prefers to remain nonaligned.
Smith's salary has been fixed at $ 2000 per month.

Antonyms:

Loose	Undo	Unfix

Examples:
This belt is too loose for your SLIM waist.
It is very difficult to undo a wrong done to the poor.
If you do not approve this draft agreement, I will unfix the whole deal.

Fatal (Adjective)

The cyclist was knocked down by the lorry and received fatal injuries.

Synonyms:

Lethal	Mortal	Deadly
Destructive	Pernicious	Baneful

Examples:
Venom of black cobra is a lethal poison.

Because of an ancient family feud, the two cousins grew up as mortal enemies from birth.
Cancer is a deadly disease.
Youth energy should not be wasted for destructive purposes.
Nowadays he is involved in the pernicious business of selling heroin.

Antonyms:

Life- giving	Helpful	Beneficial
Constructive		

Examples:
This medicine has a life-giving constituent.
His attitude was greatly helpful in the achievement of my objective.
Panchsheel is a beneficial concept for the solution of many international conflicts.

Fat (Adjective)

His fat cheeks get turned whenever he is abashed.

Synonyms:

Stout	Portly	Obese
Plump	Adipose	Chubby
Buxom		

Examples:
Winston Churchill had a stout impressive body.
He had a portly gain in his movements like those a king.
She gives an impression of an obese personality. She is known to be a glutton.

Antonyms:

Emaciated	Thin	slim

Examples:
Continued poverty has brought him emaciated looks.
He is so lean and thin; I am always afraid the next cyclone will blow him away.
This frock is too wide for her SLIM waist.

Fear (Noun)

They stood there is in fearing and trembling.

Synonyms:

Fright	Horror	Alarm
Panic	Terror	Dread

Examples:
Nuclear armament gives many a nation grave fright.
The horror of the Third World War keeps modern civilization in suspense.
The nuclear war can bring to end the human race without alarm.

Antonyms:

Trust	Courage	Calmness
Equanimity		

Examples:
Super powers must learn to trust each other, if they wish to dispel the fear of war.
They must display courage in placing their cards on the table in order to reach settlement on armament issues.
She is facing the prospect of her operation with cheerful equanimity.

Feeble (Adjective)

His pulse was very feeble.

Synonyms:

Weak	Impotent	Frail
Languid	Debilitated	Infirm

Examples:
The strong should help the weak.
His wife has sought divorce from him because she thinks he is impotent.
He has put forth a frail theory which even an average person can challenge.
The infirm conclusion was based on deliberate distortion of the evidence.
Their house has debilitated due to its long exposure to the elements.
The languid wind offered no relief from the heat.

Antonyms:

Strong	Vigorous	Muscular
Athletic	Stalwart	Robust
Sinewy		

Examples:
A strong man needs no arms to fight his way up.
The country has to make vigorous efforts to solve the unemployment problem.
His muscular body enables him to perform numerous feats.
He is a political stalwart. He has retained the Lok Sabha seat since the very first election after independence.

Filthy (Adjective)

South Africa is no more a filthy country.

Synonyms:

Dirty	Squalid	Foul
Impure	Sullied	Unclear

Examples:
A pile of dirty clothes is to be sent to the laundry.
The slum dwellers live a squalid life.

The policeman used foul language against a suspect without due confirmation of guilt.
People, unclean in mind and spirit, generally try to harm others.
I will not let my lips be sullied by the use of ugly words.
Failure of rains compelled people to drink impure water.

Antonyms:

Pure	Clean	Immaculate
Spotless	Unsullied	Unsoiled

Examples:
We must first boil the water and then claim it is pure.
Our classroom is so clean, not a speck of dust can be seen anywhere.
Your firmed John always wears immaculate and spotlessly clean clothes.
This shirt is old but unsoiled so far.

Final (Adjective)

The final chapter of this book contains a very interesting information about the author.

Synonyms:

Last	Ultimate	Concluding
Finishing		

Examples:
I did reach an agreement with him in the last round of talks.
The ultimate result of the negotiations was the retention of the premises by the company against an additional payment of Rs.1LAKH only.
In his concluding remarks the principal counselled the students to do selected reading rather than unplanned study of too many books.

Antonyms:

First	Beginning	Opening
Initial		

Examples:
My first advice to you is to develop the habit of listening to what others say and then giving your own views.
Geneva negotiations on disarmament are yet in their beginning stage.
The opening remarks of the President on the occasion were devoted to the important of religion in day – to –day life.

Find (Verb)

Did you ever find the pen that you lost?

Synonyms:

Locate	Learn	Unearth
Detect	Ascertain	Discover

Examples:
Kashmir is located in the extreme north of India.
Students should learn their lessons everyday by heart.
The police were finally able to unearth the headquarters of the spy ring.
I have detected quite a few factual errors in this book.

Antonyms:

| Forget | Miss | Mislay |
| Misplace | Overlook | |

Examples:
It is good to forget the unlucky past and start a new era with sincere effort.
I missed the train by just a few seconds.
I seem to have mislaid my passport again.

Finish (Verb)

Have you finished the book yet?

Synonyms:

Close	Shape	End
Conclude	Complete	Perfect
Finalize		

Examples:
Unless we close our ranks in society, we cannot hope to achieve socialism.
India and the United States are likely to have greater economic cooperation in future, looking at the way India's liberalization policy is shaping.
This policy may end the long standing differences between the two countries.

Antonyms:

| Begin | Start | Open |
| Initiate | | |

Examples:
Prime Minister's visit to Washington may begin a new era in Indian-US friendship.
The leaders of the two countries have already started parleys on important issues.
The Parleys if successful will open the way to manifold increase in economic exchanges of different sorts.

Foresight (Noun)

If you had had more foresight, you would have saved yourself a lot of trouble?

Synonyms:

Foreknowledge	Care	Caution
Precaution	Prudence	Forethought
Prescience	Presentiment	Foreshadowing

Examples:
Augustine's treatment of God's foreknowledge and man's free will makes an interesting reading.
He could have avoided the accident by using forethought.
She showed great prescience in selling her shares just before the market cracked.
The King's prudence saved him falling prey to his minister's designs.
The saint had a presentiment that his pupil will poison him one day.
These incidents are foreshadowing of the civil war.

Antonyms:

Narrow –mindedness	Bias	Short-sightedness
Prejudice		

Examples:
Narrow-mindedness is one of the important causes of conflict among humans at all levels.
The teacher had a bias against Mary. He, therefore, deducted his marks in the general behaviour, though she showed great improvement in overall performance.
Jane's short-sightedness in business brought him early profit but huge loss in the end.

Fright (Noun)

What a fright you look in that old hat!

Synonyms:

Apprehension	Alarm	Horror
Dismay	Panic	Terror
Trepidation	Fear	Dismay
Dread		

Examples:
His apprehensions about the difficulties inherent in the new job proved correct.
The terrorist is trying to create panic by killing innocent people.
All the members of the family were in a state of trepidation when the dacoits attacked the house at midnight.
Countless fears leaped up whenever she had to face any new situation in life.
During the international crisis everyone was filled with the dread of nuclear war.
Their utter refusal to compromise dismayed him and left him at a loss.

Antonyms:

Tranquillity	Calmness	Coolness
Equanimity	Placidity	Composure

Examples:
Installation of military guards has brought about tranquillity in the state.
The leaders have shown calmness in handling the law and order situation.
His coolness in human relations cannot be termed as his mental equanimity.

Fraud (Noun)

He got more money by fraud.

Synonyms:

Deceit	Duplicity	Stratagem
Chicanery	Guile	Hoax
Fake	Scam	Swindling
Deception		

Examples:

I was surprised at his flagrant deceit by which he kept his wife from knowing about his new love affair.

She referred to the pills as sweets in a harmless deception this made it easier to administer them to the child.

She confessed her guilt of duplicity of another engagement that evening.

His stratagem for winning her comprised of agreeing to everything she said.

Antonyms:

Honesty	Probity	Integrity
Fairness	Rectitude	Trustworthiness

Examples:

Honesty always pays its way in due course.

He puts his cards always face up. He is, therefore, known for his probity.

He believes in straight – forward dealings in society. He is, therefore, known for his integrity of character.

Former (Adjective)

She looks more like her former self.

Synonyms:

Antecedent	Anterior	Earlier
Erstwhile	Prior	Quondam
Ancient	Departed	Old
Previous-part	Aforementioned	Aforesaid

Examples:

Please telephone at your earliest convenience.

His erstwhile friends turned against him.

The aforementioned person was acting suspiciously.

The incident happened before I was married and that's all ancient history now.

Your dear departed brother was very intelligent.

It is the matter of past when people thought that the Sun move around the earth.

Antonyms:

Coming	Current	Ensuring
Following	Future	Latter

Subsequent	Succeeding	Modern
Present	Present day	

Examples:
To gain the status of permanent membership in UNO is the current issue of every Indians.
It rained on the day we arrived, but the following day was sunny.
Modern world stand at the edge of atomic war.
My present condition is better than that of past.

Futile (Adjective)

All his attempts at last turned out to be futile.

Synonyms:

Abortive	Barren	Bootless
Empty	Forlorn	Fruitless
Hollow	In vain	Ineffectual
Profitless	Unproductive	Unsuccessful
Worthless	Useless	Trivial
Idle	Trifling	Unimportant

Examples:
I was tired of their barren discussions.
It is not good to drink alcohol on an empty stomach.
Empty houses quickly take on a forlorn look.
Our efforts to persuade her proved fruitless.
I topped the wall to see if it was hollow.
She made several unsuccessful attempts to see him.
I displaced all the worthless furniture to the basement.
It is totally useless to persuade her, she is adamant and rude.

Antonyms:

Constructive	Effective	Fruitful
Profitable	Purposeful	Successful
Useful	Variable	Worthwhile
Important	Significant	

Examples:
I'm trying to be constructive because I have less time to fulfil the task.
Delhi government is trying to make the health service as effective as possible.
She spent a very profitable afternoon in the library.
Young people's energies should be directed towards more purposeful activities.

Fundamental (Adjective)

Knowledge of the fundamental rules of Arithmetic is must to get more marks in this exam.

Synonyms:

Essential	Important	Primary
Basic	Crucial	First Integral

Examples:
Always speaking the truth is an essential qualification for this job of great financial responsibility.
Fertilizers have become an important feature of agriculture productivity.
Irrigational facilities are a primary consideration for determining the value of an agriculture farm.
Food, cloth and shelter are the basic requirements of human beings.
Mathematics is made an integral part of the school syllabus now which was only an optional subject before.
To get a first division in the examination was crucial to her.

Antonyms:

Secondary	Unimportant	Non-essential
Extra subsidiary	Superfluous	

Examples:
Human labour has come down to secondary position in this age of automation.
His attendance at today's meeting is unimportant.
Many of the non-essential commodities like motor car and T.V have been upgraded to essential category in all modern advanced countries.
You don't need to give those superfluous details about the incident.
For a student all other works are subsidiary in comparison to studies.
You should take some extra health drinks in order to improve your health.

Gallant (Adjective)

He is very gallant at the ball.

Synonyms:

Bold	Brave	Courageous
Daring	Dashing	Heroic
Lion – hearted	Valiant	Valorous
August	Dignified	Glorious
Magnificent	Splendid	

Examples:
I don't feel bold enough to ask for a pay increase.
It was brave of her to go into a burning house to rescue her child.
These women are resourceful and courageous.
Deepak has a daring personality. He always speaks the truth.
Throughout his trial he maintained a dignified silence.
Soldiers always die a glorious death in the battlefield.
The bride looked simply magnificent in her wedding dress.
The hotel stands in splendid isolation surrounded by moorland.

Antonyms:

Cowardly	Fearful	Ignoble
Churlish	Discourteous	Ill-mannered
Impolite	Rude	

Examples:

It was cowardly of you not to admit your mistake.
It seems churlish to refuse such a generous offer.
It was discourteous of you to arrive late every day.
It was ill-mannered of you not to thank her.
Some people think it is impolite to ask someone's age.
It is rude to interrupt when somebody is speaking.

Gather (Verb)

A crowd soon gathered around him.

Synonyms:

Congregate	Collect	Muster
Convene	Accumulate	Amass
Flock	Group	Heap
Marshal	Assemble	

Examples:

A crowd quickly congregated round to hear their dedicated leader.
We need to accumulate enough evidence to ensure his conviction.
They amassed enough evidence to convict him.
Huge number of birds had flocked together by the lake.
The police groups round the demonstrators.
The children were marshalled into the playground by their teacher.
We should first collect the funds and then plunge into action.
The general mustered courage and plunged his army into the war.

Antonyms:

| Disband | Scatter | Separate |
| Diffuse | Disperse | Dissipate |

Examples:

As soon as the mission was over, the leader disbanded the gang.
The sun sends out the rays, scattering them throughout the horizon.
We can separate oxygen from the water. The left over is invisible gas hydrogen.

Gay (Adjective)

The gay voices of young children got the attention of the teachers.

Synonyms:

Cheerful	Jovial	Vivacious
Jolly	Sprightly	Buoyant
Joyous	Blithe	

Examples:

Although he was to undergo an operation, he was looking cheerful.
Albert Johnson was jovial old man of this neighbourhood.
The vivacious girl made a good sales executive for the advertisement agency.
She was very jolly in Pankaj's birthday party.
Our grandfather's 80th anniversary was a joyous occasion for the whole family.
He is surprisingly sprightly for an old man.
Rita's buoyant personality attracts many new friends to her.
Their child had a wonderful blithe personality.

Antonyms:

Mournful	Cheerless	Unhappy
Depressed	Gloomy	Sorrowful
Sad	Dismal	

Examples:

He is so serious in life. His looks become mournful as soon as he concentrates on a difficult problem.
Visiting his office is no pleasure. He is rich but cheerless.
Unhappy is one who is rich but unhealthy.
The low percentage of marks in the examination has made him too depressed.

General (Adjective)

The general opinion of the people about this subject is not in favour of the government.

Synonyms:

Common	Popular	Public
Universal	Accepted	

Examples:

It is common knowledge that wine is unwelcome in religious premises.
Gandhi was the most popular leader among every community in India.
An agreement contrary to public policy is unenforceable.
There is a universal agreement on this issue.

Antonyms:

Uncommon	Unusual	Queer
Specific		

Examples:
Instances of the diseases are uncommon in this country.
The meat had queer smell.
I can answer all your specific enquiries without hesitation.
His unusual behaviour outraged the employer.

Generous (Adjective)

He is generous in giving help to the needed.

Synonyms:

Liberal	Noble	Lavish
Bountiful	Magnanimous	

Examples:
It befits a gentleman to be liberal.
He was lavish with his praise.
There are very few who deserve to be called noble in this materialistic selfish world.
Nature is bountiful in India but men are lazy and lethargic due to heavy eating habits or cold.
As he was magnanimous, he did not take revenge on Ravi, though he had done great harm to him.

Antonyms:

Greed	Niggardly	Chary
Sparing	Light	Selfish
Parsimonious		

Examples:
One whose heart is made of lead cannot but be niggardly.
Selfish persons seldom care for their nations.
Businessmen always and everywhere tend to be greedy for profit.
He is a parsimonious person. People don't like him

Genial (Adjective)

He is under the genial influence of good wine.

Synonyms:

Affable	Agreeable	Amiable
Cheerful	Cheery	Congenial
Convivial	Cordial	Easy – going
Enlivening	Friendly	Glad
Happy	Hearty	Jolly
Merry	Pleasant	Sunny
Warm		

Examples:
He found her parents very affable.
I found him most agreeable at that moment.
Her parents seemed very amiable.
You are looking very cheerful today.
I think that this aspect of my job is particularly congenial.
People very often take advantages of her because of her easy going nature.
I am glad to hear he is feeling better.
I won't be happy until I know she is happy.

Antonyms:

Cheerless	Coo	Discourteous
Frigid	Morose	Rude
Sardonic	Sullen	Unfriendly
Ungracious	Unpleasant	

Examples:
It was discourteous of you to arrive late daily.
Raja is a morose. He always behaves rudely to elders.
It was rude of them not to phone and say they would be late.
All my attempts to amuse the children were met with sullen scowls.
He was distinctly unfriendly towards me.

Genuine (Adjective)

This is not a genuine picture of Rubens.

Synonyms:

Authentic	Pure	Real
Actual	True	Sincere

Examples:
Mr. Brown is an authentic person. He always speaks the truth.
The air is so pure in these mountains.
Real life is sometimes stranger than fiction.
Our guests always receive a sincere welcome.

Antonyms:

Fictitious	Spurious	Artificial
Fake	Forged	Imaginary

Examples:
The characters in this story are fictitious.
This drug is spurious. Hence it should not be taken.
That body of water is an artificial lake.
He forged the Managing Director's signature but was caught in time.
Both the roots of this quadratic equation are imaginary but quite illustrative of the

point at issue.

Glorify (Verb)

You should not glorify yourself.

Synonym:

Extol	Adore	Canonize
Enshrine	Revere	Venerate
Exalt	Commend	Appraise

Examples:

He was extolled as a hero.
He was exalted as a pillar of the community.
The students commended the greeting message of the principal.
The examiner unbiasedly appraised the papers of the students in an unbiased manner.

Antonyms:

Abuse	Depress	Reject
Debase	Defile	Degrade
Humiliate	Mock	Condemn

Examples:

One of the accused started abusing his friends in the presence of the police.
The death of Madhu's father depressed him.
The boss has rejected my application for leave.
The workers condemned the management for throwing few of their colleagues out of job.

Gifted (Adjective)

There is a separate school for the students gifted with special talents.

Synonyms:

Intelligent	Able	Apt
Skilful	Sagacious	Talented
Adroit	Expert	Clever
Ingenious		

Examples:

Dolphin is an intelligent animal.
The starving man was barely able to walk.
The doctor made a few apt remarks about nutrition and health.
Only the most skilful pilots are deployed for bombing the enemy positions.
Mr. Suresh Tiwari is the most sagacious teachers in our school.
Praveen is one of the few talented students of the class.
Fox is a clever animal.

He succeeded by a combination of generosity and adroit diplomacy.
She is an expert in hand embroidery.
Roopa is very ingenious when it comes to deal with her cunning boss.

Antonyms:

Foolish	Stupid	Idiotic
Stolid	Amateur	Dull
Inept	Remanded	

Examples:

It would be foolish on your part to change the profession at this late age.
The stupid fellow! He annoys his friends by making silly comments at the wrong movement.
His idiotic utterances now and then leave a bad impression on his colleagues.
He is a basically stolid. His face remains expressionless against anger or irritation.
I have never seen anyone so inept in writing essays on social issues.
The whole book needs re-editing by you, since it is not a job for amateurs.
All work and no play make a child dull.
He is mentally retarded.

Gorgeous (Adjective)

We have captured the gorgeous sunset in our camera.

Synonyms:

Sumptuous	Magnificent	Splendid
Grand	Brilliant	Dazzling
Elegant		

Examples:

Our host provided a sumptuous feast on his birthday.
She looked simple in her wedding dress.
The hotel stands in a splendid isolation surrounded by moorland.
The chairman received his guests in a grand manner.

Antonyms:

Colourless	Simple	Unadorned
Sombre	Ugly	Cheap
Shabby	Shoddy	

Examples:

The inauguration of the shop by the local leader happened to be a rather colourless affair.
Sonia is too simple to work in an advertising agency.
The manager is the unadorned king of this departmental store.
His sombre attitude always lets him down as a salesman.

Govern (Verb)

The President of a country has more powers to govern the country towards the overall development of the people.

Synonyms:

Rule	Manage	Control
Direct	Command	Supervise
Administer		

Examples:

A dictator thinks he can be successful only when he rules with an iron hand.
The police failed in its attempt to control the unruly mob.
He has appointed a new man to manage his business.
Our new office manager will supervise the work of several departments.
The Vice-Chancellor of our university personally administers the establishment's financial affairs.
The king commanded the guards to raise the new bridge.

Antonyms:

Misrule	Mismanage	Misgovern

Examples:

The military general misruled his country, no wonder he had to abdicate in favour of a civilian government.
Some of the public sector undertakings are still mismanaged.
The new Governor has taken personal responsibility to set right the misgoverned departments.

Gradual (Adjective)

We experience a gradual increase in the cost of living in this town.

Synonyms:

Slow	Steady	Moderate
Piecemeal	Gentle	Regular
Continuous	Progressive	

Examples:

The stratagem of slow and steady wins the race.
Rupak is regular in his studies.
The continuous outflow of blood led to his untimely death.
Only a few of the young politicians are progressive.

Antonyms:

Rapid	Momentary	Unanticipated
Unpremeditated	Unforeseen	

Examples:

English Synonyms and Antonyms 'G'

Rapid flow of river waters causes soil erosion, unless the extra flow is used for hydro-electricity.

His response to the boss's instructions was only momentary.

Quite often unanticipated circumstances beyond one's control upset the planned procedures.

Any further functioning of the unpremeditated machines would cause complete breakdown.

Grand (Adjective)

Synonyms:

Noble	Majestic	Lordly
Stately	Resplendent	August
Exalted	Illustrious	

Examples:

In the north of India stand the majestic Himalayas as its saviour.

His lordly manners angered everyone present in the meeting.

All the members of the non-aligned movement were awed by Mrs. Gandhi's stately grandeur and innate humanism.

Her resplendent necklace became the focus of attention of all her female guests.

Ashoka had an august personality.

The performance of Sania Mirza in tennis is superb.

The poet Milton wrote in an exalted style.

He has won many medals for his illustrious service in the Indian Army.

Antonyms:

Inferior	Colourless	Ignoble
Undignified	Awful	Mean
Worthless		

Examples:

A Lieutenant has inferior status compared to a Captain.

The opening ceremony of the exhibition was rather colourless.

His ignoble performance at the meeting led to his dismissal.

He is worthless person.

I had an awful time sitting under the scorching sun waiting for you.

It was mean of him to behave in that rude way.

The occasion turned out to be undignified.

Grasp (Verb)

A man who grasps too much may lose everything.

Synonyms:

Hold	Seize	Snatch

| Grip | Grab | Clutch |
| Clasp | | |

Examples:

I will hold the mirror; you look into it.
One who seizes the opportunity when it comes makes a success in life.
The thief snatched the golden necklace from the lady's neck and ran away.
But the policeman grabbed the thief and recovered the necklace.

Antonyms:

| Loose | Lose | Abandon |
| Release | Relinquish | |

Examples:

This shirt is too loose for my slim body.
Don't lose patience; I will set it right.
I have abandoned the idea of going abroad for the time being.
He relinquished his job on being criticized by the general manager.

Grief (Noun)

His taking to drugs was a great grief to his parents.

Synonyms:

Pain	Sorrow	Trouble
Grievance	Remorse	Suffering
Tribulation	Trouble	Woe
Affection	Bereavement	Distress

Examples:

The doctor gave me a tablet to relieve the pain in my stomach.
Sorrow will pay no dept. Sorrows are our best educators.
His spoiled son has become a source of great trouble to him.
Faith permitted him to endure every affliction.
His bereavement was shared by his relatives and friends.
The distress caused by her son's death can make her insane.

Antonyms:

Glee	Joy	Contentment
Satisfaction	Rejoicing	Solace
Happiness	Pleasure	

Examples:

The child experienced great glee on breaking the toy.
Taking a cold drink gives joy and contentment in the summer.
It gives me satisfaction, pleasure and happiness in declaring a net dividend of 15% on the ordinary shares of the company.

Grim (Adjective)

At last all our struggle turned out to be mere grim moves.

Synonyms:

Cruel	Ferocious	Fierce
Formidable	Frightful	Ghastly
Grisly	Gruesome	Hard
Harsh	Horrible	Merciless
Ruthless	Severe	Sullen
Surly	Terrible	

Examples:

Sometimes you have to be cruel to be kind.
The lion is a ferocious animal. It can kill you.
Damini was a formidable woman. No one dared to disagree with her.
Still now you can see a frightful prospect of nuclear war.
The grisly remains of my friend's half eaten corpse are found on the bank of the river.
We have to face up to the harsh realities of life.
Butchers are merciless. They kill animals.
Eidi Ameen was a ruthless dictator of Uganda.

Antonyms:

Amiable	Attractive	Benign
Cheerful	Easy	Genial
Gentle	Happy	Kind
Pleasant	Soft	Sympathetic

Examples:

Her parents seemed very amiable and gentle.
He is nice, but I don't find him at all attractive physically.
Anita is a very pretty and cheerful girl.
It is easy to go downward in respect of upward.
The old man is very gentle and gorgeous
I am very happy to know that my father reached home safely.

Groundless (Adjective)

It is not my responsibility to answer all these groundless rumours.

Synonyms:

False	Baseless	Unauthorized
Gratuitous	Fanciful	

Examples:

We should not make a false statement in a legal document.

His allegations were founded on a baseless rumour.
His unauthorized absence from office will be treated as a break in service.
She has a fanciful way of calling her plants by human names.
His gratuitous insult flabbergasted me.

Antonyms:

Actual	Material	Well-founded
Substantial	Positive	Real
Solid		

Examples:
I have made a statement of actual facts and figures.
There is material evidence available to prove our case.
My arguments in this care are based on well – founded legal precepts.
There is substantial weight in your new theory.

Habitual (Adjective)

He took his habitual seat at the dining table.

Synonyms:

Accustomed	Common	Familiar
Fixed	Natural	Ordinary
Standard	Customary	Chronic
Constant	Established	Frequent
Inveterate	Recurrent	Persistent

Examples:
My eyes slowly grow accustomed to the darkness.
Cigarette smoking is not only common among college students even school goers smoke cigarettes.
I am quite familiar with French
Natural calamities are very common like flood and drought.
It is ordinary to wear dhoti kurta in village still now.
Pressure of the container remains constant.

Antonyms:

Abnormal	Exceptional	Extraordinary
Rare	Strange	Uncommon
Unusual	Infrequent	Irregular
Occasional		

Examples:
It is abnormal to speak with the elders rudely.
In North India rain in winter is exceptional.
Pundit Jawaharlal Nehru was an extraordinary statesman and great politician.
Such cases of diseases are relatively infrequent.

There will be occasional showers during daytime.
It is extremely rare for the weather in April to be this hot.
The person behaved in a strange manner.

Halt (Verb)

We want to halt between two arguments.

Synonyms:

Break off	Cease	Close down
Come to an end	Desist	Draw up
Stand	Wait	Check
Curb	Nip in the bud	Terminate
Obstruct		

Examples:
He broke off in the middle of the sentence.
The factory ceased making bicycles.
At last the fight between two countries came to an end with the interference of UN.
I wish he'd desist from interacting with his friends at all hours of the day and night.
The taxi drew up outside the house.
The boss terminated my job due to carelessness.

Antonyms:

Begin	Commence	Continue
Go ahead	Maintain	Proceed
Resume	Start	Aid
Boost	Encourage	Forward

Examples:
This year monsoon will begin after June.
Our examination will commence from next week.
The desert continued as far as the eyes could see.
The unexpected win helped to boost the team's morale
She encouraged her husband to lose weight.
We have today forwarded you the new catalogue.

Hamper (Verb)

His walk is hampered by his heavy coat.

Synonyms:

Bind	Cramp	Curb
Encumber	Entangle	Fetter
Frustrate	Hamstring	Handicap
Impede	Obstruct	Prevent

| Restrain | Thwart | Hold up |

Examples:
They bound his legs together so that he could not escape.
All these difficulties cramped his progress.
Traveling is difficult when you are encumbered with two small children and heavy suitcases.
Her long hair got entangled in the rose bush.
My little sister prevents me from doing my homework.
He attempted to frustrate his political opponents by denying then access to the media.

Antonyms:
Aid	Assist	Host
Encourage	Expedite	Forward
Further	Help	Promote
Speed		

Examples:
His absence aided the rebels to gain control over the city.
I always assist to my mother in cooking whenever I have time.
The parents encouraged their child to concentrate in studies.
We must all help each other in the time of need.
A training course was provided by this company that promotes better communication between employers and its staff.
The drugs will help speed her recovery.

Handy (Adjective)

Do not throw the plastic bag away. That may come in handy.

Synonyms:
Skilled	Skilful	Accessible
Available	Useful	Adopt
Expert	Adroit	Proficient
Dexterous	Ready	Close
Near	Convenient	

Examples:
It is better to pay more to a skilled man than exploring an unskilled man.
The mason did a skilful job in building this wall.
Sanjay was an expert driver that is why he escaped the accident.
Most of the political leaders in our country are adroit speakers.
Her dexterous fingers moved effortlessly over the key board of this computer.
The children are close to each other in age.
The parking lot is convenient to the office.

Although she is a proficient typist, she takes little interest is her work.
Some of the nearer branches caught fire.
Keep your dress ready because we can start form here any time.

Antonyms:

Unskilled	Unskilful	Bungling
Clumsy	Unhandy	Awkward
Inept	Maladroit	Useless

Examples:
This factory will do better if it were to replace unskilled workers by trained mechanics.
He claimed proficiency on machines, but his handling of this machine seems unskilful.
The new management is bungling with the whole mechanism of the production process.
The cartoon was very awkward.
This book is full of information but it is useless as a GMAT guide.
The function became a failure maladroit handling of the whole affair.

Handle (Verb)

Wash your hands before you handle my books.

Synonyms:

Hold	Wield	Touch
Carry out		

Examples:
I can hold this bag in the bus without much difficulty.
The Chief Engineer wields great authority in the public works department.
The pile of books is placed in such a way that it would collapse at a slight touch.
I always carried out the orders of my teacher without hesitation.

Antonyms:

Throw	Bungle	Miscarry

Examples:
I sold my land at a throw – away price.
If you bungle with my money in future, I will throw you out.
The pregnant woman fell from the staircase and had a miscarriage.

Hard (Adjective)

Try hard to succeed.

Synonyms:

Arduous	Difficult	Laborious
Troublesome	Trying	

Examples:

This is an arduous task involving lot of efforts.

It is quite difficult for a salaried man to make his both ends meet in these days of inflation.

Suraj is a laborious boy. He will do very well in his exam.

Antonyms:

Easy	Simple	Plain
Flexible	Malleable	Pliable
Weak	Soft	

Examples:

It is easy to say but difficult to perform.

It is a simple machine, capable of being run by an unskilled person.

He made the objective of his visit quite plain.

You ought to be flexible with your old principles as the modern trends are changing.

The pillar is very weak as it was constructed years long back.

The new product launched by Lakme will make your skin soft & smooth.

Harsh (Adjective)

His voice is harsh to our ears.

Synonyms:

| Jarring | Rancorous | Discordant |
| Strident | | |

Examples:

His criticism jarred with the friendly tone.

We could hear the sound of rancorous laughter coming from the pub across this street.

The strident voice of my wife quite often bores me.

Many a couple has discordant views on the art of raising children now-a-days.

Antonyms:

| Musical | Concordant | Tuneful |
| Melodious | Mild | |

Examples:

The sweet atmosphere inspired the couple to make musical notes.

The meeting helped to create concordant views on the controversial subject.

My piano made tuneful, melodious sound in the hall.

He gave a mild answer in spite of his annoyance.

Hate (Verb)

My cat hates dogs.

Synonyms:

Abhor	Abominate	Be hostile to
Be repelled by	Be sick of	Despise Dislike
Have an aversion to	Loath	Be reluctant
Shrink from		

Examples:

I abhor her way of talking to elders.
I dislike her because of her laziness.
He is reluctant in doing his homework regularly.
Small kids shrink from bathing in winter.
I have an aversion to getting up early in the morning.

Antonyms:

Be fond of	Cherish	Dote on
Enjoy	Esteem	Fancy
Like	Love	Relish
Treasure	Wish	

Examples:

I am fond of playing football.
Let us cherish the moments we had been together.
They seem to dote on that dog of theirs.
Mon and women should enjoy equal rights.
Pearls were greatly esteemed as personal ornaments.
Good mannered students are liked by everyone.
India is a country of great variety. I love my country very much.

Hazard (Noun)

In this town, your life will be full of hazards.

Synonyms:

Chance	Danger	Jeopardy
Risk	Venture	Peril
Contingency	Threat	

Examples:

This road may not be the right one but that's chance we're going to take.
He had stayed up so late he felt the danger of oversleeping and being late for work the next morning.
Many species are already in peril of extinction because of our destruction of their natural habitat.
Mahesh Jain has insured his assets against the risk of fire and theft.
Such a gamble against odds would put their whole venture in jeopardy.
The leader has threatened to wipe him out if ever he thought of leaving the gang.
We must be prepared for any contingency.

Antonyms:

Assurance	Certainty	Necessity
Protection	Safeguard	Security
Surety		

Examples:

I wanted an assurance from my boss for security of job.
There is no certainty of a lasting career in the private sector.
There is no particular necessity for me to linger on this job
A house is the first protection from vagaries of nature.

Healthy (Adjective)
These children look very healthy.

Synonyms:

Vigorous	Strong	Robust
Sound	Hale	Hearty
Sound	Sturdy	

Examples:

The vigorous climate of North Eastern countries makes its people strong and robust.
A sound mind can exist in a sound body.
I found our neighbour hale and hearty at 78.
He has the knack of keeping well under any circumstances.

Antonyms:

Sick	Sickly	Ill
Unhealthy	Weak	Weakly
Unsound		

Examples:

Vicky has started feeling sickly of late.
I fell ill due to extreme cold.
The atmosphere of this locality is very unhealthy.
That is why you children here weak.
This plan of business is rather unsound.

Hesitate (Verb)

They hesitate to spend so much money on clothes.

Synonyms:

Waver	Tarry	Totter
Pause	Demur	Falter
Vacillate		

Examples:

He never wavered in his destination to success.

He paused long enough before each painting in order to note the painter's name.
The success of these reforms faltered in this late 1980s.
While she hesitated, he vacillated between positive and negative thoughts of her.
The majority was in favour of the plan, but a few demurred.
Don't tarry too long in coming to a decision.
The vase tottered and fell on the hard ground.

Antonyms:

Determine	Settle	End
Decide	Resolve	

Examples:
I am determined to make a success of this project.
The differences between the husband and wife need to be settled once and for all.
The controversy over political issues should be ended without delay.
We should decide about the course of action to be taken on their behalf.
This problem could then be resolved with ease.

Heavy (Adjective)

His walk is hampered by his heavy coat.

Synonyms:

Crushing	Burdensome	Onerous
Oppressing	Sluggish	Gloomy
Serious	Difficult	

Examples:
Sania Mirza gave a crushing defeat to her opponent.
It is a burdensome task to prepare a good pitch for the coming cricket match in this rainy season.
The heat of this summer is highly oppressing.

Antonyms:

Trivial	Easy	Light
Mild	Agile	Bearable
Gentle		

Examples:
Do not quarrel with you friend on this trivial matter. Sort it out immediately.
There is nothing as easy as talking and gossiping.
He is basically light-footed and light – tempered.
Finding a suitable house is no easy.
He has a mild temperament. He has never made an enemy.

High (Adjective)

After his success in the Olympic, he holds his head very high.

Synonyms:

Elevated	Tall	Lofty
Towering	Steep	Soaring
Great		

Examples:

A joint Secretary in the Ministry of External Affairs is generally elevated to the position of an Ambassador.

Date tree is usually very tall.

I am possessed of very lofty ideals. But I don't know whether I will ever get the necessary opportunities to achieve them. a toweringpersonality.

Antonyms:

Base	Low	Short
Degraded	Drafted	Stunted
Mild		

Examples:

The base of all evil in the world is selfishness of individuals.

The standard of living of the common people in India is still rather low.

I have joined a short term course in computer programming.

By demanding of special rights for all regions and all religions, we are degrading the national view point.

Highest (Adjective)

The values of shares of this company have reached the highest point this month.

Synonyms:

| Topmost | Uppermost | Supreme |
| Tallest | | |

Examples:

The president holds the top most position in Pakistan.

Disarmament is the uppermost controversy in the international discussions today.

Under the constitution of India, the President is the supreme commander of the country's defence forces.

Antonyms:

| Under most | Lowest | Deepest |
| Bottom | | |

Examples:

The President is the under most member of the administrative system in India.

He is at the lowest rung of the departmental hierarchy.

The Pacific is the deepest ocean in the world.

The bottom of the ocean has many unknown treasures of nature.

Hire (Verb)

Hire a taxi to reach the top of the mountain in time.

Synonyms:

Engage	Employ	Appoint
Commission	Lease	Charge
Rent	Enlist	Recruit

Examples:

I am engaged in the construction of my house these days.
I have employed sixty workers to do the construction work.
I may rent out one portion of my house when it is completed.
I have already enlisted a few candidates for the proposed renting of the portion concerned.

Antonyms:

| Purchase | Buy | Fire |
| Retire | Discharge | |

Examples:

I had to purchase the iron rod for construction at a very high price.
I have yet to buy the wood for the almirahs, doors and windows.
I propose to insure the house against fire and theft.
I will retire from my present job in coming October.

Holy (Adjective)

The Pope is addressed as The Holy Father.

Synonyms:

Religious	Godly	Pious
Pure	Sublime	Virtuous
Saintly	Sacred	Hallowed
Divine		

Examples:

In every civilization marriage is regarded as a religious ceremony.
The old priest was a wise and godly man.
Swami Vivekananda tried to establish relationship between the divine and material worlds.
Not only the Indian but also the foreigners were also influenced by the saintly sermons of Swami Vivekananda.
John's last wish was that he may be buried in hallowed ground.
Giriraj is a mountain near Matura thought to be scared by the Indians.

Antonyms:

Irreligious	Ungodly	Irreverent
Blasphemous	Wicked	Unholy
Sacrilegious	Profane	

Examples:

By declaring India a secular state, you cannot state that constitution – makers wanted to make the country men irreligious.

A communist society cannot be called ungodly as the actions of the people of such a society are perfectly godly.

There are churches in the USSR and the common people are not irreverent to clergymen. The churches are not used for sacrilegious or profane activities.

Horrible (Adjective)

This newspaper got its popularity by reporting the horrible crimes taking place in the society.

Synonyms:

Frightful	Appalling	Dire
Ghastly	Ugly	Fearful
Awful	Terrific	Dreadful
Hideous	Repulsive	

Examples:

As the full moon rose, frightful howls of dog pierced the air around the cemetery.
The plight of the victims of the railway accident was appalling.
Hijackers threatened that refusal to meet their demands will have dire consequences.
It was the ghastliest accident I have ever seen.
He was fearful of her psychological situation; she may harm herself.
Although he was going slowly, he met a dreadful accident.
Ravi Shankar was found guilty of the awful crime of poisoning his wife.
Every day we read in the newspaper about hideous crime in the western countries.
He is a well-educated man but his table manners are repulsive.
A terrific earthquake woke the whole town.

Antonyms:

Agreeable	Pleasant	Delightful
Pleasurable	Charming	Pleasing

Examples:

He has an agreeable attitude to every friend.
His pleasant manners have won him a large circle of friends.
It has a delightful experience to meet the President of India A.P.J. Abdul Kalam.

Hot (Adjective)

A man with a hot temper is not suitable for this job.

Synonyms:

Burning	Feverish	Scorching
Torrid		

Examples:

In India disharmony among all religions is one of the burning problems today.
The government is feverishly trying to come to settlement with western leaders.
It is not good to move in scorching heat.

Antonyms:

Cold	Cool	Calm
Soothing		

Examples:

This winter is exceptionally cold.
This medicine will calm down your temper.
The coffee is not cool enough to drink.
This music is highly soothing.

Humane (Adjective)

He is a man of humane character.

Synonyms:

Humanitarian	Philanthropic	Sympathetic
Tender	Kind	Benign
Human	Charitable	Compassionate

Examples:

Amnesty International is an organization doing lot of humanitarian work.
Some of the industrialists perform philanthropic activities just to hood wink the income tax authorities.
Our management has a sympathetic attitude towards the labour.

Antonyms:

Inhuman	Unkind	Cruel
Uncharitable	Malignant	

Examples:

Policy of apartheid practice is considered inhuman in a democracy.
It was unkind of the Boss to push out Madhu from employment just because she did not attend the marriage party of his son.
The growth is not malignant.

Humid (Adjective)

The humid nature of this hills station is attracting many tourists to this place.

Synonyms:

Wet	Moist	Close
Sticky	Oppressive	

Examples:

Don't wet my carpet. Better leave your muddy shoes outside.

Water this plant regularly to keep the soil moist.
Today the weather is rather close and sticky. There is no breeze.
The government of South Africa was indulging in oppressive acts against the black population.

Antonyms:

Parched	Dry	Arid
Sunny	Torrid	

Examples:
The draught has made even fertile land dry and parched.
The scientists have now invented chemicals which help vegetation even in arid lands.

Humour (Noun)

He wrote a story full of humour.

Synonyms:

Wit	Fun	Comedy
Factiousness	Amusement	Jocularity
Pleasantry		

Examples:
He showed a great deal of wit of handling the delicate situation.
I'm teaching myself to cook, just for fun.
We are so happy with the drollery of the game that we play it every night.
There is a time for work and a time for amusement.
He is popular for his jocularity in the company of his friends.
They exchanged pleasantries for a few minutes before saying goodbye.

Antonyms:

Solemnity	Gravity	Sobriety
Seriousness		

Examples:
We have to honour the solemnity of the occasion. Reserve your nice jokes for some other time.
It took us some time to let him wake to the gravity of the situation.
This topic needs an atmosphere of sobriety for a healthy discussion.

Humorous (Adjective)

Your humorous remarks were well received by the audience.

Synonyms:

Funny	Witty	Comic
Comical	Droll	Jocose
Jocular	Waggish	

Examples:

This story is quite funny. Let us read it again.
The main character is so witty. His dialogues can make even a priest laugh.
We can convert the play into a comic story without much difficulty.
There are a number of comical scenes in this feature film.

Antonyms:

Serious	Grave	Dull
Sedate	Gloomy	

Examples:

I have a serious interest in this business.
The situation in Beirut is very grave owing to civil war in the country.
My duties in this organization involve dull and drab study of statistical data.

Hypocrisy (Noun)

Making a claim that one did not commit a mistake is nothing but hypocrisy.

Synonyms:

Deceit	Dissembling	Duplicity
Pretence	Falsify	Deception
Cant		

Examples:

There is too much deceit practice by private companies in this country to make extra profits.
The detective managed to infiltrate into the smuggling ring by pretence.
The robber's claim that he was going to give the money to the poor was just an act ofcant.
He falsified his birth certificate in order to get a new passport.
The stage murder looked real, but it was only a visual deception.

Antonyms:

Honesty	Uprightness	Straightforwardness
Sincerity	Truthfulness	

Examples:

Pankaj has risen in life by dint of his strict adherence to the principle of honesty.
He lays cards on the table. He had nothing to hide. He believes in uprightness.
His dealings are marked by straightforwardness. He does not indulge in hypocrisy.

ICY (Adjective)

In summer we in this town experience icy wind.

Synonyms:

Arctic	Hitting	Bitter
Chill	Chilling	Chilly

Freezing	Aloof	Cold
Distant	Forbidding	Frigid
Frosty	Glacial	Indifferent
Stony		

Examples:
Black coffee leaves a bitter taste in the mouth.
By seeing the chilly welcome by the host, I become upset.
It is freezing here. Shut the window.
Throughout the conversation he remained silent and aloof.
It is very cold today. The mercury fell down to 4oC.
She had a distant look in her eyes. She obviously wasn't listing at all.
Seeing her indifferent attitude, I gave up my intention to propose her.

Antonyms:

Blistering	Boiling	Not sizzling
Cordial	Friendly	Gracious
Warm		

Examples:
The runners set off at a blistering pace.
The boiling point of water is 100oC
It is very hot today. The temperature rises to 45oC.
They were very friendly to me when I first arrived.
My grandmother is a very gracious lady.

Ideal (Adjective)

Ooty has the ideal weather for our holidays.

Synonyms:

Archetype	Model	Prototype
Example	Standard	Original
Pattern		

Examples:
Satan is the archetype of the evil doer.
The architect has prepared a model for our housing scheme.
The government has formulated a prototype scheme for constructing the houses for miners.
The teacher quoted many examples to make the lesson interesting.
His work does not reach the required standard.
Jagdish Chandra Bose gave many original ideas to science.
A good seamstress can make a dress without a pattern.

Antonyms:

Factual	Realistic	Practical

Deficient	Impaired	Imperfect
Unsuitable		

Examples:
This is the factual outlook of our scheme.
It is realistic rather than ideal, but it can be achieved and depended upon.
Let us be practical, not utopian, if you wish to be popular among the common people of average intelligence.
The boy was rather an unsuitable match to the beautiful girl.

Idle (Adjective)

When men cannot find employment, they remain idle.

Synonyms:

Inert	Unoccupied	Lazy
Inactive	Sloth	Sluggish
Unemployed	Indolent	

Examples:
Helium is an inert gas, as it neither moves nor causes any motion.
Village labourer is unoccupied for about six months in a year.
The waiters seem lazy in this restaurant as there is not much rush of visitors.
Many machines have been inactive in this office since the computer was installed last year.
Her sloth manners keep her away from good friend.
I feel sluggish and lazy after eating too much.
Due to lack of enough avenues for employment, the unemployed youth are becoming frustrated day by day.
The teacher scolded the indolent student but could not pull him up.

Antonyms:

Active	Busy	Diligent
Industrious	Assiduous	

Examples:
Deepak is a very active boy. He is good in both sports and studies.
Sarita keeps herself busy in one activity or the other all her waking hours.
John takes diligent interest in both sports and studies.
He is quite industrious in his studies.
The book was the result of ten year's assiduous research.

Imitate (Verb)

You should imitate great and good men.

Synonyms:

Burlesque	Echo	Follow

Copy	Impersonate	Mock
Mimic	Counterfeit	Forge
Parody		

Examples:
The cultural programmes and the dramas in which burlesque scenes on absent minded professors were exhibited.
The temple bells echoed across the valley every evening.
Religion teaches us to follow the footsteps of our true saints.
Don't copy everything your elder brother does.
He can impersonate many well-known politicians.
Back in the barracks the solider would mimic the platoon sergeant.
Now days counterfeit currency is in large circulation.
Everyone laughed when the comedian parodied the minister's brag.

Antonyms:

Alter	Convert	Modify
Vary		

Examples:
The old man has very much altered with age. He is no more an innocent gentleman.
Deepak has converted his religious attitude into purely materialist one.
The equipment has been modified to suit local requirements.

Improve (Verb)

He came back from holidays with greatly improved health.

Synonyms:

Amend	Correct	Reform
Rectify	Ameliorate	Better

Examples:
The official secrets act has been amended to prevent further leaks.
How can in indifferent society these policies reform desperate men?
Steps should be taken to rectify the situation.
The results of experiment proved wrong as she had not corrected her earlier findings.
Steps have been taken to ameliorate the situation.
He would better join the tuition centre to make up for his deficiency.

Antonyms:

Spoil	Deteriorate	Corrupt
Mar	Damage	Deprecate
Impair		

Examples:
You will spoil the child by increasing his pocket money.

His condition had deteriorated in this nursing home owing to negligence of the doctors.

The officials of this department are rather corrupt.

They are marring the reputation of the whole organization by their corrupt habits.

Imprudent (Adjective)

Is it not imprudent of you to marry when your salary is very low?

Synonyms:

Careless	Fool hardy	Foolish
Headless	Ill-advised	Ill-considered
Ill-judged	Improvident	Irresponsible
Rash	Reckless	

Examples:

If you want to do well in your class you should not be careless in your studies.

It was foolhardy of him to go swimming alone.

Deepak is not serious in his job. He is a headless man.

He was ill-advised to tell his manager that he is not the responsible man for the damages.

It was irresponsible of you to leave the door unlocked.

It would be rash of them to make up their minds before they have heard all the evidence.

Antonyms:

Careful	Cautions	Considerate
Discreet	Judicious	Polite
Provident	Prudent	Responsible
Wise		

Examples:

Be careful of the dog, it sometimes bites the people.

It was considerate of you not to play the piano while I was asleep.

I should make a few discreet inquiries about the firm before you sign anything.

When the fight began he thought it polite to leave.

Some farmers had been provident in the good years but others were ruined by the bad harvests.

Incapable (Adjective)

The children are incapable of telling lie.

Synonyms:

Incompetent	Inefficient	Unqualified
Inadequate	Unable	Unfit
Disabled		

Examples:
The workers went on strike as the new manager was found incompetent to efficiently control productive activities of the firm.
The inefficient workers cannot be paid as much as the efficient ones.
I feel unqualified to speak on the subject.
Inadequate supply of essential commodities in the district has caused general dissatisfaction among the people.
He is unable to walk properly owing to an old age.
He is unfit to try once again in his present state.

Antonyms:

Gifted	Capable	Qualified
Accomplished	Competent	Efficient

Examples:
Deepak is a gifted child. He invariably tops in the class.
Nehru was a capable leader. His oratory was unrivalled and patriotism too was explicit in every word he utters.
Pankaj is a qualified engineer. No wonder he makes the machine work accurately.
Deepak is an accomplished personality in every sense of the term knowledgeable, smart, sociable and healthy.

Inclement (Adjective)

You should not go into sea in this inclement weather.

Synonyms:

Rough	Stormy	Rigorous
Severe	Harsh	Draconian
Unfavourable	Unpleasant	

Examples:
His rough behaviour repels many a good friend.
His speech was too stormy, the mob proceeded to the office of the chairman to express their strong protest against the corrupt practices of the officials.
The weather today is rather unfavourable for playing tennis.

Antonyms:

Genial	Mild	Pleasant
Favourable	Balmy	Clement
Merciful		

Examples:
Saurabh has a genial personality. He makes everybody a well-wisher.
Today the weather is mild enough to let us go on a picnic.
Her pleasant manners win everybody to her side.
Don't go there until the situation becomes favourable.

Incline (Verb)

His letter inclines me to believe that he does not want to come.

Synonyms:

Dispose	Lean	Fall upon
Tend towards	Slope	

Examples:

Various objects were disposed on the desk in front of her.
The creeper tends to lean downwards in a vertical pole.
The common people have a tendency to fall upon right kind of leadership of patriotic spirit and moral strength.
The valley slopes downwards on the west side of the hill

Antonyms:

Indispose	Rise	Go upwards
Repel		

Examples:

When I went to meet him, I found him indisposed. He was lying in a bed.
The sun rise in the east ad sets in the west.
The smoke of the factory goes up in the environment.
His cold temperament repels me from any intimate talk.

Include (Verb)

Your duties include putting the children to bed.

Synonyms:

Involve	Comprise	Contain
Comprehend		

Examples:

The manufacturer of washing soap involves the use of many some chemicals.
Our country comprises of a many hill, high mountains, valleys and sea coasts.
This classroom contains a number of benches, desks, a black board and a pair of teacher's chair and table.

Antonyms:

Exclude	Omit	Leave out

Examples:

We can easily exclude the girl students from this picnic, as it is going to be too hazardous.
Don't omit the use of commas and full stops while answering your question paper in the English language. These are pertinent to accuracy.
Leave out the pans from the list of stationary as I am going to buy it wholesale from Kanpur.

Inconsistent (Adjective)

His accountant of what happened is inconsistent.

Synonyms:

Capricious	Erratic	Fickle
Changeable	Irregular	Uneven
Unstable	Contradictory	Contrary
At variance	Conflicting	Inconstant

Examples:

An erratic eating habits cause insomnia and other diseases.
The weather here is notoriously fickle and changeable.
He is an awkward, contrary child.
His behaviour is highly irregular.
Deepak is an inconstant lover. He frequently changes his girlfriend.
The Indian political system remains highly unstable.
Her theory is at variance with the known fact.

Antonyms:

Consistent	Constant	Predictable
Reliable	Stable	Steady
Coherent	Homogeneous	Orderly
Uniform	Reconcilable	

Examples:

You are not very consistent. First you condemn me and then you praise me.
This door is a constant passage. Do not block it.
The government tacks a coherent economic policy.
Opposition to the proposal came from predictable quarters.
My memory is not very reliable these days.

Incur (Verb)

His way of living incurred a lot of expenses for us.

Synonyms:

Run	Meet	Bring
Danger	Blame	Expose
Gain	Contract	Induce

Examples:

Our company has incurred a loss of $ 5, 00, 00 this year.
The loss will have to be met by raising a new loan.
The commitment to import a new machine brings danger of further temporary loss in the books of the company.
We cannot blame the management for this situation as the machine will add to the profits in due course.

Antonyms:

Shun	Avoid	Escape
Defect		

Examples:
We cannot shun new investments for the future property of the company.
We cannot avoid new schemes of workers' welfare.
The culprit escaped from the place of accident without being noticed.

Indecent (Adjective)

You should not have left the party in an indecent haste.

Synonyms:

Indelicate	Lewd	Indecorous
Unchaste	Improper	Shameless
Filthy	Foul	

Examples:
The shameless fellow passed lewd glances at every passing girl.
It was indelicate of you to mention her marriage problems.
He was forced to make a hasty and indecorous departure without his clothes.
It is considered improper for a lawyer to discuss cases with his clients outside his office.
The shameless woman flirted with many a man she met.
It is quite improper to use filthy language while talking to others.
The slaughter house was filled with foul smell.

Antonyms:

Decent	Seemly	Pure
Moral	Proper	Virtuous
Chaste	Decorous	

Examples:
His ways with women are considered always decent and decorous.
He is a man of pure, moral character above the unchaste atmosphere of modern youth clubs.
Deepa Mehta is a virtuous lady, charming and capable of proper calculated behaviour at every step.

Induce (Verb)

What induced you to do such a thing in your life?

Synonyms:

Impel	Convince	Instigate
Generate	Persuade	Cajole
Urge	Coax	Wheedle

Move

Examples:

Your role in the creation of the present circumstances in the company has impelled me to demand your resignation.
She finally persuaded us that she was telling the truth.
She was cajoled into accepting a part in the play.
My father urged me to marry a man of his choice.
But I am not convinced.

Antonyms:

Hinder	Repel	Curb
Deter	Prevent	Restrain
Discourage	Subdue	

Examples:

These new laws will hinder rather than promote prison reform.
He discouraged efficient supervisors by refusing due promotions.
Prevent water entry into your child's ears for it will cause infections.

Influence (Noun)

Many a woman has a civilizing influence upon her husband.

Synonyms:

Actuate	Draw	Excite
Inflame	Lead	Prompt
Urge	Move	Induce
Stir	Drive	Incite
Compel		

Examples:

Most of his acts are actuated by greed and selfish interests.
The strands of rubber were drawn to test their strength.
The professor's lecture on galaxy excited our interest to know more about universe.
The roof inclines over the porch without distorting its view.
The candidate's integrity and strength led the voters to support him.
Deepak was prompted by his friends to quarrel with his neighbour.
The Principal urged the parents to pay their dues promptly.
The bus was already moving when I jumped onto it.
Alcohols can induce a loosening of the tongue.
The coach's emotional pep talk stirred the teams.
The dictator's cruel decree incited the people to open rebellion.
I was compelled to acknowledge the force of his argument.

Antonyms:

| Retard | Dissuade | Hinder |
| Deter | Prevent | Inhibit |

Restrain

Examples:

His carelessness retarded progress in his studies.
I dissuaded him from his illegal activities like smuggling, bribery to officer and the like but to no avail.
His lust for beautiful women hindered his slow and steady rise in career.
Nobody can deter him from achieving his objective.
Even the lecture of priest on honesty could not prevent him from beginning rich the fast way.
Kaj Krishna side-tracked the normal inhibitions and could not be strained in his illegal proclivities. No wonder he has landed in jail.

Inner (Adjective)

Satisfying your inner man is the most difficult affair.

Synonyms:

| Inward | Interior | Internal |

Real

Examples:

Our actions do not always reflect our inward nature.
I have engaged an architect to make a plan for the interior decoration of my house.
India does not interface in the internal affairs of her neighbours.
The story is based on a real incident.

Antonyms:

| Outer | Exterior | External |

Superficial

Examples:

The outer atmosphere of the earth has many natural features which help mankind to survive and develop.
The exterior of a human body comprises of skin from top to bottom.
The external affairs of India are governed by Panchsheel i.e. five principles of mutual co-existence among sovereign countries.
He is a superficial without real talent or character but only show-off.

Innocent (Adjective)

He is not as innocent as a new born baby.

Synonyms:

| Blameless | Sinless | Untainted |
| Virginal | Guiltless | Irreproachable |

Examples:

His strict adherence to lofty principles of truth and honesty has bestowed on him ablameless personality.

His whole life can be regarded as a continuity of sinless and blameless achievements.
His face is a mirror of virginal innocence.
His poise and solitude manifest his guiltless soul.
Her behaviour in society has always been irreproachable.

Antonyms:

Blameworthy	Culpable	Guilty
Immoral	Lewd	Impure
Unchaste	Depraved	Dirty
Indecent		

Examples:
His bad company right from childhood has made him a blameworthy character.
The police have found him guilty of murdering his wife.
Virappan's life is a net-work of numerous immoral and lewd deeds, although he may have escaped the clutches of law for long.
His involvement with prostitutes, smugglers and dacoits – tell of his life of impurity, unchaste and depravation.

Innocent (Adjective)

He is not as innocent as a new born baby.

Synonyms:

Blameless	Sinless	Untainted
Virginal	Guiltless	Irreproachable

Examples:
His strict adherence to lofty principles of truth and honesty has bestowed on him ablameless personality.
His whole life can be regarded as a continuity of sinless and blameless achievements.
His face is a mirror of virginal innocence.
His poise and solitude manifest his guiltless soul.
Her behaviour in society has always been irreproachable.

Antonyms:

Blameworthy	Culpable	Guilty
Immoral	Lewd	Impure
Unchaste	Depraved	Dirty Indecent

Examples:
His bad company right from childhood has made him a blameworthy character.
The police have found him guilty of murdering his wife.
Virappan's life is a net-work of numerous immoral and lewd deeds, although he may have escaped the clutches of law for long.

His involvement with prostitutes, smugglers and dacoits – tell of his life of impurity, unchaste and depravation.

Insist (Verb)

I insisted that he should come with us.

Synonyms:

Urge	Persist	Contend
Demand	Maintain	Preserve

Examples:

The principal urged the parents to pay their dues promptly.
Despite hardship he persisted in his ambition to get college education.
The lawyer contended before the judge that the witness was not factually present at the scene of the incident;
Courtesy demands us to be polite to our seniors
The two friends have maintained their friendship for the last thirty years.
Talent is worthless unless you preserve to develop it.

Antonyms:

Relinquish	Forgo	Waiver
Renounce	Abandon	

Examples:

The retaining manager relinquished charge of his job after delivering the portfolios to the new manager.
I can forgo share of profits in his favour.
The judge announced a waiver of penalty against defaulters.
Buddha renounced the kingdom to take the meditation and to study the objective of human life.
I have abandoned the idea of going to England this summer.

Integrity (Noun)

Was not this treaty supposed to guarantee out territorial integrity?

Synonyms:

Honesty	Probity	Sincerity
Truthfulness	Rectitude	Truth

Examples:

Honesty adopted as a policy in business pays huge dividends in the long run.
Probity involves deep thinking about each and every aspect of a problem.
Sincerity brings its reward by the very law of natural relationships.
Truthfulness may cause trouble to start with but always has a happy ending.

Antonyms:

Unfairness	Dishonesty	Disunity

Diversity

Examples:
Business loses and unfairness in the management were exposed by the consultants.
The firm disrepute for dishonesty can seldom survive.
The sense of national integration among citizens is essential to avoid disunity and break up in a federation.
India is a land of diversity in religion and language but unity in economy and polity.

Intensify (Verb)

Intensify your efforts to attain what you want.

Synonyms:

| Aggravate | Heighten | Magnify |
| Increase | Enhance | |

Examples:
Wrong medicine will aggravate the pain.
These lenses can magnify the object 40 times.
It is very easy to increase the expenditure but very difficult to decrease it.
Her splendid dress enhanced her beauty.

Antonyms:

Milden	Lessen	Diminish
Attenuate	Reduce	Alleviate
Assuage		

Examples:
Condition of the patient was mildewed by the doctor's visit.
This medicine will lessen the pain in your back.
The number of students in our schools has diminished since last year.
Your donation to the orphanage will attenuate your guilt to some degree.
This exercise will help you reduce your weight.
The only thing that can alleviate your financial burden in the long run is taking to mechanization and automation at the earliest.
Resumption of duty alone will assuage your worries.

Invincible (Adjective)

It is only because of his invincible determination, he succeeded.

Synonyms:

Impregnable	Indestructible	Indomitable
Inseparable	Insuperable	Invulnerable
Unassailable	Unconquerable	Insurmountable

Examples:
Arsenals are in an impregnable position at the top of the league.

The two friends were inseparable. They went everywhere together.
Liverpool is in an invulnerable position at the top of the league.
Manchester Limited has built up an unassailable lead at the top of the premier division.
Before 1953 Mount Everest was unconquerable.

Antonyms:

Assailable	Beatable	Conquerable
Defenceless	Fallible	Powerless
Unprotected	Vulnerable	Weak
Yielding		

Examples:
The President has proved that he is fallible after all.
Being defeated by BJP now congress is powerless.
The election defeat puts the part leader in a vulnerable position.
That bridge is too weak to carry heavy traffic.
She is soft and yielding.

Jaundiced (Adjective)

Do not take a jaundiced view on this matter.

Synonyms:

Cynical	Preconceived	Sceptical
Bitter	Biased	Distorted
Envious	Hostile	Jealous
Partial	Prejudiced	Resentful
Spiteful	Suspicious	

Examples:
They have grown rather cynical about democracy.
He had no preconceived ideas about what careers his children should follow.
I am rather sceptical about his change of winning, despite what the papers say.
Failing the exam was a bitter experience to him.
He is clearly biased in the government's favour.
She cast envious eyes on her sister's dress.

Antonyms:

Credulous	Ingenuous	Naïve
Optimistic	Open-minded	Trusting
Unbiased		

Examples:
Their approach to life is refreshingly naïve.
She is not optimistic about the outcome.
Madhu wished her parents more open – minded about his friends.

Sarita has a trusting nature. She never deceives anybody.

Jest (Noun)

All his efforts have made him only a standing just.

Synonyms:

Fun	Joke	Jeer
Taunt	Amuse	

Examples:

There is nothing to joke about the present hard financial position I am in.
It took all the fun out of the occasion when we heard that you were ill.
Don't jeer at my helplessness today. I may be a rich man tomorrow.
He has no right to taunt on my failure in business.

Antonyms:

Seriousness	Thoughtful	Earnest
Sober		

Examples:

I can say with all the seriousness at my command that you can rise to the top in business.
Deepak is quite thoughtful in his investments. No wonder they always bear good dividend.
I am earnest in may endeavour to pass this examination.
My boss can maintain sober temperament under any circumstances or situation.

Joyous (Adjective)

My school-days are the most joyous moments in my life.

Synonyms:

Ecstatic	Elated	Jovial
Genial	Jolly	Glad
Happy		

Examples:

She was elated by the news of her result.
Kishore Kumar can sing the jovial songs much better.
Deepak can maintain a genial atmosphere in any place in which his jovial talk takes place.
Amana can keep jolly without effort.

Antonyms:

Gloomy	Miserable	Morose
Solemn	Sad	Unhappy

Examples:

His morose presence makes even a bright atmosphere gloomy.
Rakish feels miserable in the company of girls.

Let us take a solemn pledge to perform our fundamental duties sincerely.
It is sad that he did not live to see his book published.

Just (Adjective)

Be just to all.

Synonyms:

Decent	Fair	Good
Honest	Impartial	Pure
Right	Accurate	Exact
Faithful	Lawful	Apt
Deserved	Proper	Suitable
Legitimate		

Examples:
We must provide decent housing for poor.
She deserves a fair trial.
Manoj is poor but honest, he never tells a lie.
Every citizen should be impartial against cast and creed.
Delhi Jal Board should supply pure water to the people.
The dog is a faithful animal.
Mumbai is a suitable place for underworld.

Antonyms:

Corrupt	Devious	Dishonest
Inequitable	Prejudiced	Unfair
Unjust	Unlawful	Untrue
Inappropriate	Undeserved	Unfit

Examples:
Corrupt officials should be punished.
It would be dishonest of me to pretend that I enjoyed the evening.
The price charged to distributors was highly inequitable.
He went to the principal alleging that I was prejudiced against his daughter.
It is unfair to the candidates to raise their hopes too soon.
He was charged with unlawful possession of drugs by CBI.

Justify (Verb)

Nothing could justify your immodest behaviour in the dinner party.

Synonyms:

Absolve	Defend	Clear
Explain	Perform	

Examples:
After examining all evidence, the judge absolved the accused of all charged.

The lawyer who defended the accused felt elated at the judgment.
The accused explained the circumstances of his involvement in detail.

Antonyms:

Condemn	Accuse	Censure
Blame	Denounce	

Examples:
The government strongly condemned the extremists for their violent activities.
The opposition leaders accused the government of partiality towards notable politicians.
The judge censured the prosecution for illegal detention of the accused.
If you fail, the exam you'll only have yourself to blame.
The government denounced the opposition for open support to regional parochialism.

Keen (Adjective)

That is a knife with a keen edge.

Synonyms:

Acute	Eager	Sharp
Shrewd	Penetrating	

Examples:
Dogs have an acute sense of smell.
I am eager to take the medicine to reduce my pain.
The shears aren't sharp enough to cut the grass.
Arun Kumar is a shrewd politician. He knows the art of diplomacy and accurate judgment of human affairs.
Police inspector's penetrating eyes observed the criminal with professional thoroughness.

Antonyms:

Slow	Stupid	Bland
Languid	Dull	
Indifferent		

Examples:
He is a slow thinker, but a fast worker
Rajesh was stupid enough to miss the chance of an interview with the president.
This cheese is too bland for my taste.
She appeared indifferent to their sufferings.

Kill (Verb)

The frost killed the flowers.
Synonyms:

Assimilate	Dispatch	Massacre
Murder	Slaughter	Put to death
Butcher	Execute	

Examples:
Indira Gandhi was assassinated by her body guard.
Hitler ordered the massacre of innocent Jews to satisfy his racial whims and fancies.
Siddhartha was sentenced to death for murdering his wife.
A numbers of goats were taken to the slaughter house.
The culprit was executed for his murdering of his wife.
Even the mulch animals were butchered due to shortage of meat for the soldiers.
The injured horse was dispatched by its owner.
The king put the rebel to death when he came to know of the conspiracy hatched by the latter.

Antonyms:

Create	Produce	Fashion
Cause		

Examples:
God has created humans to love each other, not to hate and kill.
The organization has produced a booklet to help small investors.
Modern fashions do not impress the simple village folk.
Improper sanitation and drainage has caused malaria and jaundice in the city.

Kind (Adjective)

He is kind to all.

Synonyms:

Compassionate	Benign	Affable
Generous	Lenient	Sympathetic
Charitable	Merciful	Tender
Philanthropic	Complacent	

Examples:
After the death of his father Raghav was appointed as an accountant in the same company on compassionate grounds.
His benign attitude to the subordinates is appreciated by the company's management.
He has affable manners towards the fair sex.
Anita is very generous. She gives the children lovely presents on their birthday.
His lenient attitude has made his subordinates irregular in attendance.
His neighbours were quite sympathetic to his family during Ram's illness.
The charitable institutions have been exempted from the new tax.
She was merciful to the prisoner.

Our organization has benefited from the philanthropic attitude of the business magnate.
We are all much too complacent about the quality of water supply.

Antonyms:

Cruel	Callous	Unfeeling
Unkind	Hard	Hearted
Insensible	Harsh	

Examples:
The cruel king along with his cruel nobles had to surrender to the mob.
The king was callous to the genuine demands of the people. No wonder he was made to abdicate.
His attitude to the sick was marked by unfeeling and lack of human consideration.
The king was unkind to the slaves and the poor.

Kindle (Verb)

These songs kindled my enthusiasm to learn music.

Synonyms:

Ignite	Inflame	Light
Fire	Agitate	Excite
Incite	Induce	

Examples:
The malicious propaganda of the communal parties ignited fresh wave of violence.
The speeches of the leaders inflamed the high passions of the mob.
Sumitra lighted twenty-five candles on her twenty fifth birthday.
The house caught fire due to short circuit.
His appearance at the party had clearly agitated her.

Antonyms:

Extinguish	Put out
Satisfy	Satiate

Examples:
The police used new equipment to extinguish the fire in the house.
It took them five hours to put out the fire.
Of all the cold drinks, Campo Cola satisfies my thirst the best.
Journalism may be financially less paid. It does satiate one's thirst for knowledge and adventure.

Knowledge (Noun)

Knowledge of London is must to roam around the city.

Synonyms:

Perception	Science	Wisdom

Intuition	Comprehension	Cognition
Information	Lore	Light
Intelligence		

Examples:
A good driver must have a good perception of distance.
Systematic knowledge acquired after experiments is called science.
I question the wisdom of giving a child so much money.
My intuition ought to be correct.
The teacher had no comprehension of the boy's problems at home.
A copy of this report is enclosed for your information.
The judge gave no cognition to the verbal plea of the prosecution without through evidence.
The lore of Naga tribes includes many fascinating stories about their habits.
The home minister could not throw any light on the issue.
Mohan shows great intelligence though he is still very young.

Antonyms:
| Ignorance | Unfamiliarity | Misunderstanding |
| Misapprehension | Inexperience | Illiteracy |

Examples:
Ignorance of law is no excuse to commit a crime.
Mohan showed complete unfamiliarity with the topic though he was given notice ahead of a full week.
A misunderstanding has crept up between India and Pakistan on nuclear policy.
America's misapprehensions against the USSR need to be cleared by Russian leaders.

Known (Adjective)

He is known for his painting skills.

Synonyms:
Acknowledged	Admitted	Avowed
Celebrated	Common	Familiar
Manifest	Obvious	Patent
Popular	Published	Recognized
Well-known		

Examples:
Burgundy is celebrated for its fine wines.
It is not a rare bird, just a common or garden sparrow.
Such accounts of environmental pollution are now depressingly familiar.
Spending less money is the obvious answer to his financial problems.
Joggings is the most popular form of exercise among the people under 40.

Deepak Kumar is a well-known scientist.

Antonyms:

Closet	Concealed	Hidden
Secret	Unfamiliar	Unknown
Unrecognized	Unrevealed	

Examples:
I suspect he is a closet anti-nationalist.
Secret talks were held between the government and the rebel leaders.
His face was unfamiliar to me. I did not see him before.
The parts are all played by unknown actors.

Labour (Noun)

International Labour Organization, located in Geneva, is a powerful body.

Synonyms:

Work	Toil	Exertion
Drudgery	Industry	

Examples:
The work of building the bridge took six months.
The farmer toils in the field from dawn to dusk but the landlords enjoys the fruit of his labour.
This exertion will be good for him for reducing his excessive fat.
Preparing these monthly reports is nothing but drudgery.
The new supervisor was rewarded for his industry plus intelligence.

Antonyms:

Repose	Rest	Relaxation
Stillness		

Examples:
He has reposed confidence in me despite my first default.
I have taken two day's leave for rest and recreation.
Mental relaxation is a must for any original creation by an artist.
The stillness of the atmosphere awed me and reminded me of the noisy scenes of the previous evening.

Lack (Noun)

Lack of minimum knowledge of English is affecting his living in Canada.

Synonyms:

Need	Shortage	Deficiency
Want		

Examples:
Despite of the nourishing food, he needs complete physical and mental peace.
Shortage of money compelled him to stop further construction of his house.

Deficiency of iron in the blood leads to anaemia.
One wants balance diet as well as vegetables and fruits to eradicate anaemia.

Antonyms:

Sufficiency   Prosperity   WealthRiches

Examples:

Sufficiency of essential items for a reasonably good living is necessary for the growth of a balanced personality.
Tourism has brought an increase in prosperity to the islands.
Natural resources like forests, mines, water, vegetarian etc. are called the basic wealthof a nation.
The riches of the rich and the poverty of the poor are the basic contradictions in the Indian economy.

Lawful (Adjective)

Only lawful approach will help us to resolve these problems.

Synonyms:

Rightful   Legal   Fair
Legitimate

Examples:

Madhumita is the rightful heir to this property as the only survivor of the family.
Property is not more a fundamental right of the individual in society, it is only a legalwhich means one can acquire it by payment of cost of such property and not otherwise.
The principal's decision on the dispute between the two students was fair andreasonable.
The demand of the labour for participation in the management of a firm is consideredlegitimate in modern philosophy.

Antonyms:

Illegal   Unlawful   Illicit
Banned   Forbidden

Examples:

Use of violence to solve mutual disputes among individuals is illegal. There are courts to settle such disputes.
It is unlawful to use violence against other individuals in society except for self-defence.
There are numerous underground firms in the country producing illicit drugs. It is our duty to report about such firms to the police.

Leader (Noun)

He is not a leader of high repute.

Synonyms:

Guide	Guru	Teacher
Director	Conductor	Principal
Politician		

Examples:
The Gita is the greatest guide of the Hindus
The guru should be given as much respect as was given by our forefathers.
Did your teacher tell you how to do your sums?
The club needs a vigorous recreation director.
He had served as a conductor for ten years before getting his promotion.
My father retired as the principal of DAV senior secondary school.
Pundit Jawaharlal Nehru was a great leader and scholar.

Antonyms:

Follower	Trainee	Apprentice
Pupil	Henchman	

Examples:
Lal Bahadhur Shastri was a strict follower of Mahatma Gandhi.
Mahesh has been selected as an executive trainee by a multinational company.
Pankaj started his career as an apprentice in a chemical enterprise.
Srivastava is respected and revered by his pupils for his noble character.
A politician generally has to develop a good number of henchmen to keep his popularity alive.

Learn (Verb)

Learn swimming when you are young so that you will be healthy.

Synonyms:

Acquire	Memorize	Discover
Attain	Imbibe	Detect
Trace		

Examples:
Indian scientists have already acquired advanced knowledge of space technology.
Gita can memorize the Mathematical formula very fast.
She was delighted to discover a very good restaurant nearby.
The electrician soon detected the fault of the electrical wire.
The police combed the whole village to trace the dacoits.

Antonyms:

Forget	Unlearn	Miss
Misunderstand	Ignore	

Examples:
Forgive and forget is a common trait in a successful personality.

The time lag between initial lessons and the intensive course in a foreign language has made me unlearn its basic theory.
I missed the train by just a couple of minutes.
Lack of thorough knowledge about each other's view point usually creates misunderstanding among clients.
I cannot ignore the disrespect heaped on me by the new subordinate.

Learning (Noun)

Learning swimming in this shallow water is a difficult affair.

Synonyms:

Scholarship	Erudition	Knowledge
Understanding		

Examples:
The new Pope is a man of great scholarship.
His manner of prayer and the content of speeches show his wisdom.
Pankaj Kumar has good knowledge of Mathematics.
His social behaviour is always designed to create an atmosphere of understanding.

Antonyms:

Ignorance	Illiteracy	Misunderstanding
Unlearning		

Examples:
Ignorance of law is no excuse for its evasion.
Over 60% of people in South Africa are still illiterates.
Misunderstandings between any two countries can be removed by negotiation and international arbitration.

Lengthy (Adjective)

The people were enthusiastic enough to hear his lengthy speech.

Synonyms:

Tedious	Diffused	Detailed
Prolix	Spread	

Examples:
This text book seems to be a tedious one for too young students.
The Prime Minister has diffused the differences among the leaders of the district by discussing the local problems in full detail.
The task has been spread out into sections and subsections to make its implementation easy.

Antonyms:

Short	Concise	Brief
Limited	Terse	

Examples:
It is only a short walk from my house to this shop.
Let us be concise in our discussion; I have my next appointment in ten minutes.
I have given you a brief description of the incident.

Lessen (Noun)

This medicine will certainly lessen the pain to some extent.

Synonyms:

Lighten	Assuage	Allay
Mitigate	Soften	Temper

Examples:
Computer has lightened the manual work of accounting.
We have tried to assuage the feelings of our retrenched employees by assuring to absorb them in the next phase of expansion programme.
We have to allay the fear of the existing staff in respect of any further retrenchment.
The management has announced an increase in dearness allowance to mitigate the adverse effect of recent inflation. This has softened the attitude of hard core union leaders. It has also helped to temper the quality of the new staff.

Antonyms:

Heighten	Toughen	Enlarge
Escalate	Extend	Intensify

Examples:
Promotions among the existing officers have greatly heightened the reputation of the company.
But the attitude of the lower staff has toughened threatening to reduce productivity at the lower levels.
We should enlarge the sphere of cooperation among the officers and the subordinates somehow to achieve better performance.

Liberal (Adjective)

He is liberal of promises, but not of money.

Synonyms:

Plentiful	Tolerant	Profuse
Free	Progressive	Generous
Flexible		

Examples:
The current monsoons assure a plentiful crop of food grains next year.
Unless Hindus and Muslims show the old tolerant attitude, the age-long oneness may not be fully restored in Gujarat.

Madhuri shed profuse tears on hearing of her husband's death by a bomb in Jammu & Kashmir.

The new economic policy announced by the Finance minister gives a free hand to private enterprise in its day-to-day functioning.

Antonyms:

Scanty	Grasping	Low
Mean		

Examples:

The scanty rains this year in some of the state in India may adversely affect the total availability of food grains.

Our boss has a grasping temperament. He seldom looks to the other's view point.

I am feeling very low today. The news of the air crash has upset my spirits.

Liberty (Noun)

They fought to defend their liberty.

Synonyms:

Emancipation	Freedom	Independence
Licence	Permission	

Examples:

1807 was the year of emancipation of slaves in the British Isles.

Eternal vigilance is the price of freedom.

India got its independence after a long-drawn struggle for two centuries.

He has applied for a licence to keep fire arms.

The teacher will give him permission to attend the class provided he has done his homework.

Antonyms:

Captivity	Compulsion	Constraint
Imprisonment	Slavery	Serfdom
Servitude	Oppression	Obligation
Thralldom		

Examples:

Many landlords around the world openly violate the new law on bonded labour.

They keep many of their labourers in captivity.

The workers are made to bear captivity on compulsion of mere subsistence.

The landlords need to be put under constraint by strict enforcement of the new law.

Defaulting landlords should be duly punished by prescribed imprisonment.

The age-long slavery of the bonded labour must be ended in practice and not only in theory.

The country must rise above the serfdom of the 19th century political environment.

Lie (Noun)
This book is nothing but a pack of lies.
Synonyms:

Falsehood	Untruth	Prevarication
Quibble	Practice	Collusion

Examples:
Falsehood never pays in the long run.
Prosperity based on untruth can never bring happiness as your conscience always pricks you.
The report was full of lies and prevarications.
I only have a few minor quibbles about your essay. Basically it is very good.
Antonyms:

Truth	Honesty	Veracity
Authenticity	Original	

Examples:
Always speak truth if you want to be successful in business.
Honesty is the best policy in every walk of human life.
Mahesh Jain is a great businessman. The secret of his success lies in his veracity.
The authenticity of the statement is beyond doubt.

Lift (Verb)
This book is heavy for me to lift.
Synonyms:

Exalt	Erect	Raise
Elevate	Hoist	

Examples:
The Queen holds a very exalted position in Britain.
The town has erected a monument to its war heroes.
The management has raised new hopes for us in the matter of salaries.
The Vice President was elevated to the post of President of the company.
The Prime Minister hoists the flag at Red Fort on the Independence Day ever year.
Antonyms:

Drop	Lower	Sink
Let	Fall	

Examples:
I have dropped the idea of taking interest in politics.
This bad reputation may lower my prestige in business circles in the long run.
The still ball sinks when thrown in water but the ship does not.
Can you let out this room to me for week?

I fell down from the staircase and broke my leg.

Likely (Adjective)

This looks a likely field for mushrooms.

Synonyms:

Apt	Reasonable	Presumable
Liable	Credible	Possible
Conceivable		

Examples:
Our puppy is apt to knock his dish over.
My Daddy bought this chair at a reasonable price.
If you don't agree with her, she is liable to get angry.
He told quite a credible story of his adventure.
The prisoner saw only one possible way of escaping.
There is no conceivable way to unite the opposition parties in India.

Antonyms:

Doubtful	Improbable	Questionable
Unlikely	Dubious	Unreasonable

Examples:
I am doubtful of his sincere endeavour next time.
His arrival today in Delhi seems improbable due to bad weather.
His solution to this problem is questionable owing to inability to dig real facts and figures.
My visit to Mumbai in the near future seems unlikely.
His approach to this ticklish problem is rather dubious.
The company has rejected the demand of the peons for further raise in salaries as unreasonable.

Lively (Adjective)

The patient seems little more lively this morning.

Synonyms:

Vivid	Vigorous	Brisk
Keen	Vivacious	Spirited

Examples:
Amitabh Sharma gave a vivid picture of his visit to France.
His description of the luxurious living of the average citizen in France was ratheranimated.
There was brisk business today in the shares of our company at the Stock Exchange.

Antonyms:

| Listless | Languid | Languorous |
| Lethargic | Lifeless | Immobile |

Examples:
His heavy loss in business has left him rather listless.
His movements are languid and feverish.
He falls occasionally sick as he has a lethargic routine.

Lonely (Adjective)

This lonely mountain village has produced many poets of high repute.
Synonyms:
| Solitary | Desolate | Isolated |
| Deserted | Alone | Single |

Examples:
The office was completely deserted.
I was the solitary passenger in the early morning bus to the Railway Station.
He is a forlorn personality; seldom seen in the company of friends.

Antonyms:
| Escorted | Attended | Befriended |
| Popular | Together | Accompanied |

Examples:
The boss was escorted to his place of work by his assistant.
Hilary attended the marriage ceremony of her brother with great enthusiasm.
She was accompanied by a large number of her friends.

Lock (Verb)

This door locks easily.
Synonyms:
Behold	Inspect	See
Watch	View	Stare
Gaze	Discern	Observe
Regard	Survey	Arrest

Examples:
I was enchanted to behold the beauty of the rainbow.
The engines of a new ship have to be carefully inspected before it sets our on voyage.
He looked for her but could not see her in the crowd.
Watch the magician and try to figure out how he makes the rabbit disappear.
She was starting blankly into the space.
When the baby is in her arm she gazes up at the sky.
The doctor will observe the patient only when he visits him at the clinic.

The condemned prisoner regarded the jury with a look of outraged innocence.
We surveyed the countryside from the top of the hill.

Antonyms:

Ignore	Reject	Veil
Bypass		

Examples:

Janardhan ignored the presence of his rival at the ceremony.
I am sorry I cannot reject the valuable remarks of the esteemed viewers.
He tried to veil the circumstances of the accident by fleeing from the scene.
You cannot bypass the reality by closing your eyes.

Loud (Adjective)

The bomb exploded with a loud noise.

Synonyms:

Noisy	Vociferous	Clamorous
Boisterous	Sound	

Examples:

The railway station presented a very noisy scene.
He is vociferous in his views on political issues.
The worker cannot help making clamorous demands for increased wages in these days of galloping inflation.
He can keep the atmosphere around him highly gay with his boisterous personality.

Antonyms:

Peaceful	Silent	Soft
Taciturn	Subdued	

Examples:

I like to run away from the noisy atmosphere and large crowd of Delhi to the peaceful environment of a hill station.
This fan moves silently even at full speed.
My brother is too soft for taking to the police career where one has to deal with criminals and gangsters.

Love (Noun)

Show love towards yours neighbours.

Synonyms:

Affection	Fondness	Charity
Liking	Regard	Friendship
Tenderness	Attraction	

Examples:

Mother's affection for her child knows no bounds.

I have a fondness for playing cricket.
Charity is one of the five duties imposed on man by Holy Koran.
The husband should take care of the likings and disliking of his wife.
The people have great regard for their leader.
Adversity is the real test of friendship.
The new medicine will maintain the tenderness of your skin during winter.
Miss Universe Susmita Sen was an attraction to the crowd at the airport.

Antonyms:

Dislike	Abhorrence	Animosity
Disgust	Repugnance	Antipathy
Abomination	Loathing	Aversion
Detestation		

Examples:
I dislike getting up too early in the morning.
I have abhorrence for noisy and polluted atmosphere of Delhi's life.
Their friendship has turned into animosity owing to some recent developments in business.
I am disgusted with those people who deceive innocent people.
She made no attempt to hide her feelings of antipathy.

Luck (Noun)

My luck is out.

Synonyms:

Fortune	Chance	Prosperity
Good	Stroke	

Examples:
On his death he left a great fortune to his son.
He got many chances to become rich but he did not avail them as has no love for money.
He is not jealous of the prosperity of his brothers.
You must try harder for the good of the team.
A stroke of good luck turned the beggar into a rich man.

Antonyms:

Bad luck	Misfortune	Bad stroke
Unfavorable	Loss	Missing

Examples:
He is such an enterprising young man. His failure in business is sheer bad luck.
I have been denied many good chances in the career as I have the misfortune of being the nephew of a notorious politician.
I was entirely booked for a nice career abroad, but the breaking out of the war

proved a bad stroke.

My circumstances are now rather unfavourable for a career in business. I will have to take up a job for the time being.

Loving (Adjective)

Loving husbands are in heavy demand all over the world.

Synonyms:

| Affectionate | Devoted | Fond |
| Ardent | Dear | Solicitors |

Examples:
Sunny is one of my affectionate friends on whom I can depend.
Shishir is so much devoted to his wife. He will never go alone, without her.
I am fond of my hobby of plantation.

Antonyms:

Bitter	Cold	Unaffectionate
Aloof	Cruel	Hostile
Mean		

Examples:
There is nothing to feel bitter over my remarks. They are meant for your good.
Ronald is a cold person. He goes by logic, not by emotions.
Of late I have noted our uncle has become rather unaffectionate so far so I am concerned.

Magnanimous (Adjective)

Today many rich people turn out to be magnanimous.

Synonyms:

Beneficent	Big	Bountiful
Charitable	Free	Handsome
Kind	Noble	Beneficent
Selfless		

Examples:
All parents are beneficent to their children.
The bigger the crime the longer the jail sentence.
A bountiful supply of food has been sent to the earthquake victims by the central government.
You should try to be more charitable to your neighbors.
After ten years in prison, he was free man again.
I would describe her as handsome rather than beautiful.
Would you be kind enough to help me?

Antonyms:

Miserly	Petty	Resentful
Selfish	Small	Unforgiving
Vindictive		

Examples:
She can be extremely vindictive.
She felt angry and resentful at what had happened.
When you have children, you have to become less selfish.
Children learn better in small classes.
Unforgiving your children will spoil their lives.

Magnetic (Adjective)

Our voice is recorded in the magnetic tape held inside the gadget.

Synonyms:

Alluring	Captivating	Charismatic
Charming	Enchanting	Fascinating
Hypnotic	Irresistible	Mesmerizing
Seductive		

Examples:
She has a captivating personality.
Her alluring smile hypnotizes me.
She has a charismatic figure and charming beauty.
We found the scenery of Kashmir very enchanting.
The results of the survey make fascinating reading.
The music had a hypnotic effect on her.
She found his charms irresistible.

Antonyms:

Disagreeable	Offensive	Repellent
Repulsive	Unattractive	Unlikable
Unpleasant		

Examples:
Neeraj is a disagreeable person therefore nobody likes him.
You are generally very moderate but that time I found your attitude most offensive.
The idea is repellent to me.
Picking your nose is a repulsive habit.

Magnificent (Adjective)

Ambani has constructed a magnificent house near the beach in Mumbai.

Synonyms:

| August | Elegant | Glorious |
| Grand | Impressive | Lavish |

Luxurious	Majestic	Opulent
Rich	Regal	Sublime
Transcendent		

Examples:

Pundit Jawaharlal Nehru was an august statesman.
The historical monuments of Agra give us an evidence of India's glorious past.
It is not a very grand house, just a small bungalow.
His collection of paintings is most impressive.
He was lavish with his praise.
This car is our most luxurious model.
That particular business made him rich.
She dismissed him with a regal gesture.
The food was absolutely sublime.

Antonyms:

Bad	Humble	Ignoble
Lowly	Mean	Modest
Ordinary	Petty	Poor
Trivial	Undistinguished	Unimposing

Examples:

It is extremely bad to interrupt when two elders are speaking.
Be humble enough to learn from your mistake.
Don't be so mean to your little brother.
Ordinary people are seen in American villages.
Most of the people are poor in villages.
It is not wise to fight for trivial matters.

Maintain (Verb)

The improvement in his health is being maintained.

Synonyms:

Carry on	Conserve	Keep
Nurture	Retain	Uphold
Support	Claim	Contend
Justify	Vindicate	Perpetuate

Examples:

He was shouting and carrying on.
She had a lot of problems to contend with.
He claimed to have been abroad when the crime was committed.
I do wish you wouldn't keep on interrupting me.
These measures will only perpetuate the hostility between the two groups.
We retained the paintings in original place when we decorated the room.

I consider that I have been completely vindicated.

Antonyms:

Abolish	Break off	Conclude
Drop	End	Give up
Relinquish	Abandon	Suspend
Terminate	Desert	

Examples:
The fort had long been abandoned.
Death penalty should be abolished in all countries.
He broke off in the middle of the sentence.
The story concludes with the hero's death.
They ended the play with a song.
I give up. Tell me what the answer is.

Majority (Noun)

The majority of people prefer watching games to playing games.

Synonyms:

Adulthood	Excess	Superiority
Preponderance	More than half	

Examples:
If a girl is married before 16 years of her age she can declare her marriage null and void on attaining adulthood.
An excess of fat in one's diet can lead to heart disease.
He does not mix up gracefully with his classmates because he is suffering from asuperiority complex.
This deal was decided according to the theory of preponderance of probability.

Antonyms:

Minority	Smallness	Inferiority

Examples:
The Sikhs are in minority in Haryana, Himachal and Delhi. The only state where they have majority is Punjab.
His tall talk about himself shows his smallness.
Children from poor families wherever admitted in public schools are bound to carry the inferiority complex owning to obvious reasons.

Manner (Noun)

I do not like his manner.

Synonyms:

Style	Mode	Custom
Method	System	Way

| Fashion | Conduct | Behaviour |

Examples:
The new batsman has an awkward style of hitting the ball.
The mode of repayment of debt was duly described in the agreement.
A custom must be very old in order to be valid in the eyes of law.
I like his method of solving the problem of Mathematics.
Scientists have helped the farmers to try out new systems of growing crops.
I like the way you've done your hair.
She moves in a graceful fashion.
The students were fined for their disruptive conduct in the class.
The biologist studied the behavior of lions in their natural habitat.

Antonyms:
| Mannerlessness | Discourteous | Unsocial |
| Unsystematic | Unmethodical | |

Examples:
His mannerlessness caused disgust among the neighbours.
He was so discourteous to the Principal that the management committee had to rusticate him despite his high connections with the deputy commissioner.
He is extremely intelligent, but his unsocial behavior stands like a wall in his career.
He is intelligent but unsystematic.

Melody (Noun)

The melody is next taken up by the flute.

Synonyms:
| Unison | Tune | Symphony |
| Music | Harmony | Air |

Examples:
The children showed complete unison in their dance and music items.
Shankar Jai Krishna has composed many interesting tunes.
Shall we have some music during dinner?
Amaranth and I worked together in complete harmony for several years.
The rich child carries an air of extravagance around him.
This symphony is part of his new composition.

Antonyms:
| Discord | Distortion | Disruption |
| Noise | | |

Examples:
Religion is no more the root of discord in modern societies. It is the clash of economic interests that causes disharmony.
Many a dispute in society is based on distortion of facts by vested interests.

Once the society is divided among classes, disruption consequentially follows.
The music presented at the concert was pure and simple noise meant for the animal taste and not for the gentry invited for the occasion.

Mercy (Noun)

They showed little mercy to their enemies.

Synonyms:

Benevolence	Favour	Pardon
Clemency	Compassion	Gentleness
Leniency	Pity	Mildness
Grace	Kindness	

Examples:

The playground coach smiled with benevolence at the noisy children but tamed them in a few minutes by his sportsmanship.
The scheme found favour with the town planners.
May god grant you pardon for your sins!
The defendant was grateful for the judge's clemency.
The teacher had great compassion for her pupils.
The members took the advantage of the leniency of the chairman.
We feel pity on the inhuman living conditions of the slums.
His gentleness moved his opponents to appraisal.
The mildness of steel bars can be increased by heating them.
By the king's grace, the traitor was permitted to leave the country.
He can never forget the kindness shown by his neighbours during the communal riots.

Antonyms:

Cruelty	Hardness	Harshness
Vigour	Severity	Penalty
Punishment		

Examples:

The harshness of the teacher failed to reform the student.
The hardness of the metal was not in consonance with the needed quality of the motor.
Let us serve our motherland with all the vigour at our command.
The severity of this winter has bruised my skin.
The delay in return of the books compelled me to pay the penalty.
Violation of traffic rules can lead one to punishment by fine or imprisonment.

Merit (Noun)

There is not much merit in giving away the things that you do not want.

Synonyms:

| Worth | Value | Excellence |
| Virtue | | |

Examples:
The present worth of a rupee is hardly 50% of last year.
It means the value of money in relation to goods has fallen to almost half.
On the whole, however, the economy of the country has shown its excellence in terms of total national product.
The engineering exports of the country have doubled by virtue of scientific advancement.

Antonyms:

| Fault | Error | Flaw |
| Weakness | Worthlessness | |

Examples:
This computer operator has many faults in his behaviour.
He is amenable to errors of over-sophistication and artificiality.
There is, however, no flaw in his character. Every man has some weakness, and he is no exception.
The worthlessness of Darwin's ideology in human behaviour has been proved beyond and doubt.

Mild (Adjective)

He was awarded only a mild punishment.

Synonyms:

Bland	Soft	Gentle
Kind	Docile	Tender
Meek	Placid	

Examples:
These bland spring days are good for picnics.
The soft green grass of the Mughal gardens is a special attraction for the visitors to Rashtrapati Bhavan in New Delhi.
She gave the baby a gentle pat on the back.
Although he tried to act rough, he was basically a kind man.
He was criticized for being too docile to be an administrator.
The mother took good care of the tender child, yet the baby feels ill.
Even the meek students could not help speaking against the history teacher for his anti-social approach.
She has an amazingly placid disposition which appeals to one and all.

Antonyms:

| Wild | Ferocious | Blood-thirsty |

| Fierce | Brutish | Savage |

Examples:
With growing civilization, wild animals are going extinct one by one.
Tiger is a ferocious animal but humans can tame him all right.
The frustrated criminal became blood-thirsty after release from long imprisonment.
Kalinga was a fettle field which was fierce and took thousands of lives, ultimately converted Ashoka into a great Buddhist.
The policeman's brutish appearance terrified the criminal.

Mind (Noun)

Have you made up your mind about what you will do?

Synonyms:

Wit	Thought	Sense
Reason	Intellect	Disposition
Brian	Intelligence	Understanding
Spirit		

Examples:
His essays are full of wit and humour.
He had to change his plan of action when he gave a second thought to the problem.
The teacher tries to inculcate into his pupils a sense of beauty.
His arguments did not appeal to our sense of reason.
Man's intellect distinguishes him from the beasts.
The film is not recommended to people of a nervous disposition.
He died because his brain was fatally wounded in the accident.
Objective type questions are a new method of testing the intelligence of the candidates.
Few people have an understanding of international law.
He was deeply depressed and no one could lift his spirits.

Antonyms:

| Body | Matter | Brown |
| Brute force | Material | Substance |

Examples:
The hypnotist mesmerized my body and soul.
The matter in nature is divided into solids, liquids and gases.
The boy with the brown suit is my cousin.
It needs brute force to kill an enemy.
The government favours policy of importing raw materials, finishing them into products and exporting them.
There is little substance in the facts and figures to support your argument.

Miscellaneous (Adjective)

I have maintained a miscellaneous collection of books and cassettes.

Synonyms:

Assorted	Mingled	Motley
Unlike	Various	Variant
Dissimilar	Discordant	Confused
Promiscuous		

Examples:
The gift pack contained assorted biscuits.
A few goats were mingled with the sheep in the same field.
It is amazing that such a motley group has got along for such a long time.
It is the only club which gives membership to unlike persons.
This song is just a variant of a folk tune.
We have various types of cars in this show room for sale.
The two girls are so dissimilar that you won't believe they are real sisters.
The speakers had entirely discordant views on the subject. Hence they could not help quarrelling with each other.
He was so confused that he could not answer even simple questions.
She did not regard herself as promiscuous.

Antonyms:

Homogeneous	Identical	Like
Pure	Uniform	Same
Similar		

Examples:
India is composed of homogenous races.
The interests of all the states in India are identical.
Very often he behaves like an uneducated person.
This is pure diamond, not artificial.
A uniform law on citizenship prevails in most of the European countries.
I am facing the same problems in this city as you are facing.
I am happy we have similar tastes in colour and dress.

Miserable (Adjective)

This story is all about the miserable lives of the refugees in Europe after the war.

Synonyms:

Forlorn	Unhappy	Dismal
Sorry	Wretched	

Examples:
Don't look so forlorn without your girl friend.
Unhappy is the head that wears this heavy crown.

His achievement abroad was rather dismal as he fell in the company of drug addicts.
I am so sorry. I cannot help you in your financial problems.
African Blacks are leading a wretched life in South Africa where the white minority continues to reign supreme.

Antonyms:

Happy	Cheerful	Joyous
Contended		

Examples:
Deepak and Anita is a happy-go-lucky couple.
John is always cheerful come what may. I always feel joyous in his company.
Thomson is contented with his lot due to his extra spiritual attitude.

Misery (Noun)

Children suffer misery from the toothache.

Synonyms:

Woe	Wretchedness	Heartache
Distress	Anguish	Torment
Torture	Agony	Discomfort

Examples:
I am distressed at the woe of proper sections of society in the country.
Poverty is the biggest wretchedness of mankind.
Incidents like the recent Kanishka air-crash cause many possible passengers heartache.
The majority of the people in Asia and Africa suffer from anguish of one type or the other, natural or manmade.

Antonyms:

Bliss	Joy	Happiness
Pleasure	Ecstasy	Elation
Sweetness		

Examples:
It is bliss to be ignorant of mankind's agonies.
Some people get pleasure out of other people's sufferings. They are called sadists.
Real happiness lies in doing something which eradicates human suffering.
Their cultural affinity helped to get real ecstasy during their honeymoon period.

Mislead (Verb)

You mislead me to your malicious intentions.

Synonyms:

Misguide	Deceive	Delude
Misdirect	Beguile	Misled

Examples:
The members of the committee were misguided by the secretary.
The beggar deceived us by pretending that he was blind.
I may delude myself, but I think I am losing weight.
He beguiled woman into thinking that he could not pay for his night's lodging.
The stranger was misdirected by the naughty boys.
The students were misled by the teachers to take the exam without adequate preparation.

Antonyms:

Pilot	Guide	Direct
Steer	Lead	

Examples:
I piloted the plan of the new project at the general meeting of the members of the company.
The minister simply guides the policy of the Ministry. Real work is done by the members and staff of the secretariat.
The supervisors at the local level direct the activities at the grassroots.
Only a bold stance on this policy matter can steer the affairs of the country to peace and progress.
A big nation needs to be led by love and devotion, intellect and wise judgment.

Modern (Adjective)

His house is with all the modern facilities.

Synonyms:

New	Present	Contemporary
Current	Recent	Timely
Present day		

Examples:
The new policy lays down more incentives for the private sector.
There were 500 people present at the meeting.
USA keeps in mind contemporary political thought round the world while formulating its basic political philosophy.

Antonyms:

Bygone	Past	Ancient
Old fashioned		

Examples:
Let bygone be bygone. We should restore our old friendship.
India's nationalism and patriotism developed very strongly in the past century.
India's ancient history was very glorious. It keeps inspiring Indian traditions and culture.

This dress has now become old-fashioned.

Modest (Adjective)

He is modest in his requirements.

Synonyms:

Lowly	Humble	Shy
Unassuming	Unpretentious	

Examples:
Although a millionaire, he is lowly in his behavior with his subordinates.
He is humble in habits but rich in intellectual. She is beautiful in appearance but shy in public.
In spite of her great achievement in music, Lata Mageshkar is so unassuming.
Although he is 60, he is shy of public speaking.

Antonyms:

Conceited	Pretentious	Showy
Overbearing	Immodest	

Examples:
His high status in wealth has little meaning so long as he is self-conceited and pretentious.
He is showier than he really does.
Vicky is a fantastic story – teller but he becomes over-bearing after a few minutes.
His riches, unaccompanied by real talent, have made him rather immodest.

Monotonous (Adjective)

People rarely prefer monotonous works.

Synonyms:

All the same		
Boring	Colourless	Droning
Dull	Flat	Humdrum
Plodding	Repetitive	Soporific
Tiresome	Unchanging	Uniform
Wearisome		

Examples:
All the same there's some truth in what she says.
Stop! You are boring me.
There is never a dull moment when John Lever is around.
The children were being rather tiresome.
I would not take up the repetitive works.

Antonyms:

Animated	Enjoyable	Entertaining

Enthralling	Exciting	Exhilarating
Interesting	Lively	Invigorating

Examples:
I had rarely seen him so animated.
The movie was immensely enjoyable.
The play was very entertaining.
The hero of this novel is enthralling.
It is very exciting to go on a picnic.
My first parachute jumps was an exhilarating experience.
The Science fiction is very interesting.

Moral (Adjective)

The moral standards of the ordinary men have come down considerably.

Synonyms:

Honourable	Upright	Just
Fair	Ethical	Strict
Right	Virtuous	

Examples:
Honourable Finance Minister will deliver a speech on industrial policy next Monday.
He is an upright man of strong character.
The rules made by the Government on this subject are just and fair.
Our English teacher is very strict and allows no talking in his class.
He is the right man for the chairmanship of the company.

Antonyms:

Immoral	Dishonourable	Vicious
Licentious	Unprincipled	Unrighteous

Examples:
Everything is fine in society except greed for money which raises all kinds of immoral social problems.
Greed for money makes many an honourable person dishonourable.
The vicious look in the criminal's eyes made the unarmed policeman shiver with fear.
The unprincipled leader had to face his defeat in election at the hands of his voters.

Mourn (Verb)

He mourns the loss of his mother.

Synonyms:

Bemoan	Bewail	Sorrow
Lament	Regret	Grieve
Deplore	Cry	

Examples:

He bemoaned the shortage of funds available for research.
He bewailed the disappearance of his little dog.
It is a matter of great sorrow that he has lost his son in an accident.
Pankaj lamented that so many hedges had been destroyed.
Everyone regretted the death of Indira Gandhi.
Try not to grieve too much for the puppy that has died.
The boatman deplored the roughness of the sea.

Antonyms:

Be joyful	Joy	Rejoice
Triumph	Enjoy	Please

Examples:

The occasion of my brother's marriage with famous actress proved highly joyful.
The child gets a strange joy from playing with its toys.
Let's rejoice the silver jubilee of our company by holding a grand party.
The emergence of Bangladesh was a matter of great triumph for Mrs. Gandhi.
Enjoy your stay in this hotel.

Mysterious (Adjective)

They handed over the mysterious looking parcel to the Police.

Synonyms:

Abstruse	Arcane	Cryptic
Curious	Enigmatic	Hidden
Obscure	Perplexing	Puzzling
Secret	Unknown	Veiled

Examples:

Her writing is very abstruse. It is quite difficult to understand.
He is curious boy, always asking questions.
He has an enigmatic character. He may be spy.
I found the lecture very obscure.
The whole affair is rather perplexing.
Secret talks were held between the government and rebel leader.

Antonyms:

Apparent	Clear	Manifest
Open	Plain	

Examples:

Certain problems were apparent from the outset.
It is quite clear to me she is not coming.
His nervousness was manifest to all of us in the way he spoke.
The dog escaped through the open gate.

Native (Adjective & Noun)

The first meetings between Captains Cook and the natives resulted in failure.

Synonyms:

| Aboriginals | Innate | Natal |
| Original | Natural | Indigenous |

Examples:

The aboriginals of this district still live in small huts.
This beautiful woman has an innate sense of style.
Anti-natal care of the children forms a part of the new family welfare schemes of the government.
The loss of some persons even in a small war is natural and inevitable.
The original plan was good but of late it has become too complicated for implementation.
Our industrial policy lays great emphasis on indigenous production of machinery.

Antonyms:

| Foreign | Extraneous | Alien |
| Acquired | Supplemented | Extrinsic |

Examples:

Foreign policy of India lays due emphasis on five principles of co-existence called PanchSheel.
The doctor found an extraneous matter in his blood; so he referred him to a specialist.
Aliens are kept under constant watch in India these days to stop the terrorist activity.
The government can acquire any private property for public good by paying compensation to the owner.
My uncle had supplemented his income by working overtime to cover an extra family liability.
The extrinsic value of a currency is the one which matters in international dealings.

Necessary (Adjective)

Sleep is necessary to our health.

Synonyms:

| Essential | Needful | Required |
| Requisite | Undeniable | Unavoidable |

Examples:

Food, shelter and clothing are essential for life.
The home ministry has directed the police to do the needful immediately.
The defender was required to be present before the court in person.
We have reminded them to send the requisite information expeditiously.

Freedom of speech is an undeniable right of man.
He was under such compelling circumstances that his neighbour's helps became unavoidable for him.

Antonyms:

Casual	Worthless	Needless
Non Essential	Optional	Unnecessary
Useless		

Examples:
Engineering appliances are no more a casual need of the towns' man. These are becoming almost essential for day-to-day life.
All talk of luxuries for the poor is worthless unless you meet their ordinary needs first.
Needless to say I will be present at the meeting only if it is held on a Sunday.
Bus transport and electricity are no longer non-essential items of daily use in the cities.
I have chosen philosophy as my optional subject in my B.A.
My presence at the meeting was unnecessary.
It is useless to cry over the split milk.

Neglect (Noun)

Do not neglect writing to your mother.

Synonyms:

Carelessness	Neglectfulness	Negligence
Omission	Oversight	Slight
Scorn	Slackness	Inadvertence
Heedlessness	Default	Failure
Disregard	Disrespect	Error

Examples:
Saurabh's carelessness will cause him great loss one day.
His boss scolded him for his neglectfulness.
The employees took full advantage of negligence of the boss.
The accountant was regretful of his omissions and errors.
The boatman scorned his son for his perpetual fear of peddling in the sea.
The slackness of the worker irritated the boss.
The father was worried about the heedlessness of his son for studies.
I am confident he will not default in repaying your loan.
One should not be disappointed on failures, as they ultimately lead to success in life.
The king disregarded the counsel of his minister and waged the war.
He married a poor girl disrespecting the wishes of his parents.

Antonyms:

Care	Attention	Observation
Adventure	Heed	

Examples:

If you care for others, others will certainly care for you.
I drew the attention of the Minister to the sources of corruption in his Ministry.
The Minister heeded my observations while drafting his proposals for eradication of corrupt practices.
My new scheme is an adventure in the country's economy.

Nervous (Adjective)

The nervous system of the human body is a wonder of its own nature.

Synonyms:

Hesitant	Shaky	Timid
Timorous	Afraid	Agitated

Examples:

He was hesitant to go outstation in the first instant. His father, however, encourages him to join the offered post in Calcutta.
Vicky feels very timid when he sees a big dog.
He was much agitated when he heard of the accident.
His recent failures have made him so shaky. He is not ready to start even a sound business.
Deepak is afraid of going out alone at night.
She is a timorous young woman unable to live life on her own.

Antonyms:

Courageous	Bold	Manly
Undaunted	Doughtily	Valiant
Brave		

Examples:

There are very few courageous persons like Dev.
I don't feel bold enough to ask for pay increase.
His manly courage was behind for his great success in business.
Rajeev Gandhi has shown undaunted courage by concluding an agreement on Punjab.
The circus man was a doughty fellow. He was feeding the lions as if these were cats.
Valiant are those that carry on the struggle until they achieve their objective.
Richard is brave boy. He can hunt in the forest alone.

New (Adjective)

An orientation seminar has been arranged for the new members of Parliament.

Synonyms:

| Unused | Fresh | Novel |
| Recent | Modern | |

Examples:
He deals in used-cars as well as unused cars and scooters.
This is the only market in this area where one can get fresh vegetables and fruit.
Mrs. Indira Gandhi was praised all over the world for the novel ideas on international issues.
He has given the details of his recent visit of Antarctica region in his adventure story.
Our Father does not like modern music, but Ashi and I do.

Antonyms:

| Old | Ancient | Aged |
| Obsolete | Antique | Antiquated |

Examples:
At fifteen years old Deepak left the school to start his own business venture.
Ashoka was the hero of ancient time.
Richard was accompanied by an aged person when I saw him.
This handicraft is obsolete yet highly valuable.
It is an antique of the Indus Valley civilization.
Deepak is fed up with his mummy's antiquated ideas.

Nimble (Adjective)

Being as nimble as an ant is what will take you to a new height.

Synonyms:

Active	Agile	Prompt
Flexible	Quick	Speedy
Spry	Swift	

Examples:
Even at the age of 85, Khuswant Singh is very active and agile.
She is very prompt in giving salary to her workers.
His attitude towards life is quiet flexible.
The quick reply given by the child surprised all of us.
Speedy action on the part of the fire brigade saved the house from destruction.
At 75 she is very spry. She manages everything in time.
The thief made a swift exit leaving no trace of his identity.

Antonyms:

Clumsy	Unready	Sluggish
Inert	Inactive	Dull
Dilatory		

Examples:

Poor children of a slum cannot help looking clumsy. They are after all underfed and shabbily dressed.
The police was unready to chase the dacoits. No wonder the dacoits decamped.
My habits have become sluggish. This is the result of my recent sickness.
Our science teacher is rather inert, although extremely intelligent.
Anil is rather inactive for the type of quality education he is enjoying.
Our new teacher is rather dull and drab in his lecturers.

Noble (Adjective)

He has planned to build a house on a noble scale.

Synonyms:

Dignified	Lofty	Eminent
Honourable	Magnificent	Great
Illustrious	Elevated	Peer
Lord	Aristocrat	Grand

Examples:

The President received the guests in the usual dignified manner.
The Himalayas is a lofty mountain.
I met several eminent leaders in a conference yesterday.
Honourable Prime Minister has consented to chair the meeting.
Mahatma Gandhi was a great leader of India.
Shakespeare is England's most illustrious poet.
An elevated house is one that has been built on a high platform.
The defendant was tried by a jury of peers.
He keeps lording over his subordinates day in and day out.
Membership of this club is reserved for aristocrats only.
The army chief looked grand in his uniform.

Antonyms:

Ignoble	Mean	Humble
Common	Plebeian	

Examples:

His ignoble attitude has spoiled the image of his political party.
He is rather mean in his dealings with his colleagues.
Mahatma Gandhi was humble in demeanour but noble in idea and action.
The common man in India still lives below the poverty line.
The way the person behaved shows that he belongs to a plebeian origin.

Notion (Noun)

I have no notion of what he means.

Synonyms:

Conception	Impression	Imagination
Opinion	Doctrine	Belief
Supposition	Thought	

Examples:
The architect's conception of the building was a glass sky-scrapper.
He imbibed a deep impression of the Taj's lovely moonlight beauty when he viewed it for the first time.
With a little imagination we should be able to find a solution to this vexed problem.
His teacher has a very high opinion about Pankaj
Progress has swept many of the old doctrines away.
His firm belief in God helps him overcome all difficulties in life.
He acted on the supposition that the public would applaud his political manoeuvres.
What are your thoughts on this topic?

Antonyms:

Truth	Reality	Fact
Variety	Actuality	

Examples:
Truth always triumphs; falsehood never pays.
Terrorism has of late become one of the menacing realities round the world.
The fact of poverty in the developing countries continues to persist.
There is a great variety of religions in India, Hinduism, Islam, Sikhism, Christianity, Buddhism, Jainism, Zoroastrianism etc.
The actuality of divisive tendencies in the Indian social firmament cannot be denied.

Numerous (Adjective)

All her numerous friends are well settled in their respective professions.

Synonyms:

Various	Several	Manifold
Sundry	Diverse	

Examples:
Various views have been expressed on the agreement relating to the Arab Israeli conflict.
God is one but the ways of realizing him are several.
The city counsel has a manifold plan to beautiful the city.
I had to buy sundry things to equip myself for the forthcoming trip abroad.
The crowd scattered in diverse directions when the police opened the tear-gas.

Antonyms:

Few	Scarce	Scanty
Rare		

Examples:
Only a few individuals graced the silver jubilee celebrations of the political party owing to the tense atmosphere in the city.
The commodities which are scarce in supply carry more value in the market.
The western region of India has had only scanty rainfall this year.
This piece of antique has been declared a rare object.

Obdurate (Adjective)

His obdurate nature resulted in loss of his job.

Synonyms:

Adamant	Dogged	Firm
Fixed	Hard	Hard–hearted
Immovable	Inexorable	Inflexible
Obstinate	Relentless	Unending
Inexpressible		

Examples:
She was quite adamant that she would not come.
I don't want to be unkind, he said in a firm voice.
He had the fixed idea that a woman's place was in the home.
Lock your bike to something immovable like a railing or a lamppost.
She is obstinate and inflexible in her attitude.

Antonyms:

Amenable	Biddable	Complaint
Flexible	Malleable	Plaint
Soft-hearted	Submissive	Tender
Tractable	Yielding	Placid

Examples:
I find him very amenable to reason.
She is a placid and biddable child.
The government, complaint or ever, gave in to their demand.
You need to be more flexible and imaginative in your approach.
The young are mere malleable than the old.

Obedient (Adjective)

Obedient children seldom score low marks in their exams.

Synonyms:

Submissive	Subservient	Dutiful
Tractable	Yielding	

Examples:

His submissive nature leads others to believe he is a coward.
A good leader's policies must be subservient to the needs of the people.
For many years Ashutosh was a dutiful soldier before he turned a terrorist.
A green ranch needs tractable horses for its guests.
The government has been yielding to even undue demands of the rebel group.

Antonyms:

Mutinous	Stubborn	Intractable
Disobedient	Refractor	

Examples:
General Pervez Musharraf became mutinous and deposed Nawaz Sharif in Pakistan.
My son is a stubborn character. It is rather difficult for me to change his habits.
My ideas on the political system needed for India are intractable as they are based on strong logic.
It is not wrong to be disobedient to the elders if your cause is noble and lofty.
Cancer is refractory disease in India so far.

Obligatory (Adjective)

Is attendance at school obligatory or optional in that country?

Synonyms:

Necessary	Unavoidable	Needful
Imperative	Compulsory	

Examples:
If necessary, I am prepared to come again tomorrow.
It is unavoidable to pay taxes if your income is beyond $ 50000 in a year.
I am sure Sanjeev will do the needful in this matter if he possibly can.
It is absolutely imperative that we make a quick decision.
Sex education should be compulsory in schools.

Antonyms:

Desired	Willing	Voluntary
Self	Chosen	

Examples:
We should work our utmost to achieve the desired objectives.
Sorry, I am not willing to relax the rules for the sake of your son's admission in my school.
My father has taken to voluntary retirement after 20 years of service in the government, though he could still continue for few more years.
The career followed by my son is self-chosen. I have never given him serious advice or guidance.

Obliterate (Verb)
The criminals obliterated all signs of crime before they left the scene.

Synonyms:

Annihilate	Blot out	Cancel
Destroy	Efface	Eradicate
Erase	Expunge	Extirpate
Root out	Wipe out	

Examples:
She annihilated her opponent who failed to win a single game.
He tried to blot out anything that would remind him of his ordeal.
The match had to be cancelled because of bad weather.
They have destroyed all the evidence of the spot.
Time and weather had long since effaced the inscription on the monument.
Small pox has now been eradicated.
He has tried to erase from his mind all memories of the disaster.

Antonyms:

Build	Construct	Create
Establish	Form	Formulate
Generate	Make	

Examples:
Birds build their nests out of twigs.
Delhi government has constructed many flyovers in Delhi.
God created the world, the universe and every living being.
India tries to establish a good relationship with China.
They form the clay into figure of animals.

Oblivious (Adjective)
The students were oblivious of what were taking place around them

Synonyms:

Forgetful	Absent – minded	Inattentive

Examples:
Suresh is of forgetful type. One cannot entrust him serious assignments.
Our professor of Philosophy is so absent – minded that he entered his neighbour's houses instead of his own yesterday.
John is inattentive in his class. That is why he is so poor in studies.

Antonyms:

Attentive	Aware	Observant

Examples:
My son is very attentive in his lessons. No wonder he is always near the top in his class.

The people are gradually becoming aware of their rights and responsibilities as citizens. Thanks to the ever spreading T.V. media.

Our M.D. is quite observant of the activities of his rival businessmen.

Obvious (Adjective)

What the politician would do after the News Paper published the crime report was obvious to us.

Synonyms:

Clear	Evident	Visible
Distinct	Palpable	Patent
Discernible	Perceptible	

Examples:

Ranjeet is very clear in his thoughts as well as actions.
I became quite evident that he was not willing to undertake the assignment.
Nothing was visible at a distance of even 10 yards because of the thick fog.
I had the distinct impression that I was being watched.
There is a palpable difference in their ages.
His patent reply to every question is a big no.
The mediator made a discernible analysis of the problem.
The difference in their heights is hardly perceptible.

Antonyms:

Hidden	Masked	Veiled
Covered	Secret	Obscure
Concealed	Latent	

Examples:

Every idea has a hidden meaning besides the obvious one.
The leader's views seemed masked by a deeper meaning.
The creditor gave a veiled threat to his debtor to expedite his recovery.
Despite the ban on gambling, the crooks found a covert place to play cards.
Secret talks were held between the government and rebel groups.

Obscure (Adjective)

Is the meaning still obscure to you?

Synonyms:

Dark	Doubtful	Dim
Dense	Hidden	Dusky
Muddy	Turbid	Involved
Unintelligent	Deep	Darksome
Cloudy		

Examples:
He always kept his parents in the dark regarding the weakness in his studies.
It is extremely doubtful that anyone survived the explosion.
I could scarcely read by the dim light of the candle.
After looting the train the robbers ran into a dense jungle.
They had to pass though the muddy water before reaching the temple.
The government has prescribed such an involved procedure for grant of subsidy that hardly a few can make use of the scheme. What they were saying was unintelligible to me.
The sky all of a sudden turned cloudy and we had to stop our play in this ground.
I hardly recognized my friend in the dusky light.

Antonyms:

Apparent	Intelligible	Lucid
Plain	Straightforward	Transparent
Unadorned	Obvious	Evident
Distinct		

Examples:
The apparent reason for his failure in the examination is his sickness during the examination days.
His accent is not so intelligent to the class that many students laughed at him.
His thinking is very lucid but action rather complicated.
Pradeep is the unadorned king of the school sports, though the principal is the chairman of the sports council.
Pankaj was the obvious choice of the school for representing it in the state sports.
It is evident that he is intelligent in studies from his power of speech plus vast vocabulary at his command.

Odd (Adjective)

1, 3, 5, 7 and 9 are odd numbers.

Synonyms:

Queer	Uneven	Uninvited
Irregular		

Examples:
Science teacher of my school has very queer habits of always performing day-to-day routines in the irregular way.
His uneven moods make him completely unpredictable.
Do you recognize the man in the blue cap? It seems he has come uninvited to this party.
Irregular habits of diet have wrecked Silpa's health.

Antonyms:

Usual	Match	Matching
Even	Parallel	

Examples:
When the accident happened, the usual crowd gathered.
These ducks very much match in colour.
This colour is not matching with the original.
Two, four, six, eight, ten, etc... are all even numbers in Arithmetic.

Odious (Adjective)

The atmosphere in that college is odious to stay there even for a few days.

Synonyms:

Abhorrent	Abominable	Detestable
Disgusting	Execrable	Foul
Hateful	Horrible	Horrid
Loathsome	Obnoxious	Repugnant
Repulsive	Unpleasant	Vile

Examples:
Violence and communal riot are abhorrent to him.
Murders and rape are abominable crimes.
It is detestable to me to get up early in the morning.
To bite nails is a disgusting habit.
Her way of talking to elders is very execrable.
The memory of her childhood was still hateful to her.

Antonyms:

Agreeable	Charming	Congenial
Delightful	Enchanting	Enjoyable
Pleasant	Pleasing	Winsome

Examples:
I found him most agreeable.
She looks very charming today.
I find this aspect of my job particularly congenial.
I was very delightful to see the splendid arrangement in the party.
We found the scenery of Nepal very enchanting.

Onerous (Adjective)

He resigned his job because that is full of onerous duties.

Synonyms:

Burdensome	Troublesome	Backbreaking
Wearing	Oppressive	Difficult

Examples:
The old man was glad to get rid of his burdensome furniture.
A successful teacher knows how to handle the troublesome students.
Democracy cannot tolerate oppressive leaders.
Facing a corrupt bureaucracy is one of the most difficult problems of the new government.
The members of the society are tired of the wearing manners of the secretary.
Carrying the furniture to the attic was a back breaking task.

Antonyms:
Easy	Fluent	Harmless
Comfortable		

Examples:
The language paper was rather easy. I had nothing to worry.
Modern moving belt system at the airports and big railway stations has made fluent the problem of luggage placement in the luxury cars.
Taking of bed tea is harmless but only if you keep the consumption within limits.
The new luxury coach is as comfortable as your well cushioned drawing room.

Ooze (Verb)

Blood still oozes from the wounds.

Synonyms:
Drip	Drop	Drizzle
Let fall		

Examples:
The bottle glucose was dripping very small drops into the tube for transmission into the patient's veins.
Today the weather is rather dry. There is no sign of even small drops to drizzle.
The earthen pitcher filters the water drop by drop.

Antonyms:
Rush	Pour	Gush
Flow	Rain	

Examples:
During floods this river has a sudden rush of water.
The rains today let fall heavy pour of water.
The siphon allows gush of water in the can if you let off the air and use a wide connecting tube.
This tributary has a uniform flow of water throughout the year.

Opinion (Noun)

What is your opinion of our new President?

Synonyms:

Thought	Idea	Judgment
Theory	Dogma	Tenet
Mind	Notion	Speculation
Verdict		

Examples:
You must give a serious thought before resigning this handsome job.
I got a good idea last night for my mother's birthday present.
The judgment of the Umpire cannot be questioned by the players.
He has a theory that wearing hats makes man go bold.
With the progress of science the religious dogmas have lost their sway.
It is quite impossible to know his mind because he speaks very little.
His colleagues had a wrong notion about him but he is basically a very kind hearted man.
My speculation about the results of my son has come out true.
The jury will give its verdict in this case next week.

Antonyms:

| Silence | Dictation | Non-committal |
| Execution | Order | |

Examples:
There was a pin–drop silence in the hall when the Pope spoke his sermon.
He is a versatile steno. He can take down notes from the dictation of a tape – recorder.
The reply of the Management to the demands of the labourers was non-committal.
The project is now ready in all respects for being taken up for execution.
The Prime Minister has ordered for fresh elections in the state.

Opportunity (Noun)

I had no opportunity to discuss the matter with her.

Synonyms:

| Chance | Occasion | Turn |
| Scope | Window | Expedient |

Examples:
Real success lies in availing of the right chance at the right moment.
The present state of affairs is no occasion for rejoicing.
Now it is turn to get the ticket from the counter.
It is now expedient to hold the election in the Punjab in Pakistan.
Unless you have a professional degree you have a little scope of employment in a multinational company.

Antonyms:

| Omission | Lapse | Neglect |
| Leave undone | | |

Examples:
There are many errors of omission in this book.
The time for payment of the income tax has lapsed.
The case reflects extreme neglect on the part of the dealing officer.
At many places the analysis of data has been left undone.

Optimistic (Adjective)

This Journal takes an optimistic view of events.

Synonyms:

Hopeful	Confident	Brave
Bright	Cheerful	Happy

Examples:
India is hopeful of a big stride in space technology very soon.
Sachin is very confident of his success in the competition.
The coast guard men braved the storm to reach the sinking ship.
The sitting room is brighter in the afternoon.
It will make Mary cheerful if you go over and talk to her.
It makes me happy to think of the golden college days.

Antonyms:

Pessimist	Dejected	Drooping
Disappointment	Cheerless	Hopeless

Examples:
Romario is basically a pessimist. He looks at the dark side of things more than at the bright.
When I entered the house, I found my brother dejected owing to a bad interview he had in an examination.
With her marriage proposal breaking half away, she lay drooping on her bed.
Her disappointment was acute. Her demeanour was cheerless.

Opulent (Adjective)

Action should be taken to remove the opulent vegetation in this area.

Synonyms:

Affluent	Lavish	Luxurious
Moneyed	Prosperous	Sumptuous
Wealthy	Well-to-do	Copious
Plentiful	Profuse	Prolific

Examples:
Her parents were very affluent in that locality.
He was lavish with his praise.
He bought a luxurious car. It is very expensive.
The moneyed class people lead a luxurious life.

The north of this region is still more prosperous than the south.
Mangoes are plentiful at the moment.
She supports her theory with copious evidences.

Antonyms:

Destitute	Down and out	Broke
Moneyless	Needy	Penurious
Poor	Poverty – stricken	

Examples:
When he died his family was left completely destitute.
During the recession thousands of small business went broke.
Nowadays I am moneyless. Can you lend me $ 500?
We should help the poor and needy.
Due to bad policy of the government African farmers are still poor.

Orderly (Adjective)

Keats is a man with an orderly mind.

Synonyms:

Neat	Tidy	Trim
Uniform	Graceful	

Examples:
Our firm has an entirely neat system of filing.
Amarnath is always found in tidy apparels.
Leander keeps his whole personality well-trimmed.
His body and mind are generally marked by uniform smoothness of sorts.

Antonyms:

Chaotic	Disorderly	Untidy
Messy		

Examples:
Our library is in a chaotic condition since the librarian is on a long leave.
The books of the library are lying in disorderly way here and there.
The whole atmosphere is untidy.
The students and teacher who come and search their own books created a messy situation.

Ordinary (Adjective)

You can attend the function in an ordinary dress.

Synonyms:

Average	Common	Usual
Commonplace	Regular	Medium
Low	Inferior	Undistinguished

Examples:

Kishore is a student of average caliber but secures a high position in the examinations due to hard work.

The common man is hit hard by the price rise but the government has taken no steps to raise his wages in equal proportion.

My elder brother has gone out for his usual evening walk.

Horses and buggies were commonplace sight of Delhi in 1920s.

Getting up very early in the morning is my regular habit.

She is neither short nor all. She has medium height.

A Captain is inferior in rank to a Major in the Indian Army.

His military career was an undistinguished one but after retirement he has done some business and made tons of money.

Antonyms:

Extraordinary	One-in-a-million	Uncommon
Above the average	Abnormally high	First rate
Superior	Distinguished	

Examples:

My brother is an extraordinary boy, both in studies and sports.

Shahrukh Khan is an actor of uncommon caliber, one-in-a million.

Suresh is far above the average in intelligence but a middling in all-round performance.

His intelligent quotient is abnormally high.

An MP is called a first rate citizen in a democracy.

Miss Anjai has a superior position in the company.

Kapil Sibbal is a distinguished lawyer of this country.

Organize (Verb)

He is the responsible man to organize the expedition to the South Pole.

Synonyms:

Classify	Arrange	Order
Sort	Marshal	

Examples:

A dictionary is a classified arrangement of words.

Please arrange these jumble words alphabetically.

These goods need to be placed in the showroom in as ascending order.

Sort out the commercial letters from this mail.

I have marshalled the facts of the case in this notebook for your ready reference.

Antonyms:

Disorganize	Muddle	Bungle
Dishevel		

Examples:

Our college library is very much disorganized these days due to stock-taking.
Henry has muddled the whole sales programme owing to his eccentric behavior with his clients.
The new treasurer has bungled with the accounts of the society.
Never mind my dishevelled hair. Come to the brass-tacks.

Original (Adjective)

The original plan was better than the plan we followed.

Synonyms:

Aboriginal	Earliest	Initial
Introductory	Primary	Primitive
Fresh	Novel	Fertile
Inventive	First	Genuine
Authentic	Master	Prototypical

Examples:

Please, get a new telephone connection at your earliest convenience.
My initial reaction was to refuse.
An introductory chapter should be attractive. It enhances the value of the book.
The disease is still in its primary stage.
The cave provided a primitive shelter from the rain and storm..
The agricultural land of West Bengal is very fertile.
Deepak stood first in his class.
The Hindustan Times always publishers authentic news.
He is the master of his subject.

Antonyms:

Final	Last	Antiquated
Conventional	Familiar	Normal
Old	Ordinary	Spoiled
Standard	Traditional	Typical
Usual	Secondary	

Examples:

This is his last in UPSC Exam to reach his dream job.
This is a final proof of this book.
An antiquated bus is playing in the route no-85.
An old building is situated near the Lincoln square.
Spoiled food should be avoided to prevent from disease.
We provide a first standard of service.
It is usual to rain in August.

Outbreak (Noun)

The enmity between the two communities resulted in an outbreak of clashes.

Synonyms:

Commotion	Tumult	Insurrection
Outburst		

Examples:

Opposition leaders are talking irresponsibly in this district. No wonder there has already taken place a commotion among members of different communities.

The labouring class has caused a tumult in a number of factories by their agitation against rising prices.

Discontentment against the king was so great that the common people rose in an insurrection and dethroned the king.

The leader caused outburst among the masses by their burning extempore.

Antonyms:

Order	Quiet	Subsidence
Peace		

Examples:

The new leadership created order out of chaos.

The dissidents achieved what they wanted and the result was return of the quiet atmosphere.

The revolt was brought under subsidence and peace restored.

Outstanding (Adjective)

We have pictured the outstanding features of this landscape.

Synonyms:

Celebrated	Distinguished	Eminent
Great	Important	Impressive
Special	Superior	Superlative
Due	Payable	Arresting
Eye-catching	Prominent	Salient

Examples:

Amitabh Bachchan is celebrated for his good acting.

I think gray hair makes you look very distinguished.

Pankaj Vohra is an eminent journalist for his investigative journalism.

Mahatma Gandhi was a great leader of International fame.

It is very important to me that you should be there.

His collection of painting is most impressive.

She is very special in cooking food.

She is clearly superior to the other candidates.

Antonyms:

Dull	Inferior	Insignificant
Mediocre	Ordinary	Pedestrian
Run of the mill	Unexceptional	Unimpressive

Examples:
Today is deadly dull as the temperature touches a low point.
She is inferior to her sister in studies.
Very ordinary clothes were worn by the poor.
His books are distinctly mediocre.

Pacify (Verb)

We did all our best to pacify our father.

Synonyms:

Appease	Mitigate	Quench
Lull	Allay	Compose
Quiet	Assuage	Tranquillize

Examples:
He appeased his hunger with sweet dishes.
Government has taken several steps to mitigate the sufferings of the shopkeepers of this area.
I need something to quench my thirst.
There was a lull before the patient's anxiety.
She remained well composed during the hot controversy.
The teachers tried to quieten the students.
The medicine may assuage the pain, but soaking in lukewarm water will do you injury more good.
This medicine will tranquillize the restless baby and put him asleep.

Antonyms:

Irritate	Inflame	Annoy
Incense	Enrage	Exasperate
Vex		

Examples:
His criticism irritated me very much.
The fiery speech of the trade union leader inflamed the passions of the workers.
The subordinate's impertinence annoyed the boss.
They feel deeply incensed by the way I have been treated.
The peasant's rude behavior enraged the landlord.
The neglect of the civic problems in the city has exasperated the local population.
The municipal commissioner has vexed the problem by his indifferent attitude.

Pain (Noun)

Does not your laziness give pain to your parents?

Synonyms:

Throe	Pang	Ache
Grief	Distress	Throb
Agony		

Examples:

Child – birth is no joke. It causes immense throe to the mother.
The beloved lady could hardly bear the pang of separation from her lover.
The ache of my head has been greatly relieved by aspirin.
Sunny has come to great grief his constant unemployment.
Scooter accident has put him in a state of agony.

Antonyms:

| Health | Pleasure | Well-being |
| Ecstasy | Relief | |

Examples:

Health is the first requisite of a good personality.
"Duty first, Pleasure next" is the motto of good citizens.
A welfare state does a lot of work nowadays for the well-being of the common people.
Ram felt great ecstasy in the company of Sita.
It gives me great relief to be told about an increase in my salary.

Pardon (Verb)

Pardon me for giving you the wrong information.

Synonyms:

Condone	Forgive	Absolve
Exonerate	Acquit	Excuse
Overlook		

Examples:

The boss has condoned my late coming to the office.
Forgive me God for my bad deeds, if any!
The judge acquitted the accused after preliminary hearing.
Excuse me, may I borrow your pen for a minute?
We should not overlook our faults while appraising our good achievements.

Antonyms:

| Condemn | Convict | Punish |
| Penalize | | |

Examples:

His racket needs to be condemned thoroughly and brought to the notice of the government.

The court convicted the accused for his guilt.
Law punishes the people who commit social crimes.
God penalizes those who escape the legal penalties by hook or crook.

Pardon (Noun)

I beg your pardon for having given you the wrong information.

Synonyms:

Absolution	Mercy	Remission
Amnesty	Forgiveness	Acquittal

Examples:
His absolution from his partner's debts gave him great relief.
The culprit begged for mercy but to no avail.
His application for remission of fine was rejected by the principal.
The king granted amnesty to the rebels.
We must forgive our enemies if we ourselves expect forgiveness.
His acquittal by the jury has saved an innocent from being punished.

Antonyms:

Penalty	Retaliation	Punishment
Retribution	Vengeance	

Examples:
The government has imposed a new penalty for evasion of taxes.
Retaliation is no solution to the verbal attacks made in individual relationships.
All crimes against society carry a punishment under law.
Some traditions lay down retribution as a punishment for social misdeeds, intentional or otherwise.
The idea of vengeance is repugnant to the philosophy of Buddhism.

Part (Noun)

We spent a part of our holiday in France.

Synonyms:

Atom	Member	Portion
Share	Segment	Section
Particle	Fraction	Fragment
Piece	Disconnect	Disjoin

Examples:
At one time it was thought that atom cannot be split.
Only the members of the club can participate in the annual function.
Only some portion of an iceberg is visible from outside the water.
Each of the partners tried to appropriate a bigger share of the profits.
A chord is a line which divides a circle into two segments.

Government has formulated a new policy for the upliftment of the economically weaker sections of the society.
She got a particle of dust in her eye while sweeping the room.
The cup was smashed and lay in fragments on the floor.
She tore away his letter into pieces and threw it in the waste paper basket.
The guard's van was disconnected from the train.

Antonyms:

Connect	Join	Tie
Attach	Link	Combine
Couple	Cement	

Examples:
By connecting the wire of the positive charge with the negative one, we simply create a big spark.
Joining of two dots by a foot rule makes a straight line.
We can tie the knots on the rope and make a net.
His name has been attached with a spy ring.
His link with an important smuggling concern has been established.

Partial (Adjective)

Examiners were partial towards the pretty women students.

Synonyms:

Unfair	Incomplete	Limited
Biased	Inequitable	Restricted
Predisposed	One-sided	

Examples:
Many shrewd leaders have resorted to unfair means to win the election.
This clerk is in the habit of leaving his work incomplete.
In spite of the limited resources, the Indian scientists have made great inventions.
Some people have biased views against their colleagues.
His restricted approach can lead to his failure in the noble mission.
His mother's work as a nurse predisposes him for aspiring to be a doctor.
A judge cannot do justice if he takes one-sided view of the case.

Antonyms:

Fair	Complete	Entire
Equitable	Disinterested	Whole
Just	Impartial	

Examples:
The new minister has a fair view of society and its problems.
He has travelled the entire width and length of the country to obtain a practical insight of social problems.

He has a complete study of the society of India.
There is need for a more equitable distribution of wealth in India.
An internationalist is one who can take a disinterested view of international problems.
The whole town was destroyed by the earthquake.
The just demands of the student must be met.
I cannot take an impartial view in a case where my brother may be involved. Hence I advise you to seek somebody else as an arbitrator in this dispute.

Passion (Noun)

She was choking with passions.

Synonyms:

Love	Anger	Fury
Emotion	Fever	Desire
Excitement	Zeal	Fervour

Examples:

Everything is fair in love and war.
My anger grew as he continued his invectives.
She flew into a fury when I refused to land her any money.
The film did cause enough emotion among the audience.
The examination fever makes him nervous.
His only desire was to see his son married before his death.
She had to calm herself after all the excitement.
He has started his new business with great zeal and fervour.

Antonyms:

Apathy	Calmness	Coolness
Hate	Indifference	Frigidity
Unconcern		

Examples:

There is certain apathy about local elections among the public.
I noticed certain coolness between his wife and him.
In cold region, frigidity is common among women.
The indifferent attitude of local leader prevented the progressive work in this area.
Men with beards are one of my pet hates.

Passive (Adjective)

In spite of my efforts to elicit an answer from the boy, he remained passive.

Synonyms:

Patient	Inert	Submissive
Resistant		

Examples:

You'll have to be patient with my mother. She is rather a deaf.
Deepak has become rather inert since his last illness.
Rakish Jain is submissive in his business dealings.
He has lost the power of resistance to wrong decision.

Antonyms:

| Active | Alert | Vigilant |

Watchful

Examples:

Mahesh is an active and smart boy.
He is alert of his surroundings both in his business and in his private life.
Income tax authorities have of late become more vigilant to economic offences by business house.
Bhupendra advised me to be watchful of the tricks of my business partner.

Paternal (Adjective)

My paternal grand-father expired few days back.

Synonyms:

| Careful | Fatherly | Patronizing |

Kind-Hearted

Examples:

My father is careful in his business dealings. He never signs a paper without proper judgment.
My boss has a fatherly attitude to all the employees.
He is patronizing so long as my business proposals are profitable to him as well as to me.
Our principal is a kind – hearted while dealing with the students.

Antonyms:

| Careless | Rough | Rude |

Indifferent

Examples:

I try not to be careless in accounts which I consider are basic to success in any business.
Before taking a business decision I make rough estimates and then prune them before implementation of projects.
It is rude to interrupt when somebody is speaking.
My boss is not indifferent to the welfare of his subordinates.

Patience (Noun)

She has no patience with those who are always grumbling.

Synonyms:

Forbearance	Passiveness	Sufferance
Resignation	Endurance	Fortitude
Calmness		

Examples:
It takes considerable forbearance to overlook his faults.
The passiveness of the Indian farmer can be partly attributed to his religious traditions.
He cannot help but praise the sufferance of the audience who saw the full drama.
He accepted his defeat with resignation.
Sailing the Atlantic Ocean single handily requires great endurance.
He bore his long illness with quiet fortitude.
The calmness of the sea was a prelude to the storm.

Antonyms:

Wrath	Enrage	Enjoy
Infuriate	Vex	Displease
Inflame	Incite	Indignation
Irritation		

Examples:
The cyclone plundered the whole coastal areas as god's own wrath.
The behavior of the servant enraged the master.
Let's first finish our home task lest we annoy our teacher.
The boss felt infuriated on the failure of the subordinate in tackling such a simple problem.
Let's simplify rather than vex the problem.
The boss was displeased with his subordinate.
The political leader inflamed the mob without proposing patience. Hence the incident of stone – throwing took place.

Pause (Noun)

The whole discussion went on without any pause.

Synonyms:

Respite	Interval	Break
Halt	Cessation	Intermission
Lull	Suspension	Stoppage
Wait		

Examples:
The board of directors gave the candidate short respite before the next question.
There was an interval of ten minutes at the concert to give the orchestra a rest.
His absence from office was treated as a break in his service.

The troops halted for a rest.
The warring nations agreed on a cessation of hostilities.
Many of the audience left the hall in the intermission, so boring was the picture.
There was lull before the thunderstorm.
His suspension has been revoked by the new secretary.
Stoppage of work by the union leaders for their trivial demands was condemned by the press.
The chairman is waiting to begin the meeting.

Antonyms:

Continue	Continuance	Continuation
Continuity		

Examples:
We continued our journey without break.
We should inform of our new order to the firm in continuation of the earlier order.
This business is a continuance of the old one.
We must ensure the continuity of schemes undertaken by the forgoing ministry.

Peculiar (Adjective)

This was the wedding dress peculiar to the 18th century tribes.

Synonyms:

Strange	Extraordinary	Remarkable
Odd	Queer	Unusual
Rare	Abnormal	Uncommon
Irregular	Singular	

Examples:
A strange feeling came to his mind while entering the haunted house.
A snowfall as seen under a microscope is of extraordinary beauty.
Congress party has made remarkable progress in the current elections.
The giraffe is an odd-looking animal.
We heard a queer story about how a dog was changed into a monkey.
It's unusual for him to be so rude.
He has a good collection of rare art pieces.
The abnormal growth of tissues leads to cancer.
A solar eclipse is an uncommon occurrence.
Our clock is irregular and cannot be trusted.
We saw a singular sight of a dog pulling a small cart.

Antonyms:

Natural	Customary	Normal
Commonplace	Usual	Ordinary

Examples:
Hot summers are a natural phenomenon of tropical countries.

Desert is a customary dish after dinner in European hotels.
The normal life of this city should not be disturbed at any cost.
T.V. is a commonplace source of recreation for the town folk nowadays.
My usual summer dress is a blue shirt and a Terri coat pant.
Many extraordinary luxuries in India are ordinary necessities in Europe.

Peevish (Adjective)

The peevish nature of this politician is the biggest blockade for his progress.

Synonyms:

Acrimonious	Cantankerous	Captions
Childish	Churlish	Crusty
Fractions	Fretful	Ill-tempered
Petulant	Sulky	Sullen
Surly	Testy	Tetchy
Touchy		

Examples:

The acrimonious dispute between two groups was settled peacefully.
His illness has made him increasingly cantankerous.
It seems churlish to refuse such a generous offer.
She is ill-tempered so easily gets fraction.
A petulant and jealous wife always quarrels with her husband.
All my attempts to amuse the children were not with sullen scowls.

Antonyms:

Affable	Agreeable	Cheerful
Cheery	Easy-Going	Even – tempered
Genial	Good-natured	Happy
Merry	Pleasant	Sweet

Examples:

He found her parents very affable.
I was very happy to hear the news of winning our team.
She is very cheerful and agreeable by nature.
My mother doesn't mind who comes to stay. She is very easy going.
The air was sweet with the scent of lilies.

Perfect (Adjective)

She is perfect in performance of his duties.

Synonyms:

Flawless	Faultless	Ideal
Consummation		

Examples:

This scheme seems flawless if well operated.
Your thesis is faultless in language and ideas.
Your approach to the problem seems ideal.
This technique will certainly lead to consummation of the task.

Antonyms:

Deficient	Imperfect	Flawed
Incomplete	Unfinished	Defective

Examples:

India is still deficient in mineral oil.
Mary's performance in the play was imperfect at many places.
Mohan flowed in the debate at many points.

Permanent (Adjective)

This is not my permanent address.

Synonyms:

Stable	Enduring	Constant
Everlasting	Steadfast	Lasting
Durable		

Examples:

India's stable foreign policy since Nehru's time has brought international applause.
An enduring programme of rural development is necessary to boost India's economy.
This machine has been made durable enough to last a decade without repairs.

Antonyms:

Brief	Temporary	Short-lived
Changing	Mortal	Transitory

Examples:

Chairman made a brief speech on the occasion.
This arrangement is meant for a temporary period of a month or so.
We need not devote such huge investment of time and money on this short-lived problem.
All living things are mortal.
Fashion is changing day by day.
Fame attained through bad means is transitory.

Permission (Noun)

By whose permission did you enter this building?

Synonym:

Allowance	Leave	License
Permit	Liberty	Authority
Consent		

Examples:

The daily allowance paid to the government servants on tour does help them to save something after expenses.

The boss gave him leave to go home early.

His license to keep a dog has been cancelled by the Municipal authorities.

He was given a permit to go through the private park.

They give their children a great deal of liberty.

The Headmaster has no authority to administer a school in whatever way the likes.

He gave his consent for the project to get under way.

Antonyms:

Prevention	Refusal	Resistance
Prohibition	Denial	Hindrance
Opposition	Objection	

Examples:

Prevention of a disease is better than cure.

His refusal to lend me a small amount of $ 50 shocked me very much.

His resistance to my tempting invitation to a sumptuous dinner was very unusual.

The government of Maharashtra has withdrawn prohibition of alcoholic drinks.

Permit (Verb)

Circumstances do not permit me to help you.

Synonyms:

| Let | Allow | Agree |
| Authorize | Enable | |

Examples:

Let us join our heads to find a solution to this puzzle.

The government should not allow any fissiparous tendencies to raise their ugly head.

The deputy commissioner was authorized to nip the riots sternly.

Antonyms:

| Forbid | Prevent | Prohibit |

Examples:

The court gave its ruling forbidding the use of religious places for political campaigning.

We can prevent the spread of this disease by general inoculation of children.

The chairman had to prohibit demonstrations of any kind in factory premises.

Persist (Verb)

She persists in wearing that old-fashioned hat.

Synonyms:

Continue	Last	Remain
Stay	Endure	Insist
Preserve		

Examples:
He continued his speech despite hooting by the audience.
He was afraid that his money would not last to the end of his holidays.
The weather will remain cold for the next few weeks.
How long did you stay there?
The Bible says that God's mercy endures forever.
Father insisted that mother must take two hour rest in the afternoon.
Your really must tell him! All right, if you insist.

Antonyms:

Discontinue	Conclude	Quit
Finish	Terminate	End
Desist	Cease	

Examples:
My sister has discontinued her studies after graduation.
His studies concluded after 15 years under the 10+2+3 year graduation course.
Satish has quit his job as he could not pull on with his boss.
He has finished his practical training in a couple of good firms.
The boss terminated the services of his inefficient subordinate.
They decided to end their relationship.
Deepak has desisted further assaults on his reputation.
Hostilities between the two sides ceased at midnight.

Persistent (Adjective)

Persistent attacks of malaria resulted in his death.

Synonyms:

Ceaseless	Continuous	Unceasing
Unremitting		

Examples:
It requires a ceaseless journey for three months by road to reach their destination.
It was through unceasing planning an effort that he topped in the class.
They had to undertake a continuous journey for three days in order to reach the destination.

Antonyms:

Occasional	Periodic	Inconstant
Changeable	Temporary	

Examples:
It was one of the occasional chances that brought him to lime light.

Periodic check-up is always good for children.
Fever near the school final exams brought temporary set-backs in his career.

Persuade (Verb)

How can I persuade you of my sincerity?

Synonyms:

Allure	Urge	Lead
Incite	Entice	Coax
Convince	Incline	Move
Induce	Impel	
Bring		

Examples:

He was allured by her wealth and sophistication.
Mother urged Shoran to go to the dentist.
He led the horse back into the stable.
His speech incited the mob to violence.
Our Father did everything to entice our mother to go to the party.
Ram coaxed his father to let him use the family car.
The politicians' speech convinced the voters he was the man deserving to be elected.
The whole family is inclined to rise early in the morning.
He was deeply moved on hearing his cousin's death.
I tried to induce Mohan to come with us, but he would not.
Wild animals and birds are often impelled by hunger to come near the human beings, especially in winter.
I just can't bring myself to apologies.

Antonyms:

Hold back	Restrain	Deter
Repel	Dissuade	Hinder
Discourage		

Examples:

I cannot now hold back my offer of a job to him in my organization.
His remarks greatly disparaged my reputation, but I restrained myself from giving him a blow on his jaw.
Such a blow could have deterred him from making such remarks in future.
Similar magnetic poles repel each other.

Physical (Adjective)

It is physical impossibility to be in two places at the same time.

Synonyms:

| Bodily | Carnal | Corporal |

| Somatic | Real | Visible |

Examples:
He was bodily healthy but intellectually inferior.
Carnal necessities compel many a young man to stoop low.
His approach in day-to-day life is rather fleshy. There is little poetic about him.

Antonyms:
| Mental | Spiritual | Intellectual |

Examples:
His mental make-up is so strong. He invariably tops in the class.
Unless the modern youth reduce their luxurious habits, they cannot make to spiritual outlook.

Pitiable (Adjective)

His efforts to change the nature of his brother were nothing but pitiable attempts.

Synonyms:
Mournful	Moving	Grievous
Distressing	Sad	Doleful
Woeful	Sorrowful	

Examples:
What has happened to make you look so sad?
It was distressing to see him suffering from pain.
Hearing the sorrowful news she wept bitterly.
His speech was deeply moving.
The death of Martin Luther King in 1968 was a grievous loss to humanity.
The funeral involved a long and doleful ceremony.
The woeful news of the death of Mrs. Indira Gandhi grieved the nation.
The pupils and teachers are mournful today because the headmaster has died.

Antonyms:
| Pleasant | Desirable | Enviable |

Examples:
The weather is very pleasant today.
Our college encourages numerous desirable extracurricular activities after study hours.
Our new manager is an enviable personality – what a gait, manners, speech, vocabulary, health!

Placid (Adjective)

Every thing is visible in this placid water.

Synonyms:
| Calm | Collected | Composed |
| Cool | Even | Gently |

Halcyon	Mild	Peaceful
Serene	Still	Tranquil
Undisturbed	Unexcitable	Untroubled

Examples:
The city is calm again after yesterday's riots.
She always stags cool, calm and collected in a crisis.
This wince cellar stays at an even temperature all year round.
He seems very meek and mild.
Though the India is a country of diverse religious communities, the feeling of patriotism among the people makes India a peaceful country.
Throughout out the crisis she remained serene and in control.
Please stand still while I take your photograph.

Antonyms:
Agitated	Disturbed	Emotional
Excitable	Impulsive	Passionate
Rough	Temperamental	Tempestuous

Examples:
She became very agitated and started shouting.
She teaches children who are emotionally disturbed.
People get very emotional about issues like animal welfare.
The journey from Delhi to Mumbai was very excitable.
My car is a bit temperamental. It may stop working anytime anywhere.

Plain (Adjective)

After we engaged a guide, everything was a plain sailing.

Synonyms:
| Clear | Evident | Obvious |
| Conspicuous | Apparent | |

Examples:
It is better we clear our account before it is too late.
His desire for friendship with you is evident from his offer of flower bouquet on your birthday.
Spending less money is the obvious answer to his financial problems.

Antonyms:
| Hidden | Concealed | Secret |
| Imperceptible | | |

Examples:
The thief's face was hidden in a mask.
Roy concealed many of his business dealings from his partner. No wonder their

partnership broke off.
The leader's clarification made only an imperceptible impact on the public who continued to carry the grudge against his earlier stand on the issue.

Plead (Verb)

He pleaded with his son to be less troublesome to his mother.

Synonyms:

| Pray | Sue | Supplicate |
| Entreat | | |

Examples:
The advocate prayed to the court to take a compassionate view about his client.
If you do not complete the work, I will sue you.
The student supplicated to the Principal to take lenient view of his misadventure.

Antonyms:

| Command | Demand | Order |

Examples:
Nehru commanded great respect in international circles for his intellectual stance and love for humanity.
Workers demanded a raise in their wages.
The Principal ordered the dissenting students to quit the college.

Pleasant (Adjective)

Make yourself pleasant to the visitors.

Synonyms:

| Pleasing | Agreeable | Attractive |
| Enjoyable | Nice | |

Examples:
The pleasing demeanour of the wife cancelled the anger of her husband.
Agreeable manners always bring good reward.
She looked quite attractive in that red saree.
The party was enjoyable.
You look nice in this attire.

Antonyms:

Awful	Distasteful	Displeasing
Unpleasant	Repulsive	Unattractive
Obnoxious		

Examples:
The awful demeanour of the wife added to the wrath of the husband.
The clash between husband and wife caused an unpleasant atmosphere in the house.

Repulsive manners bring untoward misery, however harmless the objectives of a person.
As we crossed the Yamuna River, we felt some obnoxious smell in the air.

Pleasure (Noun)

It gave me much pleasure to hear of your success.

Synonyms:

Delight	Enjoyment	Joy
Ecstasy		

Examples:
The pleasing demeanour of the wife cancelled the anger of her husband.
Agreeable manners always bring good reward.
She looked quite attractive in that red saree.
The party was enjoyable.
You look nice in this attire.

Antonyms:

Awful	Distasteful	Displeasing
Unpleasant	Repulsive	Unattractive
Obnoxious		

Examples:
The awful demeanour of the wife added to the wrath of the husband.
The clash between husband and wife caused an unpleasant atmosphere in the house.
Repulsive manners bring untoward misery, however harmless the objectives of a person.
As we crossed the Yamuna River, we felt some obnoxious smell in the air.

Plentiful (Adjective)

To come out of this problem of scarcity of water, what we need is plentiful supply of river water at once.

Synonyms:

Abundant	Lavish	Replete
Luxuriant	Bountiful	Ample
Plenteous	Teeming	Sufficient

Examples:
Oranges are abundant in Spain.
Uncle Hari was always lavish in giving gift to his relatives.
The prince was brought up in great luxuriant atmosphere.
There is a plenteous supply of wheat in India this year.
These fishes are sufficient for the foreign market.

The cabinets were replete with valuable antiques.
The crops are bountiful this year.

Antonyms:

Scarce	Limited	Niggardly
Sparing	Skimpy	Scanty
Insufficient		

Examples:

Apples are a scarce commodity in summer.
The supply of food grain is extremely limited. Hence their price rises very high.
He belongs to rich family, yet the housewife is niggardly to their guests and visitors.
There is hardly a sparing capacity in our workshop these days.
The dancers wore skimpy dresses.

Polished (Adjective)

His polished speech failed to convince the people.

Synonyms:

Accomplished	Adept	Faultless
Fine	Impeccable	Skilful
Bright	Gleaming	Glossy
Cultivated	Finished	Polite
Sophisticated	Refined	Shining
Elegant	Perfect	Pleasant

Examples:

He is very adept in repairing computer.
Their team work was faultless.
These fine clothes are imported from China.
His editing skill is impeccable and perfect.
Tomorrow's weather will be bright and shining.
His voice was pleasant and cultivated.
It won't be finished for another hour.

Antonyms:

Amateurish	Inept	Inexpert
Dark	Dull	Matt
Rough	Uncivilized	Uncultivated
Unrefined	Crude	Unskilled
Unpolished		

Examples:

The police described the burglary as crude and amateurish.

It is too dark to play outside.

I have never heard anyone so inept at making speeches.

The output of the product has reduced due to inexpert and unskilled worker in the factory.
Will this paint give a glosser a matt finish?
The rough surface of the mirror produces vague image.

Polite (Adjective)

Just a polite remark is enough to correct his mannerism.

Synonyms:

Elegant	Polished	Urbane
Genteel	Gallant	Courtly
Courteous	Civil	Complaisance
Chivalrous	Cultivated	

Examples:
The table was covered with an elegant lace cloth.
My aunt Mary was the most genteel woman I ever knew.
The old man was esteemed for his courtly manners.
They wrote us a courteous thank you note.
Martin Luther king devoted his life to civil rights.
The boss's complaisant manners made every one feel at home.
Chivalrous men usually treat women with respect.
She cultivated her mind by reading many books.

Antonyms:

Awkward	Bluff	Untaught
Unpolished	Uncouth	Brusque
Ill-bred	Clownish	Raw
Insolent	Insulting	Discourteous

Examples:
He asked many awkward questions to my boss which in fact put me to shame.
His claim of getting high position in the Government Service proved a bluff.
He was nice to look at but when it came to speech his untaught mannerism came into focus.
His jokes are rather crude and unpolished.
His education has not lifted him from uncouth mannerism.
His advice was sound but it was rather brusque.
He played the role of an ill-bred rustic in the new play.
His clownish behavior at the office party cost him his job.
His is too raw for a show boy job in this emporium.
Very often our servant becomes to insolent. I wish to terminate his services.

Poor (Adjective)

The poor little puppy had been abandoned.

Synonyms:

Hard up	Destitute	Meager
Unfortunate	Inferior	Under-privileged
Ordinary		

Examples:

The depression brought down his income and made him feel hard up.
The government has chalked out many schemes for the betterment of the under-privileged.
Majority of the village folk in India live below the ordinary standard.

Antonyms:

Rich	Privilege	Excellent
Fortunate	Happy	
Extraordinary		

Examples:

In India the rich have becomes richer and the poor become poorer since independence.
Mohan is a rich man. He belongs to the privileged class.
By topping in the University, Sohan has given evidence of an extraordinary brainy chap.

Possess (Verb)

What possessed you to do that?

Synonyms:

Have	Command	Seize
Own	Hold	Obtain
Enjoy		

Examples:

We have a small garden which meets all our needs of fruits and vegetables.
I command complete authority over the workers of this factory.
He seized my bag and ran off with it.
Do you own this beautiful tennis racket?
Where from did you obtain your tennis racket?
We shall enjoy the dinner after the variety show.
The girl was holding her father's hand.

Antonyms:

Want	Forfeit	Lose
Need	Dispose	Relinquish

Examples:
We want at least a two-room flat for residence.
If you do not attend the function, you will forfeit the right to a special gift.
I need all your blessings for the success of my new venture.
The government disposes the owners of a property useful for public purpose.
The manager has relinquished his charge in favor of the new incumbent.

Possible (Adjective)

Are you insured against all possible risks?

Synonyms:

Likely	Potential	Conceivable
Practicable	Feasible	

Examples:
An accident is likely to happen at this intersection anytime due to its defective signal system.
Always watch out against any possibly potential dangers.
There is no conceivable way to raise ten thousand rupees immediately.
It is not feasible to make the trip to Kanpur from Delhi and back in one day.
The Secretary was unable to suggest any practicable solution to the problem.

Antonyms:

Impossible	Incredible	Unfeasible
Impracticable	Unachievable	Inconceivable

Examples:
The word impossible did not find a place in the dictionary of Napoleon.
This scheme is absolutely impracticable in the present circumstances.
Some of the targets laid in the seventh plan seen unachievable unless law and order position greatly improves.
The possibility of a no-war pact with Pakistan is inconceivable so long as Pakistan continues to plan an atomic bomb.

Praise (Verb)

Our guests praised the meals as the best they had had for years.

Synonyms:

Acclaim	Flattery	Plaudits
Laudation	Approval	Cheers
Cheering	Compliment	Applause
Approbation		

Examples:
The Football team was highly acclaimed on return for winning the championship.
It is not necessary to indulge in flattery to win friends.
I will not give my approval to any proposal in which my role is not clearly delineated.

Players won the plaudits of the critics.
Children cheered when the teacher announced the holding of the prize distribution ceremony.
Mrs. Indira Gandhi was greeted by large cheering mobs in the USSR.
He was complemented for establishing new records in swimming.
The audience applauded Lata's song. There was loud applause.

Antonyms:

Abuse	Vituperation	Slander
Scorn	Repudiation	Obloquy
Reproof	Hissing	Disparagement
Contempt	Blame	Condemnation
Slander-mongering		

Examples:
The master abused his servant for shopping wrong articles.
The meeting of the political parties was marked by personal vituperation and slander-mongering.
The members scorned each other and indulged in attacking their mutual repudiation and in obloquy.
Some members were seen in disparaging contempt for their opponents indulged in hissing sounds.

Precarious (Adjective)

You will make only a precarious living as an author.

Synonyms:

Doubtful	Dubious	Hairy
Hazardous	Insecure	Perilous
Risky	Shaky	Slippery
Touch and go	Tricky	Uncertain
Unreliable	Unsafe	Unstably

Examples:
I feel doubtful about whether to go or not.
I remain dubious about her motives.
Driving on icy roads can be pretty hairy.
The government has prohibited the import of hazardous chemical.
She feels very insecure about her marriage.
It is very risky to drive without driving license.
Her hands are shaky because, she is nervous.

Antonyms:

Certain	Dependable	Reliable
Safe	Secure	Stable
Steady		

Examples:
One thing is certain that I am not coming.
My memory is not reliable these days due to prolong illness.
Will the car be safe outside?
She was happy and secure to know that her family loved & respected her.
The patient's condition is stable out of danger.

Predominant (Adjective)

This is a forest in which oak-trees are predominant.
Synonyms:

Main	Chief	Important
Leading	Paramount	Prominent
Superior	Dominant	Ruling
Prevalent		

Examples:
My main concern is the welfare of these children.
The most prominent building in the Janpath is the Rastrapati Bhawan.
Shahrukh enjoys a superior position in his office.
India has become a dominant power of Asia and Far East.
The ruling class everywhere exploits the poor masses.
Superstition is still prevalent in some communities of Rajasthan.

Antonyms:

Minor	Inferior	Unimportant
Junior	Petty	Subsidiary
Subordinate		

Examples:
There were numerous major and minor issues raised in the meeting of the shareholders of the company.
This pen is much inferior to the one I bought last time.
This subject is too important to occur to the examiners.
He is junior partner in my business firm.
Asha is a petty officer in the bank.
This bank is a subsidiary of the State Bank of India.
There are quite a few officers and many subordinates in this firm.

Predicament (Noun)

His efforts to help his friends landed him only in an awkward predicament.
Synonyms:

Plight	Puzzle	Strait
Fix	Difficulty	Jam
Perplexity		

Examples:

Madhu lost her purse during the journey and was in bad plight.
The Straight of Gibraltar lies between the Mediterranean Sea and the Atlantic Ocean.
After losing all his money Deepak was in a great fix.
He has won the first prize for solving a puzzle.
I am in a jam due to financial shortage.
He found himself in perplexity when he reached the cross road.
His one difficulty in getting a house is getting a house on reasonable rent in a good locality.
He was in a fix owing inability to help his close friend at the right moment.

Antonyms:

Assurance	Self-satisfaction	Rest
Decision	Ease	Comfort
Calmness		

Examples:

I can hand over the tape-recorded to him for repairs on your assurance.
He is working hard these days for self-satisfaction and for the satisfaction of his loss.
The doctor has set at rest my doubt about the disease.
Your decision in this matter is as good as mine.
We can solve this problem with ease.
My uncle lives in great comfort at this old age, thanks to his savings!
Mahatma Gandhi was a picture of calmness at the most difficult situation.

Prediction (Noun)

Your prediction of her success in this exams may prove wrong.

Synonyms:

Announcement	Prophecy	Forecast
Augury	Foreboding	Warning
Fortune-telling	Foresight	Divination

Examples:

The announcement of the Indian Civil Services Examination was published quite late this year.
Many prophecies about the future of mankind are mentioned in the Bible.
Leading newspapers publish the next day's weather forecast daily.
The rainbow was an augury of clear weather.
She had a sense of foreboding that the plain would crash.
The boss has issued him a warning for coming late to office so often,
In India you can find a good number of persons engaged in fortune – telling.
Mrs. Indira Gandhi was one of the few world leaders with keen foresight.
The divination of Swami Vivekananda came to limelight after his visit to America in 1893.

Antonyms:

Mystery	Secrecy	Hiding
Occult	Concealment	

Examples:
The fate of the deposed Iraqi President was kept a mystery by the Americans.
The secrecy of the defence establishment was violated by a military officer. He was, therefore, sacked.
The accused remained in hiding for a few months but was then caught.
The occult view of the dacoit helped the police to nab him.
The underground leader was in due course recovered from concealment.

Prejudice (Noun)

Listen to this new poem without any prejudice.

Synonyms:

Unfairness	Presumption	Preconception
Bias	Partiality	

Examples:
Although the step-daughter was so much neglected, she never complained against the unfairness of her parents.
Your presumption that he will return your loan will prove wrong.
The partiality of the reference helped the guest team to win the match.
Europeans had a pre-conception that India was a country of snake – charmers.
A Judge should be completely without bias.

Antonyms:

Certainty	Reasoning	Conviction
Demonstration	Evidence	Proof
Reason		

Examples:
There is no certainty of good rains this year.
The finance Minister has changed the financial policy of the government with enough reasoning and conviction.
The workers held a demonstration outside the gates of the factory to demand increase in wages.
The court has sought more evidence against the accused before admitting the prima-facie case.
There is no proof that he stole the pen.
There is no reason for us to worry about this affair.

Premature (Adjective)

Taking more sweets will result in premature decay of your teeth.

Synonyms:

Rash	Unreasonable	Previous
Early	Precipitate	Untimely
Unjustified		

Examples:

It was rash of John to stand on the pond when the ice was too thin.
Their demand for hike in wages is unreasonable and unjustified.
Their previous visit to the Taj had been highly pleasant.
He leaves for work early in the morning.
Fall of shower in so early a summer is untimely.
The oppressive measures adopted by the Government helped to precipitate the liberation movement.

Antonyms:

Reasonable	Overdue	Late
Slow		

Examples:

It we put a reasonable price for this product we can go fast on sales.
The balance payment from his buyer is long overdue. Please remind him in strong language.
Because of the cold weather the crops are late this year.
She was not slow to realize what was happening.

Preserve (Verb)

These social activities will preserve old people from the loneliness of old age.

Synonyms:

Care for	Conserve	Defend
Guard	Keep	Save
Secure	Shield	Continue
Retain	Sustain	Conserve
Maintain	Protect	

Examples:

Pankaj did not think she cared for him anymore.
Conserve your strength for coming world matches.
When the dog attached me, I define myself with a stick.
The watch man guarded our houses at night.
The notice said, keep off the grass.
It was too late for the doctors to save her and she died that night.
Secure all the doors and windows before leaving.
The ozone layer shields the earth against harmful radiation.

Antonyms:

Assail	Assault	Attack
Leave unprotected	Abandon	Discontinue
Drop	End	Give up
Consume	Spend	Squander
Waste		

Examples:
A feeling of panic assailed him.
He got two years imprisonment for assaulting a police officer.
A woman was attacked and robbed by a gang of youth.
They abandoned their land and property to the invading force.
The fire quickly consumed the wooden hut.
I spend lot of money to decorate my new house.

Pretend (Verb)

They pretended not to see us.

Synonyms:

Fabricate	Make-believe	Sham
Feign	Simulate	Profess
Allege	Counterfeit	

Examples:
He fabricated a good excuse for absenting from the class.
We have taught our dog to lie down and sham being dead.
The boy feigned headache to escape school attendance
He alleged that the clerk had sought bribe for doing the job.
He professed to be an expert of labour laws.
He was arrested for supplying counterfeit currency.

Antonyms:

Verify	Substantiate	Establish
Authentic		

Examples:
I have verified the facts of the statement by comparing them with official statistics.
We can substantiate our claim by facts, figures and documents.
It was with due evidence that we established our claim to the official premises.
Here is an authenticated copy of his statement supporting our claim.

Prevent (Verb)

Who can prevent us from getting married?

Synonyms:

Anticipate	Avert	Avoid

Balk	Bar	Block
Check	Foil	Frustrate
Hamper	Hinder	Obviate
Preclude	Restrain	Stave off
Thwart	Ward off	Stop

Examples:
We anticipated their complaint by writing a full report ourselves.
I tried to avert my thoughts from the subject.
I just avoided running over the cat.
His parents balked at the cost of the guitar he wanted.
Poverty bars the way to progress.
You must check the flow of blood from a wound.
Progress has been hindered by financial difficulties.

Antonyms:

Allow	Encourage	Help
Incite	Permit	Support
Urge		

Examples:
My boss doesn't allow me to use the telephone for private calls.
Her parents always encourage her in her studies.
Please help me up the stairs with this heavy trunk.
He was accused of inciting his manager to hold a driving licence.
She is below the permitted age to hold a driving licence.
The American public stopped supporting the war in Iraq.
He urged me to reconsider my decision.

Primary (Adjective)

More than five hundred students are studying in this primary school.

Synonyms:

Best	Capital	Cardinal
Chief	Dominant	Elementary
First	Greatest	Highest
Leading	Main	Paramount
Prime	Principal	Top
Essential	Radical	

Examples:
The best thing about the party was the food.
Smoking is one of the chief causes of lung cancer.
The caste stands in a dominant position above the town.
The questions were so elementary that he easily passed the test.

She won first prize in the competition.
Mount Everest is the highest peak of the world.
Oxygen is essential for every living being.

Antonyms:

Inferior	Lesser	Lowest
Subordinate	Supplementary	Unimportant
Ensuring	Following	Later
Secondary	Subsequent	Succeeding

Examples:
The new term of employment may be inferior to those they previously enjoyed.
He is stubborn, and so is she but to a lesser degree.
The reservoir was very low after the long drought.
He is in a subordinate position to the head of the department.
His first and subsequent visits were kept secret.

Privilege (Noun)

Do not grant anyone the privilege of fishing in this trout stream.

Synonyms:

Favour	Charter	Grant
Licence	Immunity	Exemption
Right	Prerogative	

Examples:
He is always ready to do anyone a favour.
The government helped small fishing villages with grant for building hardboards for their boats.
He has already obtained a licence from the government for setting up a small scale industry in the industrial estate.
The charter of demands given by our union will be considered by the cabinet today.
Penicillin grants immunity against several diseases.
Income from National Saving Certificates is exempted from taxation.
The right to speak has been guaranteed under the constitution of India.
The princely states enjoyed several prerogatives under the patronage of British rule in India.

Antonyms:

| Inhibition | Veto | Prohibition, |
| Department | | |

Examples:
The modern society has given up many old social inhibitions that stood in the way of healthy growth of young persons.
UN has no real power of military action against warring states as any on the five permanent members – US, UK, USSR, France and China can veto such action.

The Parliament of India has so far never issued any intermittent on the taking of alcoholic drink, though some of the states have enforced prohibition now and then.

Prohibit (Verb)

Children are prohibited from buying cigarettes.

Synonyms:

Ban	Prevent	Preclude
Inhibit	Hinder Disallow	
Debar	Forbid	Interdict

Examples:
Smoking is in all public places banned in India.
Mother fastens a strap round the baby to prevent him from climbing out of his pram.
Ill-health has precluded him from the list of the competition.
Doctor has inhibited him from taking tea.
Our bus was hindered by a large herd of cows on the road.
Forbid him to bathe in the river till he can swim.
He can't take the examination because the University has barred him for two years.
His statement was interdicted by his own colleagues.
The teacher disallowed him to attend the class as he came very late.

Antonyms:

Authorize	Consent to	Direct
Suffer	Tolerate	Warrant
Order	Permit	Give consent
Enjoin	Employee	Command
Allow		

Examples:
The authorized capital of this company is $ 2 million.
The father of the boy did not consent to the matrimonial offer of the girl's father.
I have established direct contact with the client to avoid any mid-between agents.
The firm has suffered heavy losses due to the uncertain law and order conditions in the state.
I have tolerated his behavior so far but will not do any longer.
The judge issued warrants of arrest of the accused who was continuously absent from the court.
The department ordered the suspension of the absenting employee.

Prolong (Verb)

Only after prolonged questioning, the culprits admitted their role in this crime.

Synonyms:

Lengthen	Continue	Protract

Extend	Stretch	Sustain
Quicken	Accelerate	

Examples:
The days are starting to lengthen again.
In spite of difficulties, he is determined to continue his studies.
He got a positive reply for recovery of money after protracted correspondence spread over two years.
The garden was extended to include a little stream that ran beside it.
Mary's new gloves had to be stretched before she could put them on.
Their courage was sustained by the cheerfulness of the younger members of the party.
The car driver had to accelerate before coming up the hill.
Adoption of modern technology will quicken the space of our progress.

Antonyms:

Contain	Lessen	Shorten
Diminish	Abridge	Decrease
Contract	Abbreviate	Delay

Examples:
This utensil can contain about one litre of milk.
You will have to lessen the quantity to make use to this can.
Your uniform is too loose. Why not shorten it yourself?
We will have to diminish the use of sugar if you want to avail only the rationed amount.
This book is good but too long. Why don't you abridge it and reduce the price.
The value of the rupee has decreased in the domestic marked by 44% in one year.
The metals contract in winter and expand in the summer.
Your ideas need to be abbreviated to make them pleasant reading.

Prominent (Adjective)

The rose-garden is the most prominent feature in this landscape.

Synonyms:

Conspicuous	Distinctive	Marked
Celebrated	Distinguished	Leading
Eminent	Notable	Principal

Examples:
The Eiffel Tower in Paris when viewed from an aero plane is conspicuous for its beauty for miles and miles.
Mutual respect is a distinctive feature of our foreign policy.
Amitabh Bachchan is a celebrated actor.
She is a woman of marked intelligence.
Jagdish Chandra Bose has done notable work in the field of Botany.

Harbinger is an eminent professor of English language.
He has distinguished himself as an artist also.
The Hindustan Times is a leading daily newspaper in India.
He is the Principal of a very large institution.

Antonyms:

Inconspicuous	Minor	Union
Unimportant	Petty	

Examples:
I am an inconspicuous guy in this small firm.
I play a minor role in the production department.
Here comes the junior partner of our firm. He is the son of the proprietor.
No one of us is considered unimportant so long as we do our respective duties honestly.
The salaries paid to us may be petty cash very month, but we get best regard and love of our boss every moment of our working.

Promote (Verb)

He was promoted to the rank of sergeant.

Synonyms:

Advance	Help	Push
Urge on	Raise	Further
Exhort	Assist	Excite
Elevate	Foment	Advocate
Encourage	Foster	

Examples:
Property values contribute to advance rapidly.
It helps the government in the promotion of new schemes of development.
We always have to push our son to do his homework.
It urges on the people to lay emphasis on better contribution to national causes.
It raises issues in the public mind for assimilation of healthy ideas.
It furthers the cause of the common man.
It exhorts business houses to take up faster production processes.
Mother urged Raja to go to the dentist.

Antonyms:

Allay	Hinder	Retard
Prolong	Discourage	Divert
Degrade		

Examples:
We should allay the fears of the public on good activities of the government.
Some people tend to hinder the progress of development projects by unhealthy criticism.

Vested interests retard productive activities in the country of their selfish motives. When people at large fall in their trap, they prolong the production processes of the nation, discourage the workers by aggressive policies, divert resources to anti-national activities and degrade popular ideologies.

Protect (Verb)

This room is well protected against cold weather.

Synonyms:

Save	Covered	Event
Guard	Harbour	Shelter
Shield		

Examples:

The government must equip itself militarily to save the country from foreign attack.
In winter I cover my head with a cap and in summer with a solar hat.
The girls in the country should be taught to defend their honour in emergency.
Our armed forces guard our borders from foreign infiltrations.
Let us harbour goodwill among different communities.
House gives us shelter from heat and cold.

Antonyms:

Expose	Betray	Assail
Assault	Expose to danger	Endanger
Threaten	Attack	

Plunder

Examples:

Pakistani nuclear equipments expose India to a danger of destruction.
U.S. has betrayed India by providing defence and offensive equipments to Pakistan.
There is a constant danger of attack on India from Pakistan.
The dacoits plundered the village and ran away with booty.

Prove (Verb)

I shall prove to you that the witness is quite unreliable.

Synonyms:

Attest	Justify	Verify
Demonstrate	Establish	Show
Confirm		

Examples:

His concern for the famine victims is an attested fact.
Marxists believe that ends justify the means.
His bonafides were got verified by the police before he was granted the gun licence.
He failed to establish the truth of the facts mentioned in his statement before the

judge.
He was required to show his identity card at the gate of the office.
I have asked him to confirm the date of his arrival in New Delhi.
The lawyer demonstrated how the witness was lying.

Antonyms:

| Refuse | Negative | Deny |
| Refute | Disprove | |

Examples:
I have refused to part with my books at any cost.
There is always a negative side to any issue in any matter.
I have never denied that my knowledge is limited.
He may refute his earlier statement but he cannot disprove it.

Provide (Verb)

He has a large family to provide for.

Synonyms:

Supply	Prepare	Furnish
Get	Arrange	Care
Procure	Purvey	Cater

Examples:
It is statutory duty of the municipal corporation to supply drinking water.
They are preparing themselves to launch a new project in the village.
The court has directed the police to furnish full details of the case.
Do you have time to get the house white-washed?
The secretary tries to cater to the Minister's every wish.
Father has at last procured the kind of television set he wants.
Our firm purveys frozen and dried meat in the Army.

Antonyms:

| Consume | Spend | Dissipate |
| Exhaust | Use | |

Examples:
We consume 200 watts of electric power every month.
I spend 20% of my salary on rent.
A lot of money gets dissipated on items whose prices have raised rocket high.
My budget gets exhausted on the 25th day of the month.
I am left with nothing for use during the late five days.

Prudent (Adjective)

We are blessed with a prudent house keeper.

Synonyms:

Canny	Careful	Cautions
Circumspect	Discerning	Discreet
Judicious	Politic	Sagacious
Sage	Shrewd	Vigilant
Wary		

Examples:

Be careful about what you say to him.
You should be cautions about spending money when you are away from your home.
We must be extremely discreet. My father suspects something.
When the fight began, he thought it is politic to leave.
Amitabh is a shrewd businessman. He never trusts anybody.

Antonyms:

Careless	Heedless	Imprudent
Inconsiderate	Indiscreet	Irrational
Rash	Thoughtless	Unwise
Extravagant	Wasteful	

Examples:

Deepak is very careless in his studies.
It is not good to be heedless when your teacher teaches you.
The child sitting in next bench is very imprudent.
One indiscreet remark could rich the whole plan.
She is rather extravagant when it comes to buying perfumes.
You shouldn't make rash promises.

Publish (Verb)

Today News Paper has published news about our achievement.

Synonyms:

Proclaim	Disclose	Disseminate
Advertise	Declare	Divulge
Promulgate	Broadcast	Announce.

Examples:

India proclaimed itself a Republic on 26th January 1950.
The old lady would not disclose to anyone how she made her cherry jam.
Television and radio disseminate ideas and information.
Only big companies can afford to advertise their products through television.
The government will declare its new export policy very soon.
Amarnath would not divulge what he has been told.
President of Pakistan has promulgated a new constitution for his country.
The Princes announced her engagement.

The special election broadcast will be on the local station at eight tonight.

Antonyms:

Suppress	Extinguish	Smother
Repress	Conceal	Check
Cloak	Stifle	Restrain

Examples:

It is wise for the government to sometimes suppress inflammatory news and views.
Men from five fire brigades came and extinguished the fire in our locality.
The fire left behind smothered debris.
The dictatorial governments always try to repress the people's feelings of freedom and liberty.
The earthquake left lot of broken bricks and debris with dead humans concealed underneath.

Punish (Verb)

How would you punish somebody for stealing money?

Synonyms:

Afflict	Chasten	Subdue
Humble	Chastise	Correct
Discipline	Castigate	

Examples:

Poverty and unemployment still afflict the youth in India.
An unemployed youth was greatly chastened by his failure.
The police used tear gas to subdue the rioters.
The king's forces were humbled by the peasant revolt.
His father chastised Vicky for not attending the schools regularly.
Being one of his close friends, you should correct him whenever he goes wrong.
The teacher disciplined her students by holding them for one hour after the school time.
The accountant was castigated by his boss for his frequent absence from office.

Antonyms:

Recompense	Indemnify	Reward
Repay	Compensate	Remunerate

Examples:

The office recompensed me for my touring expenses.
I filled the indemnity bond to take an advance from the bank.
The principal rewarded the boy for saving his colleague from drowning.
If you lend me $ 500, I'll repay it to you tomorrow.
I will compensate you for interest in due course.
What remuneration do you seek for this job?

Purpose (Noun)

For what purpose do you want to go to Canada?

Synonyms:

Aim	Object	Plan
Intention	End	Meaning
Resolve	Intent	

Examples:

Character building should be the aim of education.
What was steno's object in leaving so early?
Does he plan to stay with us tonight?
Their intention is to make the area a public part.
All is well that ends well.
Since his wife died, his life has had no meaning.
He was charged with intent to kill his boss.
John resolved to work hard so as to win a prize.

Antonyms:

Vague	Meaningless	Aimless
Unplanned		

Examples:

Ram has to build a mission of life. His actions are therefore, generally vague.
The play of the evening showed aimlessness of the theme and unplanned direction of the story.
To me life is meaningless without art and recreation.

Push (Verb)

Please push the table near to the wall.

Synonyms:

Press	Thrust	Shove
Jostle	Urge	Drive
Propel	Impel	

Examples:

His parents are pressing him hard to get married.
Harish thrust his hand into a hole in a tree to find out how deep it was.
When you are standing in a queue, don't shove.
Mother urged Mohan to go to the dentist.
Our troops drove away the enemy.
My invalid uncle can propel his wheel chair by its handles.
Wild animals and birds are often impelled by hunger to come near the human beings.
The audience jostled each other as they entered the hall as the entry gate was rather narrow.

Antonyms:

Pull	Haul	Drag
Tow	Draw	Trail
Jerk	Deter	Tug

Examples:
The horse pulled the Tonga with ease.
The police hauled the smuggler with their drugs at the railway station.
If you park you car here the police might tow it away.
Our school played a tug of war game yesterday.

Put Up (Verb)

Are you going to put up for John again?

Synonyms:

Accommodate	Construct	Erect
Entertain	Present	Raise
Float	Nominate	Propose
Put forward	Recommended	Instigate
Prompt	Endure	

Examples:
The hotel can accommodate up to 500 guests.
Delhi government has constructed many fly-overs.
They are planning to demolish the house next door and erect a block of flats in its place.
Could you entertain the children for an hour while I make supper?
He endured three years in prison for his religious beliefs.
The police have instigated an official enquiry in to the incident.

Antonyms:

Demolish	Destroy	Flatten
Knockdown	Level	Pull down
Raze	Object to	Oppose
Protest	Stand against	Reject

Examples:
The earthquake demolished many buildings in the city.
They have destroyed all the evidences.
Several buildings had been flattened in the blast.
The old houses are going to be knocked down.
The ground should be levelled before you plant flowers.
During the war all the villagers were razed to the ground.

Qualified (Adjective)

He is qualified for this job.

Synonyms:

Able	Accomplished	Adept
Competent	Efficient	Eligible
Equipped	Experienced	Expert
Proficient	Skilful	Talented

Examples:

I have never been able to understand such complicated things.
Madhu is an accomplished dancer. She dances very well.
This garage provides very good service. It has many adept mechanics.
She is not competent to look after young children.
He revealed himself to be surprisingly practical and efficient.
If you have finished your graduation you are eligible to appear for UPSC exam.

Antonyms:

Amateur	Apprentice	Self-styled
Trainee	Uncertified	Unqualified
Untrained	Outright	Unconditional
Unequivocal		

Examples:

He is an amateur football player.
There are many apprentice workers recruited in the factory.
I feel unqualified to speak on the subject.
To the untrained eye, the picture is simply a mass of colored dots.
Her answer was an unequivocal no.

Quantity (Noun)

I prefer quality to quantity.

Synonyms:

Measure	Amount	Bulk
Number	Sum-total	Volume
Aggregate		

Examples:

The government is introducing new measures against tax fraud.
Government has to spend large amount on armaments.
The old man left bulk of his estate to his wife.
The number of students appearing in the Indian Civil Services may exceed our estimate this year.
What is the volume of water in the tank?

The aggregate to his marks in all the papers exceeds five hundred.
He was astonished to know the sum total of the value of his estate.

Antonyms:

Shortage	Deficiency	Insufficiency
Deficit		

Examples:
There is no shortage of food grains in India now. Thanks to better seeds, better irrigation facilities and tractors!
You can remove the deficiency of blood in your body by better diet and some regular exercise.
Insufficiency of electric supply stands in the way of quicker industrialization in India.
This year's budget is again a deficit budget, the deficit to be made up by larger borrowing and public deposits.

Quality (Noun)

I prefer quality to quantity.

Synonyms:

Excellence	Property	Brand
Nature	Trait	Characteristic
Attribute		

Examples:
She deserves praise for her excellence in sports.
The chemical properties of gases help us to distinguish one gas from another.
Which brands of tea do you prefer?
John has a very kind and friendly nature.
Boldness and resolution are two of the traits of a good leader.
Hot summers and heavy rains are the characteristics of this place.
Generosity is one of his many fine attributes.

Antonyms:

Ordinary	Flat	Commonplace
Colourless		

Examples:
A man of ordinary intelligence, Rupesh owes his success to hard work and determination.
This valley has a sizable flat surface for agricultural development.
As a democrat, I believe in commonplace ways of living. I rather despise luxuries.
Although a rich man, he is rather colourless in social behaviour.

Quarrel (Noun)

His is always having quarrels with somebody about something.

Synonyms:

Wrangle	Fray	Contest
Enmity	Fight	Riot
Row	Strife	Controversy
Brawl		

Examples:

Deepak wrangles with his colleagues on trivial issues.
During riots many people jump into fray for no good reason.
There was a great contest between them for the election.
They have no enmity for each other now.
She was given a tough flight by her opponents on the tennis court.
Government had to call the military to control the riots.
The history of strife has left its marks on the tiny nation.
There is some new controversy over the ownership of this piece of land.
Most cowboy movies include a scene of a bar room brawl.

Antonyms:

Agreement	Assent	Consent
Acquiesces	Harmony	Friendship
Peace	Amity	Equanimity
Concord		

Examples:

India and Pakistan are trying to reach an agreement on trade and cultural relations.
The President has put his assent on the 46th amendment of The Constitution of India.
The subordinate acquiesced to the wishes of his boss on the question of transfer from the headquarters.
There is now perfect harmony among Hindus and Sikhs in the Punjab, Haryana and Delhi.
India's friendship with the USSR is beyond any controversy.
The non – aligned movement is responsible for a new desire for peace among nations round the world.

Queer (Adjective)

His queer way of talking attracted all of us.

Synonyms:

Eccentric	Abnormal	Strange
Odd	Curious	Peculiar
Extraordinary	Unusual	Singular
Fantastic		

Examples:

The old lady is becoming very eccentric. She loses temper on minor issues.

He would be an abnormal boy if he did not want to run about and play at this carefree age.

It feels strange to be visiting the place again after all these years.

The Giraffe is an odd-looking animal.

She had a curious way of expressing herself.

The tribes have peculiar customs of marriage.

It seems quite extraordinary that the Prime Minister can claim these figures as a triumph.

A singular glow came from the unidentified flying object.

Rains in January are unusual in northern India.

The story of "Sindbad, the Sailor" is a fantastic one.

Antonyms:

Ordinary	Habitual	Everyday
Normal	Common	Usual
Commonplace		

Examples:

Deepak has ordinary average habits. But he has a sterling character.

Danny is a habitual drunkard.

He drinks alcohol every day.

Joseph has a normal habit of going for walk every morning.

Morning walk is a common feature among both the old and the young in our locality.

Question (Noun)

They questioned the Conservative candidate on his views.

Synonyms:

Doubt	Query	Investigation
Interrogation	Inquiry	Inquisition

Examples:

The latest scientific discoveries cast doubt on earlier theories.

The science teacher put a query to Vicky to check out weather he had been paying attention to his lecture.

Scientists are now investigating ways of producing more and more food over the world.

The police have found some new clues after interrogation of the person's detainment in this case.

He has finished his inquisition in this case and submitted his report.

A commission of inquiry has been set up to probe into the cause of Kanishka air crash in which 239 lives were lost.

Antonyms:

| Reply | Answer | Rejoinder |
| Respond | Rejoin | Response |

Examples:
I have yet to reply to the queries of the income tax authorities.
The answer he gave was quite surprising.
His advocate is preparing a rejoinder for submission to the court in response to a charge of the complainant.
The government has not yet responded to my appeal for assistance under the new scheme.
I have decided to rejoin the college for higher studies.
I received an encouraging response to my letter.

Quick (Adjective)

The flashes of lightings came in quick succession.

Synonyms:

Active	Sudden	Deft
Alive	Agile	Alert
Fast	Rapid	Swift
Perceptible		

Examples:
It is advisable not to drive too fast on a crowded road.
India has made a rapid progress in agricultural development during the last decade.
He was swift to condemn the terrorist violence.
The governor is trying to precipitate the solution of the Assam problem after having settled the Punjab controversy.

Antonyms:

Listless	Slow	Inexpert
Calm	Patient	Lazy
Sluggish	Calm	Calculated

Examples:
Russell has become listless in his studies and sports since his last sickness.
I always prefer to driver slow in the crowded streets of the city.
The efforts of the government in solving national problems should be calm and calculated.
Everyone dislikes his sluggish behaviour.

Quicken (Verb)

The child quicken in the womb.

Synonyms:

Hasten	Urge	Speed
Make-haste	Further	Drive
Advance	Accelerate	Expedite
Dispatch		

Examples:
She hastened to put the teapot out of the boy's reach.
The mother urged Mohan to go to the dentist.
The speed of an aero plane is much greater than that of a car.
His support furthered my career.
Our troops drove away the enemy.
They have advanced their programme for Delhi by one week.
The car driver had to accelerate before climbing the hill.
Using postal code number always expedites the delivery of your mail.
American warships have been dispatched to the areas.

Antonyms:

Check	Obstruct	Retard
Drag	Hinder	Impede
Delay		

Examples:
Will you please check the mistakes in this paragraph?
The opposition party is meant to obstruct the taking of rash decisions by the ruling party.
Sometimes it retards the progress of health and constructive decisions.
The discussion on a controversial issue may drag on for hours in the Parliament without any decision.
It is under such circumstances that the work of the state gets hindered by the opposition parties.
This impedes the speed of work done by the departments at various levels. Hence government work is said to be delayed.

Quiet (Adjective)

In the quiet of the night, the stillness is audible.

Synonyms:

Repose	Stillness	Compose
Lull	Modify	Calm
Soothe	Still	Allay
Appease	Hush	Calmness
Quietude	Rest	

Examples:

The baby is in repose when he is asleep.
She remained composed even during the loud thunder and lighting.
There was a lull before the thunderstorm.
The angry man was mollified when Tom expressed he was sorry for bumping into him.
Baby cried when he was taken out of his bath, but mother soothed him with delicate powder.
The doctor was able to allay the mother's anxiety.
His hunger was soon appeased.

Antonyms:

Excitement	Tumult	Commotion
Turmoil	Exasperate	Disturb
Aggravate	Disquiet	Enhance

Examples:

Scenes of love and violence provide excitement to the viewers.
The news of the lottery in favour of Jim to the value of $ One million caused a great tumult in his family.
The little controversy on an academic subject led to a commotion in the college.
The news of the war caused turmoil round the whole world.
The failure of his son very much exasperated the old mind but he did not express adversely to the young boy.

Race (Noun)

The future world will be full of only fixed races

Synonyms:

Tribe	Blood	Bread
Clan	Progeny	People
Family	Caste	Nation
Ethnic group		

Examples:

Each tribe has some customs which are observed by its members compulsorily.
Politicians generally believe that the people have a short memory.
Now a day the government is laying great emphasis on family welfare schemes.
The caste system was a very rigid in India until independence.
A period of hundred years is not a long period in the history of a nation.
In India all ethnic groups enjoy constitutional rights to maintain their identity.

Antonyms:

Unit	Individual	Humanity
Mankind	Generation	Global
Brotherhood		

Examples:

All tribes of this region have formed a common unit.

There has to be a reasonable reconciliation between the interests of the individual vis-à-vis his society.

Disarmament is necessary for saving the humanity from atomic warfare.

Mankind cannot enjoy permanent peace unless the nations join together to form a World Federation.

Modern generation everywhere is becoming over materialistic.

Unless the feeling of universal brotherhood is inculcated among all people, achievement of global peace is out of question.

Racy (Adjective)

No one likes his racy style of speaking.

Synonyms:

Flavourful	Rich	Spicy
Spirited	Poignant	Lively

Examples:

The tomato soup is so flavourful that it has aroused my appetite.

Banana is rich source of iron and vitamins.

At launch they serve very spicy dishes.

I'm afraid I don't feel very lively today.

Although our team was defeated, it exhibited a very spirited game.

The critic wrote a poignant review of the biography.

Antonyms:

Cold	Vapid	Dull
Flat	State	Prosy
Insipid	Tasteless	Stupid

Examples:

My office being 50 km away from my residence I have to do with only a cold lunch on working day.

The vapid conversation between Deepak and Manoj bored me very much.

The dull atmosphere of my office repels my attendance.

This dish is not only state but also tasteless.

Deepak often tells stupid stories of his colleagues.

The hotel charges flat rate for snacks.
Only state meals are served here at night.
She tells her tones in a rather prosy style.

Radical (Adjective)

What we need is a radical change in this scheme.

Synonyms:

Basic	Complete	Entire
Essential	Native	Extreme
Natural	Primitive	Thorough
Total	Perfect	Positive
Innate		

Examples:

The basic ingredient of this dish is hamburger.
He has a complete set of Bertrand Russell's books.
His entire home was damaged by the rioters.
Air and water are equally essential for the survival of living being.
Political views of the communists looked rather extreme at the time.
Success demands a good idea of natural talent and lot of hard work.
The cave provided a primitive shelter from the storm.
His new policies will bring about a thorough change in the administration.
Mahatma Gandhi believed in total prohibition of alcohol.
She is the perfect choice for the job.
He always had at his command many positive ideas on company's affairs.
An innate flaw doomed the plan from the very start.

Antonyms:

Trial	Tentative	Inadequate
Conservative	Partial	Slight
Superficial		

Examples:

Only a trial will convince you of the utility of this product.
We have made a tentative programme for the meeting on the 11th of next month.
In my opinion the arrangements made for the function are inadequate. There are still many flaws to be removed.
We have nowadays conservative governments in the UK and the USA.
The USA seems partial to Pakistan and prejudiced against India for some reason.
A slight move on your part will help me to get the job.
His contribution to the club is rather superficial. He should have been more considerable and sincere.

Raise (Verb)

We did our best to raise the sunken ship to the surface, but in vain.

Synonyms:

Lift	Hoist	Exalt
Increase	Collect	Grow
Breed	Cultivate	Develop
Nature	Elevate	Uplift

Examples:

The government is trying to lift the common people from below the poverty line.
The Prime Minister hoists the national flag at the Red Fort on August 15 every year.
The nationalized banks are supposed to elevate the poor farmer to a bit higher level of working and giving.
The government has floated a few ambitious projects to uplift the scheduled castes.
Democracy is meant to promote the cause of the people at large.

Antonyms:

Depress	Lower	Decrease
Diminish	Lessen	Reduce
Descend		

Examples:

The scene of floods and the havoc depressed the Prime Minister.
It orders to raise the standard of living of the poor, it is necessary for the richer classes to lower theirs a bit.
The bird killed by Joe with his toy gun descended on the ground with its injured wings.

Rare (Adjective)

It is very rare for her to arrive late to school.

Synonyms:

Curious	Odd	Peculiar
Scarce	Unique	Infrequent
Remarkable	Unusual	Uncommon
Precious	Incomparable	

Examples:

Children are very curious to know everything.
The youth earned pocket money doing odd jobs.
His attitude towards his subordinates is very peculiar.
Qualified workmen were scarce during the war.
Kohinoor is one of the most unique diamonds.

Such cases are relatively infrequent.
Congress party has achieved remarkable success in the recent elections.
Appearance of a Comet is an unusual phenomenon.
A solar eclipse is an uncommon occurrence.
Richard has a good collection of precious stones.
Have you seen the incomparable beauty of the Dal Lake?

Antonyms:

Common	Usual	Frequent
Familiar	Hackneyed	Customary
Trite		

Examples:

The Government of a country is meant to solve the common problems of all the citizens?
The usual price of a good second hand car in India nowadays is Rs.40, 000.
I go to this hotel quite frequently.
I am quite familiar with you boss. I will speak to him for your promotion if you want.
This college has hackneyed methods of teaching instead of the novel methods prevalent in modern colleges elsewhere.
She gave the customary thank to the chairman of the board.
This salary seems a trite in these days of high inflation.

Rash (Adjective)

We do not need a rash young man.

Synonyms:

Hasty	Venturesome	Foolhardy
Indiscretions	Reckless	Precipitate
Incaution		

Examples:

Manu always repents for his hasty decisions.
Deepak has been challenged several times for his reckless driving.
The oppressive measures adopted by the British Government in early 20th century precipitated our freedom movement.
The indiscreet remark could ruin the whole plan.
The truck driver was incautious in driving at the curve. No wonder he ran into a car coming from the opposite direction.
It was foolhardy of him to go swimming alone.

Antonyms:

Careful	Wary	Discreet
Canny	Prudent	Considered
Cautions		

Examples:

I am very careful in my driving at the hilly area.
You should be wary of trusting someone like that.
The court is expected to take discreet judgment on vital matters.
Ravinder is cautions in his business dealings. He checks twice before he signs an agreement.

Rate (Verb)

Do you rate Mr. Raja among your friends?

Synonyms:

| Appraise | Compute | Estimate |
| Reckon | Assess | Price |

Examples:

He computes the interest meticulously and charges every single paisa from his clients who buy things on instalments.
The cost of constructing the house will very likely exceed your estimates.
The tax department always assesses a property on the higher side.
The agent priced the house at the right level for the market.
The secretary has apprised the Minister of the latest developments in this district.
The government may have to reckon with new forces of communalism in the near future.

Antonyms:

| Miscalculate | Underrate | Undervalue |

Examples:

I do not generally miscalculate figures as this leads to basic flaws in the pricing of products.
I do not wish to underrate your talent but I wish I had the necessary outlet for its full utilization.
A good salesman should neither undervalue nor overvalue products to conduct his marketing targets.

Ration (Noun)

Go and draw ration.

Synonyms:

Allotment	Dole	Measure
Provision	Quota	Part
Portion	Share	

Examples:

The allotment of houses will be made after the society gets the approval of the Registrar of Cooperative Societies.

It is likely that the quota of sugar of the ration shops will be doubled soon.
Each part of the body is important for its smooth functioning.
You give this portion of the ticket to the inspector and keep the other.
Some of the members were not satisfied with the number of shares allotted and requested the chairman of the society to give them more.

Antonyms:

Totality	Aggregate	Entirety
Whole	Sum total	

Examples:
The computer can indicate the totality of a number of calculations in a few seconds.
My aggregate marks are 66% although my marks in English are over 75%.
I have described to you the situation of the problem in its entirety.
As member of society we are all part of greater whole.
The sum-total of voter cast by votes in the late elections was 32 crores.

Ready (Adjective)

Are you ready to come with us to cinema?

Synonyms:

Quick	Speedy	Alert
Prepared	Disposed	Willing
Set		

Examples:
She was quick to point out all the mistakes she had committed.
Computer helps speedy disposal of work.
Duties of a fire brigadier can be performed only by an alert person.
The salesman is prepared to visit his client at the time of the latter's convenience.
You are most welcome to join us if you feel so disposed.
I am willing to set apart some money for purchase of shares of your company.

Antonyms:

Unwilling	Slow	Clumsy
Unprepared	Inexperienced	

Examples:
He is an unwilling worker. Let's dismiss him.
Slow and steady wins the race is an old wise saying.
His clumsy look shows he must not be a smart worker.
If you go unprepared for the interview, you may fumble in the midst of discussion.
The new employee may be inexperienced but he is quite shrewd.

Readiness (Noun)

Have everything in readiness to have an early start.

Synonyms:

| Promptitude | Willingness | Eagerness |
| Alacrity | Quickness | |

Examples:
Indira Gandhi was praised by all for her promptitude in introducing the 42 amendment bill.
The boss will assign him a new job only after he has ascertained his willingness.
Rajesh is looking forward to his new job with great eagerness.
His alacrity to overpower the thief surprised us all.
She answered his call for assistance with pleasurable quickness.

Antonyms:

| Unwillingness | Reluctance | Disinclination |
| Aversion | Tardiness | |

Examples:
Your unwillingness to help me at the present moment shows your lack of faith in me.
My reluctance to buy the new soap disappointed the sales girl.
I told her the reason of my disinclination, yet she clung to her salesmanship.
I have an aversion for luxury products which pinch my pocket.

Real (Adjective)

Things that happen in real life are stranger than the things happen in fiction.

Synonyms:

Actual	Demonstrable	Genuine
True	Positive	Developed
Veritable	Essential	Certain

Examples:
His actual income far exceeds the income shown in his tax returns.
She seems genuine, but can I trust her?
This picture depicts the true image of typical Italian Village.
The Anti-Defection bill indicates the positive intention of the Government to curb defection among politicians.
Fundamental rights are the essentials of our democracy.
One thing is certain – I'm not coming here again.
The company has made no demonstrable progress during the crisis-period.
Let's have these pictures developed.

Antonyms:

Conceived	Reported	Visionary
Untrue	Unreal	Imaginary
Fiction	Fanciful	Illusory

Examples:

I have conceived an idea of a story for my next picture, but it will require deep thinking and imagination to give a final shape to the plot.

The newspapers have reported about the extent of black money in this country.

Pundit Jawaharlal was a visionary. His book Discovery of India shows the potentiality of Indian youth.

His basic themes are always true although in developing them he delves into untrue imagination.

Reasoning (Adjective)

He surpasses most of us in power of reasoning.

Synonyms:

Rationale	Thinking	Logic
Analysis	Exposition	Generalization

Examples:

What is the rationale behind this decision?
What is your current thinking on this question?
Science is based on logic and reasoning.
The chemical analysis of the food taken by the deceased has proved that he was poisoned.
The tent far away from the picnickers had to face exposition of heat and rain.
This is not all a true exposition of his views.
His generalization that most of modern youth are corrupt is wrong.

Antonyms:

Illogicality	Stupidity	Nonsensical
Senselessness	Foolish	

Examples:

The illogicality of his arguments sometimes irritates me beyond the point of tolerance.
The actions of the present manager are marked by stupidity of the highest order.
Only God can save him from bankruptcy. His decision of finance is all nonsensical.
Many of the well-wishers of the firm are becoming aware of the senselessness of the manager's dealings and are feeling insecure.
Discussing among themselves, they regard the manager's decisions as foolish.

Rebellion (Noun)

The first rebellion against the dictator moved all of us.

Synonyms:

Sedition	Insurgence	Disobedience
Heresy	Mutiny	Uprising
Insurrection	Revolt	

Examples:
In the army the punishment for sedition is death.
The first mutiny in the Indian army took place in 1857 at Meerut.
Any uprising against his regime was suppressed ruthlessly by President Saddam Hussein.
The Tamils have been charged of insurrection by the Government of Sri Lanka.
Only the President can grant pardon to a person who revolts against the Government.

Antonyms:

Loyalty	Patriotism	Devotion
Faithfulness	Nationalism	Toadyism

Examples:
Anti-defection Bill provides for loyalty by members to the party which sponsored them for election.
Extreme form of patriotism is despised by right thinking people as something obstructing the growth of internationalism.
Devotion to one's duty is always rewarded one way or the other.
His faithfulness to his country is beyond any doubt.
Nationalism is welcome only so long as it does not contradict internationalism.
Toadyism stands for toeing the line of your boss blindly without regard to the merit or demerit of an action.

Recalcitrant (Adjective)

The recalcitrant tendency of the workers resulted in loss of job for many workers.

Synonyms:

Contrary	Defiant	Insubordinate
Intractable	Obstinate	Refractory
Stubborn	Uncontrollable	Unmanageable
Unruly	Unwilling	Wayward
Wilful		

Examples:
The results were contrary to all expectation.
The child is a defiant. He does not obey his parents.
I was in my childhood very disobedient to my father.
The obstinate and stubborn old man refused to go to hospital.
The public are usually unwilling to accept change.

Antonyms:

Amenable	Complaint	Docile
Obedient	Submissive	

Examples:
I find him very amenable to reason.

The government, compliant as ever, gave in to their demands.
The party is naturally obedient to the will of its leader.

Recover (Verb)

I doubt whether he will recover.

Synonyms:

Heal	Improve	Recapture
Recoup	Redeem	Restore
Recruit	Reposes	Retrieve
Regain	Resume	Cure

Examples:

The mother is always able to heal the troubles of her children.
The famous old painting stolen from the National Museum was repossessed from abroad and restored.
The police have managed to retrieve some of the money from the thief.
Pinky soon regained her health during the holidays.
After several months she left hospital and tried to resume a normal life.
These medicines will cure the mother's fever in a couple of days.
A team of officers had come to our village to recruit soldiers.
Our cricket team has succeeded this year. It has regained the trophy.

Antonyms:

Die	Sink	Worsen
Grow	Fail	Deteriorate
Abandon	Forfeit	Lose
Replace		

Examples:

The old man died of paralysis of the brain.
The cargo ship sank in the high seas due to a severe cyclone.
Of late the health of the old man has gone for the worse.
You must invert if you want your business to grow.
Rajesh's new business project has miserably failed.
I wish to replace my old car by a new one.

Refuse (Verb)

They refused me permission to enter the music festival.

Synonyms:

Veto	Renounce	Withhold
Decline	Exclude	Deny
Repudiate		

Examples:
The Permanent Members of Security Council can veto on decision taken by the General Assembly.
He has renounced the world and become a Sanyasi.
His increments have been withheld for three years as a penalty for negligence of duty.
He declined to help his friend at the critical juncture.
Children under ten were excluded from the film show.
Many women were denied the opportunity of having a career.
He has repudiated the charges of corruption levelled against him by the department.

Antonyms:

Acquiesce	Agree	Grant
Cede	Admit	Accede
Assent	Allow	

Examples:
The management had to acquiesce to the demands of the workers to avoid a strike.
They had to agree to a 20% raise on each salary.
The workers were also granted a 20% annual bonus.
The government had to intervene to make the management accede to the demands of the workers.

Release (Verb)

This medicine will release your father from his sufferings.

Synonyms:

Disentangle	Exempt	Liberate
Unloose	Relieve	Free
Disengage	Extricate Emancipate	

Examples:
Students who attended the evening lecture were exempted from doing homework.
The bonded labours were beaten severely when they tried to liberate themselves from the clutches of the landlord.
The thief unloosed the knots of the rope and escaped.
The doctor relieved him of the headache by a single dose.
India was freed from the foreign yoke after a prolonged struggle.
The leader disengaged him from the fury of the mob with great difficulty.
He has disentangled himself from party politics.
The fox tried desperately to extricate itself from the trap put up by the jackal but failed.
The fox tried desperately to free itself from the trap put up by the jackal but failed.
The government has emancipated a large number of agricultural workers from serfdom.

Antonyms:

Bind	Confine	Enthrall
Restrain		

Examples:
I had to restrain myself from saying something rude.
I have confined myself to pure research for the next two years.
The magician enthralled the audience for full one hour.
The bind between the father and his sob is so deep that they live together for a long time.

Remarkable (Adjective)

He is a boy who is remarkable for his stupidity.

Synonyms:

Extraordinary	Conspicuous	Striking
Famous	Noticeable	Strange
Distinguished		

Examples:
India has been an extraordinary progress in the field of space technology in the last decade.
There is a striking contrast between his two novels.
There is a conspicuous similarity between the two brothers.
It is strange we haven't heard from him.
His joy knew no bounds when the distinguished guest accosted him.
His elder brother is a famous cricket player.

Antonyms:

Ordinary	Commonplace	Customary
Normal	Average	Habitual
Medium		

Examples:
This is no ordinary achievement- topping in the Indian Civil Service Examination.
The design has become a commonplace affair in cities.
It is customary in Europe to remove one's hat before bowing to ladies.
The normal temperature of human body is 37oC.
The average height of a Nepalese is 5'-4' a little lower than that of an average Indian but the Nepalese are good soldiers.

Reluctant (Adjective)

He seemed reluctant to help us now.

Synonyms:

Unwilling	Averse	Slow
Opposed	Indisposed	Backward

Examples:
He was unwilling to be transferred to Mumbai but his boss did not consider his protest.

He seems to be averse to hard work.

My tenant's rent payments are always slow.

She seems violently opposed to your going abroad.

The master was indisposed to give him permission.

He is a little backward in his studies.

Antonyms:
Desirous	Inclined	Willing
Eager	Disposed	Favourable

Examples:
John is desirous of going to the United States for higher studies in computer programming.

We can go for a walk, if you feel so inclined.

He is eager to return to India after higher studies as a big boss.

He has disposed of his guests with great difficulty.

His interview has been favourable but the result would be known after a month.

Repeal (Verb)

The Commission repealed the rule which was brought into force by the Divisional Manager.

Synonyms:
Abolish	Revoke	Nullify
Reverse	Annul	Rescind

Examples:
Britain passed an Act of Parliament in 1870 to revoke slavery.

There is a campaign afoot to abolish current restrictions on immigration at least from the Indian side.

Law commission has recommended to nullify a number of antiquated laws.

You can reverse this table-cloth and it will still look nice.

Both the countries have decided to annul the previous agreement.

The Supreme Court rescinded the High Court judgment.

Antonyms:
Substantiate	Ratify	Endorse
Confirm	Assent	

Examples:
In order to quality for immigration, you have to substantiate your claim by showing evidence of academic standing.

The bank has endorsed my bill of exchange. This confirms my claim from the foreign buyer.

Head of the twelve European governments will meet to ratify the treaty.

Repentance (Noun)

It is a crime to show repentance to him for his involvement in this looting.

Synonyms:

Contrition	Regret	Compunction
Sorrow	Penitence	Grief

Examples:

He feels contrition for betraying his mother?
The businessman seemed to have no compunctions about cheating the innocent – peoples.
There was great regret in the village at the death of the head of the village.
The children felt great sorrow when their pet dog died.
Deepak felt deep penitence for disobeying his teacher.
His heart was filled with too much grief when he heard of his brother's death by drowning.

Antonyms:

Satisfaction	Complacence	Pleasure
Gratification		

Examples:

The parents expressed satisfaction with his son for his excellent performance in the examination.
India may be well prepared for defence, yet there is need to avoid any complacence in the examination.
I feel pleasure in presenting my book at a function to the Honourable Minister for release.
The unscrupulous car owner offered gratification to the traffic policeman to evade the fine for wrong driving.

Resign (Verb)

He resigned his post from the Cabinet.

Synonyms:

Renounce	Yield	Abandon
Quit	Leave	Surrender
Abdicate		

Examples:

He has renounced the world and become a Sanyasi.
I have abandoned the idea of becoming a Charted Accountant.
Manoj has decided to quit his present job.
He has sought the permission of his boss to leave the station.
After the battle, the enemy troops surrendered.
King Edward VII abdicated in 1936 on grounds of his romance with the daughter of

a commoner.

My mother yielded to my wish and agreed to attend the annual function of my school along with my father.

Antonyms:

Hold	Stay	Continue
Remain	Maintain	Retain
Keep		

Examples:

Our forces held the ground despite heavy bombing.
I have decided to stay in the hostel to continue my higher education in this city.
Only about half original workforce remains.
I will maintain myself by taking part-time job of accounts in a local firm.
This will help to retain my self-respect in my family circle.
You should keep to your lane while cycling on a city road. That is the traffic rule to be observed.

Respect (Noun)

The Prime Minister is held in the highest respect.

Synonyms:

| Esteem | Regard | Consideration |
| Accept | | |

Examples:

I have a great esteem for my teachers in the college.
They also give me due regard for my deep interest in studies.
I have due consideration for the ability of all my teachers.
My teachers have accepted me as a good student.

Antonyms:

| Contempt | Disregard | Disown |
| Ignore | | |

Examples:

I feel nothing but contempt for people who treat children cruelly showing regard for the good ones and disregard for the bad ones.
We may disown responsibility for wrongs done by others.
We should ignore the bad things we see around but accept the good we come across.

Retain (Verb)

This dyke was duilt to retain the flood water.

Synonyms:

| Employ | Contain | Grip |
| Maintain | Preserve | Memories |

| Recall | Recollect | Engage |
| Maintain | Keep | Hold |

Examples:
Under this Act nobody can employ the workers on ad hoc basis.
The accused was allowed to engage a lawyer for his defence.
It is very difficult to maintain two establishments within the limited resources.
I do wish you wouldn't keep on interrupting
Mother asked the nurse to hold the child for another couple of hours.

Antonyms:
Give up	Cede	Surrender
Relinquish	Renounce	Forsake
Abandon		

Examples:
Edmund had given up his studies before graduation.
I have ceded a part of my property to an orphanage.
The Pakistani forces surrendered to Indian forces in Bangladesh in 1971.
I have not yet relinquished charge to my successor in the company.
I have abandoned the idea of taking up a government job.

Riddle (Noun)

I do not know the answer to this riddle.

Synonyms:
| Mystery | Puzzle | Problem |
| Paradox | Enigma | |

Examples:
There is a mystery about the habits of migrant birds in this part of the world.
Arun has won several prizes for solving puzzles.
The government has solved the Punjab problem and is now devoted to the solution of the Assam problem.
It is a paradox, but with age Rekha is becoming young and smart.
Whether there is life on any other planet besides the Earth, is still an enigma.

Antonyms:
| Answer | Explanation | Solution |
| Proposition | Axiom | |

Examples:
The Prime Minister answered the questions of a large number of journalists at the Press conference.
His answers presented his views for the solution of pending problems.
He made a proposition for peace in the Indian Ocean region.
He used a few axioms to compare international problems between super powers.

Risk (Noun)

To succeed in business, one must be prepared to run risks.

Synonyms:

Hazard	Jeopardize	Venture
Peril	Danger	Imperil
Stake	Endanger	

Examples:

The ascent of the Mount Everest was a great hazard for the early mountaineer.

Nancy jeopardized her life but saved a drowning child.

John ventured to stake on the ice only after it was fully frozen.

These birds are able to survive the peril of arctic winter.

He was not aware of the danger of touching a live wire.

The fireman endangered his life to save the lives of persons trapped in the burning house.

In International trade the stakes are high, but so are the profits.

He has imperilled our investments by staking them on the new issues of a limited company.

Antonyms:

Security	Secure	Save
Harbour	Safety	Defend
Shelter	Shield	

Examples:

The bank has refused to advance me a loan without a proper security.

You can secure 80% marks if you work hard.

Let us save something every month for a rainy day.

I have a feeling that Ralson is harbouring evil designs in money matters.

We ran to safety when bombing took place during the last war.

India can defend herself from neighbours but what would happen if there is a nuclear war among super-powers.

Where would humans then run for shelter?

Will any place be good enough as a shield from nuclear effects?

Rot (Verb)

One of the pieces had rotted off.

Synonyms:

Decay	Corrode	Faster
Perish	Decompose	Putrefy

Examples:

The matter over and under the ground decays in due course to become fossils.
The earthquake left a number of bodies under the debris found decomposed on digging.
One could smell the stink of putrefied junk months after the earthquake.

Antonyms:

Flourish	Bloom	Expend
Flower	Increase	Grow

Examples:
During the rainy season green plants get flourished.
The flowers bloom in the spring season.
Vegetation grows profusely in tropical countries.

Rough (Adjective)

Keep away from the rough quarter of the town to have a peaceful life.

Synonyms:

Severe	Course	Irregular
Blunt	Indelicate	Hard
Tough	Difficult	Uneven

Examples:
We had a very severe winter last year.
The knife was so blunt that she had difficulties in cutting vegetables.
I had tough time dealing with him.
The floor of this room is very uneven.

Antonyms:

Calm	Regular	Delicate
Elegant	Graceful	Pleasant
Glossy	Smooth	Even
Fine	Straight	

Examples:
There is no wind today. The weather is hot and calm.
The surface of this material is glossy and shiny.
The best path to a smooth career for a young man is appearing in a competitive examination of one's choice and trying to get selected.
The surface of land in this region is even, hence there is good slope for provision of fast local transport.

Rude (Adjective)

It is rude to interrupt at people.

Synonyms:

Discourteous	Impudent	Unmannerly

Saucy	Churlish	Impertinent
Impolite		

Examples:

We felt sorry to observe that the son was rather discourteous to his father's guests.
Mrs. Laxmi complained to her friend that the errand boy had been impudent to her.
These children are too unmannerly to be invited to a party.
Her saucy remarks raised many eyebrows.
The churlish brute muttered menacingly when my friend asked him to leave.
The customers were unhappy with the impertinent waitress.
It is considered impolite for a man to receive guests in informal night dress.

Antonyms:

Civil	Cultivated	Polished
Courteous	Elegant	Genteel
Refined	Sophisticated	

Examples:

Raman knows how to be civil with lady quests.
I am trying to cultivate friendship with Neha my classmate.
His polished manners win him new friends with ease.
His courteous behavior has made him quiet popular among the local elites.
Richard is elegant enough to make high level contacts in politics.
Graham is too refined and sophisticated for a rough life of the village.

Sacred (Adjective)

Nothing is sacred to these wild youths.

Synonyms:

Holy	Sanctified	Dedicated
Consecrated	Inviolable	Hallowed
Divine	Blessed	

Examples:

The Ganga is a holy river in India.
The Ramayana and the Mahabharata are sanctified scriptures of ancient India.
The shrine was consecrated by the local philanthropist.
He is a dedicated social worker.
For Sikhs the sermons of Guru Granth Sahib are inviolable.
The church graveyard is a hallowed ground.
Quran is a divine scripture of the Muslims.
God blesses those who bless the poor and the downtrodden.

Antonyms:

Profane	Impious	Irreverent
Irreligious	Blasphemous	Sacrilegious
Temporal	Worldly	Lay

Examples:
The government has taken up to check the profane activities of the smugglers.
Modern picture of violence and nudity give impious ideas to the youth.
The attitude of the students to their teacher has become irreverent.
There is nothing irreligious in the secular policy of the government.

Sad (Adjective)

John is sad because his dog has died.

Synonyms:

| Dull | Grave | Dejected |
| Depressed | Downcast | Melancholy |

Examples:
The conference was deadly dull.
This is a grave problem for the government to cope with terrorism.
Repeated failure had left him feeling very dejected.
The news of Jame's failure in the examination depressed his mother.
Since his failure in the examination Subhash is looked like a downcast in his family circle.

Antonyms:

| Glad | Gay | Joyous |
| Cheerful | Excited | Lively |

Examples:
I am glad your college has improved its all round atmosphere by introducing co-education.
Everybody looks gay in your birthday party.
Every student seems smiling and talking jovially.
The teachers as well as students looked joyous and cheerful in annual day function.
The whole premise gives a lively look of academic brilliance.

Sanction (Verb)

Would you sanction flogging as a punishment for crimes of violence?

Synonyms:

Allow	Support	Approve
Ratify	Endorse	Authorize
Permit	Confirm	

Examples:
The teacher allowed the student to go home early today.
Amarnath works hard to support his family.
She doesn't want to take her boy friend home in case her parents don't approve.
Most nations of the world have ratified the U.N. character.

I am sure his boss will endorse his view on the issue.
He has been authorized to issue letters on behalf of the principal.
Anthony was given a permit to go through the private park.
The hotel confirmed our reservations by telegram.

Antonyms:

Disallow	Debar	Veto
Ban	Interdict	Forbid
Prohibit		

Examples:
The Principal has disallowed the use of college premises for political activities.
The retired officers of the commerce ministry have been debarred from doing liaison work for private firms.
The UN Security Council has vetoed the General Assembly's decision to impose economic and political sanctions against North Korea.
The government has banned the use of religious shrines for accumulation of weapons.
The government has interdicted the publication of educational books calculated to cause communal disharmony.

Satisfy (Verb)

Riches do not always satisfy.

Synonyms:

Appease	Assuage	Feed
Indulge	Pacify	Quench
Sate	Satiate	Meet
Slake	Surfeit	Serve
Fulfill	Suffice	

Examples:
He assuages my hunger by feeding me.
I fed and watered the horse before I left home.
House wives indulge in gossiping most of the time.
The leader of this locality pacifies the dispute between two groups.
I need two glasses of water to quench my thirst.
I felt satiated after Christmas dinner.
We slaked our thirst in a stream.

Antonyms:

Annoy	Displease	Dissatisfy
Exasperate	Frustrate	
Give cause for complaint	Fail to meet	Dissuade
Fail to persuade		

Examples:

My younger brother always annoyed me by asking questions.

Her insolence greatly displeased the judge.

I failed to persuade her to go to movie.

He tried to dissuade me from going to live abroad.

His constant whistling exasperated her.

Scatter (Verb)

The police scattered the crowd.

Synonyms:

Sprinkle	Disperse	Spread
Broadcast	Propagate	Dissipate
Distribute	Disseminate	

Examples:

The people who believe that man becomes pious by sprinkling holy water on him are great frauds and fakes.

The class dispersed as soon as the bell rang.

The news of the Indian Gandhi's assassination spread like wild fire.

The special election broadcast will take place on the local station at eight every evening for twenty days before the date of election.

The missionaries propagated the teachings of Christianity throughout the island by establishing educational institutions.

The fog dissipated when the sun came out.

Plato's philosophy has been well disseminated throughout the western world.

The postal department distributes the mail by Pin code.

Antonyms:

Hoard	Gather	Store
Collect	Amass	Pick
Garner	Accumulate	

Examples:

The black market makes money by boarding scarce products and essential commodities.

We are used to celebrate musical evenings with the whole family gathered round the piano.

We need to accumulate enough evidence to ensure his conviction.

The little girl picks flowers in the garden for making garlands.

Scanty (Adjective)

The shortage of rice this year is because of scanty paddy harvest.

Synonyms:

Narrow	Skimpy	Inch
Sparing	Slender	Meager
Limited	Small	

Examples:

The lane was so narrow that two cars could not pass at the same time.

The dancers wore skimpy dresses.

If you add a pinch of salt, your dish will become tastier.

They have grown a number of slender birch trees.

The utensils of the cottage were very meagre.

Father gives him a limited pocket money every month.

Our teacher believes in sparing use of the stick.

The Chartered Accountants have instructions to check even the small details of their firms thoroughly before preparing the balance sheet.

Antonyms:

Profuse	Abundant	Lavish
Unlimited	Sufficient	Ample
Copious	Absolute	

Examples:

The philanthropist was quite profuse in his gifts to the poor.

Tata has abundant resources of men, money and materials to start new projects successfully.

He makes lavish expenditure on his kitchen to keep his family members healthy.

No body has unlimited and absolute powers in the Indian constitution, not even the Prime Minister.

There is sufficient provision for mutual checks and balances of the powers of the executive, legislature, and judiciary in the constitution.

India has ample resources but limited organizational infrastructure to deserve being called a rich country.

Scold (Verb)

He scolded his child for being lazy.

Synonym:

Reprimand	Castigate	Hearten
Nag	Censure	Reprove
Chide	Rebuke	Admonish

Examples:

Father reprimanded him for his negligence in study.

The clerk received a strong censure for his carelessness.

When the child giggled over the remark of a visitor, her mother reproved her with a stern look.

He was harshly rebuked by his boss for misplacing important files.

Our Manager chided us for having lost in the international championships.

Antonyms:

Compliment	Applaud	Praise
Extol	Acclaim	Approve
Commend		

Examples:

The President complemented the Indian Lawn Tennis players for excellent performance at Wimbledon.

The Principal applauded the work of his teachers who won first positions in the Secondary Board results.

This movie deserves high praise for its story and direction.

I should commend good work of our salesman who has doubled the sale of this product in one year.

Seek (Verb)

He is going to Canada to seek his fortune.

Synonyms:

Hunt	Court	Inquire
Look for	Search	Solicit
Follow	Ask	

Examples:

It requires a great deal for courage and experiences to hunt a tiger.

The union leader will court arrest today to press their demands.

May I inquire who the singer among these girls is?

Prabhat is looking for an opportunity to go abroad.

Nowadays Hamish is in search of a handsome job.

The old man solicited our help for his sick wife.

The detective followed the gang to its hide-out.

Antonyms:

| Shun | Avoid | Eschew |
| Evade | | |

Examples:

I always try to shun the company of bad characters.

He's been avoiding me like a plague since quarrel.

The Principal advised the students to completely eschew political discussions in college.

He managed to evade all the difficult questions.

Selfish (Adjective)

He reacted from his selfish motives.

Synonyms:

Sordid	Greedy	Mercenary
Ungenerous	Illiberal	Mean
Selfish		

Examples:

The boy had lived in sordid home for decades.

Nobody likes a greedy child.

The mercenaries face a tragic death when they are defeated in war.

His boss is rather ungenerous in granting leave to the employees.

Illiberal policies always tend to cause hardship to the people.

Even his colleagues do not like him because he is mean and selfish.

Antonyms:

| Generous | Liberal | Charitable |
| Bountiful | Lavish | |

Examples:

Deepak is generous to a fault. No wonder his so called friends exploit his friendship.

Our government has launched liberal policies towards businessmen for expanding their ventures.

Some businessmen have a charitable attitude towards their employees and help to live better.

This year the rains have helped the crops to be bountiful.

Modern businessmen have a charitable attitude towards their employees and help them to live better.

Modern businessmen can afford to pay lavishly to their sincere employees.

Sensible (Adjective)

He is sensible of the danger of his position.

Synonyms:

Judicious	Wise	Aware
Conscious	Observant	Intelligent
Sane	Rational	Sagacious
Cognizant		

Examples:

The President of a country has to be man of judicious temperament.

It is wise to keep the child indoors when he had a cold.

Are we aware of the developments taking place in our neighbouring courtiers?

I became conscious that someone was moving about upstairs. I, therefore, checked but found only a car.

He is intelligent enough to understand the problem instantly.

It is necessary to have a rational approach to our family budget in these days of high inflation.

Be observant to this mischief of your neighbour.

The court reached a sagacious decision on this complicated case.

Is the accused cognizant of his rights?

Antonyms:

Unaware	Senseless	Idiotic
Stupid	Asinine	Foolish
Unconscious	Doltish	

Examples:

Our masses are yet unaware of their rights and duties provided in the constitution.

All talk of ideal and fair election is senseless in the light of their money role.

Anil's idiotic behavior in the interview let him down. It is highly stupid of him not to read a good books on interviews.

The new teacher was rather asinine for the clever and mischievous students.

Separable (Adjective)

These scissors are made of separable parts.

Synonyms:

Divisible	Classifiable	Branched
Group into		

Examples:

Ten is divisible by two.

The books in my personal library are classifiable.

The different parts of this computer can be branched separately and again assembled when necessary.

Class X of our school shall be grouped into 3 parts on the basis of merit.

Antonyms:

Indivisible	United	Inseparable

Examples:

Earlier scientists thought that an atom is individual but atomic theory has disproved the old theory.

India is a federation of states united by one common constitution.

The states of India are inseparable parts of one country.

Separate (Verb)

England is separated from France by the Channel.

Synonyms:

Detach	Cleave	Remove
Sever	Sunder	Estrange
Disconnect	Disengage	Disunite

Examples:

Somebody has detached the battery from my car.

If you don't pay your bills they will disconnect your electricity.

The receptionist told me she would connect me with her boss as soon as he is disengaged from a previous caller.

The Kapoor family stands disunited with two of their sons migrating to the United States.

Antonyms:

Combine	Connect	Consolidate
Engage	Amalgamate	Joined
Unite		

Examples:

Hydrogen combines with oxygen to form water.

The two towns are connected by excellent bus service.

The Finance Ministry is formulating new schemes to consolidate the country's developing economy.

I will engage him in talks while you can have a look into the inner office.

The two parties have united to form a coalition.

Settle (Verb)

The Dutch settled in South Africa.

Synonyms:

Conclude	Establish	Fix
Colonize	Liquidate	Finish
Domicile	Adjust	Decide
Determine		

Examples:

We will conclude the concert with the National Anthem.

A new thermal power plant was established at the far end of our village.

I have fixed the next meeting with union leader at 4 P.M. on Saturday.

The company has decided to liquidate all its dues this year.

Two of the runners failed to finish.

The Hindu Marriage Act applies to those Hindus only who domicile in India.

He needs to adjust the brakes of his bicycle.

The Gaon Panchayats can decide upon petty cases only.

The Supreme Court alone can determine inter-state disputes and constitutional interpretation.

The Dutch were the first among Europeans to colonies new territories in Africa and Asia.

Antonyms:

Ruffle	Dismantle	Confuse
Derange	Disorder	

Examples:

The new manager has ruffled all the organization.

The new mechanic has dismantled my car with a view to overhaul and cleanses each part.

The speaker confused the different issues of the debated subject. No wonder he was hooted down.

The untimely death of the son has seriously deranged the mother.

When I visited the place of accident I found every thing in disorder.

Shallow (Adjective)

He lost in the oratorical competition because of his shallow argument.

Synonyms: Trifle

Superficial	Slight	Trivial
Foolish	Unintelligent	Simple

Examples:

His mother keeps telling David not to cry over trifle things.

The new teacher seems to have superficial understanding of mathematics. He never goes deeper into any chapter.

He is no indifferent to studies; he misses his college on slight excuses.

Hema is so sensitive, even trivial things upset her.

It was foolish to quarrel with his best friend.

His unintelligent handling of the situation has implicated him in the losses of the financial deal.

The machine is quite simple to use.

Antonyms:

Recondite	Clever	Wise
Intelligent	Shrewd	Astute
Discerning	Deep	

Examples:

Chandra is a wise and intelligent boy.

His intelligent talks have impressed his teachers and friends.

The business man proved too shrewd for the fake salesman.

The astute handling of the labor problem enabled the management to avoid the lockout.

There is a discerning resemblance between the two brothers.

Danny is a deep thinker. He thinks twice before he speaks or acts.

Shame (Noun)

What a shame to deceive a girl!

Synonyms:

Disgrace	Modesty	Dishonour
Shyness	Abashment	Mortification
Coyness	Abasement	

Examples:

Smith felt disgraced when he split the ink on the table cloth of his boss.

Jack was filled with abasement when he was asked by the principal to stand up on the bench.

Her modesty kept her from wearing a mini-skirt.

His collusion with the enemy brought dishonour to the whole family.

His son was refused admission in the school for his shyness.

I forgot to preface my speech owing to stage shyness. What mortification indeed!

Antonyms:

Honour	Grace	Flare
Courage		

Examples:

I felt greatly honoured on receiving the trophy from the sports minister.

The principal showed due grace to let me present the gift to the minister.

I shook hands with my friend with smooth flare.

It needs courage to face a huge audience from the stage.

Sharp (Adjective)

His sharp intelligence has got him a great respect in the college.

Synonyms:

Acute	Cutting	Pointed
Serrated	Abrupt	Extreme
Alert	Apt	Astute
Bright	Clever	Discerning
Observant	Penetrating	

Examples:

There is an acute shortage of water in this area.

When I asked about her new job she was quite abrupt with me.
Although he was over eighty his mind still remarkably alert.
His choice of music was most apt.
He is the brightest child in the class.

Antonyms:

Blunt	Dull	Rounded
Even	Moderate	Blurred
Dim	Slow	Stupid
Simply	Amicable	Courteous
Friendly	Bland	Mild

Examples:
Police said he had been battered with blunt instrument.
The weather of hot summer in Delhi is deadly dull.
The boundaries between east and west have become blurred.
An amicable settlement has reached.
The child is very stupid. He doesn't even know how to speak with elders.

Shelter (Verb)

Dig trenches to shelter the men from gunfire.

Synonyms:

| Guard | Protect | Screen |
| Defend | Shield | |

Examples:
India has recently deployed more troops to guard its borders with Pakistan.
The hen-house needs to be protected from the prowling foxes.
The atmosphere screens the earth from infra-red rays coming from the sun.
Tom defended his dog when it was attacked by a fox.
In a hot country men and women often wear large hats to shied their heads from the sun.

Antonyms:

| Betray | Expel | Reject |
| Surrender | Refuse | Expose |

Examples:
Smugglers are the worst enemies of the country as they betray its interests.
The government has decided to expel the foreign spies caught red handed.
The boss has rejected the demand of the employee for a rise in salary.
The culprit surrendered to the police to save his life from the bullet shot.

America has refused to hold parleys with Iran without any conditions.

The enemy spies, on being cross-examined, have exposed their intention to run the terrorist movement in India.

Shock (Noun)

If you touch the live wire, you will get a shock.

Synonyms:

Scare	Dismay	Offend
Outrage	Blow	Collision
Tremor	Disgust	

Examples:

She was scared to see a thief under her bed.

The news of his failure in the examination dismayed him.

My refusal to lend him the bicycle offended him.

Cruelty to children is an outrage punishable under law.

The failure of his business was a terrible blow to him.

The collision of the bus with the truck coming from the opposite side was heard for a kilometre.

A slight earthquake tremor was felt in Delhi yesterday morning.

He could not hide his disgust at the sad news.

Listening of the gruesome stories horrifies small children.

Antonyms:

| Delight | Gladden | Please |

Examples:

It was a matter of great delight for me to shake hands with the President.

The award of the Academy Merit Certificate gladdened the father of the boy.

The visit of my friend from Shimla greatly pleased me.

Shoddy (Adjective)

His book is nothing, but a shoddy piece of work.

Synonyms:

Cheap	Junky	Poor
Rubbishy	Second	Rate
Slipshod	Tacky	Tatty
Tawdry	Trashy	

Examples:

Their woollen clothes are cheap in quality.

Rajeev's poor performance in the examination made his parents upset.

The rubbish T.V. serial bored me badly.
You are too slipshod in your presentation.

Antonyms:

Accurate	Careful	Craftsman – like
Excellent	Fine	First – rate
Meticulous	Quality	Superlative
Well-made		

Examples:
He is very accurate in mathematics.
You should be careful lifting glass vase, it may fall.
She speaks excellent French.
This earthen pot was well-made.
These fine clothes are imported from America.

Signify (Verb)

Do dark clouds signify rain?

Synonyms:

Denote	Intimate	Mean
Show	Proclaim	Indicate

Examples:
The hosting of the flag at mast denoted the origin of the ship.
The headmaster intimated the students about the half holiday on Saturday.
He does not mean to hurt you.
His face showed he had taken otherwise of you joke.
A public holiday was proclaimed in honour of the coronation.
His high temperature indicates he is seriously ill.

Antonyms:

Veil	Mask	Dissemble
Cloak	Cover	Hide
Conceal		

Examples:
The veiled dress she is wearing shows she is either a nurse or nun.
The robbers who looted the bank were wearing masks.
The motor mechanic dissembled my car for repairs and then reassembled it.
I covered my head with a hankie before entering the shrine.
The thief hid himself under a bed in a servant quarter.
He kept his face expressionless to conceal his excitement.

Silly (Adjective)

How silly of you to do that?

Synonyms:

Absurd	Senseless	Foolish
Unwise	Non-Sensual	

Examples:

It is absurd to say that this text book is useless only because some of its lessons make dull reading.

It is senseless for parents to compel their wards to study the subjects which don't suit their taste and interest.

It was foolish of him to openly quarrel with his boss.

It is unwise to think that trade unions should be banned.

He is fed up of listening to the non-sensical sermons of his boss.

Antonyms:

Sensible	Clever	Wise
Sapient	Intelligent	

Examples:

Rita is a sensible girl. I have never observed anything irrelevant in her talks.

John is a clever boy. He could make a successful businessman.

He remembers the wise sayings of all great men by heart.

Our new science teacher is quite a sapient learned man.

His lectures are all very intelligent.

Sincere (Adjective)

Are they sincere in their wish to disarm?

Synonyms:

Genuine	True	Frank
Heart	Honest	Open
Wholehearted		

Examples:

This book is a genuine research work of the first order.

All the statements made in the book are true and frank.

The principal spoke out his heart-felt views about the rash activities of some the students which could bring bad name to the college.

Modern politicians are supposed to be honest at least to their party ideology.

The Prime Minister has made an open statement to the opposition parties to keep him apprised of their view point on major national issues.

The government has decided to work whole-heartedly for the welfare of the poorer sections of society.

Antonyms:

Affected	Untrue	Feigned
Half-hearted	Hypocritical	Insincere
Pretended		

Examples:

The disturbed law and order situation in some states has affected the clean thinking of many politicians in the country.

The allegations made in some quarters about India's aggressive designs against Sri Lanka have proved untrue.

Pakistan's feigned views about India's efforts to prepare for war are being exploited for going nuclear.

Pakistan's approach to sole differences with India is half hearted and hypocritical.

Skill (Noun)

Is learning a foreign language a question of learning new skills?

Synonyms:

Artistry	Adroitness	Finesse
Mastery		

Examples:

The artistry of India's handraftsmen of Muradabad and Varanasi is appreciated the world over.

The adroitness of the new management can save the company from bankruptcy.

The ivory carvers of Delhi are reputed for their finesse.

The carpet weavers of Jammu and Kashmir have perfect mastery and monopoly over their trade.

Antonyms:

Clumsiness	Incompetence	Ineptitude

Examples:

The clumsiness of some of the engineering products of India brings bad name to the country's craftsmanship.

Incompetence and ineptitude of Indian management in some textile mills has brought them into the red.

Skilful (Adjective)

He is very skilful at using chopsticks.

Synonyms:

Competent	Ingenious	Adroit
Clever	Experienced	

Examples:

His father is a competent surgeon.

The way in which the parts of a watch are put together is very ingenious.
He manages the business in a very adroit way.
The thief was so clever he left no clues.
My uncle is an experienced chemical engineer.

Antonyms:

Inexperienced	Bungling	Incompetent
Clumsy	Awkward	

Examples:
Although inexperienced, my assistant is proficient in accounts.
The new treasurer has been charged of bungling the funds of the cooperative society.
The manager is honest but rather incompetent for the high responsibility.
No wonder his handling of some affairs has been rather clumsy.
This has proved awkward for the person who recommended him.

Slander (Verb)

He is punished with fine because he slandered.

Synonyms:

Decry	Defame	Aspersion
Opprobrious	Accuse	Malign
Disparage	Defamation	

Examples:
The Captain decried the lack of support he received from his team.
Politicians defame each other to win public support.
It's not fair to caste aspersions on someone you know nothing about.
The liaison officer of the company was reprimanded for his opprobrious conduct.
The servant was accused of stealing utensil from the kitchen.
A fair politician debates the issues and does not malign his opponent.
His father always disparaged his attempts to better himself.
He sued the newspaper for defamation of his character.

Antonyms:

Praise	Eulogize	Commendation
Laud	Laudation	Commend

Examples:
The local public lauded the achievements of the Municipal Commissioner Your conduct in negotiating settlement between warring brothers deserves high praise.
The readers eulogize Shakespeare for his brilliance of expression and characterization.
The book has much to commend it.

Slapdash (Adjective)

His slapdash approach resulted in total failure of the project.

Synonyms:

Slovenly	Clumsy	Disorderly
Haphazard	Hasty	Hurried
Messy	Negligent	Perfunctory
Slipshod	Thoughtless	Untidy

Examples:

It is not easy walking in these clumsy shoes.

He was arrested for being drunk and disorderly.

The government's approach to the problem was haphazard.

I don't want to make a hasty decision.

She is very negligent in her studies.

She gave this factory only a perfunctory inspection.

The goal was a result of slipshod defence.

I haven't offered you a drink. How thoughtless of me!

Antonyms:

Careful	Conscientious	Fastidious
Meticulous	Ordered	Orderly
Painstaking	Precise	Punctilious
Thoughtful	Tidy	Clear

Examples:

Be careful that you don't hurt his feeling.

This essay is a most conscientious piece of work.

She is meticulous about her appearance.

The Hindustan Times gave a clear and precise description of the incident.

His face took on a thoughtful expression.

Slavery (Noun)

Gandhi was a great man worked for the abolition of slavery.

Synonyms:

Subjugation	Thralldom	Bondage
Forced Labour	Submission	Drudgery
Servitude	Captivity	

Examples:

Subjugation of poorer classes by the richer elite is a historical phenomenon which continues its way even today in most countries around the world.

Since money is power, the rich can always hold the poor in thraldom.

One form of slavery in villages is bondage of agricultural labour by the landlord. Once in bondage the labour class is forced and exploited by the landlord forever.

The bonded labour is under submission to the landlord who keeps the former in very poor condition so that he may not raise his voice of rebellion or run away.

All the drudgery of work is done by the labourers while the landlord enjoys the fruit of their labour. Thus the system of servitude and captivity has continued ever since but it is being shaken off by the democratic wind blowing round the world today.

Antonyms:
Freedom
Emancipation
Liberty
Independence

Examples:
Modern democracies are taking legal action to bring about the freedom of the bonded labour and the emancipation of the poor workers from serfdom.

He is being given the liberty of movement from the clutches of the landlord and independence in the choice of work.

Slick (Adjective)

The roads were slick with wet mud.

Synonyms:

Glib	Meretricious	Plausible
Polished	Smooth	Sophisticated
Adroit	Deft	Dexterous
Professional	Sharp	Skilful

Examples:
She could find no plausible explanation for the disappearance of my car from my shed.

She succeeded by a combination of adroit diplomacy and sheer good luck.

With deft fingers she untangled the wire.

The doctor was accused of professional misconduct.

The shears are not sharp enough to cut the grass.

Marble is so smooth to touch.

Antonyms:

Amateurish	Clumsy	Crude
Inexpert	Unaccomplished	Unpolished
Unprofessional		

Examples:

Detectives described the burglary as crude and amateurish.

Walking in these clumsy shoes is very difficult for him.

He was dismissed for unprofessional conduct.

The company appointed few unskilled workers.

Smart (Adjective)

We have tried our best to make this site as informative as possible. It will certainly help in broadening the horizons of knowledge of the visitors. We also apologize for the mistakes which are not deliberately committed. Both suggestions and criticisms to enhance the quality of this site are sincerely welcomed. Use our Contact Us form to submit both your suggestions and criticisms.

You look very smart with this dress.

Synonyms:

Spruce	Trim	Elegant
Well-dressed	Immaculate	Neat
Showy		

Examples:

In advanced countries majority of the people can maintain spruce, trim and elegant personalities on the strength of high wages earned by them.

The common people cannot afford to be well-dressed, neat and smart.

In poorer countries which were under the domination of the white man for countries, the economic condition are only gradually improving but only a minority class of elites can maintain immaculate clothes.

Antonyms:

Rugged	Worn	Untidy
Shabby	Unkempt	Threadbare

Examples:

Most of the people in poor countries are seen in undeveloped villages or industrial townships in rugged and worn clothes.

The workers employed in industries can afford only shabby clothes while their working conditions are untidy.

Their personalities are therefore unkempt and they live threadbare below the poverty line.

Slow (Adjective)

He is slow to make up his mind.

Synonyms:

Gradual	Leisurely	Retarded
Slack	Sluggish	

Examples:

There is a need for gradual automation in the electronic industry in Argentina.

The Indian engineers work in a rather leisurely fashion, otherwise our Public works departments and utility undertakings would be more efficient.

The demand for T.V. sets has slackened owing to high prices and the inability of the common people to afford it.

Antonyms:

Agile	Fast	Quick
Rapid	Speedy	Lively

Examples:

The Japanese engineers are much more agile when working in advanced countries as they have better opportunities of showing their worth.

India has been fast developing its industries since last two decades.

The horse runs more quickly in the morning.

Some of the Indian rivers flow rapidly down the stream and so they are good for producing hydroelectricity.

Sociable (Adjective)

She is not sociable after she joined a new school.

Synonyms:

Companionable	Festive	Affable
Genial	Convivial	

Examples:

My uncle is such a companionable personality; you can never feel bored in his presence.

The festive season starts in India after harvesting of the crops.

Mary's affable manners attract the young and the old.

The Retired old man has genial way of amusing his vision.

Antonyms:

Secluded	Inimical	Hostile
Sequestered	Puerile	Giddy
Peevish		

Examples:

Ever since his brain injury, Robin has become a secluded personality. I think it will take a few months before he restarts mixing with people.

The dispute among brothers on property matters has made them inimical.

Even their children are affected to be hostile to each other.

The old age has made Ranjit a sequestered person. Gone is all his old joviality and sociability.

Although rich in money, he is a puerile person, small hearted and peevish.

Soft (Adjective)

She likes a soft pillow and hard mattress.

Synonyms:

Elastic	Flexible	Pliable
Pulpy	Spongy	Ductile
Yielding	Mouldable	Malleable
Supple	Smooth	

Examples:

The dough should be smooth and elastic.

I believe in following a flexible approach in human affairs in view of the changing framework of society.

Plastic is a pliable material capable of being converted and mixed with numerous materials.

The young are more malleable than the others.

An actor has to be highly mouldable and volatile in his emotional expression.

Antonyms:

Hard	Firm	Unyielding
Compact	Rigid	Stiff

Examples:

The alloy of metals is very hard and can be used in sophisticated super-strong structures.

It is firm in nature and it does not bend nor melt except at 100oC temperature.

Andrews is such a hard fellow to bend on principles. He is unyielding in his temperament.

This machine is so compact that it can last for decades without repairs.

India follows a rigid foreign policy measured strictly by principles of non-alignment.

The government is prepared to take stiff measures to curb the terrorist activity in the country.

Soil (Verb)

He refused to soil his hands.

Synonyms:

Stain	Spoil	Dirty
Smear	Pollute	Taint
Contaminate	Sully	

Examples:

George never does anything which may stain his character.

Deepa is a spoiled child, always making mischief, never serious.

Smoking is a dirty habit. It affects health adversely.

Coal and oil based industries tend to pollute the atmosphere.

Antonyms:

Clarify	Clean	Purge
Wash	Cleanse	Purify

Examples:

The Principal clarified many controversial issues raised by the students and the teachers.

The new government has promised to give a clean administration to the country.

It has been decided to purge the government of inefficient and corrupt officials.

The washer man washes the dirty clothes of the people.

In these days of good washing soaps and powders, most families prefer to clean their clothes themselves as an economic measure.

Solemn (Adjective)

There is a solemn silence prevailed as the coffin was carried out of the church.

Synonyms:

Traditional	Dignified	Grand
Grave	Majestic	Thoughtful
Ceremonial	Devotional	Pious

Examples:

Sonia's marriage involves performance of traditional ceremonies.

The national flag will be hoisted on the Independence Day at the Red Fort in the usual ceremonial way.

Devotional music is played at this Gurudwara early morning every day.

The opening ceremony of the Bhakra Dam was performed in the background of pious national anthem and parade.

Antonyms:

Impious	Irreligious	Sacrilegious
Irreverent		

Examples:

There is nothing impious in performing the opening ceremony without the usual mantras.

There is nothing irreligious in departing from the traditional pattern so long as the objective of a mission is noble and pure. The sanctity of a programme lies in its overall benefit to the common people.

The ceremony does not become sacrilegious so long as the spirit of the occasion is fully imbibed and enthusiasm aroused.

If we can call agricultural and industrial projects as temples of modern age, it is not irreverent to compare the manager of such an industry with the head-priest of the religious temple.

Solid (Adjective)

When water freezes and becomes solid, we call it ice.

Synonyms:

Sound	Compact	Dense
Hard	Serious	Safe
Religious	Trustworthy	Strong

Examples:

This project is based on sound principles of management. Those principles are sincere and based on strong technical know-how.

They enjoyed their vacation safe in the knowledge that their friends were looking after the home.

We must ensure the selection of reliable supervisors and trustworthy financial officers for running the project.

It is not safe for girl to travel all alone.

It is not easy to find out a trustworthy friend.

Antonyms:

Unreliable	Hollow	Crumbling
Decoying	Precarious	Undependable
Unsafe		

Examples:

The statistical data prepared by foreign sources of people killed in pro and anti-reservation clashes in Ahmedabad are entirely unreliable.

The arrangements made for the organization of sports clubs in every locality in the district seem undependable.

The sheds constructed for use by visitors to the hot spring at Gurgaon are unsafe.

The hollow pipes are needed to take water to this area from that lake.

Solitary (Adjective)

The solitary life that he lives now is the punishment for his mistake.

Synonyms:

Unfrequented	Uninhabited	Secluded
Lonely	Isolated	Sequestered
Deserted		

Examples:

The palace, although well situated on the shore of this island, is unfrequented as there are a few mysteries concerning its history.

Many parts of Canada are yet uninhabited.

There are many secluded parts even in northern Australia although it is very rich in natural resources.

Manoj has been feeling very lonely since the death of his wife.

He has isolated himself from many of his old friends to keep his sorrow to himself.

Antonyms:

Inhabited	Popular	Well frequented
Sociable		

Examples:

This land is inhabited by red Indians.

The President has become quite popular since his last press conference.

This restaurant is now well-frequented by military personnel.

The Chairman of this club is a very sociable person.

Solve (Verb)

Solve this SUDOKU puzzle and win the prize.

Synonyms:

Decipher	Decode	Unravel
Uncover		

Examples:

I can't decipher the inscription on the pillar.

The captain has decoded the message received from the army headquarters.

Central Bureau of Investigation has unravelled many mysteries in his new investigation.

The doctor uncovered the body of the dead patient to ascertain the cause of his death.

Antonyms:

Baffle	Confuse	Unsolved
Puzzle		

Examples:

One of the exam questions baffled me completely.

Let us not confuse the numerical puzzle with the help of the teacher in the class today.

Soothe (Verb)

It is difficult to soothe a crying baby.

Synonyms:

Palliate	Alleviate	Ease
Appease	Solace	Assuage
Calm	Deaden	Tranquillize

Examples:

The announcement of financial assistance has palliated the victims of the earthquake.

The 20-point programme of the Prime Minister has alleviated the living condition of the poorest of the poor in many parts of the country.

The banking institutions are helping to ease the financial handicaps of the farmers.

Land reforms are designed to appease the more restive of the farmers.

Today's rains have provided great solace to the draught ridden parts of the region.

Antonyms:

Irritate	Nettle	Inflame
Agitate	Animate	Excite
Stimulate	Exasperate	Enrage

Examples:

The sulky weather today is rather irritating.

The trade union has nettled the workers to resort to a pen-down strike.

The union's leaders have been warned against inflaming the workers against the company.

The workers are planning to agitate for an increase in their wages.

Modern dress fashions which are marked by nudity tend to animate violence and crime among the youth.

Sordid (Adjective)

In India, still many people live in sordid poverty.

Synonyms:

Dirty	Filthy	Foul
Seamy	Sleazy	Skimpy
Squalid	Wretched	Debauched
Degraded	Low	Shabby
Shameful	Vicious	Vile
Malicious	Selfish	

Examples:

Dirty water is not fit for drinking.

Don't use filthy languages while talking to your elders.

I have had a foul work to do today.

The water level in the reservoir was very low after the long draught.

You look pretty shabby in these clothes.

It is shameful of you to deceive your teacher.

Antonyms:

Clean	Fresh	Pure
Spotless	Unblemished	Decent
Honourable	Noble	Pure
Upright		

Examples:

The water is clean. You can drink it.

Fresh air blows in the morning. So you should go for walk.

Pure milk is not available here.

His spotless character helps him to win the election.

She was admired for her decent manner.

Soul (Noun)

He eats hardly enough to keep his body and soul together.

Synonyms:

Mind	Heart	Life
Animation	Incarnation	Ardour
Ego	Essence	Vital
Principle		

Examples:

Let us devote our mind and body to the welfare of our country.

Unless we put our heart and soul into our work, we cannot achieve success.

Ego is the enemy of self-realization among men and women.

Discipline is the essence of a successful personality.

Self-determination and strong will-power are vital for optimum achievement in life.

Antonyms:

Body	Matter	Materialization
Embodiment		

Examples:

A sound mind can flourish only in a sound body.

Matter representing mode of living is bringing about materialization of the soul.

A pure heart, conscious of the omnipresence of God, is the embodiment of a dynamic personality.

Spiteful (Adjective)

When our neighbours let their radio blare, our days are spiteful moments.

Synonyms:

Rancorous	Malevolent	Venomous
Vindictive	Malignant	Malicious

Examples:

Only constructive use of scientific advancement can bring about a society in which rancorous behavior of individuals which sets the individuals against each other or in conflicting groups, can be ended.

The malignant attitude of nations against each other can be ended only by bringing about a classless society in which the interests of individuals cease to clash but are reconciled in the framework of a peaceful united mankind.

Nationalism and narrow patriotism are concepts which lead to the propagation of malicious propaganda that divides the worlds into conflicting groups and races.

Antonyms:

Benign	Beneficent	Benevolent
Benignant		

Examples:

Educational systems in different countries should teach international citizenship to the students as a compulsory subject from the early age so as to make all humans and individuals develop a benign attitude.

Only a universal spirit of benignity can make everyone work for the beneficent functioning of a new world order of peace and mutual cooperation.

If the world's newly attained knowledge in sciences and humanities could be applied in full force, the universal feeling of benignancy would make the world live in peace, amity and prosperity.

Spread (Verb)

The rumour quickly spread through this village.

Synonyms:

Circulate	Expand	Escalate
Multiply	Proclaim	Publish
Development	Escalation	Distribute
Propagate		

Examples:

The college authority has circulated the admission notice in the newspapers.

The government has registered over 2 lakhs fair price shops in the country to distribute essential commodities, including food grains and sugar, among the people at fixed prices.

The government propagates its policies in different manners to elicit the co-operation of the people in their implementation.

Antonyms:

Accumulate	Contain	Control
Curb	Repress	Restrain
Gather		

Examples:

The black marketers try to accumulate scarcity goods in their godowns to sell them at higher prices whenever there is a chance.

I was so furious that I couldn't control my feelings and I hit him.

In this way they gather a lot of black profit for building more property.

Splendid (Adjective)

We thank you for this splendid dinner.

Synonyms:

Resplendent		
Magnificent	Grand	Impressive
Luxurious	Superb	Radiant
Brilliant	Beaming	Shining

Examples:

The bride looks resplendent in her red Banarsi Sari and precious ornaments.

They shed their radiant look from a distance.

The new car is available in a variety of brilliant colours.

Julie came out of her house beaming glamorously at her boy friend.

The new boot polish is shining reflectively on my shoes.

Antonyms:

Dull	Dark	Dim
Tarnished	Depressing	Disgusting
Mediocre	Pathetic	Sordid
Cloudy		

Examples:

Modest people prefer to wear clothes of dull colour.

Don't always look on the dark side of things.

She was in dim spirits today owing to the absence of her lover.

The unearthing of smuggled goods has tarnished the good name of my uncle's family.

The weather is cloudy today with prospects of heavy downpour soon.

Statement (Noun)

Clearness of the statement is much more important than the beauty of the language.

Synonyms:

Account	Narration	Declaration
Avowal	Assertion	Announcement
Utterance		

Examples:

The statement of accounts of the company shows the good progress made during the year.

Her narration of the grim story of the fatal accident of her husband brought tears to my eyes.

Indo-Chinese declaration on future trade has been hailed by the people of both countries.

Settlement of Punjab and Assam problems has been possible owing the avowal of all parties to the basic integrity of India.

The regional parties of the two states have asserted their right to develop their respective languages and cultures.

The announcement of the new commercial policy of India has heartened the business circles.

Antonyms:

Refutation	Disavowal	Contradiction
Denial	Negation	

Examples:

The integrity of the country lies in the refutation of regional claims for autonomy.

The Akali Party has expressed disavowal for violent activities of extremist elements.

There are certain fundamental contradictions in the U.S. foreign policy. On the one hand U.S. claims to support democratic movements in different countries; on the other it lends support to undemocratic regimes like that of the South African Republic.

Spontaneous (Adjective)

He made a spontaneous offer of help to us.

Synonyms:

Extempore	Free	Impromptu
Impulsive	Instinctive	Natural
Unbidden	Uncompelled	Unforced
Unprompted	Voluntary	Willing

Examples:

His extempore speech was admired by the audience.

After ten years imprisonment he was free again.

Earthquake and flood are natural calamities.

The firm went into voluntary liquidation.

Are you willing to accept responsibility?

Antonyms:

Arranged	Calculated	Contrived
Deliberate	Forced	Mannered
Orchestrated	Planned	Premeditated
Preplanned		

Examples:

It is a calculated risk to break your leg when you fell from the tree on the ground.

It is obviously a contrived incident to mislead the newspapers.

The deliberate killing of innocent civilians is the motto of terrorists.

I found this reasoning rather forced.

The attack was clearly premeditated by the terrorist.

Steady (Adjective)

Are Tony and Jane going steady?

Synonyms:

Constant	Undeviating	Stable
Regular	Firm	Consistent
Uniform		

Examples:

Our forces keep a constant watch on the country's borders in the north, east and west.

India's attachment to the non-aligned principles is undeviating.

Rajeev Gandhi was trying to provide stable government at the centre and in the states.

We must expand the production of hydroelectricity if we have to assure regular supply of electric power to industries.

India has firm policy on non-alignment.

It has consistently held to the principles of PanchSheel, since Nehru's time.

Antonyms:

Irregular	Unstable	Wavering
Changeable	Variable	Unsteady
Inconsistent		

Examples:

Pamela has been irregular in her attendance in the college.

Alexander's interest in studies has been unstable right from the beginning.

The subject Sachin has taken is not changeable at this stage. Hence his educational progress has been unsteady.

Steep (Adjective)

That story is rather steep. I find it difficult to understand it.

Synonyms:

High	Headlong	Sheer
Exorbitant	Sharp	Abrupt
Precipitous		

Examples:

Harry has reached a high peak in his career.

His rise in his profession has been sharp during the last five years.

This hall has an abrupt ending at the top.

If one were to look down from the hill top, one will observe a precipitous slope on all sides.

Antonyms:

Gradual	Low level	Straight
Easy	Gentle	

Examples:

In our valley there are hills round with gradual ascent.

Some hills look like descending below to the lower levels becoming plain-like, straight and easy to get down and gentle to walk.

Stiff (Adjective)

She was scared stiff.

Synonyms:

Brittle	Firm	Hard
Rigid	Solid	Taunt
Tense	Tight	Clumsy
Crude	Arduous	Formidable
Tough	Cruel	Drastic
Extreme	Strong	

Examples:

Non-metals are brittle. They can break when hammered.

We have no firm evidence.

Finding the right person for a job can be hard work.

She sat in her chair rigid and strong.

Metals are solid and heavy due to their low level of inter molecular space.

The cap of this bottle is very tight. It is very difficult to lose it.

A formidable task lies ahead of us.

Antonyms:

Ductile	Elastic	Flexible
Pliable	Plaint	Limber
Supple	Casual	Easy
Informal	Natural	Relaxed
Spontaneous		

Examples:

Metals are ductile. You can make wire from it.

Rubber is elastic. It can spread when pulled.

You should be flexible in your attitude and ideas.
I do a few exercises to limber up before a running-race.
Moisturizing cream keeps your skin soft and supple.
It is easy to drive in a free road rather than in a crowded one.
Now I feel relaxed after completing the tedious job.
It is only natural to worry about your children.

Still (Adjective)

He still hopes for a letter from her.

Synonyms:

Motionless	Calm	Peaceful
Serene	Stagnant	Quiet
Stationary	Pacific	

Examples:

When I reached his room, I was shocked to find his body lying in a motionless state.
I checked his pulse but it was calm and stationary.
His face was serene and peaceful as ever as if he were asleep. But his half open eyes frightened me.
When I looked at the sea beyond the window, I found the water stagnant and quite.

Antonyms:

Moving	Flowing	Excited
Disturbed	Troubled	Agitated
Running	Flustered	

Examples:

The train was moving on the plains at a terrific speed.
I was excited by the scenery around and by a large river flowing by the side of the rail track.
I was disturbed by the sheer memory of the death of my friend in the hostel.
My troubled thoughts agitated me in my dreams.

Stimulate (Verb)

He stimulated his son to make greater efforts.

Synonyms:

Instigate	Whet	Purr
Inflame	Inspirit	Good
Provoked	Incite	Motivate

Examples:

The police have instigated an official enquiry into the incident.

Attendance of public meetings held by the Arya Samaj at the local hall has always whetted my thoughts about society and humanity.

The purr of our pet dog is highly amusing though it disturbs when I am studying.

The union leader inflamed the workers against the managements.

He goaded them to go on a weeklong strike to press for demand for reduction in tuition fees and hostel rent.

Our teacher motivated us properly to score high marks in this international exam.

Antonyms:

Prevent   Hinder   Deter
Dissuade

Examples:

Nowadays the parents cannot prevent children from doing what they like.

More freedom to children need not necessarily hinder their progress provided they get nice educational facilities.

Enforcement of strict discipline does not deter children from going wrong if their minds are not put on the right track by their own free will.

The processes of guidance to children should not include dissuasion but indirect discouragement of wrong deeds.

Stimulus (Noun)

She worked very hard under the stimulus of monetary award.

Synonyms:

Spur   Incitement   Inducement
Incentive

Examples:

Modern films spur ideas of violence and sex among children and young students, but such incitement does not necessarily make them bad individuals as their dormant feelings find only theoretical expression through such spur and not practical demoralizations.

Science and technology provide inducement to more and more products of comfort in society. They are a great incentive to the economic development of a country.

Antonyms:

Deterrent   Dissuasion   Hindrance

Examples:

Sophisticated armaments are as much as deterrent to wars as they are a danger to mankind.

While science and technology help produce atomic and hydrogen bombs, developments in social sciences act as dissuasion factors against their use.

Hence science and technology are not a hindrance to human progress.

Strange (Adjective)

What a strange dress you are wearing!

Synonyms:

Queer	Extraordinary	Unique
Unnatural	Unusual	Uncommon
Odd	Eccentric	Inexplicable

Examples:

Stephen is an extraordinary person with very high intelligence, but his behavior is queer at times.

One unique feature of this T.V. is the remote control with which you can set its volume or focus your chair without going near the set.

Today's cool atmosphere is quite unusual and unnatural for these days of the hot season.

The scene of almost a vacant cinema hall is not uncommon these days because of competition with T.V., but it is quite odd.

An eccentric wife is never an asset in a family.

Antonyms:

Normal	Common	Familiar
Habitual	Standard	Everyday
Usual	Natural	Ordinary

Examples:

Delhi has normal temperature today.

Every day is not a hay day even for the richest man.

This crowd represents a usual phenomenon of this super market's evenings.

That he returns very tired in the evening after day's hard work is quite natural considering his age.

Stop (Verb)

The earthquake stopped all the clocks.

Synonyms:

Block	Arrest	Cease
Halt	Prevent	Discontinue

Examples:

The police arrested the smuggler for selling hashish in bulk to a scooter driver.

The law in India provides for the arrest of a person taking unhealthy drugs. This provision is designed to check the use of such drugs and their international smuggling.

Hostilities between these two sides ceased at midnight.

Antonyms:

Begin	Activate	Continue
Quicken	Purr	

Examples:

I began my schooling when I was five

We will have to activate our enthusiasm and will-power to achieve this higher position.

Let us continue to go up at the speed of 20 km an hour.

We can quicken our pace on less steep slopes.

Let us purr away the journey to the destination by sweet songs.

Strong (Adjective)

His breath is rather strong.

Synonyms:

Muscular	Fit	Healthy
Robust	Stalwart	Shout
Sturdy	Reinforced	Athletic
Powerful	Tough	

Examples:

It requires a muscular body to play wrestling and boxing.

Your punch has to be powerful enough to unbalance the opponent.

Sturdy bodies make more successful boxers.

Their tough punch has to carry a strong impact.

Antonyms:

Powerless	Delicate	Feeble
Faint	Mild	Timid
Pale	Weak	
Soft		

Examples:

I am powerless in this game.

People can make use of my weak points to their advantage.

I am reputed for my soft yet strong character.

She looks very delicate these days.

Sublime (Adjective)

To find a snack bar at the top of Mount Olympus would be to go from the sublime to ridiculous.

Synonyms:

| Superb | Grand | Lofty |

Majestic	Noble	Glorious
Exalted	Splendid	Resplendent
Beautiful		

Examples:

This computer set is superb. What a performance? What a design?

It was a grand reception from every angle.

Our principal has inculcated lofty ideals among the youth of his college.

Mrs. Sonya has exalted manners which bewitch her friends and relatives.

The hotel stands in splendid isolation surrounded by moorland.

Antonyms:

Powerless	Lowly	Mundane
Ordinary	Poor	Ridiculous
Bad	Common place	Mean
Insignificant	Weak	Soft

Examples:

Mrs. Sharma is mean to her servants, doubts their integrity, casts aspersions on their intentions and charges them of little thefts and so on.

We were dressed up for the party but she was still in her ordinary cloth.

Her behavior with servants is generally ridiculous.

No wonder she is socially insignificant in her neighbourhood.

Western clothes are now commonplace in Beijing.

Submissive (Adjective)

Mary is not a submissive wife.

Synonyms:

Abject	Accommodating	Acquiescent
Amenable	Complaint	Deferential
Docile	Dutiful	Humble
Obedient	Passive	Plaint
Tractable	Unresisting	

Examples:

I found the officials extremely accommodating to foreign visitors.

The government complaint as ever gave in to their demands.

Deepak is very dutiful. He performs his duty diligently.

Be humble enough to learn from your mistakes.

Pankaj is very obedient to his teachers and also to the elders.

Antonyms:

Awkward	Difficult	Disobedient

| Head strong | Intractable | Obstinate |
| Stubborn | Uncooperative | Unyielding |

Examples:
Please arrange the meeting at a less awkward time.
It is quite difficult to stay here without proper supply of drinking water.
Disobedient children are not liked anywhere.
The obstinate child refused to go to school.
She can be stubborn as mule. She never changes her idea.

Substantial (Adjective)

Were what you saw something substantial or only a ghost?
Synonyms:
Actual	Material	Tangible
Palpable	Perceptible	Corporeal
Real	Existing	

Examples:
Modern acting involves living the actual role to make it interesting.
The material side of the problem is not so serious. It is its psychological offshoots that are bothering me.
There is no tangible picture of the business project in view yet.
Bribing an officer to get a work done is a palpable offence as serious as the acceptance of bribe.

Antonyms:
Illusive	Unsubstantial	Illusory
Unreal	Chimerical	Shadowy
Fanciful	Farcical	

Examples:
The problem of poverty is illusive of solution due to lack of enthusiasm on the part of the administrators who run the relevant schemes.
The reasoning furnished by you for obtaining official support for your business project is unsubstantial.
You cannot win your point in a debate by giving illusory arguments.
The facts presented by you in support of your case for loan are unreal and shadowy.

Stubborn (Adjective)

He was stubborn in his attempt to go abroad.
Synonyms:
| Adamant | Fixed | Bull – headed |
| Obdurate | Tenacious | Unhanding |

Examples:

Norman is adamant in his demands. Unless he is given what he wants, he keeps the obsession.

The General of the regiment is headstrong. He moves heaven and earth to achieve what he wants.

His objective military strategy is inflexible.

Antonyms:

Adaptable	Complaint	Irresolute
Malleable	Pliable	Vacating
Pliable	Headstrong	Inflexible
Obstinate	Docile	Flexible

Examples:

The military policies of the government are adaptable to the demands of each situation.

My complaint behavior was appreciated by my principal.

Our new teacher is rather docile. The students do not listen to her with due reverence.

Plastic and rubber are flexible raw materials capable of being moulded to desired pattern.

Stupid (Adjective)

Do not be stupid enough to believe that.

Synonyms:

Dense	Dull	Slow
Thick	Unintelligent	

Examples:

How can you be so dense?

This colour is too dull to match your face.

Samson is a slow learner. His tutor is fed up with his thick memory and unintelligent grasp of lessons.

Antonyms:

Bright	Clever	Intelligent
Keen	Smart	

Examples:

Robin is a bright student, always topping in his class.

Rajesh is clever in his studies and intelligent in grasping faces and figures.

He takes keen interest in general knowledge and the world around him.

His action is firm but not obstinate.

Suitable (Adjective)

Ooty is the most suitable place for our summer picnic.

Synonyms:

Appropriate	Eligible	Pertinent
Relevant	Befitting	Seemly
Convenient	Becoming	

Examples:

Arthur gave appropriate replies to most of the questions asked by the interviewers.

Edwin is eligible for the post, he applied for, in every respect.

Members of Parliament asked questions to the minister pertaining to the departments under his charge and the latter gave pertinent replies.

He gave relevant facts to prove his replies.

The District Magistrate was given a reception befitting his status

Antonyms:

Unsuitable	Inappropriate	Irrelevant
Unseemly	Untimely	Improper
Contextual		

Examples:

The dress worn by the leader on the occasion was entirely unsuitable.

In his reply to the welcome address, the leader made many inappropriate remarks which offended the hosts.

He made quite a few irrelevant statements which damped the chances of the leader's election.

He made an unseemly scene at the house of the host.

Summon (Verb)

The Queen has summoned The Parliament.

Synonyms:

Call	Bid	Arouse
Assemble	Convene	Invite
Rouse	Convoke	Invoke
Send for		

Examples:

The Speaker of the Lok Sabha is responsible for calling the meeting of the House.

Some members of UN General Assembly have invoked special emergency session to condemn the Apartheid policies of South African government.

The principal has sent for application by students for free scholarships.

Antonyms:

Dismiss	Postpone	Adjourn

Examples:

The President has dismissed quite a few officers on charges of corruption and negligence.

The match was postponed to the following Saturday because of bad weather.
The meeting was adjourned for the next weak.

Superb (Adjective)

His performance in the musical competition was superb.

Synonyms:

Admirable	Breathtaking	Brill
Choice	Divine	Excellent
Exquisite	Five	Gorgeous
Grand	Magnificent	Marvellous
Superior	Superlative	

Examples:
The construction of Asdherdham Temple is admirable.
The performance of Shahrukh Khan in the feature film Veer-Zaara is really breathtaking.
Mathematical skill of this student is excellent.
The quality of these imported machines is fine.
Lal Qilla is a grand and magnificent movement of Mughal period.
Natasha Kumar is superior to his elder brother in studies.

Antonyms:

Abysmal	Awful	Bad
Disappointing	Dreadful	Inferior
Mediocre	Pathetic	Poor quality
Run-of-mill	Terrible	Woeful

Examples:
Indian farmer's condition is abysmal due to central government's biasing policy.
The plight of starving people is too awful to think about.
It is very bad to disobey your parents.
The weather this summer has been very disappointing.
I am afraid it is all a dreadful mistake.
After the death of his father, the child leads a pathetic life.

Superficial (Adjective)

He scored very low marks in the exam because of his superficial knowledge of the subject.

Synonyms:

External	Shallow	Slight
Outward	Hasty	Casual
Cursory	Empty	Frivolous
Lightweight	Silly	

Examples:

External factors play their role in the fixation of prices within a country.

This well is rather shallow. Its water is therefore, a bit saltish.

Let us not slight this problem, as on its solution depends the future of the country.

Don't go by her outward look. She is the master of a golden heart and soul.

Antonyms:

Penetrating	Deep	Thorough
Profound	Detailed	Serious
Comprehensive		

Examples:

This book is a penetrating study of the problem of poverty.

This well is very deep. Its water is sweet, cold in summer and hot in winter.

A thorough look at the picture shows that modern painting is becoming more and more abstract.

The leader of the opposition in a legislature is supposed to cast a profound influence on some of the policies of the government.

Sure (Adjective)

I think he is coming, but I am not quite sure.

Synonyms:

Certain	Assured	Clear
Confident	Accurate	Trustworthy
Persuaded	Positive	Satisfied
Definite	Doubtless	Positive

Examples:

I am certain I can perform this job nicely.

There is a definite move in the economy towards rapid progress.

There is doubtless flaw in the project at the engineering level.

There are positive indications of corrupt practices in the implementation of the project.

Antonyms:

Doubtful	Uncertain	Unsure
Wavering	Improbable	Vague
Unreliable	Insecure	

Examples:

Your presumption seems doubtful, because I have made foolproof arrangements against corruption.

However, I am uncertain about the technical flaws in their planning of the foundations.

I am also unsure about the quality of engineers appointed in the project.

He gave a vague idea about the attackers.

Surprising (Adjective)

His failure did not cause much surprise to all of us.

Synonyms:

Unexpected	Marvellous	Startling
Striking	Astonishing	Amazing
Suddenness		

Examples:

This unexpected turn in the events has upset the original planning of the foreign inspired terrorists.

The suddenness of the Rajeev – Longowal accord has provided a marvellous development which has startled the extremist elements, striking at the very root of their evil designs.

The accord can bring about astonishing results by way of normalization of Hindu – Sikh brotherhood.

The return of the business situation in Punjab and Delhi to normalcy has been amazingly rapid.

Antonyms:

Everyday	Ordinary	Usual
Normal	Customary	Habitual

Examples:

The distribution system in India provides sufficient stocks of everyday needs of essential commodities through fair price shops.

There is a difference in the standards of living between an ordinary citizen and the privileged classes.

There is always the usual class struggle going on between the two categories of people.

Only political leaders can discern this normal phenomenon of this class struggle.

It is customary for this college to hold its annual prize distribution function in August every year.

My grandfather was a habitual drinker of tea and coffee.

Suppress (Verb)

This News Paper has suppressed the truth about the crime.

Synonyms:

Subdue	Overpower	Bridle
Quash	Restrain	Quell
Check	Moderate	Repress
Impede		

Examples:

If the weaker sections are not brought up in society with grace, they would overpower the privileged classes in due time.

The horseman bridled his horse to give a pick up to his speed in the race.

The understanding reached between the management and the workers has quashed on the issues of bonus.

The workers are being restrained from going on a total strike with the help of the labour commissioner.

The Prime Minister appointed extra military force to quell the agitations.

Antonyms:

Inflame	Encourage	Incite
Promote	Stimulate	Spread
Gee up	Excite	Provoke
Agitate	Kindle	

Examples:

The feelings of the labourers were inflamed by the union leaders.

The teachers roused among the student's enthusiasm for keen interest in studies and sports.

Modern so – called blue films excite the young viewers to sex and violence.

The pornographic films provoke the students to take to undesirable drugs.

The labour union has decided to agitate for higher wages.

Suspend (Verb)

He was fined $ 2000 with a suspended sentence by the High Court.

Synonyms:

Debar	Stay	Hinder
Stop	Withhold	Interrupt
Discontinue	Fall	Defer
Delay		

Examples:

Ronald has been debarred from reappearing in the examination on grounds of indiscipline.

The tenant has obtained stay orders from the court against the landlord.

Financial circumstances have hindered his plan of higher studies.

I stopped my car at the crossing owing to the red signal.

I am withholding my opinion on Kim until the result of his last examination.

The phenomenon of occasional strike by teachers interrupts the coverage of the course.

Antonyms:

Begin	Keep up	Urge on
Protract	Continue	Expedite
Prolong		

Examples:

Sam has begun his studies in right earnest.

Keep up the courage my boy. You will be able to face better next time.

I have urged on my younger brother to work harder.

Centre – Assam accord on foreigner's issue was signed after protracted negotiation.

I will continue playing badminton every evening to achieve my ambition of becoming Delhi champion.

Surrender (Verb)

We advised the hijackers to surrender themselves to the Police.

Synonyms:

Leave	Resign	Yield
Waive	Let so	Leave
Give up	Over	Code
Alienate	Abandon	

Examples:

The plane leaves Delhi for Mumbai at 12.35.

I may resign from my present job to take more seriously the banking probationers examination.

The applications of new machines in industry can yield highly revolutionary impact on productivity.

I would have obtained the contract for the construction of the building if the commissioner had the power to waive the condition of Master's degree in architecture.

Antonyms:

Withhold	Hold	Defy
Oppose	Resist	Withstand
Reserve	Retain	Detain

Examples:

The government should not withhold information about the smugglers from the newspapers.

He told us to reserve our strength for the next days match.

The accused offered to retain the famous lawyer for advocating his case in the High Court.

The police are detaining the culprits in their custody until the case is brought to the court.

Swell (Verb)

His heart was swelling with pride.

Synonyms:

Distend	Enlarge	Extend
Increase	Rise	Bulge
Bloat	Billow	Belly
Magnify	Bungle	Amplify
Dilate	Enhance	Expand

Examples:

He increased his speed to overtake this bus.

This looking glass magnifies one's face beyond proportion.

Mr. Raja has so bungled the accounts of the firm that it cannot help being closed.

His securing the top position in the IAS has enhanced him prestige.

This transistor is meant to amplify the sound.

The metals contract in the winter as they expand in the summer.

Antonyms:

Shorten	Contract	Reduce
Decrease	Diminish	Abridge
Attenuate		

Examples:

The habit of drinking wine shortens one's life.

The metals contract in the winter as they expand in the summer.

I have reduced the consumption of sugar in my diet as per the advice of my doctor.

The demand for record-players has greatly decreased with the arrival of cheap tape – recorders.

The demand for a product diminishes with increase in production.

This book has been abridged in its new edition.

Sympathy (Noun)

I have some sympathy with their views.

Synonyms:

Kindness	Pity	Condolence
Commiseration	Tenderness	Harmony
Rapport	Warmth	Love
Fellow – feeling	Compassion	

Examples:

We should show kindness to the downtrodden.

We should love our country and our countrymen as our brethren.

Fellow-feeling for our countrymen does not mean hatred for outsides or people of other countries. It implies universal brotherhood.

We should carry compassion for our subordinate, employees or the poorer brethren.

Antonyms:

Pitilessness	Cruelty	Hard – heartedness
Selfishness		

Examples:

In Germany and Italy, patriotism reached its negative climax. It manifested itself through pitilessness on outsiders, non-citizens and Jews.

The Nazi Germans perpetrated untold cruelty on the Jews.

Italians under Mussolini manifested hard-heartedness towards the French neighbours and Africans.

Systematic (Adjective)

You should take a systematic attempt to attain your objective.

Synonyms:

Methodical	Efficient	Organized
Precise	Standardized	Regular
Orderly		

Examples:

Modern management implies methodical performance of business activities.

I have arranged for a regular supply of kerosene oil in the village.

Why don't you arrange for the holding of the proposed exhibition in an orderly fashion?

Antonyms:

Irregular	Casual	Fortuitous
Unmethodical	Occasional	

Examples:

If you become so irregular in attendance in your new job, you may not be able to maintain it.

Allan has taken casual leave for two days in order to look after his ailing mother.

This source of income is fortuitous for him. It comes his way once a while.

His functioning is so unmethodical. It can never bring a lasting success.

You should make occasional social calls to keep up your popularity.

Taciturn (Adjective)

He is taciturn to talk in front of a large audience.

Synonyms:

Mute	Quiet	Reserved
Reticent	Silent	Tight – lipped
Unforth coming	Withdrawn	

Examples:

She remains mute all the time in prayer meeting.
Please can you keep the children quit while I am on the phone?
She is reserved by nature. She prefers to say alone.
He seemed strangely reticent about his past.
There are several questions I wanted to ask but I kept silent.

Antonyms:

Chatty	Communicative	Forth coming
Garrulous	Loquacious	Open
Outgoing	Sociable	Talkative
Verbose	Voluble	Wordy

Examples:

This small kid is very chatty. He always speaks something or the other.
I don't find Sandeep very communicative. He is reserved.
He always becomes garrulous after a few glasses of wine.
Indian women are loquacious by nature.
He has an open heart, he doesn't hide anything form his friends.
Deepak has never really been the sociable type.
What's wrong with you? You are not talkative this evening.

Tact (Noun)

Have great tact in dealing with people.

Synonyms:

Finesse	Diplomacy	Adroitness
Finesse	Discretion	Skill
Cleverness	Consideration	

Examples:

Thomson deserves to be a diplomat. He has a needed finesse.
She acted with considerable discretion.
Conversational skill is by itself a rare qualification.
It is only his cleverness that has saved him from death and destruction.
My application for import licence is receiving due consideration in the commerce ministry.

Antonyms:

Discourtesy	Frankness	Awkward
Clumsy	Gauche	Untoward
Roughness	Bluntness	Simplicity

Examples:

Discourtesy is the enemy of civilization and culture.

Frankness means being fearless and straight forward not blunt and rude.

He is a capable person, well-skilled in his job but his roughness of a rustic nature devalues his achievements.

His bluntness has made enemies of many friends.

He was deprived of his legal right just because of his over simplicity.

Talent (Noun)

This is an exhibition of local talents.

Synonyms:

Ability	Capacity	Flair
Endowment	Power	Knack
Genius	Aptitude	Skill

Examples:

His ability to control emergencies of any type by the dint of his alert mind is admirable.

Making cake is easy once you have got this knack.

It is rare to find such genius nowadays.

His aptitude in mathematics enables him to computerize every problem and solve it.

His skill in designing modern dresses is unmatched.

Antonyms:

Inefficiency	Unskillfulness	Idleness
Stupidity		

Examples:

His all-round inefficiency will one day bring a crash in his business.

His stupidity very often lets him down in emergencies.

He has chosen a craft in which his unskillfulness makes title difference. He is good salesman.

Tasty (Adjective)

This dish is not as tasty as the one we had few days back in New York.

Synonyms:

Appetizing	Luscious	Delicious
Palatable		

Examples:

For some tea acts as an appetizing agent, for others as the opposite

The hero looked at the luscious curves of the heroine and started dancing and signing.

This is a delicious dish of Nepal.

It is not only tasty but also palatable.

Antonyms:

Nasty	Sickening	Nauseous

Flavourless   Insipid

Examples:

I could never imagine such a popular restaurant will serve much a nasty dish.

It is sickening to see a slow movie like this.

Our kitchen is giving out a nauseous smell. What sort of meat is in the oven?

The lecture of today's visiting professor was rather dull and insipid.

Tear (Verb)

He did tear the parcel open.

Synonyms:

Rip	Rend	Shred
Sunder	Dust	Dash
Speed	Seize	Snatch
Pluck	Split	Lacerate
Sever	Rupture	Division

Examples:

In the middle ages the peers would play duels with swords and the women usually ripped the loser.

Differences among brothers have led to the split of the land left by their father.

The fight among the hoodlums of the neighbourhood led one to lacerate the other. The police had to intervene and arrest the offender.

The rupture among the partners has led to the division of firm. They have severed business connections altogether.

Antonyms:

Repair	Patch	Rectify
Restore	Mend	

Examples:

I have got my motor – bike duly repaired.

The partners have patched their differences and recombined their split firm.

The losses suffered during the split are being gradual rectified.

The profits of the old firm will get restored in due course.

The partners have mended their ways by working out a new division of responsibilities.

Tease (Verb)

She teased her father about his bald head.

Synonyms:

Irritate	Chafe	Provoke
Bait	Goad	Pester
Taunt	Vex	Plague

Torment   Annoy

Examples:

The rash decisions of my partners in business are irritating me these days.

The passengers sat chafing at the long delay of train.

If you provoke the dog, it will attack you.

Continued unemployment greatly vexed me.

Extremists and terrorists plagued some parts of the country last year with violence.

Antonyms:

| Hush | Compose | Conciliate |
| Appease | Calm | Mollify |

Examples:

The corrupt officer tried to hush up the case of smuggling against the accused.

I never lose my composure, come what may.

He has developed an attitude of conciliation with adverse circumstances.

The management has adopted a policy of appeasement towards the agitating workers in order to keep production going.

The manager calmed down the workers, by offering a 10% increase in the salary of each worker.

This soothed the resentment of the workers.

Tedious (Adjective)

The tedious work took our whole day to complete it.

Synonyms:

Banal	Drab	Dreary
Dull	Irksome	Laborious
Monotonous	Prosaic	Soporific
Tiresome	Tiring	Vapid
Wearisome		

Examples:

The clown dressed himself in drab clothes.

Bonded labour in many villages leads dreary life.

The weather of Delhi in winter is quite dull and dreary.

He found it irksome to have to catch a bus to work.

Sonia was a laborious girl. She secured 98% in board exam.

Everybody wants changes in life rather than monotonous job.

Antonyms:

| Enjoyable | Enthralling | Exciting |
| Exhilarating | Imaginative | Inspiring |

Interesting   Quickly   Finished
Short   Stimulating

Examples:

The picnic tour was really enjoyable.
The prize distributing ceremony was very exciting.
My first parachute jump was an exhilarating experience for me.
Pundit Jawaharlal Nehru was an inspiring leader.
I find his work very stimulating.

Temperamental (Adjective)

His temperamental dislike for study resulted in low marks in the final exam.

Synonyms:

Capricious	Easily	Upset
Emotional	Erratic	Excitable
Fiery	Highly strong	Hypersensitive
Impatient	Irritable	Moody
Neurotic	Passionate	Petulant
Sensitive		

Examples:

Her departure was an emotional affair.
Delivery of goods is erratic.
The circus was really very excitable.
She is hypersensitive about her weight.
You are too impatient with her. She is only a child.
The sound of loudspeaker is very irritable. It disturbs my study.
She is very moody. She does get irritated easily.
Cool-headed person always win the race.

Antonyms:

Calm	Cool headed	Easy going
Phlegmatic	Unexcitable	Constant
Dependable	Reliable	Stable
Steady		

Examples:

She is very calm. She – doesn't get irritated easily.
Cool – headed person always with the race.
My mother doesn't mind who comes to stay. She is very easy going.
Pressure in the container remains constant.

I am still dependable to my parents.

Amar is not reliable person. He doesn't keep secret of anyone.

If you are stable and steady in your attitude you will achieve your goal.

Tempt (Verb)

Nothing could tempt him to such an action.

Synonyms:

Reduce	Decoy	Inveigle
Entice	Contrive	Wheedle
Coax	Invite	Lure
Attract	Allure	

Examples:

Some of the multinational companies seduce talented young men by offering higher salaries.

In this way they decoy even some to those selected by the UPSC for the IAS by offering fabulously attractive salaries and other facilities.

The married woman, enticed by the charms of the strong Youngman, inveigled him into her home on a contrived pretext, when her husband had gone outstation.

The Youngman first invited the young woman to a dinner and then wheedled her to his bachelor apartment.

Antonyms:

Deter	Disincline	Discourage
Care	Restraint	Dissuade

Examples:

India's defense potential deters its enemies from taking an aggressive posture.

India is herself disinclined to take any aggressive attitude unless she is first attacked.

Anita found out the intentions of her college-friend and decided to discourage his advances in future.

Care of health is better than the cure of disease.

Anita put her friend's overtures under restraint.

She has not yet succeeded in dissuading her boy friend from meeting her.

Temporary (Adjective)

His job is only temporary. It may take few more months to make it permanent.

Synonyms:

Fleeting	Evanescent	Passing

Ephemeral	Momentary	Transitory
Transient		

Examples:

A woman's youth is more fleeting than that of the man.

The glory of a leader is evanescent unless he rises to the status man on immortal deeds.

The economic depression comes to many non – socialist countries as passing phase.

Some of the insect have an ephemeral life, just a few moments or at the maximum a few hours.

Antonyms:

Everlasting	Immortal	Invariable
Permanent	Persistent	

Examples:

Mrs. Gandhi has left an everlasting impact on India's history for many of her achievements.

A few names in every country's history become immortal for their everlasting contribution to human thought.

Certain scientific concepts are regarded as permanent and invariable as they will continue to be applied for the millennium.

The Synonyms and Antonyms form an integral part o

Tendency (Noun)

My Business is showing a tendency to improve.

Synonyms:

Prone	Inclination	Predilection
Leaning	Penchant	Trend
Bias	Proclivity	Propensity

Examples:

Revolutions in some countries are prone to cast their influence on the social, economic and scientific progress or others.

A persistent trend towards materialization of societies is discernible in the world today.

The socialist bias which started with the Bolshevik Revolution which started in 1917 has continued to persist.

The whole world is now inclining towards the concept of welfare state.

Modern proclivities of the people resolve round getting at more and more money for maximum comforts in life.

Antonyms:

Aversion	Distaste	Dislike
Disinclination	Antipathy	Detestation

Examples:

I have an aversion for pessimists.

This brand of fish is distasteful.

I dislike being goaded to do things. I like to be on my own.

I can appreciate your disinclination to life marked by acute materialism.

I have an antipathy for pets, especially they become a problem when they are sick.

I detest a person who is given to moods of depression.

Terse (Adjective)

He made a terse talk about the policy of this company.

Synonyms:

Neat	Short	Succinct
Laconic	Compact	Summary
Sententious	Condensed	

Examples:

We managed to get the garden looking neat and tidy.

I telephoned Mary a few minutes ago. It was a lively short conversation I will always remember.

His replies were to the point and succinct.

This description of the happenings at the airport is too laconic. Will you mind giving me more details?

This is a compact, handy dictionary of synonyms and antonyms perfectly illustrated with the usage of words.

It helps in the making of summary of long passage by expanding your vocabulary.

The ideas contained in this book are sententious and condensed.

Antonyms:

Diffuse	Circumlocutory	Confused
Discursive	Rambling	Verbose
Lengthy	Wordy	

Examples:

This is story is a diffused version of a little incident. It teaches the art of expanding ideas and expressions.

Huxley's book is verbose yet interesting.

Some of Thomas Harry's stories are unnecessarily lengthy.

It is desirable to avoid wordy letters. Brevity in correspondence pays.

Theory (Noun)

Naval officers must understand both the theory and the practice of navigation.

Synonyms:

Belief	Postulate	Assumption
Speculation	Doctrine	Conjecture
Hypothesis	Supposition	

Examples:

I admire his passionate belief in what he is doing.

The postulate on which this conclusion is based has little foundation.

Your assumption that she passes this way every Sunday morning may or may not prove true.

The upwards swing in share prices is based on speculation trends let loose by the Stock Exchange.

The doctrine Divine Right of Kings does not hold valid in this age of democracy.

Antonyms:

| Practical | Realistic | Actual |
| Happening | | |

Examples:

Practical considerations carry more weight than theoretical.

Modern logic as applied to computers is based on realistic facts and figures of statisticians.

In the fast moving life of modern society, actual considerations are more important than hackneyed theories of the gone by days.

The happenings of day-to-day life provide the base for futuristic literature.

Thick (Adjective)

The air was thick with dust and snow.

Synonyms:

Broad	Bulky	Deep
Solid	Substantial	Close
Clotted	Opaque	Abundant
Brimming	Bristling	Covered
Crawling	Replete	

Examples:

The road is broad enough to pass the heavy vehicles.

The bulky figure of Seth Diana appeared at the door.

The Ganga River is very deep at Prayaga.

We have abundant proof of this guilt.

Iron is solid whereas water is liquid.

The two buildings are close together

Clotted blood prevents bleeding the blood from the wound.

Opaque glass windows in car are prohibited in Delhi road.

Antonyms:

Narrow	Slight	Slim
Thin	Clear	Diluted
Runny	Weak	Bare
Empty	Free from	Sparse
Distant		

Examples:

You shouldn't narrow in your attitude.

A slight mistake can cause a big damage.

The water of this pond is clear.

After his prolong illness he fees weak, so he avoids physical work.

Empty mind is 'Devils workshop' is a famous saying.

Now he is free from all anxiety and distress.

Don't go outside bare headed in scorching sun.

Thin (Adjective)

He seemed to vanish into thin air.

Synonyms:

Diluted	Narrow	Slim
Bony	Lean	Slender
Delicate	Weak	Meager
Films	Scanty	Sparse

Examples:

The sad realities of the poor are much more tragic than what reaches us through diluted versions of the news media.

His servant is paid too meagre a salary for the enormously manual work he does for the company.

The boss got rid of his impertinent subordinate on a flimsy charge.

The western part of India has very scanty rainfall.

Antonyms:

Strong	Sturdy	Heavy
Thick	Bulky	Adequate
Plentiful	Abundant	Profuse
Bountiful	Wholesome	

Examples:

This tractor is really strong and solid for the heavy work it is supposed to do.

Adam is quite sturdy to undertake the strenuous manual work if we pay him adequately.

This year's Kharif crop is bountiful, thanks to the high yielding varieties programme of the agricultural institute.

This hotel serves a wholesome meal for its charges.

Thoughtful (Adjective)

It was thoughtful of you to warn me of your arrival.

Synonyms:

Attentive	Circumspect	Heedful
Provident	Careful	Considerate
Mindful		

Examples:

Suzan listens to his class lectures attentively.

A CID inspector has to be extremely circumspect these days of criminal proclivities of respected class of businessmen and the beaurocrats.

An entrepreneur of consumer products has to be heedful of the health of the consumers.

Indian women have been very provident in keeping their budgets in trim.

They have to be prudent in the choice of goods for consumption by the family.

I have to be careful with my razor while shaving owing the hardness of my skin.

Modern family life expects the husband to be considerate to his wife's feelings and vice versa.

Antonyms:

Carefree	Gay	Remiss
Reckless	Negligent	Neglectful
Giddy		

Examples:

Pankaj is a carefree boy. He studies deeply when on table and plays freely in the play ground.

He does not entertain any worries and keeps gay and humorous in company.

Alfred is always remiss in both studies and games.

Mr. Anil Jain is a reckless businessman. He gambles higher stakes for his greed for money, but most of the time suffers losses.

Robin is negligent of his games. Hence he often falls sick. He is neglectful of his bodily health.

I feel giddy due to prolong illness. I must take bed rest.

Timely (Adjective)

Your timely arrival to the function saved us from troubles.

Synonyms:

Appropriate	Convenient	Punctual

Prompt	Early	Seasonable
Opportune		

Examples:

Prompt payment of the invoice would be greatly appreciated.

I get up early in the morning to be in time for duty.

John Abraham is very punctual in his duty.

He makes use of every opportune moment in his researches.

Antonyms:

Tardy	Unseasonable	Late
Inopportune		

Examples:

Rajendra is very lazy in his studies. Therefore his progress is tardy.

This quality of teak seems to be only fit for fuel. It looks unseasonable for furniture.

Being late Sunny missed the train.

The time is yet inopportune for the inauguration of the new library in our college.

Timid (Adjective)

That fellow is as timid as a rabbit.

Synonyms:

Bashful	Afraid	Coward
Coy	Nervous	Diffident
Shy	Chicken-hearted	Timorous
Submissive		

Examples:

She is too bashful to aspire to be a model girl.

Rupak is diffident of conversing with great men due to lack of confidence.

Rupak is too shy to speak to a strange girl.

Rajeev is chicken-hearted. He can't face the circumstances with courage.

His timorous behavior at the meeting with his girl friend's father proved disastrous for his love.

Shekhar is too submissive to be a group leader.

Antonyms:

Audacious	Brace	Daring
Confident	Poised	Aggressive
Arrogance	Fearless	Shameless

Examples:

The audacious always helps him pull through nicely.

He is confident of what he wants and how he will have it.

He remains poised in turbulent circumstances.

He is often condemned for his arrogant nature.

He becomes aggressive when he is heavily drunk.

Tired (Adjective)

He was a tired man when he got back from the long walk.

Synonyms:

Drained	Drowsy	Enervated
Fatigued	Flagging	Sleepy
Weary	Exasperated	Irked
Irritated	Exhausted	Weary
Worn-out		

Examples:

Poverty has exhausted him at the young age.

The long journey has fatigued my nerves.

His job involves a combination of physical and mental work throughout the day. Hence he gives a weary look.

His worn-out suit gave him away in the eyes of his would-be in laws.

Antonyms:

Invigorated	Refreshed	Rested
Relaxed	Strengthened	

Examples:

The new job has invigorated her all-round existence.

I feel quite refreshed by a cup of coffee after every few hours.

These two months after illness have rested my tired limbs.

My work relaxes me instead of tiring me, as it is interesting and to my liking.

It strengthens my body and soul.

Toleration (Noun)

Your toleration of criticism shows your emotional maturity.

Synonyms:

Tolerance	Temperance	Endurance
Laxity	Forgiveness	Clemency
Moderation		

Examples:

Rats have developed a tolerance for certain poisons.

The temperature of this stall suits the cooking range of this pressure cooker.

He showed remarkable endurance throughout his illness.

No laxity will be allowed to political parties indulging in violence in this region.

She shows love and forgiveness for her enemies.

He appealed to the judge for clemency.

The government expects all political parties to practice moderation in their election campaigns.

Antonyms:

Irritation	Heating up	Wearing off
Rigidity	Overbearance	Dogmatism
Fanaticism		

Examples:

Over medication during my last illness has caused me irritation.

The elections have heated up the political atmosphere in the state.

The effect of the ennobling speeches of The Prime Minister is wearing off.

The rigidity of the metal caused it to crack.

The democratic wind is manifesting some over-bearance in India's political atmosphere.

The socialists have loosened their old dogmatism and fanaticism.

Torture (Noun)

If you put him to the torture, he will tell you what happened.

Synonyms:

Anguish	Afflict	Crucify
Pain	Persecute	Pain
Agony	Torment	Distress
Persecute		

Examples:

There is anguish in world circles over the lack of concrete agreement among superpowers over disarmament.

I have developed a severe pain in my legs since the last accident.

An atmosphere of agony prevailed in the family over the untimely death of the head of the family.

It has caused particular torment in the heart of the old mother.

I am distressed over my failure in the IAS examination.

The government of Iran has persecuted a number of Shiates in the country.

Antonyms:

Allay	Soothe	Alleviate
Console	Solace	Mollify
Relief	Comfort	Palate

| Ease | Deaden | Lessen |

Examples:

Akali-Government accord has allayed the fears of business in the whole of northern region.

Government assistance to the poorest of the poor in tribal areas has soothed the feelings of the tribal communities.

Government is providing relief to the draught ridden farmers in Bihar.

Modern scientific inventions have given quite many comforts to the people of the world.

The feeling of the poor can be palliated by floating new schemes for their upliftment.

I felt at ease on knowing the favourable result of my interview for a job in the bank.

Touchy (Adjective)

His touchy nature repelled him from his friends.

Synonyms:

Bad tempered	Captious	Cross
Grumpy	Irascible	Irritable
Peevish	Petulant	Querulous
Oversensitive	Surly	

Examples:

I am often bad tempered early in the morning. She is oversensitive. She cannot bear even a little pain.

The scorching sun in May & June is very irritable to me.

Grumpy women are not liked in good society.

The child is looking slightly peevish.

Strong cross wind makes it difficult for boats to leave harbour.

Antonyms:

Affable	Cheerful	Easy-going
Genial	Imperious	Indifferent
Insensitive	Pleasant	Sunny
Sweet	Unconcerned	

Examples:

I found my girl friend's parent very affable.

For having secured good marks in board exam, she is very cheerful.

My mother is very easygoing. She doesn't mind who comes to stay in our house.

She appeared indifferent to their sufferings.

Light music is always pleasant to my ears.

The air was sweet with the scent of lilies.

Tragedy (Noun)

The tragedy in this drama is the talk of the town.

Synonyms:

| Misfortune | Disaster | Affliction |
| Adversity | Calamity | Catastrophe |

Examples:

It was great misfortune for India to lose Mrs. Indira Gandhi on October 31, 1984.

It was treated by the people as a national disaster.

The country was afflicted by a wave of violence for a few days. It seemed some great calamity had befallen the country.

The leader's assassination proved to be a great catastrophe.

Antonyms:

Farce	Happiness	Joy
Prosperity	Success	Comedy
Humour	Drama	

Examples:

The dialogue between India and Pakistan for the resumption of trade proved to be a farce.

He didn't appreciate the comedy of the situation.

He has a good sense of humour.

A thing of beauty is a joy forever.

Material prosperity is what he needs at present.

His success in this board exam is a great surprise to all of us.

Transparent (Adjective)

Gandhi is a man of transparent honesty.

Synonyms:

Clear	Lucid	Obvious
Apparent	Distinct	Limpid
Crystalline		

Examples:

This picture depicts its themes in a clear way.

This piece of literature is lucid in its morals.

This mirror shows the image limpidly.

This container is made of crystalline. One can observe the item contained from outside.

Antonyms:

| Foggy | Obscure | Cloudy |
| Muddy | Opaque | Thick |

| Hidden | Vague | Uncertain |

Examples:

The weather is foggy this morning. It is better to avoid driving the scooter.

This essay is very obscure. It does not bring out the subject matter clearly.

The ideas expressed are vague and do not show any logical sequence.

Treacherous (Adjective)

Do not rely on my memory. It is treacherous.

Synonyms:

Disloyal	Deceitful	Duplicitous
Faithlessness	False	Perfidious
Unreliable	Untrue	Unfaithful
Unreliable	Not trustworthy	Perfidious

Examples:

Citizens who prove disloyal to their country are liable to punishment under law.

Madhu is unfaithful to her husband.

This brand of the motorbike part is unreliable for durability and accuracy.

Some of the employees in my firm are not trust worthy.

Some of the terrorists have been arrested by the government for their perfidious activities.

Antonyms:

| Faithful | Loyal | Trustee |
| Devoted | Reliable | Trustworthy |

Examples:

Deepak remained faithful to his beliefs.

He is a loyal devotee of the congress ideology.

I am one of the trustees of this institution.

I am devoted to the cause of education.

He is a reliable member of the Managing Committee of this college.

Mr. Robinson is a trust worthy businessman, always selling and rendering honest dealings.

Transient (Adjective)

The child enjoyed only transient happiness. Soon it was wounded in a minor accident.

Synonyms:

| Brief | Fleeting | Fugitive |
| Short | Transitory | Livid |

Momentary	Flying	Passing
Evanescent	Temporary	Ephemeral

Examples:

His stay in our college hostel was very brief but memorable.

For a fleeting moment I thought the car was going to crash.

Mr. Singh stayed with us in 1942 as a fugitive from British law. He was a freedom fighter during the Quit India movement.

Causes of disharmony among groups have been successfully removed by a discreet approach.

Antonyms:

Long lasting	Detailed	Permanent
Persistent		

Examples:

She expected a long-lasting relationship from her husband but due to her husband's drinking habit the relation broke off.

Nothing is permanent in this world.

The writer gives a detailed description of various philosophical postulations.

It is very hard to deal with persistent peoples who hardly compromise with their principles.

Tremble (Verb)

The bridge trembled as a heavy lorry crossed it.

Synonyms:

Vibrate	Shake	Quake
Shiver	Shudder	Tester
Totter	Shudder	Oscillate
Quiver		

Examples:

The whole house vibrates whenever a heavy truck passes.

Just thinking about the accident makes me shudder.

The pendulum of the clock oscillates consistently.

The earth quivers whenever there is an earth quake.

Antonyms:

Stiffen	Petrify	Steady

Examples:

I stiffened when the policeman gave a whistle seeing me riding double on a bicycle with my friend.

The suddenness of accident on the opposite pavement petrified me with horror.

Her elder sister has a steady influence on her.

Trick (Noun)

He got the money from me by a trick.

Synonyms:

Wiles	Deception	Dodge
Fraud	Swindle	Play
Skill	Ruse	Guile
Imposture	Cunning	

Examples:

The wiles of the monkey greatly amused the onlookers.

This mechanic has the skill of rectifying a blocked engine.

The ruse of the horse-rider in the circus amused the children.

The salesman guiled us to buy a carton of imitation soap at exorbitant price.

In fact he was an imposture holding the forged card of a salesman of a reputed company.

Antonyms:

Innocence	Frankness	Guilelessness
Truth	Sincerity	

Examples:

The innocence of the visitor impressed us into giving him a good hearing.

She spoke about her fears with complete frankness.

Guileless persons never beguile anybody. They are frank and fair.

Truth and sincerity are the most welcome traits of good humans.

Trust (Noun)

Can I trust you to get the money safely to the bank?

Synonyms:

Reliance	Confidence	Keeping
Credit	Office	Duty
Expectation	Hope	Credence
Belief		

Examples:

My reliance on the parents for further studies is not in keeping with my values in life.

I have confidence in my own ability to earn and learn at the same time.

The credit for affording my early education goes to my parents who sacrificed their own comforts to pay for my expense.

Antonyms:

Distrust	Faithlessness	Breaking of pledge
Deception		

Examples:

There is not question of distrust in my parents but it is one of self respect and self determination.

I am not accusing myself of faithlessness for my parents. I am simply trying to fulfill my own ambition of becoming self-reliance.

I am not causing any deception to myself or breaking any pledge to others.

Try (Verb)

He did not try to do that?

Synonyms:

Strive	Effort	Seek
Struggle	Undertake	Endeavour
Attempt		

Examples:

We must strive to do the best in life to ourselves and to others as far as possible.

We must endeavour to serve our motherland to the best of our ability.

We must attempt to develop maximum capability to do so.

Antonyms:

| Leave | Drop | Quit |
| Give up | Relinquish | Abandon |

Examples:

We must leave no stone unturned to achieve greatness.

We must drop the selfish elements from our existence in order to be useful to others.

I will quit the present job if it does not help to fulfill my ambition of serving well my motherland.

Tyranny (Noun)

Living in that country is nothing but living under tyranny.

Synonyms:

| Totalitarianism | Autocracy | Oppression |
| Despotism | Rigor | Harshness |

Examples:

Totalitarianism is a political concept which thrived during first part of the century up to Second World War in Germany and Italy.

The power in these countries was held by Hitler and Mussolini in its totality. They are autocrats.

Hitler and Mussolini let loose oppression of the people and made them to obey the government in their wrongful activities.

They were despots of the harshest variety.

They ruled with all the rigor and harshness at their command.

Antonyms:

Pity	Love	Compassion
Softness	Sympathy	

Examples:

Opposite to the tyranny of the dictators is the government of the democracies in which pity and love are the key policies for the people at large.

The rich should have a compassion for the poor in a country where the rich show sincere sympathy for the poor, the government adopts a policy of softness for the rich.

Topical (Adjective)

A new topical news film has been released today. Shall we go to that film?

Synonyms:

Indicative	Symbolical	Regular
Illustrative	Normal	

Examples:

A mixed economy is a system which is indicative of the existence of the public & private sectors side by side.

It is a universal phenomenon symbolical of the co-existence of the rich and the poor.

There is regular competition among the private entrepreneurs on the one side and a regulated coordination between the public and private sectors on the others.

The system is illustrative of the logical pattern that runs the economy of all countries in mutual relationships in economic life.

Antonyms:

Abnormal	Singular	Divergent
Peculiar		

Examples:

In the middle ages, the relationship among human was abnormal. There were feudal and serfs, aristocrats and the common.

There was emphasis on the singular interest of the feudal, the kings and the nobles.

Some of the peculiar philosophies held away few other philosophies. The philosophy of divine right of kings and sub divine right of the nobles were started as destined by God!

Ugly (Adjective)

The news in today's newspaper is ugly.

Synonyms:

Homely	Distasteful	Frightful
Hideous	Repugnant	Terrible

Baleful	Menacing	Evil
Dark	Nasty	Spiteful
Sullen	Plain	Unattractive
Unsightly		

Examples:

Rita is healthy but a homely type of beauty.

She has plain features, not so beautiful.

I find his use of bad language extremely distasteful.

It's rather dark in here – can we have the lights on.

Ameeta is rather unattractive. She had odd features, no good figure, emaciated cheeks.

Some people call her unsightly. She repels charming boys.

Antonyms:

Attractive	Beautiful	Cute
Gorgeous	Handsome	Lovely
Pretty	Pleasant	Agreeable
Charming		

Examples:

Sophia is a very attractive young lady.

Nancy has a beautiful face, knows manners, has sharp features, a stub nose, a resounding voice. She can be called a real charming person and will have all the virtues of an ideal lady.

She is pretty much to be the cynosure of our class.

Unanimity (Noun)

We are in unanimity to support the government policy.

Synonyms:

Harmony	Assent	Concert
Concurrence	Unity	Unison
Like-mindedness	Agreement	Accord
Concord		

Examples:

There is scope for greater harmony among the people of India.

Businessmen, servicemen, employees of firms, workers of factories, farmers, landlords, and others you want to go to beach? Yes they shouted in unison.

Rajeev Gandhi has been able to achieve quite a few agreements with dissidents – Akalis in Punjab, ULFA in Assam to quote a few.

Accord in Assam has solved the six-year old dispute over foreigners who migrated to the state from Bangladesh. It has brought concord among the people of the state.

Antonyms:

Disagreement	Contention	Difference
Variance	Disharmony	

Examples:

Recent accords have considerably reduced areas of disagreement on vital issue of autonomy and reconciliation of economic interests of different regions in the country.

Numerous bones of contention have been removed by peaceful negotiation.

Differences among political groups have been removed by rational discussion.

Points of variance among politicians have been clarified to mutual satisfaction.

Causes of disharmony among groups have been successfully removed.

Uncertain (Adjective)

I am uncertain whether he will come to this meeting.

Synonyms:

Fluctuating	Inconstant	Fitful
Irregular	Unreliable	Changeable
Precarious		

Examples:

The world economic situation keeps fluctuating from one period to another.

The circumstances of the world are generally inconstant.

The economies of different countries are often fitful, depending on various national and international factors.

The curves of prosperity and depression in a free economy are always irregular owing to ups and downs in trade and commerce.

The factors of production and consumption are unrealizable in an unplanned economy.

Antonyms:

Reliable	Stable	Trustworthy
Unchangeable	Regular	Steady
Permanent		

Examples:

There is a need to introduce a reliable system for the working of demand and supply condition in a regulated manner.

This system provides for stable mechanisms in different sectors of an economy.

A controlled economy however succeeds only if the country has at its disposal a trust worthy team of efficient economists.

Unconcerned (Adjective)

The teachers remained unconcerned about the welfare of the students.

Synonyms:

Nonchalant	Easy	Apathetic
Cool	Disinterested	Indifferent

Examples:

He is a person of such a cool mind. He remains nonchalant under most provoking circumstances. He is above small emotions of worldly type.

Judges has to take disinterested view and measure the facts of both sides in terms of law.

In modern societies, Judges have to interpret the law but they need not remain indifferent to the basic tenets of the constitution whenever a point comes up for their discretion.

Antonyms:

Solicitous	Interested	Concerned
Anxious		

Examples:

The solicitous enquirers paid a personal visit to the scene of rail accident to know the fate of their lives.

Interested parties responded to the advertisement by the Central Housing Board for allotment of new flats in the major cities in the country.

I felt keep concerned over the death of such a prominent leader.

I had a few anxious moments before the plane landed safely.

Unconquerable (Adjective)

No company is unconquerable in this century.

Synonyms:

Insuperable	Invincible	Indomitable
Insurmountable		

Examples:

The moon remained insuperable until 1969 when it was first reached by Neil Armstrong.

Indian army has shows indomitable courage during all the wars with Pakistan.

The problems created by the new management are becoming insurmountable day by day.

Antonyms:

Weak	Powerless	Feeble
Conquerable		

Examples:

Man is still powerless before the vagaries of nature.

The power of man is feeble compared to that of nature despite recent achievements in science.

The common diseases that perpetrated death on men have been conquered or made conquerable.

Undertaking (Noun)

Could you take undertaking of this loss-making company?

Synonyms:

Contract	Endeavour	Trade
Enterprise	Promise	Engagement
Venture		

Examples:

Gamin India Ltd has secured the contract for the construction of roads and flyover in New Delhi.

They have been in that sort of an endeavour for over two decades and their financial standing and technical know-how are quite sound.

They are an old enterprise with good record and a promising future.

They have a sister concern engaged in the manufacture of road making equipments.

The car hire firm is their latest business venture.

Antonyms:

Irresponsibility	Refusal	Truancy
Escapade	Avoidance	

Examples:

Sense of irresponsibility can make a fool of even an intelligent businessman.

Your refusal to entertain your boss is going to cost you your job.

Your truancy to the boss is likely to spoil your impression.

You cannot always find escapade as a protection from routine.

Avoidance of duty is crime both in social and religious lives.

Unfair (Adjective)

The unfair competition that prevails in India between The Multinational Corporations and the Indian Companies has to be changed.

Synonyms:

Unjust	Bigoted	Discriminatory
Unethical	Inequitable	Partial
Dishonest	Wrongful	

Examples:

The social order in India will remain unjust unless there are fixed legal upper and lower limits on incomes of citizens.

The social order will remain inequitable so long as an upper limit on the property owned by an individual is not fixed.

The fixation of minimum wages is only a partial step towards the goal of social equality.

The country has a large number of dishonest officials in the government.

There are still many wrongful laws coming down from the pre-independence days.

Antonyms:

Fair	Just	Honest
Unprejudiced	Natural	Impartial
Equitable		

Examples:

Fair deal must be meted out to the poor.

The administration should be just and honest in its objectives.

We must take unprejudiced view of things in our decisions.

The judges must be neutral and impartial in their judgments, not ignoring the spirit of the constitution.

The constitution needs to be amended to provide for more equitable social order.

Unite (Verb)

Unite the student community to fight poverty and disease.

Synonyms:

Combine	Amalgamate	Link
Meld	Ally	Associate
Collaborate	Pool	Coalesce
Blend	Join	Knit
Merge		

Examples:

It is now a fashion for the workers to combine into unions and the businessmen into chambers of industry and commerce.

A number of political parties have coalesced to form a united opposition in the Parliament.

Oil and water do not blend together.

Let our firms merge immediately to save themselves from unhealthy competition.

Antonyms:

Scatter	Disjoin	Break
Detach	Disunite	Divide
Part	Separate	Unconnected

Examples:

The rays tend to scatter on all sides as the distance from the source of light increases.

Disjoin the wires and then test their respective electrical strength.

The two unconnected elements have a different capacity from those duly connected.

Universal (Adjective)

War causes universal misery.

Synonyms:

All embracing	International	Complete
General	Whole	Comprehensive
Entire		

Examples:

God is almighty and all – embracing.

Educational institutions of higher level should provide for the teaching of international citizenship.

Any atomic wars between US and USSR can cause complete annihilation of mankind.

Our college provides comprehensive training in business management.

Antonyms:

Parochial	Sectarian	Partisan
Sectional	Factional	

Examples:

The growth of parochial tendencies in the nation should be checked from the very beginning.

Sectarian politics in some states are raising their ugly heads.

A judge is never expected to take a partisan attitude in his judgments.

Sectional heads of this department are supposed to supervise their sections as effectively as possible.

Unusual (Adjective)

He has a nose of unusual size.

Synonyms:

Extraordinary	Remarkable	Peculiar
Uncommon	Exceptional	Rare
Singular		

Examples:

This is an extraordinary monument of ancient time. There are many carved walls and ceilings.

He has a remarkable personality. He becomes the centre of conversation wherever he goes.

I had a peculiar feeling that I had been there before.

He has an uncommon lovely gait which attracts every onlooker.

Mr. Mehta is an exceptional medical man. There is no disease he cannot cure. His medical excellence is singularly rare.

Antonyms:

Usual	Common	Hackneyed
Habitual	Commonplace	

Examples:

The usual procedure as laid down in the election law will be followed in the elections in the states.

The common man is regarded as a VIP during elections.

Indian farmer still follow the hackneyed technology. Hence some of them do not flourish the way they should.

He is a habitual liar. Hence nobody trusts him.

There is nothing commonplace about Deepak who has sophisticated tastes in every walk of life.

Uphold (Verb)

I cannot uphold such a conduct.

Synonyms:

Champion	Back	Support
Maintain	Defend	Sustain

Examples:

India has always championed the case of the poor countries at all international forums.

The Congress Party sponsors and backs such candidates in elections who stand for the upliftment of the poor.

I supported the Court which maintained the judgment of the high court on the issue of property rights of individuals in the country.

The Prime Minister Claims can defend themselves adequately against any foreign attack.

Antonyms:

Betray	Drop	Destroy
Demolish	Destruct	

Examples:

Never betray your friend for a temporary benefit.

Drop bad habits in your day-to-day life.

It is good to destroy evil thoughts from your mind.

The building is demolished by bomb blast.

Upset (Verb)

The cat has upset its saucer of milk.

Synonyms:

Disturb	Disorder	Spoil

Agitate	Dismay	Grieve
Perturb	Trouble	Disconcert
Disrupt		

Examples:

My present arrangements are too good to be disturbed.

The withdrawal of your support can disconnect all your political friends.

The earthquake disrupted the life of the city for decades.

Antonyms:

Soothe	Calm	Relieve
Relax		

Examples:

Indian classical music greatly soothes my tired nerves.

The daily prayer every morning helps to calm our day-to-day life.

The new drug relieved me of my pain.

A brief nap in the afternoon relaxes me for hours.

Urgent (Adjective)

The earthquake victims are in urgent need of medical helps.

Synonyms:

Critical	Pressing	Important
Insistent	Imperative	

Examples:

His sickness has reached a critical situation. It needs best possible medical attention.

His pressing need is finance which he cannot raise.

It is important for all of us to cooperate with the government in constructive programme.

The need of funds to initiate more public undertakings is insistent and imperative.

Antonyms:

Minor	Inconsiderable	Unimportant
Trifling	Insignificant	Petty
Trivial		

Examples:

I have no spare time to attend to minor problems.

I am too busy to deal with matters of inconsiderable importance.

This matter is too unimportant and trifling to receive my attention.

Usual (Adjective)

Tea is considered the usual drink of England people.

Synonyms:

Common	Accustomed	Customary
Familiar	Regular	Ordinary
Regular		

Examples:

TV has become an object of common use by the middle classes all over the world.

People have become accustomed to some kind of recreation after their day's work.

It is customary to go for the morning walk among the old people.

Suresh is no ordinary boy. He always tops in his class.

He has regular habits of study and exercise.

Antonyms:

| Occasional | Specific | Unusual |
| Exceptional | Peculiar | Unparallel |

Examples:

I do pay in occasional visit to relatives living in my city.

There is no specific purpose for which I have come to you. I was just passing by and thought to wish you good health.

My visit is unparallel for his certain virtues in literature and sport.

Utility (Noun)

The utility van has not yet arrived.

Synonyms:

Service	Use	Advantage
Profit	Policy	Benefit
Avail	Usefulness	Serviceableness

Examples:

It is the responsibility of the local government to provide utility services like drinking water, sanitation, health centres and electric supply.

These services are of immense use to the public. It is through these that humans enjoy the advantages of modern science.

These services help businessmen run business to make profit, although these are provided on the principle of no-profit no-loss.

In this way organized societies enjoy the benefit of civilization.

Antonyms:

| Disadvantages | Worthless | Useless |

Examples:

My high caste has proved disadvantageous to me because the job I was to get has been reserved for a scheduled caste.

In the next century, sun energy will be so well developed that it may make petroleum worthless.

A car is useless without petrol or any other fuel.

Vacant (Adjective)

Apply for the vacant positions in this company.

Synonyms:

Unoccupied	Waste	Vacuous
Unfilled	Leisure	Blank
Empty	Devoid	Unemployed
Untenanted		

Examples:

This palatial house has remained unoccupied for several years.

It means a national waste of $ 10 million, even if you rate it at $ 5000 a month.

He is so mad that he can keep his face vacuous under any circumstances.

This tank has remained unfilled for lack of pressure in the Yamuna River.

Antonyms:

Occupied	Jammed	Replete
Packed	Filled	Full
Brimful	Brimming	Busy
Crammed	Gorged	

Examples:

I may not be able to attend today's meeting as I am fully occupied in the afternoon.

A small accident jammed the whole stream of traffic in Connaught Palace.

The cricket team was brimming with confidence that they will be victorious.

The article was crammed with lot of superstitious concepts.

Vague (Adjective)

I have not even a vague idea about what they want.

Synonyms:

Haze	Dim	Obscure
Indistinct	Indefinite	

Examples:

His speeches have put a haze on the political objectives of the party

There are dim prospects of his success at the polls.

This leader has obscured the basic economic issues on which controversies have raged in recent decades.

His views on putting limitations on individual property have remained indistinct.

The workers pf the factory have gone on strike for an indefinite period.

Antonyms:

Clear	Defined	Plain
Definite	Exact	Lucid
Well- defined	Sensible	

Examples:

The Prime Minister has given a clear indication of his future policies.

He has defined precisely the aims of his administration.

They elected a leader who was almost the exact opposite of the previous one.

He has had negotiations with opposition leaders in plain and sensible words.

Valid (Adjective)

This ticket is valid for one single journey between London and Dover.

Synonyms:

Binding	Defensible	Powerful
Efficacious	Cogent	Logical

Examples:

An agreement usually has clauses binding the parties singing it.

An agreement arrived at between any two or more parties within the framework of law of the country is defensible in a court of law if and when violated by any of the parties.

Trade and Labour unions have become powerful institutions in modern societies.

They are efficacious in bringing about harmony among managements and their workers at different levels.

He produced cogent reasons for the change of policy.

Antonyms:

Invalid	Unconvincing	Unsound
Lame	Feeble	Weak
Illogical		

Examples:

The Supreme Court has the power to declare as invalid any law passed by a legislative body outside the frame work of the Constitution.

The stance taken by the opposition on this controversial issue is unconvincing.

The project seems unsound in its practicability.

Sam made a lame excuse for absenting himself from the class.

It seems illogical to change the time table so often.

Various (Adjective)

He is a criminal who is known to the police under various names.

Synonyms:

Different	Multitudinous	Numerous
Variegated	Sundry	Manifold
Many	Several	Multiform

Examples:

There are different solutions to this problem. Each solution has multitudinous dimensions.

Our country is facing numerous problems in political and economic spheres.

Mr. Henry is a variegated personality. He is a writer, speaker, manager, singer, actor and sportsman combined into one.

Antonyms:

Identical	Alike	Same
Similar	Uniform	Few
Exceptional		

Examples:

These twins have such an identical face. It becomes difficult to identify them from their look.

There are only a few instances of such twins in the world.

They are alike but they don't look at all alike.

It is one of the exceptional cases in human history.

We have lived in the same house for twenty years.

Vehement (Adjective)

He is man of vehement desires.

Synonyms:

Ardent	Emphatic	Fervent
Forceful	Eager	Earnest
Passionate		

Examples:

I am eager to join your club but you must accept my subscription in instalments.

I earnestly request you to accept my application for membership of the club.

He was most emphatic that I go with him

I am passionately in love with the billiards game practiced in your club.

Antonyms:

Feeble	Mild	Affected
Cool	Moderate	Apathetic
Calm		

Examples:

My desire to join your club is feeble.

The city is calm again after yesterday's riot.

His application is, therefore, coined in mild language.

You club has now a reputation which is adversely affected by the haughty behavior of the richer members.

Victory (Noun)

He was the responsible man who lead the team to victory.

Synonyms:

| Triumph | Supremacy | Success |
| Achievement | Mastery | Conquest |

Examples:

The Punjab accord implies the triumph of forces of national integrity and communal harmony.

It proves supremacy of good over evil.

It means success of the efforts of sane thinking people and failure of those who stood for secession and breakup of the country.

It is an achievement of the Prime Minister and the leader of the Akali Party.

The conquest of Mount Everest by Edmund Hillary and Tensing Norkey shows their mastery of the art of mountaineering.

Antonyms:

| Defeat | Subservience | Failure |
| Frustration | Descent | Fall |

Examples:

Brave people do not accept defeat come what may.

Everything also is subservient to the child's welfare.

They accept failure easily as their power or resistance is low.

A few failures cause frustration in a man by gradual degrees of descent.

Violation (Noun)

Your company has acted in violation of the treaty.

Synonyms:

Trespass	Breach	Encroachment
Sacrilege	Infraction	Infringement
Transgression		

Examples:

This is a military area. Our going through this road may mean trespass. Hence we will have to take to the longer route to reach our destination.

Infraction of law brings one due punishment.

Infringement of rights of others has its adverse impact on one's own rights

Blaring radio are a sacrilege in such a secluded part of the countryside.

There is a distribution of functions among different departments of administration so that there is no transgression or overlapping of responsibilities.

Antonyms:

| Compliance | Adherence | Concurrence |
| Observance | Acquiescence | |

Examples:

Compliance of our duties is as important as the enjoyment of our rights.

As citizens we are expected to adhere to the obligation laid down in the constitution of our country.

To pass, a law the Lok Sabha must obtain the concurrence of the Rajya Sabha and vice versa.

Void (Adjective)

The agreement, not being signed, is null and void.

Synonyms:

| Abolish | Negate | Nullify |
| Cancel | Repeal | Revoke |

Examples:

The system of Sati was abolished among the Hindus in the 19th century with the efforts of Raja Ram Mohan Roy.

The role of money in elections more or less negates the functioning of democracy in India.

Corruption in bureaucracy also nullifies some of the good points of democracy. It fails to cancel the creation of black money by businessmen.

Antonyms:

| Establish | Endorse | Legalize |
| Permit | Renew | Uphold |

Examples:

The public sector was first established on an ambitious scale in the second plan.

The president has endorsed the anti-defection bill and it has since become law.

Men of the new economic reforms are designed to legalize the black money.

I have obtained an all-India permit for my new deluxe tourist bus.

I have renewed the license of my old car.

Voluntary (Adjective)

The Voluntary Retirement Scheme introduced by the Government has been immensely welcomed by the servants.

Synonyms:

Gratuitous	Discretional	Intentional
Spontaneous	Willing	Unconstrained
Optional	Automatic	Instinctive

Examples:

In some cases the judges have to make discretional judgments with a view to interpret the law in the height of each case involved.

I am willing to join the picnic party provided you also join.

In a free country you can take up unconstrained activities without fear of infringement of law.

His response to our activities is purely spontaneous.

We made several phone calls to his number. But we got only an automatic reply.

Participation in this sports event is only optional.

His intentional reply to my letter wounded me deeply.

Antonyms:

Enforced	Imperative	Compulsory
Automatic	Instinctive	Obligatory

Examples:

The membership of the party is enforced on all government servants in communist states.

It is imperative that the government of India took up the enforcement of land reforms more vigorously.

It is obligatory to remove your shoes before entering the mosque.

Education up to the 8th grade has been made compulsory in India.

Vulgar (Adjective)

His vulgar display of riches repelled him from his friends.

Synonyms:

Coarse	Crude	Dirty
Impolite	Indecent	Rude
Nasty	Gaudy	Gross
Obscene		

Examples:

This is very coarse cloth material. I want a softer one.

His crude behavior compelled me to slap him on the face.

His way of talking to his elders is positively indecent.

My gross income exceeds the net income by over 25%

This film has a few obscene shots.

Antonyms:

Exquisite	Polite	Aristocratic
Elegant	Genteel	Refined
Polished		

Examples:

This is an exquisite design suiting my taste.

He is polite salesman. Let us give him some business.

I want refined coconut oil, not the unclean crude like this one.

Wilson has polished manners. No wonder he makes friends in no time.

Wages (Noun)

The Postal Workers have asked for an increase in their wages.

Synonyms:

Payment	Hire	Compensation
Remuneration	Salary	Reward

Examples:

I have not yet made the payment for the last insurance premium.

I have hired the new house for two years to start with.

The government has decided to pay compensation for the acquired building.

I have asked for remuneration of $ 250 per day for my services.

My monthly salary is $ 1500.

Mrs. Indira Gandhi has received the Bharat Ratna award posthumously in 1984.

Antonyms:

Rewardless	Unproductively	Fruitless
Waste		

Examples:

This job can be called rewardless for the little money paid for too much laborious work involved.

This firm has introduced a new machine to end its unproductivity.

This effort will prove fruitless unless better management techniques are employed.

Wane (Verb)

After his defeat in the election, his reputation started to wane.

Synonyms:

Abate	Atrophy	Decrease
Diminish	Drop	Dwindle
Fail	Lesson	

Examples:

Public interest in this issue seems to have abated.
The idealism had become totally atrophied.
The government has decreased the size of grants.
His strength has diminished over the years.
Their savings have dwindled away to almost nothing.
His influence was already lessening.

Antonyms:

Blossom	Brighten	Develop
Expand	Grow	Improve
Increase	Rise	Strengthen
Wax		

Examples:

The gulmohar trees are in full blossom.
He was brightened up when he heard the good news.
The plot for the novel gradually developed well.
A tyre expands when we pump air into it.
You must invest more money if you want your business to grow.
Her health is gradually improving.

Want (Noun)

The plants died from want of water.

Synonyms:

Indigence	Penury	Poverty
Privation		

Examples:

The magnitude of indigence is rising year by year in India despite so much economic development owing to inability of the administration to run the welfare activities efficiently.

Continuing penury circumstances of the common man in India make a mockery of the socio – economic system.

The government has yet to eradicate poverty in India though a number of programmes have been undertaken. People are still suffering from inadequacy of provisions of various types.

Antonyms:

Affluence	Plenty	Prosperity
Wealth		

Examples:

Affluence of the elite is in sharp contrast with the poverty of the lower classes.

Despite a situation of plenty of foodstuffs in the country, the poor cannot enjoy two wholesome meals a day.

India can enjoy its prosperity only if a more equitable distribution of the country's national wealth could be established.

Wasteful (Adjective)

We have to cut the wasteful expenditures to save money for the rainy days.

Synonyms:

Prodigal	Spendthrift	Lavish
Improvident	Imprudent	Unthrifty
Reckless		

Examples:

Those who possess black money tend to be prodigal.

The black – marketers easily develop spendthrift habits.

They spend lavish sums on dresses and jewellery.

They forget the existence of God and become improvident.

They have so much money and they become imprudent and reckless in expenses.

Antonyms:

Sparing	Miserly	Economical
Prudent	Frugal	Provident
Thrifty		

Examples:

Those who become prosperous by dint of hard work or organizing capability have economic habits as they value the hard earned money.

Such people are prudent in their budget and thrifty in expenditure on luxuries.

Of frugal temperament, they spare some money for their poorer brethren.

They may be miserly on avoidable luxuries. They do save some money regularly for the rainy day.

Wavering (Adjective)

We captured those wavering flames in our camera.

Synonyms:

Oscillating	Unsteady	Fluctuating
Undecided	Undetermined	Inconstant
Vacillating	Faltering	Quivering

Examples:

In this computer the oscillating disk completes a full circle and returns to its original position at the end.

Deepak's position in politics is unsteady. He is too poor to float his ideas through the media with speed.

He keeps fluctuating from socialism to communism and again from communism back to socialism.

He is undecided about his future course of action.

Antonyms:

Steady	Unwavering	Determined
Firm	Resolute	Unhesitating
Steadfast		

Examples:

He is steady like a rock in his ideology.

There are newspapers which welcome this ideology and they give him unwavering publicity.

They are determined to push him up to political power.

This manager is firm in his determination to translate his deals into reality.

He pursues it resolutely through the media.

Weak (Adjective)

I am too weak to walk to the hospital.

Synonyms:

Decrepit	Feeble	Delicate
Effete	Faint	Enervated
Frail	Inform	

Examples:

Sumit's mother is now in a decrepit condition. She has to lean on other members of the family even for going to the bath room.

This transistor has feeble sound perhaps its battery has exhausted.

My grandfather has become frail and infirm after crossing the age of 80.

Antonyms:

Energetic	Hardy	Healthy
Strong	Stout	Sturdy
Tough		

Examples:

In his young days, my grandfather was known to be a very energetic and hardy man.

He was healthy and strong although his profession was mechanic.

My father is stout and sturdy but occasional illnesses have made him anemic.

He is not as tough as my grandfather was at his age.

Weaken (Verb)

Long illness has weakened his health.

Synonyms:

Attenuate	Enfeeble	Sap
Impair	Debilitate	Universe

Examples:

Daily prayer attenuates the errors and opinions of day to day life. God, however, does not attenuate serious crimes against society.

The angry remarks of the teacher enfeebled the weaker students instead of encouraging them.

Years of failure have sapped his confidence.

The principal advised the teacher to deal with children sweetly and not to impair their originality by harsh handling.

Antonyms:

Strengthen	Fortify	Brace
Boost	Enhance	Improve
Invigorate	Harden	Create

Examples:

The aim of education is to strengthen the character of the students.

The unexpected win helped to boost his team's morale.

The sweetness of the teacher should fortify the intellect of the learners instead of debilitating them.

The extra-curricular activities are designed to brace the young children and create in them courage.

He said nothing but I saw his face getting hardened.

Wealth (Noun)

This is a book with a wealth of information.

Synonyms:

Abundance	Substance	Riches
Profusion	Money	Pelf
Plenty	Prosperity	Property
Possessions		

Examples:

Developed countries possess abundance of wealth. Hence they can afford old – age pensions to even non government citizens.

There is enough substance in your argument that abundant wealth is necessary to launch more and more welfare schemes.

We should not feel unhappy over the riches of the rich but over the poverty of the poor.

Roses grow in profusion against the old wall.

Money dominates every walk of social life today.

Harry does not own any property but he has plenty of mental ability and intelligence.

Antonyms:

Poverty	Destitution	Privations
Distress	Want	Impecunity
Insufficiency		

Examples:

Poverty has sapped the energy and opportunity for development of the teeming millions.

The government has launched a few schemes for the care of the destitute but these are only a drop in the ocean.

The poor people continue to suffer from privations of day-to-day life.

The scene of poverty distresses all balanced people bestowed with patriotism and fellow – feeling.

Wet (Adjective)

Her cheeks were wet with tears.

Synonyms:

Drenched	Damp	Humid
Rainy	Showery	Moist
Soak		

Examples:

I was suddenly caught by the downpour which drenched my clothes.

The monsoon makes the atmosphere damp.

Towns on the sea coast generally have humid atmosphere all the year round.

The rainy season generally precedes the autumn.

Rain clouds brings showery weather in their trail if there is wound, it will give immediate relief.

Antonyms:

Dry	Arid	Parch
Parched	Dehydrate	

Examples:

In the plains the weather is dry and cold during the winter.

The deserts have arid atmosphere all the year round. However new technology of agricultural growth in arid zones is being developed.

Dry surface when burnt by sun rays gets parched and cracked.

New technology is being developed to dehydrate the over moist regions so to provide for smooth agricultural growth.

Wide (Adjective)

Keep the doors wide open.

Synonyms:

Expansive	Spacious	Large
Broad	Extensive	

Examples:

The stream is expansive for the water carried. Hence it is not deep.

This spacious bungalow belongs to the state government. It is used as a guest house.

A large crowd gathered at the boat club to listen to the esteemed opposition leader.

This article gives a broad outline of the agreement reached between India and the USSR.

The agreement provides for extensive cooperation between the two counties in science, trade and economic fields.

Antonyms:

Narrow	Cramped	Confined
Circumscribed	Close	Limited
Small		

Examples:

A narrow lane connects the two main roads in the city.

The houses built in this colony are cramped and unventilated.

The development here is confined to the provision of drinking water and electricity. There are no good roads, streets or sanitation.

This lake is circumscribed by a wide road on all sides.

The children are close to each other in young age.

I have only a limited use for my truck. Shall I hire it to other farmers?

Mine is a very small house a bed cum-drawing room; a kitchen and a bathroom.

Wicked (Adjective)

It was wicked of you to torment the poor cat.

Synonyms:

Iniquitous	Criminal	Vile
Villainous	Corrupt	Evil
Immoral	Bad	Heinous
Sinful		

Examples:

Socio – economic system in India continues to be iniquitous as there is not linking of maximum and minimum incomes and wealth by a just ratio.

The criminal activities of the rich go unspotted owing to corruption at high levels.

The vile deeds of the black – marketers are keeping the poor people half starved.

The beaurocrats are playing their villainous role in keeping the social order as unjust.

Antonyms:

Virtuous	Benevolent	Ethical
Honourable	Noble	Incorrupt
Chaste	Moral	Upright

Examples:

The virtuous deeds of the brave inspire the young.

Its behavior has not been strictly ethical.

However incorrupt the political leadership, it has so far not succeeded in chastening the government officials to any moral or upright ideals.

Wild (Adjective)

He was wild with anger.

Synonyms:

Ferocious	Fierce	Uncivilized
Barbarous	Rude violent	Furious
Savage		

Examples:

The tiger is a ferocious animal.

There was a fierce battle at Panipat between the Muslim invaders and the Rajputs in the beginning of the 11th century AD.

The priest's murder was condemned as barbarous.

The savage activities of the dacoits have frightened the villagers of the region.

Students were involved in violent clashes with the police.

Antonyms:

Gentle	Timid	Harmless
Domesticated		

Examples:

Cow is the gentlest animal in the world.

The timid behavior of the policeman encouraged the robbers to slip away.

The Camel is harmless animal. It has been tamed to be useful in deserts.

Marc and Suzie have had an unhappy married life as Suzie has proved too domesticated for Christopher's ideals of a married woman.

Wisdom (Noun)

The wisdom of our ancestors is amazing.

Synonyms:

Knowledge	Intelligence	Discretion
Sense	Learning	Erudition
Discernment	Sagacity	
Prudence		

Examples:

My knowledge of Biology is very much limited.

The UPSC nowadays tests the intelligence of candidates to various competitive examinations by putting multiple – choice questions.

Wise people use discretion in their vocabulary while speaking to men of culture.

My sense of hearing has been weakened by the noisy atmosphere in my factory.

I am learning to write commercial letters.

The judge uses erudition and discernment while delivering his judgment.

The official used his power with sagacity and prudence. Hence he earned the reputation of an ideal civil servant.

Worthless (Noun)

He is the only worthless student in our class.

Synonyms:

Cheap	Base	Degraded
Valueless	Dissolute	Despicable
Paltry	Contemptible	

Examples:

This is no cheap invention. We have to test its applicability in modern industry.

This is a base coin. It won't circulate.

Don't feel degraded simply because you have missed the first class by a few marks. Try your luck next time.

This is a valueless invention. It can't be practiced economically for many decades.

This share brings you only a paltry profit of 1% only.

Antonyms:

Excellent	Good	Transcendent
Estimable	Costly	Valuable
Admirable		

Examples:

Your suggestions are excellent, but we have to determine their practicability before giving them a trial.

The wise man is one who can discriminate between good and bad.

Buddha performed his transcendental meditation for a number of years until he achieved Nirvana.

His achievements are too many to be estimable.

It would be too costly to repair.

The principal gave me a valuable gift for being the topper in the examination.

Xanthic (Adjective)

The Xanthic nature of this flower attracted all the children.

Synonyms:

Light – skinned	Golden – haired	Yellow – haired
Fair – haired	Blonde	Fair

Examples:

The Europeans are a light – skinned race.

She is a golden – haired blonde from Switzerland.

Some of the females in Australia and New Zealand are yellow haired. This is again a physical phenomenon.

Antonyms:

Brown	Black	Wheatish
Skinned		

Examples:

Mary has matching brown eyes and hair.

The original residents of Africa have a black skin.

Most Indians have a wheatish complexion.

Some people are thick skinned. They do not react to the indignities perpetrated on them.

Xanthous (Adjective)

The Xanthous nature of this flower attracted all the children.

Synonyms:

Light – skinned	Golden – haired	Yellow – haired
Fair – haired	Blonde	
Fair		

Examples:

The Europeans are a light – skinned race.

She is a golden – haired blonde from Switzerland.

Some of the females in Australia and New Zealand are yellow haired. This is again a physical phenomenon.

Antonyms:

Brown	Black	Wheatish
Skinned		

Examples:

Mary has matching brown eyes and hair.

The original residents of Africa have a black skin.

Most Indians have a wheatish complexion.

Some people are thick skinned. They do not react to the indignities perpetrated on them.

Yawn (Verb)

There is a gulf yawned at the end.

Synonyms:

Gape	Open	Wide
Part	Split	

Examples:

I gaped at the way the monkey carried out his trickeries at the circus.

I opened my mouth wide to yawn.

I could hardly part with my beloved when the bell rang.

I split the coins into two parts and gave an option to my wife to choose one.

Antonyms:

Close	Shut	Abridge
Shorten	Peephole	

Examples:

If you close yours eyes you can't see anything.

Never shut your eyes on duty.

The journalist abridged the speech of the politicians.

The Suez Canal has shortened the distance between Europe and Africa by over 500 miles.

I have affixed a peephole at my entrance.

Yield (Verb)

We will never yield to negative forces.

Synonyms:

Give – way	Submit	Accede
Waive	Surrender	Renounce
Abandon	Forgo	Crop
Harvest		

Examples:

The bridge was defective and gave way as soon as the train passed over it.

He has submitted the requisite documents to the college. His mother acceded to his demand for a holiday tour.

The enemy could not resist our forces and had to surrender.

He has decided to renounce the world and become a Sanyasi.

I have abandoned the idea of becoming a singer.

Mary was willing to forgo the pleasure of the trip and let July go instead.

The beans cropped very well this year.

The farmer has sold his year's harvest in the market at good profit.

Antonyms:

Resist	Withstand	Refuse
Keep back	Withhold	Restrain
Oppose	Assail	Contend
Confront		

Examples:

I could not resist the temptation of cold coffee and accepted his kind offer.

I could not withstand the heat of the summer and proceeded to Shimla for relief.

I could not refuse the kind offer of a lucrative job in my friend's firm.

I am keeping back some savings for the rainy day.

The judge withheld his decision to the next sitting.

The government has built sufficient reservoirs of good stock for an emergency.

Yoke (Noun)

In this film, the HERO did his best to break the yoke of the tyrant.

Synonyms:

Link	Connect	Harness
Couple	String	

Examples:

India has broken the link of imperialism with Britain, though she continues its link with the Common Wealth Countries as a fully fledged member.

The two towns are connected by an excellent bus service.

There are two parts of this machine come into operation when coupled.

There is no string attached to the foreign aid coming to India.

Antonyms:

Release	Divorce	Abandon
Disconnect		

Examples:

The government released all political prisoners after attaining independence.

The question of political system prevailing in a country cannot be divorced from foreign relations.

Samson and Lucy have agreed to divorce each other on certain mutually settled terms.

I have abandoned the idea of marriage for the time being.

Young (Adjective)

Young James is always ready to help his old parents.

Synonyms:

Youthful	Boyish	New
Fresh	Childish	Recent

Examples:

He is old but has youthful habits which everyone can appreciate.

He is above forty but still has a boyish look.

He makes new friends in no time with his sociable outlook.

Their memories of the wedding are still fresh in their minds.

Maria behaves in a childish manner sometimes and offends her boss.

This is a recent publication on Today's Society.

Antonyms:

Mature	Elderly	Aged
Ripe	Late	Full

Examples:

His mature ideas have benefited the company in a big way.

Though he is an elderly person, he is active and energetic like a young man.

Being aged, he has ripe judgment on matters of life and death.

The person was very sad because his children deserted him in his late years.

Yell (Verb)

He greeted us and yelled with laughter.

Synonyms:

Scream	Screech	Howl
Shrink	Cry	Bawl
Holler		

Examples:

Anita screamed to prove her innocence.

The car screeched to halt.

I feel very irritated when I hear the shriek of chalk on the black board.

"Shut up and stop this nonsense!" the man bawled.

There women cried aloud for help.

Holler when you're ready.

Antonyms:

Mumble	Mutter	Murmur
Whisper		

Examples:

Please don't mumble. I cannot understand what you're saying.

Rajeev muttered asking an apology for being late.

Speak out. Just don't murmur.

The boy whispered that he is afraid.

Zeal (Noun)

Her letter expressed her zeal for the cause of the development of the poor people.

Synonyms:

Zest	Dedication	Eagerness
Devotion	Earnestness	Warmth
Energy		

Examples:

Hope is the zest of life.

His dedication to work has earned him very good repute.

His eagerness to make friends was exploited by the other boys.

His earnestness to bring an improvement in the system is clear from the actions taken by him.

The parents were gratified to see the devotion of the nurse to the care of their child.

The sun is the most important source of energy.

Antonyms:

| Coolness | Weakness | Laziness |
| Carelessness | Apathy | |

Examples:

His coolness often dwindles to the level of indifferences.

His calm face has often been exploited as his weakness.

His laziness will cost him his job some day.

His carelessness is now matter of habit. But his other virtues keep him safe in his job.

Zenith (Noun)

He took voluntary retirement at the zenith of his career.

Synonyms:

Acme	Apex	Climax
Crest	Peak	Pinnacle
Summit	Top	Apogee

Examples:

By dint of hard labour he reached the acme of success.

At 45 he'd reached the apex of his career.

Her intervention brought their quarrel to climax.

He was riding the crest of a new wave of popular fame.

The climbers made camp half way up the peak.

Antonyms:

| Base | Bottom | Depths |
| Lowest point | Nadir | Rock bottom |

Examples:

She used her family's history as a base for her novel.

There are tea-leaves in the bottom of my cup.

Water was found at a depth of 40 feet under ground.

Company losses reached their nadir in 1995.

Prices have reached rock bottom.

Zest (Noun)

He entered into our plan with zest.

Synonyms:

Enjoyment	Gusto	Relish
Charm	Pungency	Taste
Delectation		

Examples:

Children seem to have lost their enjoyment in studies now a day.

His mind was filled with delectation after receiving the news of his niece's arrival.

Adventurous books suits my taste.

The garden is full of charm.

I don't relish the prospect of coming to office on Sundays.

Antonyms:

Abhorrence	Apathy	Indifference
Lack of enthusiasm	Weariness	Loathing
Distaste	Disinclination	Aversion

Examples:

She has strong abhorrence for racism.

There is a lack of enthusiasm among the players as on other days play made them lethargic.

He had an aversion to playing hockey.

His indifferent towards my feelings frustrated me.

I have distaste for politics.

There was a general disinclination to return home after the movie late at night.

Zip (Noun)

They have the right zip to stand against the tyrant.

Synonyms:

Energy	Drive	Gusto
Vitality	Fly	Shoot
Zoom	Vigour	Enthusiasm

Examples:

The children are always full of energy.

For many weeks they zoomed around Disneyland enjoying the creations of Walt Disney.

He worked with fresh vigour and enthusiasm.

She is coming up with vitality and new ideas.

They sang the chorus with gusto.

Antonyms:

| Inertia | Apathy | Listlessness |
| Laziness | Sluggishness | Lethargy |

Examples:

There was wide spread apathy among the election campaigners as there occurred lot of bomb blasts these days.

I can't seem to throw off the feeling of inertia.

Laziness makes a person dull.

He is disliked by everyone for his sluggish nature.

He was sick for more than a month and his listlessness due to sickness hampered his official works.

★★★

Printed in Poland
by Amazon Fulfillment
Poland Sp. z o.o., Wrocław